Research Processes in Physical Education

second edition

David H. Clarke
Indiana University

and

H. Harrison Clarke
University of Oregon

PRENTICE-HALL, INC., Englewood Cliffs, New Jersey 07632

Library of Congress Cataloging in Publication Data

CLARKE, DAVID H.
　Research processes in physical education.

　Rev. ed. of: Research processes in physical education,
recreation, and health. [1970]
　Includes bibliographies and indexes.
　1. Physical education and training—Research.
I. Clarke, H. Harrison (Henry Harrison), (date)
II. Title.
GV361.C56 1984　　613.7′072　　83-13653
ISBN　0-13-774513-3

Editorial production, supervision,
　and interior design by Lisa A. Domínguez
Cover design by Jeannette Jacobs
Manufacturing buyer: Harry P. Baisley

Printed in the United States of America

10　9　8　7　6　5　4　3　2　1

ISBN 0-13-774513-3

Prentice-Hall International, Inc., *London*
Prentice-Hall of Australia Pty., Limited, *Sydney*
Editora Prentice-Hall do Brasil, Ltda., *Rio de Janeiro*
Prentice-Hall Canada Inc., *Toronto*
Prentice-Hall of India Private Limited, *New Delhi*
Prentice-Hall of Japan, Inc., *Tokyo*
Prentice-Hall of Southeast Asia Pte. Ltd., *Singapore*
Whitehall Books Limited, *Wellington, New Zealand*

Contents

Preface

With the second edition of this book, the title is changed to *Research Processes in Physical Education*; thus, the content concentrates specifically on this field. However, much of the material continues relevant for investigators in health education and recreation. The various research methodologies are presented in sufficient detail so that they can be applied by both the neophyte and the experienced scientist. Selected completed studies are described throughout in order to illustrate the various research processes considered. The edition is completely revised and updated.

The book is divided into five parts. Part I, Initial Considerations in Research, contains materials common to all research. Chapter 1, Importance and Meaning of Research, considers the nature of research, the place of research in our society and in graduate education, and the influences that have developed and shaped research in physical education. Chapter 2, The Problem, deals with locating and defining the research problem, including criteria in selecting, limiting, and delimiting the problem, and evolving the problem statement. Chapter 3, Literature Search, presents the need for surveying related literature, major sources of literature, and methods of library reading and note taking.

In Part II, Nonlaboratory Studies, investigations in physical education that do not require laboratory sources are presented. These studies do not usually require the testing of subjects, the conducting of experiments, or the analysis of quantitative data. The subdivisions of Part II are: Chapter 4, Methodology in Historical Research; Chapter 5, Philosophical Studies; and Chapter 6, Surveys.

Part III, Statistical Applications, is devoted to statistical computations—interpretations and applications to studies in physical education. In any scientific research, test data must be analyzed in ways proper to the research design; to do so, a knowledge of statistics is absolutely essential. The emphasis in this part is on statistical computations, an understanding of the basic assumptions underlying the various statistics, and the interpretation of statistical data. These chapters have been streamlined considerably over the previous edition of the text. The chapters are: Chapter 7, Central Tendency, Variability, Normal Probability; Chapter 8, Inferential Statistics, Chapter 9, Correlation.

In Part IV, Laboratory Research, laboratory resources are considered as a formally established laboratory but also as a gymnasium, athletic field, track, or swimming pool when utilized for conducting scientific investigations. Such studies involve the adoption of a study design with appropriate hypotheses and the use of proper tests to measure the essential elements under investigation. The first chapter in this part, Chapter 10, presents Laboratory and Experimental Research. Methods given are common to the various types of studies considered in subsequent chapters. This practice was adopted in order to avoid unnecessary duplication of methodology. The other chapters are devoted to five broad areas of investigation: Chapter 11, Physiology of Exercise; Chapter 12, Motor Learning/Motor Control; Chapter 13, Psychological Studies; Chapter 14, Biomechanical Research; Chapter 15, Growth and Development. In each chapter, the testing instruments unique to the area are evaluated. Illustrated studies are presented, although a review of the literature in each area is not intended; these examples of research studies should help the novice researcher by showing how successful investigators have formulated hypotheses, established experimental designs, applied evaluation procedures, analyzed data, and drawn appropriate conclusions.

Part V, The Research Report, has only one chapter, Chapter 16, Preparation of the Research Report. The main topics consider the organization of the thesis, the use of written and oral sources, the construction and use of tables and graphs, forms for footnotes and bibliography, and publication based on the thesis.

D. H. C.
H. H. C.

Initial Considerations in Research

1
Importance and Meaning of Research

INTRODUCTION TO PART I

In Part I, the initial considerations that are common to all research are presented in three chapters. The importance and meaning of research are considered, including historical and current developments and the influences shaping investigations in physical education. Criteria to apply in selecting problems for study and processes for evolving the problem statement are included. The need to survey literature germane to the problem area and methods of doing so are indicated. The chapters are: 1, Importance and Meaning of Research; 2, The Problem; and 3, Literature Search.

RESEARCH IN OUR CIVILIZATION

Our life is permeated, saturated, and maybe even surfeited with research. At Hiroshima, the atomic age was blasted into existence. Now, we have the atomic powered submarine that has sailed under the Arctic polar cap. We have sputniks and satellites, systems-guided aircraft and missiles, and a space station in prospect. Society today respects science and readily accepts its findings; but this was not always so. An overview of research in our civilization is presented in order to provide a perspective of how research has affected mankind throughout the ages. Such a perspective serves to identify the niche of the neophyte researcher in this scheme of things.

Historically, research in our civilization has been profoundly influenced by early discoveries. The discovery of fire, the wheel, numbers and the alphabet, paper and the process of printing; the development of metals and agriculture; and the use of steam and electricity have all been milestones in the development and refinement of civilization. More recently has come the use of atomic power and the penetration of outer space, which in a very real sense is the culmination of long years of research and development.

Dr. Frank Porter Graham, speaking on "Machines and Ideas in World Cooperation" before an annual meeting of the Department of Higher Education, National Education Association, stated that close to the center of three great economic transitions of modern times are three mechanisms.

1. *Compass.* The compass released trade from the narrow confines of navigation routes established and used for thousands of years and made worldwide the great Commercial Revolution. It was two simple but basic ideas that entered into both the substance and the value of the compass: the idea that the earth was round and the idea that the earth was a giant magnet.

2. *Steam engine.* The steam engine was the dynamic element of the Industrial Revolution, which has changed the way men have worked and lived in the last two centuries more than they had changed in the preceding 3,000 years. It was based upon the expansive power of latent heat, developed by Professor Joseph Black of the University of Glasgow. "When James Watt took the pure theory from the mind of Joseph Black and rearranged the ideas of the steam engine in his own mind, he rearranged the whole structure of the modern world."

3. *Atomic mechanism.* The long-accepted idea that the atom was the irreducible substance of the universe gave way in the last half century to the idea that the atom itself was a little universe of whirling bodies of tremendous energy and power. The Atomic Revolution received its revolutionary meaning and source of power from the minds of men and women working quietly and brilliantly in university laboratories.

The following statement, made twenty years ago, takes on special significance relative to the "knowledge spiral" that we are witnessing today:

> Physical changes such as the elevation of a range of mountains take a matter of a million years. Changes of climate are measured in terms of 5,000 years. Technological change, such as from fire to domesticated animals to metallurgy, are 500-year steps. . . . Since the turn of the century, however, we have seen a rate of change unlike anything the world has seen before. Knowledge has doubled each decade. Some 90 percent of all the scientists who have ever lived on this planet are still alive. Within the span of one lifetime we have witnessed the development of electricity, air travel, radio, the automobile, television, antibiotics, atomic energy, and space flight. This is a far cry from 500-year steps.[1]

These observations forcefully emphasize the contention that gigantic technological advances that are being made daily must have profound influences on our lives. Whereas for early man they were few and far between, for modern man they have come with an overwhelming rush. It has been estimated that the advances of 100,000 stone-age years are surpassed in a single year now. The upward spiral must indeed be exponential with no end in sight.

Historical Perspective

In the beginning such study as might be termed research was in reality trial and error, perhaps only the astute observation of nature, that resulted in discoveries of far-reaching significance, although a most personal and practical need was the primary stimulus. The details of much of early civilization are lost, with the exact accounting being speculative and inconclusive and the subject of interesting legend. Nevertheless, the modern development of science was helped immeasurably by the early ideas expressed, especially in such fields as mathematics, astronomy, physics, and biology. In such social and humanistic sciences as literature, art, and philosophy, the study of the Greek and Roman classics—paintings, poetry, and philosophy—became essential and integral parts of the newer era.

The scientific method was difficult to establish and was hampered by the pronounced lack of interest in natural phenomena in the Middle Ages. The reliance upon the supernatural, the dependence

---

[1] William P. Tolley, "What Does It Mean to Be Educated?" *Journal of Health, Physical Education and Recreation*, 33, No. 7 (October 1962), 26. Reprinted by permission of the author and *JOHPER*.

upon the mystical, and the dominance of religious dogma prevented the full development of a freethinking society. Medieval practice of witchcraft attested to the nonscientific reliance upon magic and miracles rather than the encouragement of naturalism and experimentation. From this atmosphere, modern science emerged, stimulated in part by two great forces. The first force was the intelligence of the individuals at the time; their insight and perception of reality plus the environment provided a powerful impetus. The second force was the heritage of knowledge and writings left from pagan antiquity, which gave evidence that scientific activity was not without precedent and that it was possible to have free and independent thinking along many intellectual fronts. These forces, together with the apparent rejection of the medieval outlook and dissatisfaction with that antiquated way of life, gave birth in the sixteenth and seventeenth centuries to the modern period in science.

To suggest that the emergence of free scientific thought was met with universal enthusiasm is to belie the facts. Medieval Christendom usually managed to suppress attempts of scholars whose findings were at variance with the beliefs of the Church or who challenged existing religious doctrine. To experiment was to reject the Divine Being; consequently, such attempts at scientific inquiry were often met with persecution. For instance, Roger Bacon, a thirteenth-century philosopher who stressed the importance of experience as a source of man's knowledge was credited by many as being the first European to emphasize the value of the experiment. Writing on such topics as anatomy, medieval chemistry, and literature, he spent the last years of his life in jail as a "reward" for offering the fruits of his experiments.

Parcelsus (1493-1541), a Swiss alchemist and physician, taught that the activities of the human body were chemical, that health depended upon the proper chemical composition of the organs and fluids, and that the purpose of chemistry was to prepare medicine. He introduced the use of many drugs and was the first to point out the relation between goiter deficiencies and resulting cretinism in the child. He was persecuted for his revolutionary ideas.

Copernicus (1473-1543) challenged the teachings of Ptolemy, who said that the earth existed as a fixed body in the center of the universe and that the planets and the sun revolved around it every 24 hours. He believed in the heliocentric theory that the sun was the center of the solar system; because of the opposition of his views, he refrained from publishing his findings until on his death bed. His discoveries were so profound that they became the foundation of what is known as the Copernican Revolution; he laid the theoretical framework for the later works of Galileo, Brahe, and Newton.

Galileo (1564-1642) became a follower of the Copernican theory and was the first to use the telescope as a scientific instrument. He found four moons revolving around Jupiter; he discovered that Venus had phases like the Moon; he identified the nature of the Milky Way and first observed the sunspots. He also contradicted the Aristotelian belief that if two bodies of the same substance fell from the same height the heavier body would reach the ground first; that a body twice as heavy as another must reach the earth in half the time. His advocacy of the Copernican theory gained for him an accusation of heresy from the Church.

Subsequently, scientific advances followed in rapid succession. Astronomy led the way, followed by physics, chemistry, and the biological sciences. Early research was largely an individual effort, a fact that contrasts markedly with the trend today in all fields. Modern research is more a group effort that is spawned by the tremendous development of scientific talent and fanned by the availability of financial support. It has cultivated a new skill, sometimes called "grantsmanship," which functions not only in industry and government but in the universities as well. Full-time administrative positions have been created with the major responsibility of providing advice and counsel to scientists as they make applications for extramural grants.

Governmental and industrial agencies or private institutes may be funded by more or less primary sources. Universities, on the other hand, provide very little of the total research money spent on campuses from the general operating fund, but they depend upon the faculty to attract grants and be rewarded with research contracts. This practice has increasingly become an important phase of university operation because of the overhead allowances gained from the grants. In fact, many operations of universities today would be drastically affected if a wholesale withdrawal of such fiscal sources were to occur.

No longer is it feasible under such conditions for one individual to work alone on projects, as was formerly the case; rather, he or she must gather together a number of colleagues, perhaps a sizable group of graduate students, and very likely cut across departmental lines to bring in ancillary disciplines. The principal investigator may then become the administrator of the project, directing the efforts of others, controlling the disbursement of funds, recruiting technicians, and supervising data collection and analysis. He or she is the "idea person" with the theoretical knowledge and ingenuity to identify the problem and to see that it is attacked properly; he or she has major responsibility for preparing technical reports and submitting manuscripts for publication.

Modern Developments

Modern research developments are astronomical in their scope and mind boggling in their sophistication. These developments show an essential and intricate blending of basic and applied research. As can be seen from the following limited number of illustrations, the results have been dramatic and far-reaching.

Airplane.   The history of air travel is long and distinguished. It is difficult to place exactly the date when the possibility of flying first occurred to man, but legends and pictures reveal early concern with such a venture. Roger Bacon suggested the principle of balloon flights with hot air; Leonardo da Vinci in the fifteenth century made drawings of parachutes, propellers, and helicopters. After the Wright brothers' flight in 1903, developments came very rapidly. However, it was not until World War I that airplanes were improved to any considerable extent. What began as crude, open bodies became closed, maneuverable crafts. The valuable use of airplanes for warfare spurred further research and development into aerodynamics that resulted in numerous technological improvements. World War II encouraged research to increase speed and range of flight. Now jet aircraft have moved to the research frontier, and a whole range of developments for civilian and military use is apparent, including the penetration of outer space. Who 50 years ago could seriously have predicted that one day it would become a matter of daily routine to fly between London and New York in 3½ hours?

Radar.   Early radio discoveries made in the late nineteenth century preceded the actual development of radar. The reflection of radio waves from distant objects permitted the detection of ships and planes; radar became extremely effective in aiming antiaircraft guns. Research since that time has adapted radar for such uses as detecting channel markers or ice fields in navigation of ships, for highway speed control, and for forecasting the intensity of tornadoes, hurricanes, or other storms.

Atomic Energy.   The power of atomic energy was forcefully demonstrated at the close of World War II; since that time, major efforts have been made to convert the ideas developed for destruction to peaceful uses. Such prospects as use for the generation of electricity or for various uses in medicine, industry, and agriculture signal the potentially widespread peaceful employment of atomic energy.

Computer.   There is almost no phase of life today that is not touched by the computer. Modern retail establishments tap computer technology in various ways, and airline personnel make instantaneous flight reservations and seat assignments. Many supermarket checkout counters now have electronic eyes that read coded prices on cans and packages and tabulate the bill much more quickly than a cash register—and in the same process give stores better control of inventories. Now available are home computers that play games, turn on TV programs, store recipes, do household accounting, start the dishwasher, and do other tasks. *Time* magazine for January 3, 1983, honored the computer as the machine, rather than the man, of the year and prognosticated a revolution that would computerize America. And, for readers of this book, who do studies requiring the analysis of test scores, statistical computations can be made with tremendous speed and accuracy by computer operation. For example, a graduate student of one of the authors completed a dissertation requiring the computation of nearly 10,000 correlations; this stupendous task would have been virtually an impossibility for a graduate thesis without the use of an electronic computer.

Laser beam.   During the past 20 years, the laser beam has grown from a laboratory curiosity into a major tool of industry, science, and weaponry. Laser is an acronym for its technical definition: Light Amplification for Stimulated Emission of Radiation. It is the most powerful light in existence, as it does not diffuse and dissipate, but is coherent and concentrated, oscillating at only one magnetic frequency. As many as one trillion watts of laser light have been produced in a billionth of a second—the equivalent of six times the power produced in the same time span by all the electric power plants in the United States. Applications of laser beams are just now being realized. They are widely used in eye surgery; they are used to cut concrete and steel, create three-dimensional photographs without lens, and track moving plates of rock along geological faults to help predict the approach of earthquakes. Laser devices are being developed to knock out enemy missiles and earth-orbiting satellites, as well as for laser guns, space bazookas, and other kinds of "star war" hardware. Studies are underway to provide cheap, unlimited, relatively clean energy by using the concentrated power of light to initiate thermonuclear fusion.[2]

Medicine.   Advances in medicine have been of astronomical proportions in recent years. Poliomyelitis has been conquered and progress toward subjugating cancer has been made. Perhaps nowhere have developments been more dramatic than in the diagnosis and treatment of heart diseases. In 1967, surgeons performed the first

[2] Lee Edson, "Laser 'Death Ray' That Improves Life," *New York Times Magazine*, May 26, 1978.

bypass operation on a human patient with a coronary artery blockage; from 1975 to 1980, over a half million of these operations occurred in the United States. Heart and lung transplants have been performed, and artificial hearts have been implanted. Calcium blockers are now used to lower blood pressure and raise cardiac output; they are effective in treating arrhythmics and angina. Nuclear scanners examine the heart's pumping performance and check for evidence of obstruction in the coronary arteries. An implantable automatic pacemaker is used to help patients with severe rhythmic disruption of the heart's contraction. Other developments by cardiac scientists are too numerous to mention here.

Comments

An important lesson can be learned from the beginnings of many research products. They were crude, almost impossible contraptions, but they developed over the years to marvels of intricate and effective mechanisms. In your mind's eye, contrast the first automobiles with today's cars; do the same for printing presses, airplanes, ships, locomotives, radio, television, and the like.

In *The Doctors Mayo*, Clapsattle described an early form of aseptic surgery thus:

> Walls of the room were lined with large jars full of many kinds of antiseptic solution, each a different color. The operating table was covered with rubber and flanked all around with drain pans to catch pail-fulls of boiled water that were sloshed generously over everything in sight. The surgical staff wore rubber boots.

When the budding scientist in physical education becomes discouraged with the crudity of his instruments, with the ineptness of experimental procedure, with the tentativeness of his generalizations, let him remember what it once was and take heart.

RESEARCH AND GRADUATE EDUCATION

Gradually, Europe emerged from the Middle Ages with a deep and enduring appreciation for the role of the scholar. Universities became true centers of learning, with the professor at the center of attention. The European tradition involved more direct contact between professor and student; the student had to satisfy the professor in charge that he had mastered the appropriate subject matter before being granted his degree. Graduate work became research oriented, and the primary concern was the student's mastery of his chosen research area; when he had established himself in his speciality, he was considered worthy of the degree.

Although today in this country graduate education retains some of the traditional aspects of European programs, typically there are too many students for the student-professor ratio to be so favorable. Instead, the student is exposed to a variable sequence of courses that often give more breadth than depth, and a number of credits are reserved for the thesis. In its most favorable light, therefore,it could be argued that research is still the center of graduate work, supported by certain courses that would lead to competence in the subject matter.

Research is carried on in other types of institutions, centers, or laboratories, but the university alone blends the two in a partnership that is at once more highly creative and intellectually stimulating than would be possible if they were separate. An opportunity is provided for the student to be a part of new developments, to watch new knowledge being obtained and new theories examined, and, more important, to watch the frontiers of knowledge pushed forward. Further, the professor involved will be intellectually stimulated by the inquiring minds of his or her students; not infrequently, he or she will be challenged by new and fresh insights into problems that research has spawned. This is a primary function of the university; it is what characterizes graduate study.

One of the most dramatic new developments in recent years has been the rise of the industrial research laboratory sponsored by manufacturers for devising specific retail products. Some industries that at one time were solely concerned with the invention of new sales items, almost entirely applied research, now have laboratories with corresponding freedom of activity for the scientist to study basic problems without the necessity of providing immediate practical applications. These industries realize that the broad base of factual knowledge culminates in far more sales products than does restricted applied research. What is missing in large measure here, however, is the dissemination of knowledge to students of the research worker, who could in turn carry his or her work forward. This continuation of projects is performed primarily in colleges and universities at the graduate level.

It has sometimes been said that teaching and research are not compatible, that the researcher is far more interested in research than in his or her students or teaching to the extent that the teaching suffers. Such statements seem to have been made more often in the fields of education than in other physical or social sciences, a fact that alone should be worth serious examination. Unfortunately, however, an undercurrent of mistrust exists relative to the marriage of these two purposes. Possibly such comments should be relegated to the role of a cliché; certainly, the evidence in support of this belief is flimsy and inconclusive. The overwhelming opinion in higher education on university campuses today holds that the most effective and stimulating teacher is the one who is continuously active in research, one who is most prone to have a thorough knowledge of and insight into his or her field.

A rather practical problem, which concerns the manner in which faculty research is to be evaluated, may be raised at this point. This evaluation is especially difficult in the various fields of education where straightforward experimental studies in the classical sense are not always undertaken. As will be seen, the measurement of several parameters or the application of a variety of procedures must often be made to a rather substantial number of subjects. When these subjects are humans, perhaps students, whose lives cannot always be ordered to suit the convenience of the investigator, a number of months may elapse between inauguration and end of data collection. The most rigorous timetable involving data reduction, analysis, and writing of the paper will require even more time. Thus the report may not appear in publication for a year or more after data have been collected.

In physical education, this situation is realistic; the evaluation of scholarship should not necessarily be based upon the same criterion as for other sciences. Numbers of reprints of worthy papers, for instance, are certainly indicative of productivity, but for an estimate of true scholarship the extent of activity and involvement in scholarly efforts should be appraised. When such is not done, serious injustice may result, or, even worse, poor scholarship may actually be encouraged. There is a sparseness of long-term studies that review aspects of longevity, training, detraining, growth and development, retention of learning, and other areas of basic concern. The urgency of publication tends to destroy efforts in these directions, particularly on the part of the younger research worker or faculty member, and it encourages a reliance upon short-term studies. Pressures of time might justly be placed on the graduate student; however, the professor should be free to make a contribution in the manner of his or her choice.

If one were to adopt the point of view that research is any activity that broadens or deepens the base of humanity's knowledge through independent scholarly means, then one must be willing to accept as research any form that is truly creative—that is, it must be new, and it must strive to enhance the future activity of the field. For physical education, much of modern research employs the experimental method, but also pertinent are historical and philosophical processes. Moreover, a special need exists to consider "creative expression" as an art form in the dance, in much the way it is accepted in departments of art and music. Just how such efforts are to be evaluated may well rest upon the interpretation given to research from one institution to another.

RESEARCH IN PHYSICAL EDUCATION

Overview

The production and dissemination of scholarly knowledge are efforts essential to the field of physical education. This field includes professional content peculiar to the utilization of its activities, mostly in educational institutions but by no means so confined. Further, this field logically includes aspects of such diverse established disciplines as anatomy, physiology, physics, chemistry, anthropology, psychology, nutrition, growth and development, and sociology. The focus of attention is on the study of man as an individual engaging in motor performances. Physical education is also inextricably associated with the well-being of a human's total organism, physical fitness, mental alertness, sociopersonal adjustment, and emotional stability.

A person could be well educated in the traditional disciplines and yet be quite ignorant with respect to comprehensive and integrated knowledge of the motor behavior and capabilities of humans and to the application of physical activity for organismic effectiveness. The areas of knowledge that are vital to physical education receive haphazard and peripheral treatment, rather than systematic development, since the focus of attention is directed toward the traditional curriculum. Furthermore, physical education over the past century has developed a body of knowledge of its own, which would be largely, if not totally, disregarded if its graduate study and research were allocated and dispersed to other disciplines.

The study of physical education does not consist of the application of the disciplines of anatomy, physiology, psychology, sociology, and the like to the study of physical activity. On the contrary, physical education, as a discipline in its own right, utilizes appropriate aspects of these associated disciplines. The graduate student in physical education will not become a physiologist or an anatomist or a psychologist. Moreover, the emphasis must frequently be placed on special areas within each of these fields, areas that receive little or no attention otherwise.

One may well raise the question: Where is the demarcation between physical education and associated disciplines? No simple definitive statement is possible, but examples may be given as illustrations. For example: What causes oxygen debt is physiology; the role of oxygen debt in various physical performances is physical education. The study of skeletal maturity is anthropology; a consideration of the nature, extent, and significance of skeletal and bodily maturity for physical activity of boys and girls of the same sex and age is physical education. The origin and attachments of muscles are functions of anatomy; the identification of the muscles involved in various physical performances is physical education. How the individual learns is a function of psychology; how this knowledge can be applied to complex motor performances is physical education. Physical fitness is more than freedom from disease and handicap; the physical educator is vitally concerned with strength and stamina and how they may be properly and effectively developed. Cultural anthropologists have long been aware of the role of physical games and sports in all cultures; however, comprehensive treatment of this topic, so intimately related to physical education, seldom appears in anthropology textbooks.

It would be unfair to say that scholars in various traditional disciplines feel that it is unimportant to study the person as an individual engaging in physical activity. Rather, the neglect is because this aspect is of peripheral rather than of central interest to the scholars in those other fields. Further, the physiologist, the anatomist, and the psychologist do not adequately understand the person as an individual engaging in motor performances; in general, they have not studied the relationship of a person's muscular and physiological status to his or her physical fitness, mental alertness, sociopersonal adjustment, and emotional stability. *They are not scholars of physical education.*

Present Evidence

Most research in physical education is done by graduate students.[3] Adequate training in research methods, experimental design, utilization of quantitative methods of treating data, and understanding and evaluation of laboratory testing and of research processes are required of doctoral candidates in the more stringent graduate programs in this field. Adequate resources both of faculty and facilities are available for proper research in physical education at many universities. There is no reason to believe that these institutions consider research to be less important for physical education than for other disciplines.

[3] H. Harrison Clarke, "Graduate Study and Research as Related to Physical Education," *Physical Fitness News Letter*, XII, No. 1 (September 1965), 1.

Probably the best way to assess the quality of graduate work in physical education is to determine how effectively its purposes are accomplished. From the standpoint of preparing college teachers and administrators the record is impressive. Many of those who have received doctorates in physical education are serving with distinction in colleges and universities. Hundreds have been called upon by federal, state, and local governments; by the armed services; by industry, business and medicine; by various youth-serving agencies; and by the Veterans Administration for consultation services in the field of their specialization. An appreciable number have achieved eminence as scholars by any definition of that term.

Evidence is available of the acceptance and contribution of graduate research in physical education; many studies have made significant scientific contributions. The following illustrations are presented in support of this contention:

1. Scientific studies in physical education have been conducted in institutions of higher learning since 1861, when the first chair in this field was established at Amherst College. Early scholars were Edward Hitchcock, Amherst College; Dudley A. Sargent, Harvard University; William G. Anderson, Yale University; R. Tait McKenzie, University of Pennsylvania; James H. McCurdy, Springfield College; and others.

2. Specific research organizations have been associated with physical education since the Athletic Research Society was formed in 1907. This society was superseded in 1928 by formation of the Research Section of the American Physical Education Association, now known as the American Alliance for Health, Physical Education, Recreation, and Dance.[4] In 1942, a Research Council was also formed within the association, which has been a working organization since its inception, with membership limited to individuals who meet specific research-related qualifications. To better serve the broad and varied research interests of the present alliance membership, a Research Consortium was formed recently; the consortium replaced both the former research section and council and now serves as the research arm of the AAHPERD. The general purpose of the consortium is "to provide a coordinating organization for research, charged with promoting the development of policy, standards, and terminology and the improve-

---

[4]H. Harrison Clarke, "History of the Research Section of the American Association for Health and Physical Education," *Research Quarterly*, 9, No. 3 (October 1938), 25.

ment of programs, materials, and methods in the areas of concern of the Alliance."[5]

3. A *Research Quarterly*, now named *Research Quarterly for Exercise and Sport*, has been published since 1930 by the AAHPERD. In the field of publishing, an international research monograph series in physical education was sponsored for several years by Prentice-Hall, Inc. Seven hard-cover monographs were published in this series, mostly authored by physical educators; physical educators also composed the editorial board.

4. Many graduate departments of physical education now have well-established, comprehensive research laboratories. Associated with these laboratories are well-prepared and experienced professors with local, national, and international reputations as scientists in this field.

5. As a service to health, physical education, and recreation, the School of Health, Physical Education, Recreation, and Dance, University of Oregon, publishes in microfiche form master's theses and doctoral dissertations, back issues of professional journals, and out-of-print scholarly works. Current bulletins contain over 3,000 titles; over 150 university libraries throughout the United States and foreign countries subscribe to this service.[6]

6. Physical education scientists have published in many journals outside their particular field, including those in medicine, rehabilitation, physiology, psychology, child growth and development, and the like. Such publications are respected throughout the world.

7. A number of physical education scientists have received grants from federal agencies, including the Department of Defense, National Institutes of Health, and the U.S. Office of Education. Physical educators in the United States have played prominent roles in international scientific conferences, especially since 1952 at all Olympic Games Symposia.

8. Physical education scientists have served jointly with the scientists of other disciplines in the application of research to the solution of human problems. An apt example is the formation of the American College of Sports Medicine, a national branch of an international organization. Many physical educators are fellows who are associated in membership and professional efforts with those from medicine and exercise physiology.

[5] Research Consortium Operating Code, 1981.

[6] H. Harrison Clarke, "Microcard Publications," 20, No. 7 (September 1949), 440; and "Microcards," *Journal of the American Alliance for Health Physical Education, Recreation, and Dance*, 22, No. 5 (May 1951), 34.

9. In recent years, athletic performances have been transformed. Skilled techniques and training regimens have been vastly improved; performance standards and records are being constantly improved. Although outstanding coaches and trainers have been effective innovators, physical education scientists have contributed significantly to these developments.

10. Knowledge developed by physical education scientists has been applied effectively in many ways outside education. For example, physical educators have served as human performance consultants to industry. Physical educators were engaged extensively by the armed forces medical services in the physical reconditioning of battle casualties during World War II; since then, they have been utilized as corrective therapists in Veterans Administration hospitals. For many years, physical educators have been associated with the psychiatric care of patients in mental hospitals. Physical educators have served on staff and as consultants to the President's Council on Physical Fitness and Sports.

Nature of Research

In research, a careful, systematic, and objective investigation is conducted to obtain valid facts, draw conclusions, and establish principles regarding an identifiable problem in some field of knowledge. As can be seen from this textbook, research in physical education has a very broad application. Thus, problem solving in this field may relate to historical accounts, philosophical conceptions, surveys of practices and administrative procedures, and scientific studies pertaining to all phases of the human organism affected by exercise.

Early in the emergence of civilization, problem solving was mostly a trial-and-error process, in which individuals tried out various procedures essential to daily living in order to decide which one worked best. Invention showed ingenuity and astute observation of natural phenomenon. History was passed on orally and by legend. Later, tradition and authority formulated "truths," which many times were followed unquestioningly and unconsciously. Preliterate people turned to tribal leaders when seeking knowledge; in medieval times, people believed that scholars and churchmen had the ultimate answers to questions, and their pronouncements could not be challenged. In such matters as dress, speech, worship, and etiquette, the automatic acceptance of approved patterns of behavior proved economical and often necessary in an orderly society. The opinions of experts and experienced leaders are still utilized in "solving" problems today, when other means of problem solving are unavailable. However, accepting unconditionally the validity of the opinions of experts is a dubious if not dangerous practice.

This textbook is concerned with appropriate formal procedures applied to the solution of various types of problems in physical education. Some characteristics of these processes follow:

1. Research is based upon observable experience or empirical evidence. It accepts only evidence that can be verified.

2. Research demands accurate observation and description. The most precise means of description is through the use of valid quantitative measuring devices.

3. Research gathers new data from primary sources or analyzes existing data for new purposes. However, merely reorganizing or restating already available materials is not research, as it adds little to what is known.

4. Research is characterized by carefully designed systematic procedures and by vigorous analysis of resultant data. Although trial and error may be involved in some situations, research is seldom just a blind, "shotgun type" solution—simply trying something to see what happens; rather, some logical notion or hypothesis is expressed and tested.

5. The researcher is knowledgeable in the area of investigation. He or she has searched the related literature and is thoroughly grounded in the terminology, concepts, and technical skills necessary to collect and analyze the data. He or she is competent to relate results to existing knowledge and to draw justified conclusions as related to hypotheses being tested. He or she should be able to suggest implications from his or her findings for professional significance and practice.

6. Research requires a logical and objective approach to problem solving. Personal bias is totally subjugated in procedures employed, in data collected, and in conclusions stated. The emphasis is on testing, not proving, relevant hypotheses.

7. Research necessitates careful and precise recording and reporting. The problem is exactly expressed, limitations are clearly stated, procedures are described explicitly, references are accurately documented, results are objectively recorded, and conclusions drawn are justified by the evidence obtained. From the written report, any competent scholar should be able to analyze and evaluate the study, and even to replicate it if that is deemed desirable.

8. The researcher is reluctant to give up an old position before a better one has been justified, not close his or her mind to new facts,

but being genuinely humble, having observed firsthand the expanse and inadequacies of the field of investigation. The researcher shuns the "sin" of holding an untenable position on any issue; avoiding prejudice, intolerance, and bigotry.

NEED FOR RESEARCH
TRAINING

The basic premise on which research rests is that through the scholarly investigation of specific subject matter areas the body of knowledge of the various disciplines will be revealed and developed. This is particularly true for physical education, where the extent of the academic discipline is not so widely known outside the field. The subject matter will be defined according to the direction provided by the published research studies. This should not be permitted to occur in a haphazard manner; however, there is serious doubt that any priority for the subjects to be published could be successfully proposed.

The most significant development in research today is the engagement of the university professor in scholarly study. Such participation will have upgrading effects upon his or her teaching. It will serve to assure that proper research methods will be employed and that subject matter will be developed systematically, at least within the abilities and interests of the faculty member. But perhaps the greatest asset will be the progressive and logical development of the field. Certainly, the reverse can be argued, for with increasing competition in the academic marketplace, the concern of the thoughtful individual is to support and define his or her subject matter. The graduate approach today must be through the avenue of scholarly investigation.

This text, therefore, is dedicated to the assumptions that research areas in physical education have been identified, that means available for the solution of many of the problems have been developed, and that training and academic backgrounds of the researchers are adequate for solution of these problems. The preparatory training of laboratory and scientific personnel can be made available for conducting sophisticated research in this field. Such preparation requires the careful blending of major and minor subject matter for the graduate student so that his or her preparation supports the research problem. This is more vital to the doctoral candidate than to the master's degree student, primarily because of the nature, extent, and scope of the dissertation, but also because doctoral degree study provides basic preparatory training for the college and university professor. The doctoral student should be prepared not only for university teaching but also for university research.

At many colleges and universities, too, academic promotions depend largely upon how soon and how well the physical educator is able to blend teaching and research. This situation is not so crucial for master's degree candidates; for many of them, this degree will be terminal. In such cases, the thesis way not be required for the degree; additional courses and examinations may be substituted. Placed in proper perspective, the master's thesis prepares the graduate student for the doctoral dissertation, and it points toward a greater understanding of the science and discipline of the field.

Related to the graduate program is the less scientific approach to physical education for the students who do not contemplate research careers but who anticipate teaching and administration in public schools or in the service programs of colleges and universities. Even so, a substantial number of these graduate students will still be required to complete an independent research study. Three justifications for this course of action seem valid.

First, the progress of any discipline is dependent in part at least upon the ability of its graduates to be knowledgeable in the current developments of its subject matter. As knowledge is created and theories are developed and tested, not only must a means for dissemination be available, but a receptive audience that can read and evaluate the current developments is essential. Inasmuch as all academic fields are becoming more technical and detailed, the need for informed practitioners is readily apparent. The ability to read and to evaluate critically the scientific literature of the field is a primary requisite in physical education.

A second justification stems from observation of the academic trend of our times, which sees more and more younger men and women pursuing graduate work, stimulated perhaps by a desire to improve themselves, either for promotional reasons, or for financial gain, or both. The short-range view for the young student might be to finish graduate study as quickly and as easily as possible, but this may be a very hasty decision. With maturity may come a desire to go further in the academic world; a premature determination not to do research might very well place him or her at a disadvantage later should he or she desire to undertake further graduate work or contemplate a research or university teaching career.

The third justification is experiencing the discipline of completing a research study. Probably never before has the tyro in research been held so completely to the logical formulization of a problem statement, to the critical examination of the sources of data and their application to problem solving, to the accurate collection of appropriate valid and objective data, to an exact report of a study's results, and to drawing only conclusions justified from the evidence obtained. A lasting value to many professional students in completing the master's degree thesis has been the strict adherence to facts and to the exact, succinct expressions required in writing the thesis report.

It may be added that physical educators at all levels of research competency should be strongly urged to apply research results to their programs. If this practice were universally followed, physical education could well be accepted universally as a highly respected discipline. Its services to students in schools, colleges, and elsewhere would be greatly enhanced.

Thus, the scope of this text must of necessity be directed primarily to the graduate or advanced undergraduate student who is to learn the techniques of research in order to formulate a problem, collect data, analyze data, and, finally, write the report. In so doing, certain basic elements that permeate most categories of research will be noted, but perhaps more striking will be the realization that a properly formulated problem is a very specific undertaking. The formats may look very familiar when one scans a number of studies, but upon careful inspection the similarities are more apparent than real. This situation is entirely proper because each problem should be mostly original. Certainly the problems presented are many and varied.

Hopefully, the attainment of a degree will not terminate research; rather, for any field to be a functioning one, the reverse must be true. An exposure to all forms of research may well stimulate a genuine interest in, or at least a wide appreciation of, the many problems facing physical education.

PREPARATION FOR RESEARCH

Logically, undergraduate courses should provide a foundation for research competency in the sciences associated with or related to physical education. Strong undergraduate professional preparation programs include courses and laboratory experiences in physics, chemistry, biology, anatomy, kinesiology, physiology, physiology of exercise, and tests and measurements. Advanced courses in appropriate fields should be pursued for those interested in a chosen scientific discipline or contemplating college and university teaching, such as exercise physiology, mechanics of movement and sport, growth and development, and motor learning. In addition at the graduate level, courses and experiences in research methods, experimental design, research laboratory measurements and procedures, elementary and advanced statistics, and computer data processing are indicated for strong scientific preparation. For the graduate student interested in such fields as the history, sociology, psychology, or philosophy of physical education and sport, advanced preparation in the chosen field would be essential.

Some universities have recognized that undergraduate preparation leading eventually to a scientific career in physical education is feasible and desirable. As a consequence, an undergraduate specialization has been established as an alternative to preparation for teaching physical education activities, administering physical education programs, and coaching. At the University of Maryland, such a sequence is called kinesiological sciences.

Other universities have employed various ways to inject research exposures into many undergraduate courses. Pollock has pointed out that if major students miss a research experience as undergraduates, many physical educators will miss it altogether.[7] He suggested that the research laboratory should serve several purposes, including providing an opportunity for research by the staff and students, serving as a training ground for students, and orienting undergraduate students in laboratory research, Strong proposed that research should be integrated into all appropriate undergraduate experiences, beginning with the introductory courses and continuing throughout the student's college career.[8] Most of the theory courses and many of the skill courses permit instructors to introduce research findings, interpret the findings, and involve students in consulting the literature related to the content of the various curricular areas. This observer presented several ways by which undergraduate physical education programs could be enhanced through appropriate use of scientific materials.

Marley described a physical education laboratory associated with the service program for men and women students at North Carolina State University, in the absence of a major program in this field.[9] The purposes of this laboratory are to serve as the center for a Physical Fitness Classification Test, to present laboratory demonstrations for physical education classes, and to conduct small sample research in the physical education program.

[7]Michael L. Pollock, "Expose Undergraduates to Research Early," *Journal of Health, Physical Education and Recreation*, 41, No. 5 (May 1970), 25.

[8]Clinton H. Strong, "Research Methodology as Part of Professional Preparation—How and When," *Proceedings, 79th Annual Meeting, National College Physical Education Association for Men*, 1976, p. 54

[9]William P. Marley, "The General Physical Education Laboratory," *Journal of Physical Education and Recreation*, 46, No. 8 (October 1975), 34.

SUMMARY

This chapter has considered the importance and meaning of research. Discovery and research have profoundly influenced the emergence and development of our civilization from the earliest discoveries to the present utilization of nuclear power. Although the process has been continuous for many centuries, it now occurs with tremendous speed. Science is a dynamic force in today's society.

The long-established role of the university has been to foster research and scholarly activity as well as to disseminate knowledge. Other institutions and centers conduct research, especially industrial research sponsored by manufacturers for the development of their products. However, the university is unique in the training of research workers. Further, in physical education most research is being conducted at the graduate level at colleges and universities.

The production and dissemination of scholarly knowledge are essential to the increasing effectiveness of physical education and to its acceptance as a distinct discipline by the scholarly community. This field contains professional content unique to the utilization of its activities; it also contains elements of such related disciplines as anatomy, physiology, physics, chemistry, psychology, sociology, and growth and development. Evidence of the acceptance and contributions of the science of physical education has been presented. The nature of research was considered in this chapter, as well as the need for research training.

SELECTED REFERENCES

BEST, JOHN W., *Research in Education* (4th ed). Englewood Cliffs, N.J.: Prentice-Hall, Inc., 1981, Ch. 1.

CLARKE, H. HARRISON, "Focus on the Future," *Washington A.H.P.E.R.*, 17, No. 2 (February 1960), 9.

CLARKE, H. HARRISON, "Graduate Study and Research as Related to Physical Education," *Physical Fitness News Letter*, XII, No. 1 (September 1965), 1.

HENRY, FRANKLIN M., "Physical Education: An Academic Discipline," *Journal of Health, Physical Education and Recreation*, 35, No. 7 (September 1964), 32.

LOCKE, LAWRENCE F., *Research in Physical Education: A Critical Review*. New York: Teachers College Press, Columbia University, (no date).

PARK, ROBERTA J., "The Research Quarterly and Its Antecedents," *Research Quarterly for Exercise and Sport*, 51, No. 1 (March 1980), 1.

STEINHAUS, ARTHUR H., "Why This Research?" in *Research Methods in Health, Physical Education, and Recreation* (3rd ed), ed. Alfred W. Hubbard.

Washington: American Alliance for Health, Physical Education, Recreation, and Dance, 1973.

TOLLEY, WILLIAM P., "What Does It Mean to Be Educated?" *Journal of Health, Physical Education and Recreation*, 33, No. 7 (October 1962), 26.

VAN DALEN, DEOBOLD, B., *Understanding Educational Research: An Introduction* (4th ed). New York; McGraw-Hill, Inc., 1979, Ch. 1.

VAN HUSS, WAYNE D., and WILLIAM H. HEUSNER, "Significance of the Space Program to Health, Physical Education, and Recreation," *Journal of Physical Education and Recreation*, 50, No. 3 (March 1979), 26.

2
The Problem

This chapter provides suggestions for locating research problems and planning procedures for their solutions. This may well be difficult for the graduate student in meeting the requirements for a master's thesis or doctoral dissertation. The process cannot be standardized, since many problems present unique features and require individual approaches for their resolution. Fortunately for the development of scientists in any discipline, problems beget problems. Almost invariably, the pursuit of one research problem reveals other issues that suggest additional work; in fact, some large or global research projects require a series of studies that systematically explore an area over a period of time. This pattern of coordinated research, followed for a number of years, perhaps for a lifetime, marks the careers of true scientists. Illustrations of such sustained research endeavor may be seen in the seven volumes of the International Research Monograph Series in Physical Education by Prentice-Hall, Inc.[1]

Team research has many advantages to commend it. In many disciplines today, especially in industry and in university grant research, researchers work in groups, pool their knowledge and ideas, and share the results of their efforts. Highly significant discoveries are apt to occur from the cumulative efforts of several investigators working together over a long period. Further, as is discussed later in

[1] See Chapter 3 for presentation of this series of monographs.

this chapter, longitudinal studies over many years are possible, in which the research efforts of individual degree candidates can be directed toward restricted phases of the major problem.

Usually, graduate students are required to develop a research plan, submit it for approval, and then pursue it to completion. The various steps are followed in a sequence under the guidance of a professor. Therefore, the premium for many graduate students is the identification of a suitable problem as early as possible in the program. This is especially true at the master's level because the degree program covers such a short period of time. If knowledge of the subject matter is essential, and there is little doubt that this is so, then the thesis topic may require development before the discipline itself is mastered. For the doctoral dissertation, the program of study is longer, the subject matter has greater depth, and the student is apt to be more mature. In addition, the student may already have completed a master's thesis that has provided knowledge of the essential ingredients of research and scholarly study. In turn, the research problem will have greater depth and thus reflect advanced training and theoretical development.

It is a mistake to think of the master's thesis as some sort of substandard problem. Although it may be the student's first research effort, this may mean simply that a more scientifically valid report requires greater attention to detail and closer supervision rather than that the study is a compromise of scientific standards. As a matter of fact, any lessening of essential procedural controls will remove the effort from the category of research altogether. The primary difference between the master's thesis and the doctoral dissertation is the scope of the study. Typically, the dissertation has greater breadth or depth or both than the thesis; as a result, it takes longer to complete, and the student may be more thorough in the selection of parameters. However, both must be scientifically sound.

BASIC PURPOSE AND METHOD OF SCIENCE

The basic aim of science is the achievement of understanding. In the final analysis, scientifically speaking, knowledge is the equivalent of confirmed theories. Research provides information as to why and how certain things affect other things and explains how it works, what are its properties, and so on. Facts, as such, do not represent knowledge; rather, they are the raw material that can lead to knowledge. Thus, the accumulation of facts is one step in research, an important contribution to the total picture but only a means to the main purpose—the formulation and confirmation of theory.

Some time ago, Dewey enunciated five steps as constituting the method of science; this process was subsequently accepted as a classical approach to scientific investigation.[2] The steps are summarized as follows:

1. A felt difficulty occurs, in which one encounters a puzzling experience or problem. This difficulty may arise from perceiving unexplained gaps in the understanding of an event or phenomenon; it may be manifested in a curiosity as to why a given relationship apparently exists.

2. The felt difficulty is identified and defined in terms of a problem statement. The problem is stated in some reasonably manageable form, so that the research process can continue logically and systematically. Such a statement may be difficult to formulate, but it must be done if the researcher is to progress further and to expect the study to be fruitful.

3. Suggested solutions to the problem are proposed as hypotheses. An hypothesis is a conjectural statement, a tentative explanation of tenable reasons for the difficulty. An hypothesis is stated for the purpose of testing its validity; it should result in its acceptance or rejection.

4. Suggested hypotheses are expanded and developed through deductive reasoning. The investigator deduces the consequences of a formulated hypothesis in solving the problem as related to available relevant facts or as based upon what seems reasonable and worthy of investigation.

5. Hypotheses are tested through valid observations and experimentation leading to their acceptance or rejection. Never should an investigator set out to *prove* an hypothesis. Many great discoveries are strewn with rejected hypotheses until the right one finally emerges.

Scientists systematically build theoretical structures, test them for consistency, and subject them to empirical testing. Scientists also systematically and empirically test their theories and hypotheses. They guard their research against preconceptions and against selective support of their hypotheses. Scientists discover new facts and add them to existing knowledge; they should contribute to the present state of hypotheses, theories, and principles. To accomplish this purpose, a theoretical framework is essential. In presenting a problem, this reasoning should be clearly stated. Further discussion of this approach appears in Chapter 5.

[2]John Dewey, *How We Think* (Boston: D.C. Heath & Company, 1933), p. 12.

LOCATING THE PROBLEM

A number of suggestions are offered that will help the student make an appropriate choice of a research topic. A variety of areas are available where investigation is needed, but it would be at once hopeless, biased, and promptly out-of-date to give a list of specific research topics. The following suggestions, then, are given as guides for effective study:

1. *Systematically record unsolved problems.* This suggestion is intended to be nonspecific, for as the student pursues his or her study, professional reading may point out several unsolved problems that could serve as research projects. These should be noted systematically with the source, along with notes of explanation, and perhaps suggestions for solution; add any circumstances that make a particular problem unique, particularly with reference to the type of sample or data obtained.

   Class discussion often yields ideas for unsolved problems. The attuned student should make note of any such propositions and immediately prepare brief notes of explanation. If the whole problem is not amenable to solution, perhaps part of it can become a side issue for study. At times professors will indicate areas that have not been thoroughly studied; these leads can be seized upon and developed.

2. *Analyze literature in an area or subject field.* An analysis of the literature in a particular field is a most important source of research problems and is perhaps the one that is most difficult for the beginning student to master. Some of the specific techniques of library work will be discussed in the next chapter, but effective scholarship is accomplished by thoroughly knowing the literature. Obviously, no one person can know everything; therefore, as the student plans his or her academic course of study, he or she should emphasize those areas that have the greatest interest. Important suggestions that can be made here are as follows:
   (a) Note the distribution of research completed in the area. Do all facets of the problem seem to be well covered? What gaps exist? Where is the greatest interest?
   (b) Discover any trends that may become evident. Have all aspects been investigated? Do deficiencies exist in any of the research completed? Do new avenues of interest appear as possible sources of research?
   (c) Examine critiques of a given field. Often key areas of neglect can be ascertained either explicitly or implicitly in critiques of various facets of the field. It may be possible to note deficiencies and strengths in this way.

(d) Analyze statements of needed investigations. Occasionally authors indicate areas or specific studies that are currently needed. If their review is comprehensive, this may be an excellent lead. Writers of theses or dissertations may include such a section as a parting gesture to indicate related studies that they feel should be undertaken.

3. *Analyze thoroughly an area of special interest.* Although related to the previous category, the intent here is to recommend that the student select an area of special interest and pursue it diligently to determine the items that require further study. The student may intuitively sense that certain aspects are not adequately understood; so the first task is to list problems that are germane. Next, it is necessary to review completed research to discover gaps in knowledge. This, in all likelihood, will cause the list of problems to grow and will require that a priority be established. When this has been accomplished successfully, the last step is to become thoroughly familiar with the research concerning the topic. One literally becomes a scholar in a specialty, and suddenly the problems become obvious. This usually requires that a number of revisions be made in the original selection of a topic in light of the more thorough understanding that has occurred from the literature review. Students must be flexible at this point and actually seek out alterations that will make the study sounder. At the same time, they must be prepared to accept the fact that their original idea may not be appropriate for investigation or that it is not an acceptable problem.

4. *Consider corroboration of former studies.* Frequently, graduate departments insist that students' studies be original. Adherence to such a requirement, however, may be unnecessarily restrictive. There may be instances when corroboration is justified, if not definitely desirable. This suggestion is not intended to advocate irresponsibly repeating studies by others; the student should have a sound reason for doing so in each instance.

In a strict replication, a former study must be duplicated in the exact manner that the original investigator conducted it. For example, Clarke obtained a correlation of −.38 between the strength and relative endurance (load proportionate to strength) of the elbow flexor muscles.[3] This correlation was completely at variance with the projected hypothesis that the correlation would be positive and high. So the study was repeated; a comparable

[3] H. Harrison Clarke, *Muscular Strength and Endurance in Man* (Englewood Cliffs, N.J.: Prentice-Hall, Inc., 1966), p. 185.

correlation of −.40 was obtained, verifying the original finding. Subsequently, however, a correlation of .90 was found when a gross muscular endurance measure (same load for all subjects) was utilized.

Other illustrations of corroborations follow. In the first, Kraus and Hirschland reported that United States children had a high incidence of failures on the Kraus-Weber Test of Minimum Muscular Fitness, especially as compared to European children. Their sample was from the "eastern seaboard," so comparable normative surveys were conducted by others in various areas of the United States and in other countries.

In the second example, a similar spate of studies followed the Hettinger-Muller report of 50 percent strength improvement in ten weeks from daily six-second contractions against a resistance equal to two-thirds of each subject's maximum strength.

5. *Examine controversial issues.*   Controversy may exist concerning various practices in physical education and sport; when present, they may provide problems for research. In the past, controversy revolved around such issues as the desirability of competitive athletics for young boys and for girls, the validity of maximum oxygen intake as a measure of aerobic fitness, the role of exercise in the reduction of serum cholesterol and tryglicerides in the arteries, the effect of wheat-germ oil and other dietary supplements upon athletic performances, and the kind, frequency, intensity, and duration of exercise to improve the various components of physical fitness. Controversy still exists in some of these areas and, of course there are others; at any given time, new controversies may erupt.

It should be recognized that solving the major complex issues of the day is a multidimensional problem. Therefore, the student needs to determine the specific facet to be researched. Such delimitations of research problems will be considered later in this chapter.

6. *Become informed of research going on at the university.* A logical suggestion for the student in seeking a research topic is to become acquainted with research underway in his or her department at the university. Large-scale research projects may frequently be sponsored and conducted in physical education or in conjunction with other departments. Quite often, graduate students can gain valuable research experience by becoming part of the enterprise, sometimes aiding as a member of the testing or laboratory team or assisting in data reduction and statistical treatment. Even in such situations, the student should exercise

initiative and propose a topic that is in line with the objectives of the overall project. This would be of help to both parties, as the project director is committed to completion of the broader study, in many instances welcoming the help of graduate students in developing certain aspects. The student also benefits from the opportunity to observe a large and integrated research study and to appreciate the depth of knowledge that is being explored; as a member of the team, the student can learn more advanced techniques of measurement and gather data that would be impossible when functioning alone. Such an approach has much to commend it as a learning research experience.

The graduate student's search of pertinent literature and other processes connected with thesis or dissertation provide a unique background from which his or her own future activity can grow. Much the same can be said for participation in research institutes, where a group of scholars from several disciplines work together on multidimensional research studies that are supported by a common thread but held together by rather diverse interests. Quite often facilities, equipment, and funds can be made available to qualified graduate students to work on problems of interest to their field. Financial support of this type is important, for it sometimes makes possible the pursuit of projects too costly for a single department.

7. *Consult with faculty members.*   Consultations with the student's adviser, course instructors, or major professors may be helpful in locating a research problem. It should be understood that the initial assignment of a graduate adviser is not usually for the purpose of thesis advisement, but, rather, for developing a program of courses to fulfill degree requirements. This adviser may or may not serve the student's thesis needs. Therefore, when the thesis topic is developed and approved, a different adviser, who may have specialized in the thesis area, may fulfill this function.

In any event, the student should not expect the faculty member to provide the research problem. Prior to consultation with a professor, the student should become acquainted with his or her research interests and should acquire a background in the field through appropriate reading. It is highly desirable to have considered possible thesis topics and to have developed tentative research approaches to them. An important function of the research adviser is to help the student clarify his or her thinking, achieve a sense of focus, and develop a manageable problem from one that may be vague or too complex.

8. ***Discover interests of associations or societies.*** Frequently, various professional groups have expressed interests in furthering specific kinds of research. Therefore, such groups may provide a source of ideas for the student, as each represents current concern for certain studies. Examples of such efforts in the past have been the following:

   a. The Research Council in 1954-56 urged research on the effects of athletics on young children.
   b. The Research Council in 1964-65 encouraged research on specific sports in an effort to assist coaches of various sports.
   c. The Oregon State Education Department stressed the need for a motor fitness test with norms.
   d. The California State Department of Education cited the necessity of acquiring a physical performance test.
   e. The School District at Coos Bay, Oregon, desired a fitness survey of all boys and girls in the system.
   f. The President's Council on Physical Fitness has urged research efforts in the area of physical fitness for a number of years and has generally indicated the problems that need solution.
   g. The American Alliance for Health, Physical Education, Recreation, and Dance has sponsored a physical fitness testing project and has encouraged research in some related areas.

CRITERIA IN SELECTING A PROBLEM

A number of factors should be considered in deciding whether or not to proceed with a particular study. The following criteria are given:

1. ***Is the problem of interest to you?*** Very likely, in the chronology of events, interest in the problem is a primary consideration of the student. Naturally drawn toward questions that interest him or her, or that the student feels should be done, he or she will not be as enthusiastic about subjects that hold no interest. For example, some individuals would find working on animal studies less than enjoyable, especially if dissections were required. Others would find the library study required for historical research too boring or the repetitious testing necessary for experimental research distasteful, particularly if it were to involve a great deal of statistical analysis. However, the advice to novice researchers at the graduate level is to adopt a permissive attitude—assume that interest is not an overriding factor and consider any worth-

while project to be acceptable. As long as the research area is not completely repulsive, experience has shown that most students become enthusiastic about their work once they are involved with it. To spend an inordinate amount of time in search of some magical combination of factors would seem ill-advised if progress in a positive direction could be made with a second order of priority. The accent must still be on the topic being acceptable, because no amount of interest can supplant scientific validity.

2. *Is it possible to obtain data appropriate to the solution of the problem?* This is a question of major concern to the researcher, as it is obvious that if the question cannot be answered affirmatively, there is little use in proceeding with research. No amount of skill can justify the project if the data are inappropriate. In many cases, especially in the psychological or sociological areas, certain assumptions, which are roughly equivalent to establishing validity of the testing instrument, must be made. Thus, for example, in assessing the emotional health of junior high school students, Lawrence not only found it necessary to define emotional health as the state of adjustment of the individual as related to himself or herself, others, and the environment, but also the validity of a prepared questionnaire as indicator of emotional health had to be established.[4] Similar procedures were used by Kenyon to assess certain psychosocial and cultural traits of prospective physical education teachers.[5] In these instances, the issues were not completely straightforward but required careful establishment of measuring instruments. Contrast these situations with the assessment by Sinclair in determining the stability of somatotype components of boys ages 12 through 17 and their relationship to physical and motor factors; in this instance, all essential ingredients in the study were more precisely stated and measured.[6]

3. *Are techniques available for the solution of the problem?* Akin to the previous question is the additional one of the techniques available for solving a problem. Examples of inadequate means for research abound in the area of laboratory

[4]Trudys Lawrence, "Appraisal of Emotional Health at the Secondary School Level," *Research Quarterly*, 37, No. 2 (May 1966), 252.

[5]Gerald S. Kenyon, "Certain Psychosocial and Cultural Characteristics Unique to Prospective Teachers of Physical Education," *Research Quarterly*, 36, No. 1 (March 1965), 105.

[6]Gary D. Sinclair, "Stability of Somatotype Components of Boys Twelve through Seventeen Years of Age and Their Relationships to Selected Physical and Motor Factors" (Doctoral Dissertation, University of Oregon, 1969).

experimentation, where scientists had to wait for the development of precise instruments. Every discipline has experienced this difficulty. With the advent of new devices has come a resurgence of interest in various phenomena heretofore left unexamined. The electron microscope permitted more detailed analysis of muscular contraction; the cable tensiometer permitted readily usable techniques for gross strength assessment; the electromyograph provided quantitative data on muscular activity; and the electrogoniometer gave greater validity to range of joint movement studies. These examples and others illustrate the development of measurement techniques that have advanced the research possibilities in physical education. It is a truism that the absence of accurate, precise instruments retards research efforts. If the techniques are unavailable for solution of a given problem, then the project must be revised or abandoned.

A secondary consideration involves the perplexing situation whereby the techniques required by the research design are known and have been adequately documented, yet the instruments themselves are not available to students at their institutions. Assuming that they cannot be purchased immediately, the solution may be found in either borrowing the equipment from another university or perhaps going to another department on campus where help may be obtained. This latter course of action has proven quite successful, particularly when blood analysis, animal tissue analysis, or other technical procedures not only require special equipment, but also trained assistance. Such interdepartmental cooperation is usually encouraged in universities, for it enlarges the research possibilities of a single department.

4. *Can the research be completed within an available time frame?* If the researcher has no particular deadline to meet—as would be true with the full-time research worker or the professor engaged in his or her own scholarly pursuits—then time may not be a crucial factor. On the other hand, the student ordinarily has a deadline to meet, which means there must be consideration given to the length of time it will take to complete the study. No meaningful standards can be set in this regard, except, possibly, for the longer time it usually takes for completion of the doctoral dissertation as against the master's thesis.

Some studies simply take longer to complete. This is particularly true of certain types of research where the investment of time is the key factor. For example, it has been known for years that more longitudinal data need to be obtained on factors of growth and development; yet, few such long-range studies exist in physical education. The Medford Boys' Growth Study, inaugurated in 1956 and continued for 12 years, is an example of such sustained research.[7] When such a continuous project is sponsored by the university, it does have the built-in advantage that the time factor for any one thesis is condensed; the student need not necessarily have collected data for each year or each age group, although he or she should have been a participant in the project for one or more years.

Conditioning or training studies over a time period have also been lacking, and yet physical fitness has always been a primary objective in physical education. Studies designed to progress for several weeks, whether the subjects are human or animal, should be encouraged. Often the studies on conditioning follow a basic 10-week plan and thereby fit into university calendars for activity classes, or they utilize members of athletic teams, in which case the studies may be seasonal. Another area of importance that requires extended time is the study of retention learning. Sometimes requiring several months for completion (perhaps even years), these investigations on motor learning are receiving more attention as the field becomes better understood.

5. *Is the cost involved feasible?*   The question of cost may be an essential factor for the student researcher. If a contemplated study is expensive to conduct and the cost must be borne by the student, an insuperable burden may be imposed. It is the rare student who is able to underwrite large expenses for the completion of his or her study; in fact, students should neither be expected nor required to do so. A function of the department should be to supply the necessary equipment and supplies to carry on research at the graduate level. If the necessary tools are not available and cannot be borrowed or purchased in time, then the problem considered should be revised or discarded.

Occasionally students become involved in studies where the true expenses are obscure, as in those that involve large surveys where considerable paper and postage costs may accrue, or those in which on-the-spot interviews are to be held individually, causing traveling and lodging expenses to be rather large.

A prevalent practice in physical education has been to obtain volunteer subjects for research studies. If the investigation is endorsed by the activity instructor, sufficient subjects can be obtained for almost any project. However, with the advent of research grants, many departments or project leaders are able to

---

[7] H. Harrison Clarke, *Physical and Motor Tests in the Medford Boys' Growth Study* (Englewood Cliffs, N.J.: Prentice-Hall, Inc., 1971).

remunerate the subjects for their time and effort spent on the research project. At many institutions, the time has apparently come when subjects are sophisticated enough to expect to be paid for their involvement. If the graduate student must do this alone, the cost can be rather substantial. If there must be some sort of monetary reward, then perhaps the researcher should give some thought to providing an incentive for participation and try to ensure full cooperation and completion of all assignments.[8]

Advance attention should be given in the research design to possible use of computers in data analysis. Quite often the amount of data obtained is substantial; with the availability of computers to assist in statistical analysis, the student might well investigate all facets of this facility. In many cases, no charge is made to the student; in others, he or she may have to pay for such items as computer operating time or card-punching time.

6. *Do you have adequate training and experience to interpret results?* A hierarchy of laboratory skills in research does exist; some skills require extensive training, whereas others need relatively little experience. This observation is not to be confused with the validity of the study, for the sole criterion here is based upon whether the tool or technique provides valid and reliable data. Whether it is a simple chronoscope or a complicated gas analyzer is irrelevant so long as the appropriate device is used for the problem at hand. The more difficult the procedure, the more time and training will be required proportionally for its use in research.

Other techniques may require an extensive theoretical background and perhaps demand that the student have courses of advanced study. The subject of intergroup relations is not approached without proper academic preparation, nor are studies involving advanced psychological techniques. If the student has not planned well in advance for this exigency, it would seem ill-advised to propose them for research purposes. Thus, some kinds of research are closed to students until adequate preparation is achieved. At the doctoral level such preparation should be expected and, in fact, encouraged.

From time to time among historians in education and physical education, the advisability of encouraging historical or philosophical research at the master's degree level has been

[8] William J. Tomik, "The Effects of Speed, Load, and Repetition of Interval Training Bouts on Endurance Performance" (Ph.D. diss., University of Maryland, 1968).

questioned. Not only are too few students academically readied for this task, but the difficulty of the subject matter puts the student who is not adequately prepared at a serious disadvantage. Certainly such studies have been satisfactorily accomplished by master's degree students, but frequently the student must be prepared to study the subject matter in some depth. On the positive side, however, those students whose backgrounds and interests qualify should be encouraged to follow such depth research, as physical education must be developed more fully in the historical and philosophical areas.

A somewhat similar situation exists concerning adequate training and experience for utilization and interpretation of statistics in experimental studies. Formal training in statistics at the graduate level should be required for anyone using an experimental design. Without this competency, an undue burden is placed upon the advisor, the student, or even some outside party to oversee every computational step in the analysis of data. Thus, the researcher must not only know the appropriate statistics to use and be able to calculate the correct answer, but must also have the ability to interpret the results.

7. ***Will the problem make a significant contribution?*** This question may be approached in two ways. First, does it add significantly to the field of knowledge, and second, does it make a significant professional contribution? In some respects, these may not be separate issues, but some differentiation may be apparent. In any case, studies contributing to both are needed, and certainly no attempt is made here to set up a hierarchy of research. Perhaps the differentiation is best observed if the basic research problem contributes primarily to the field of knowledge and if the applied research supports the professional literature.

The question of whether or not the research problem is significant is difficult to assess at the time; certainly, the investigator is in a poor position to evaluate the future and ultimate value of his or her work. To decide on the value of a research problem, a number of questions may be considered. How well does it fit into the current state of knowledge? How timely is it? Does it make a significant improvement over studies of a similar nature? Does it fit into existing gaps in current knowledge? Does it open new avenues of investigation? These and other questions are important, but perhaps one of the universal criteria can be mentioned: Is it likely that the study will meet the standards required for publication? For anyone seriously engaged in research, this is a key consideration.

DEFINING AND DELIMITING PROBLEMS

Once the problem has been selected and found to be generally acceptable, the next step is to establish the proper limits and extent of the study. The problem must be defined and delimited so that it is not too broad or unmanageable.This is frequently a problem encountered in the initial research efforts; the tendency to want to do too much must be resisted, although each problem will have its own separate limits that defy generalization. Each research study is a highly individualistic enterprise, and broad statements must be regarded entirely within the framework of the study itself.

As a matter of fact, many of the simpler topics have been treated so that in order to progress the student occasionally must propose a larger problem to be able to obtain sufficient data. Sometimes this can be done by narrowing the scope of the study to allow more intensive investigation in one limited area. The main problem is to keep the study within the limits established by the prevailing criteria selected. In some way, a balance of factors must be achieved so that the student is not burdened with an impossible task that would involve an extraordinary effort to complete alone. On the other hand, the problem should not be so narrow or trivial that it amounts to nothing more than an interesting little project lacking in real substance.

The delimitations of a study should be clearly stated so that the reader understands the nature of the topic. Quite often this is done formally in a section labeled "scope" or "limitations" or "delimitations"; they may also be shown in the title, although there are restrictions on length, as will be discussed later. Perhaps a clarification is in order concerning the terms *limitations* and *delimitations* in a research study. They are often confused and frequently used interchangeably in theses.

Limitations.   Limitations of studies are usually those items that encroach on the study in some substantive way. As applied to the thesis, a section of limitations should reflect any drawbacks to the study that should be known to the reader at the outset. Very frequently, a problem of instrumentation or procedure may be present that bears on interpretation of the data. For example, the study of specific gravity from underwater weighing—key to the measurement of lean body mass—raises the question of residual air determination.[9] It is essential to indicate whether residual air was measured or estimated; if esti-

---

[9] David H. Nielsen, "Body Composition and Its Relationship to Selected Measures of Muscular Strength" (Master's thesis, University of Maryland, 1967).

mated, the extent that this is likely to influence the data should be indicated. Physiological maturity can be estimated from bone growth, by pubic hair assessment, or by both.[10] Whichever is used, it is helpful once again to make this clear to the reader.

The limitations section is probably one of the most abused parts of the thesis study. Examples can be found where nearly every problem encountered was mentioned, whether or not it had a direct bearing on the study. The general rule should be to give only those items that indeed limit the acceptability of the data or impinge on the applicability of the findings. In the planning of the research, the investigator should make every effort to eliminate any serious limitations before beginning. Certainly, if there are major shortcomings in procedure, it is unwise to continue. Merely stating the limitations later does not absolve the investigator from responsibility, and it certainly does nothing to improve the validity of the study. Occasionally, however, things come to light very late in the study or occur suddenly during data collection, or a new finding is published after the study has begun. Perhaps the solution here is to indicate the extent that this affects the present study and enter it in the limitations section.

Delimitations.   Delimitations should be interpreted to mean the boundaries of the study. This is a section, often called the scope of the study, that gives the reader a brief idea of the restrictions imposed on such items as the number and kind of variables to be used, the number and type of subjects employed, or other important features that place the study in the proper frame of reference. In a brief space, the essential ramifications of the data can be made clear in order to avoid any misunderstandings created by the title. For example, it is not a limitation to the study for the subjects to be college-age males (necessarily); in fact, the type of subject may be an asset. It may be a limiting factor if there are too few subjects, but when extraordinarily difficult data are obtained on few individuals, this may be a strong point. As will be made clear in later chapters, the size of the sample is important; but, if it can be assumed that an insufficient number of subjects is employed for adequate statistical treatment, this then becomes a delimitation. What will be done with the subjects and what variables will be examined are also delimitations and may or may not need to be placed in a special section.

The first place where the scope of the study appears is in the title. This is very important, as it must accurately reflect the nature of the

[10] H. Harrison Clarke and Ernest W. Degutis, "Comparison of Skeletal Age and Various Physical and Motor Factors with the Pubescent Development of 10, 13, and 16 Year-Old Boys," *Research Quarterly*, 33, No. 3 (October 1962), 356.

work, but it cannot be excessively long. Occasionally a compromise can be made with the hope that the title will lead the reader to a section, preferably in the first chapter, that sets forth the delimitations more exactly. No general consensus of opinion exists as to just how long the title should be nor what it should contain, but it is clear that every feature of the data cannot be mentioned. Perhaps the best guideline is that it should be long enough to cover the subject, yet short enough to be interesting. It should not be misleading or so vague and general that it is not helpful to the individual searching for literature of related topics.

Thus, great care should be taken to formulate the title so that it does reflect adequately and concisely the topic to be studied. Such phrases as "an investigation of" or "the measurement of" are usually superfluous in the title, and naming of specific variables used in the data collection probably should be done only when it is crucial to the understanding of the content. Certainly, when multiple variables are utilized, a general category can be given such as "strength measures" or "anthropometric variables." The reader can be expected to look further in the study to determine just which ones were employed.

Evolving the problem statement. Suppose the graduate student is interested in studying "the coaching of athletics." This statement is hopelessly vague, although it does tell two things: the study will be concerned with coaching and with athletics. However, athletics can cover many sports, so a delimitation could be "coaching of football." But football is coached at many levels: in school and out of school, professionally, Pop Warner style, and so on. The student must again restate: "coaching of interscholastic high school football." Two delimitations have now been added: interscholastic football and high school football. The delimitation may well continue with profit. For example, note the additional delimitations in the following title: "Coaching of Football in Class A High Schools of Massachusetts."

The title can tell a great deal. However, limitations may also be listed, or the converse, the items to be covered. Thus, clarification should be made relative to the inclusion or omission of duties performed by the coach—the kinds of drills he uses, the emphasis he places on various aspects of the game, numerous details of equipment and facilities, and a host of other related facets. All such details, of course, cannot be carried in the title, although a qualifying word or phrase to "coaching" may be included such as "On-the-Field Coaching of Football in Class A High Schools in Massachusetts."

BASIC VS. APPLIED RESEARCH

This text does not promote one form of research at the expense of another, for there is a place for all types. It is essential, though, that whatever is done be done well; excellence in research should be the ultimate consideration. A controversy prevails, particularly in physical education, however, that may affect the direction that discipline will take in the future. Although not unique in this field, the question centers around the merits of basic vs. applied research.

Applied research seeks some immediate practical outcome; the student typically wishes to "solve a problem." Interest is stimulated as a result of his or her teaching or athletic background in which "problems" are numerous and real. The results of the study, the student would hope, would be to end this difficulty once and for all. It is suspected that this is the genesis of the many studies dealing with the methodology of teaching skills or the best techniques for strength development that have been popular over the years.

On the other hand is basic research, which in the purest sense seeks no immediate practical outcome. It seeks to increase humanity's understanding of its environment—to provide new insights into the way people live. Obviously, new knowledge can result from both forms of research, but it is not always so obvious that ultimately basic research can also be practical. Examples may be found wherever humanity's search for knowledge has laid the foundation for our very way of life and made it possible to exist in a modern society.

Perhaps the difficulty in a field such as physical education is that the differentiation between the two forms of endeavor is not easily recognized or not emphasized early enough in the student's undergraduate preparation. Consequently, the student begins a graduate program without a full understanding of the depth of knowledge that is available. Also, the curriculum of most undergraduate programs is education centered; the preparation of teachers is a primary obligation and the driving motivation of prospective candidates. The focus of attention, therefore, may be on the solution of problems related to teaching of activities, development of curricula, or administration of programs. In addition, the avid enthusiasm of most male physical education students for coaching is often apt to reveal a number of practical problems in the area of their sports specialty.

Unfortunately, the solution of such problems is beyond the ability of most individuals at the early stages of their research careers. A common misconception is that the problems solved "in the field" can be done more easily than the so-called more sophisticated laboratory experiment. What is not anticipated so frequently is that the field approach may neglect the necessary control and standardization that are required to draw sufficient generalizations from the data. Not only is there danger that the immediate question may not be solved properly but there is also the possibility that the evidence may not impart the fundamental nature of the point in question.

The impression is not intended that all research should be done in the confines of a formal laboratory, although many problems can only be solved there; rather, the site of research must be entirely appropriate to the specific nature of the study. Those experiments undertaken on the track or in the swimming pool may be just as basic as those in the laboratory. What is common to the basic research plan is that, rather than being specific to one skill or technique of teaching, it seeks to broaden the base of knowledge common to all skills or techniques, or it seeks to obtain information about some unknown phenomena relative to humanity and its environment. It is the acceptance of the doctrine "knowledge for its own sake," without recourse to the question "Is it practical?" It should be seen, then, that when the basic problems are solved the practical applications will come along naturally. When enough is known about learning of skills or performing of complex coordinative acts, the utilization of these results should be obvious.

The decision to undertake the more practical study or to follow a basic research design will ultimately be conditioned by a number of factors. It is not the intent here to favor either form but to present the emerging picture with respect to physical education. Whether historical or experimental, the field is aligning itself and patterning its activities more and more along the lines of other physical, social, or biological sciences. More particularly, the aim of physical eduction is to study all pertinent aspects of humanity in action, whether it be the study of basic movement patterns, physiological adaptations to exercise, psychological manifestations related to performance, or the historical or sociological analysis of contemporary sports and the dance. The exact definition of this form of research can be made once the various fields of knowledge within physical education are made clear.

THE FIELDS OF KNOWLEDGE

Several subdisciplines exist in physical education, some of which are of long standing while others are of recent development. The following constitute fields of knowledge in which courses of study have been established and research studies are being conducted:

1. *Physiology of exercise.* The cellular organization and the theory of muscular contraction as well as the functional study of the human organism are classed as physiology and would typically be studied in departments of physiology. The study of the role of these factors as they relate to human movement, performance, or training is within the purview of physical education and would come under the more specific heading of physiology of exercise.

2. *Motor learning.* The area of motor learning generally encompasses neuromotor coordination, kinesthesis, learning of motor acts, retention, and transfer. The emphasis is on the use of gross motor activity rather than fine motor skills; the terms *motor learning* or *psychological basis of physical activity* designate this research area.

3. *Biomechanics.* The field of biomechanics, involving kinesiology, has been developed to analyze movement and skill performance particularly with respect to laws of motion and anatomical capabilities. Also included are pertinent aspects of body mechanics.

4. *History.* Historical studies in physical education serve to preserve its heritage. They involve many aspects of the field, including histories of organizations and associations, biographies of leaders, and accounts of the development of various sports, games, and dances.

5. *Philosophy.* In this subdiscipline, philosophies are developed, aims and objectives are formulated, and principles are proposed as related to the purposes to be achieved and directions to be taken in physical education, sports, and dance.

6. *Sports sociology.* The goals of sociological inquiry are the discovery, description, and explanation of social behavior as related to sports. The social dimensions of sports and sports groups are considered.

7. *Sports psychology.* More concerned with the personality, emotional, or motivational aspects of sports and physical activity, sports psychology employs many of the techniques used in psychology, but it is a research area developed to serve physical education.

8. *Growth and development.* From the standpoint of physical education, studies in growth and development are directed toward physical and motor characteristics and their relationships to mental achievement, sociopersonal effectiveness, and emotional stability.

9. *Rehabilitation and medicine.* The development of knowledge in rehabilitation and adapted physical education is reflected in career fields of physical therapy, corrective therapy, and recreation therapy; it is also related to abnormal psychology, motor development, and sports medicine.

It may be seen from this list that a wide latitude is present for research related to physical education and sport. This is immediately evident when one reviews the studies presented over the years in the *Research Quarterly* of the American Alliance for Health, Physical Education, Recreation, and Dance, now named the *Research Quarterly for Exercise and Sport*. The scope of former studies may also be seen from the listing of several thousand theses in Health, Physical Education, and Recreation Microform Publications bulletins. Fortified by appropriate background courses in the specific field of his or her interest, the student decides upon an area of interest and then pursues it to a conclusion. The conclusion in this case is the research report.

SUMMARY

This chapter has indicated the process of locating and defining the research problem, including criteria in selecting the problem, limiting and delimiting the problem after the problem area is located, and evolving the formal problem statement. Most problems emerge from a systematic recording of unresolved issues, an analysis of the literature in a subject area, the study of research already completed, the examination of controversial issues, and an inquiry into continuous research at the graduate student's institution. Criteria in the selection of a problem for study include the specific interests of the student, the availability of appropriate testing techniques and data, the feasibility of the proposed research, and the training and experience of the investigator. Once the problem is selected and found to be generally acceptable, it must be defined and delimited so as not to be too broad and unmanageable.

The basic purposes and methods of science were considered in this chapter. The hierarchy of scientific knowledge exists as hypothesis, theory, and law. Differentiation was made between basic and applied research. The investigative fields were identified as exercise physiology, motor learning, sports psychology, history, biomechanics, philosophy, sports sociology, sports psychology, growth and development, and rehabilitation and medicine.

SELECTED REFERENCES

BEST, JOHN W., *Research in Education* (3rd ed.). Englewood Cliffs, N.J.: Prentice-Hall, Inc., 1977.

BROER, MARION R., and DOROTHY R. MOHR, "Selecting and Defining a Research Problem," in *Research Methods in Health, Physical Education, and Recreation* (3rd ed.). Washington, D.C.: American Alliance for Health, Physical Education, Recreation, and Dance, 1973, Ch. 3.

HENRY, FRANKLIN M., "Physical Education: An Academic Discipline," *Journal of Health, Physical Education and Recreation*, 35, No. 7 (September 1964), 32.

LOCKE, LAWRENCE E., *Research in Physical Education: A Critical Review.* New York: Teachers College Press, Columbia University, (no date).

VAN DALEN, DEOBOLD B., *Understanding Educational Research: An Introduction* (4th ed). New York: McGraw-Hill, Inc. 1979, Ch. 7.

3
Literature Search

Before completing a plan for a research undertaking, a person needs to conduct a literature search in the area of the proposed investigation. In fact, the student should become a scholar in that area.

REASONS FOR SURVEYING RELATED LITERATURE

The following purposes should be served by an early perusal of literature related to the research problem:

1. ***Determine if a study has already been completed on the proposed research topic.*** Obviously, if a study on the proposed topic has been completed, the investigator should know it and adjust his or her approach appropriately. The student may wish to abandon the topic altogether, or to restate the problem in a way which avoids duplication, unless a replication of the original study can be justified. Also, different approaches to a problem area may be acceptable. Where little research has been done in an area, extensions of completed research may be relatively easy to recognize. However, this might be difficult if the literature search revealed a plethora of studies in the area. Examples from the realm of weight-training methods can be cited to illustrate this

point; a search of the literature would reveal many studies to determine the effectiveness of various combinations and permutations of procedures to increase muscular strength and endurance. In this situation, more care would be necessary in order to avoid unwarranted duplication.

2. ***Determine if a study of a similar nature is in progress.*** Much more difficulty is experienced in finding related research that has not been completed, the study of which is in progress. Technically, the point may be valid that a student's current project can still be undertaken even if some work of a similar nature is underway. Theoretically, no problem is the sole right of a single investigator, and the chances of exact duplication of effort would seem remote. However, if such a study is found, the wisest choice of action would be to try to add significantly to the problem in some valid way. On the other hand, examples from scientific literature can be found where studies of a similar nature were being conducted simultaneously in laboratories separated widely by geographic location. Where scientists are concerned with certain fundamental phenomena, such duplication is inevitable and even welcomed. Consider the advancement in theory that is made when the data are in agreement.

Several means are available for locating similar studies that may be in progress. As like studies tend to attract similar projects, a check of the ongoing research at the investigator's institution could be made. Because the interests of faculty members are reflected in their research, if the project seems allied to these interests, it may be that such a study is already underway either by the professor or one of his or her students. A discussion with the appropriate individual should elicit this information.

3. ***Discover research allied to the problem.*** Frequently, the investigator will find it essential to examine published accounts of research that are allied to the problem, although these may be somewhat peripheral in nature. More will be said about this later, but the search for literature must entail a wide variety of articles that give the student more breadth of understanding. In this way, the investigator is able to place his or her own study in a proper frame of reference. For example, the study of certain personality traits must inevitably lead to perusal of the literature on mental health. Likewise, the concern with problems of circulatory endurance would be incomplete without an understanding of other cardiovascular variables.

Examples can be given of beginner researchers who view their problems as narrow and thereby unduly restrict their survey of literature. For instance, the student who wishes to examine various means of providing movement through the water must keep in mind that the basic phenomenon under investigation is propulsion. The review of completed research might very well entail studies that shed light upon this concept, whether or not they meet the exact specifications of the current study. In this way, the individual develops greater sophistication in the subject matter itself.

4. *Provide ideas, theories, explanations, or hypotheses valuable in understanding and formulating the problem.* In addition to understanding the results of other studies, the investigator must depend upon the interpretation and discussion of the data provided by other authors in an effort to formulate adequately the problem and to place exactly the right frame of reference on the theory involved. This is the precise point where reliance upon textbook analysis for development of theory comes to an end. Although textbooks are acceptable as background reading for comprehension of elementary theory, it is essential for the graduate student to progress beyond this level and to rely in part at least upon the published research literature for hypothesis formulation and theoretical background for problem development. If the studies reviewed have been carefully prepared, considerable theoretical discussion should be contained in the publication so that an adequate expression of the author's concept of the results is provided. Ordinarily, the discussion section of the paper will contain this information, and a careful reading of this section is essential for a thorough appreciation of the problem.

5. *Identify research procedures and statistical analyses of data employed by others.* As the research problem is being planned, it will be helpful in making procedural decisions to know the techniques employed and the statistical applications made by others who have conducted studies in the same investigative area. In this regard, items to observe are: research or experimental design employed; forms used in recording and presenting data; selection of subjects; sources of data; methods of collecting, classifying, and analyzing data; graphic presentations of data; and the format employed in writing the report. If results by others were meager or nonsignificant, reasons may be sought to account for that situation; possibly a different approach to the problem may yield better results. The more a person knows about research that has been done and the more aware he or she is of the gaps and

weaknesses of past research in the area, the more apt the person is to plan his or her own problem well.[1]

6. *Locate comparable material useful in interpreting the results.* The review of the literature may serve as an important adjunct to the investigator by assisting in the interpretation of his or her own study. Often, possible interpretations of the investigator's findings will be suggested, so that the results are placed in proper perspective in light of the published body of knowledge. The investigator's own discussion section is enhanced by knowing available theory relevant to his or her findings; the researcher should be prepared to restudy the pertinent references following his or her analysis of the data. A properly conceived study, then, requires that the researcher refer to the literature in an effort to show either support or refutation of his or her results. It is incumbent that the investigator discuss the pertinent theory involved—not in an effort to justify his or her results but to point out the logic involved. If the data are in agreement with the expected outcome, then this should be shown with appropriate references. On the other hand, if there seems to be a conflict between what has occurred and what theoretically should have happened, the disagreement should be pointed out as well. Also, some idea as to the reasons for such disagreement should be indicated. If, in fact, no logical answer can be found, this also should be stated.

7. *Understand the significance of the research.* The investigator may be able to develop sufficient insight to understand the significance of his or her research; in any event, such would only be possible if the results obtained by other researchers on the same problem were also known. Timeliness and appropriateness are helpful factors to know, especially if the problem is of current interest. Quite often, those studies that help to settle a controversial point are welcome. Also, those research endeavors that open up new areas of study hold a particular distinction, as they may foster a number of studies to follow. The extent of this reaction may be dependent upon how much theory is involved. When an important theoretical concept is exposed, it often permits attack of investigation from many sides, and the ramifications

[1]Carolyn W. Bookwalter and Karl W. Bookwalter, "Library Techniques," in *Research Methods in Health, Physical Education, and Recreation*, 2nd ed., ed. M. Gladys Scott (Washington, D.C.: American Alliance for Health, Physical Education, Recreation, and Dance, 1959), p. 20.

may be felt for years. However, the extent and significance of the challenges will very likely be dependent upon how well done the research is in the first place. Although there are examples of studies that have achieved considerable notoriety because they were not carefully conducted, it is safe to say that a research effort merely for the sake of attacking a writer should be avoided assiduously; reasons for such an effort should be well justified.

It is a prevalent tendency for theses to contain a section on the significance of the study; in this section are stated the author's views on the importance of the work or, at least, on the importance of the topic. The ultimate acceptance and appraisal of a study will depend upon a number of factors, chief of which is the extent that a theory has been further explicated. In turn, this will be reflected in the care and precision of testing and adequacy of problem development. Years may elapse before the true significance of a study can be known, and then the evaluation will be made by a "jury" of the author's peers.

8. *Be included as a background for the written research report.*   Eventually, the research will culminate in a written report, whether it is in thesis form, article form, or both; the results of the review of literature will become apparent at this time. Most of this material will appear in the thesis in the section on review of the literature, but it should not be felt that this is the only place where research studies may be cited. The major substantiation of the state of knowledge should be reviewed carefully and completely, but many times key studies should be cited early in the report in order to justify the problem or to formulate the hypothesis or hypotheses. Thus, for the thesis, reference to some of the literature will appear in introductory material where the problem is stated; the bulk of it, however, will be presented in the formal review section.

The author may also need to refer to other related studies using similar procedures or instruments in the description of method and perhaps to justify the inclusion of specific techniques or variables in the study. Not only does this indicate just why the investigator proceeded as he or she did but it serves to supplement the report. Quite often, lengthy descriptions of instruments or techniques may be bypassed by referring to published accounts where additional material can be found. Beyond this, the author may wish to return to the literature after presenting his or her own results, in order to place them in the appropriate frame of reference and to discuss the findings.

The preparation of a manuscript for publication is usually

approached in a different manner from that of a thesis. As a matter of fact, research journals do not publish theses but only research articles; therefore, any study done in partial fulfillment of the requirements for a higher degree must be rewritten to conform to the editorial policies of a particular journal. The manner of organization should be sufficiently flexible to permit a high degree of individuality in presentation; it is seldom possible to present a complete review of the literature in an article. The author must reduce the review to the essentials that give an appropriate and clear account of the study under investigation. He or she may begin with an introduction of other studies that have reviewed past work and then base his or her review on studies that have subsequently been completed. At any rate, it seems inappropriate to formalize a review of the literature in a research journal, for it tends to segregate or separate a portion of the work that seems to require complete integration into the written report. Actually, this should probably be the writer's choice.

MAJOR LITERATURE SOURCES

It is impossible to present here a discussion of all the pertinent sources of information available to researchers in physical education, as the scope is as broad as the type of problems undertaken. However, there are certain sources that are uniquely appropriate to this field, and these will be discussed.

The first important decision the investigator must make in deciding what to search is to differentiate between critical and allied sources. To the beginner, this is often bewildering, as the ramifications of his or her study may still be hazy and the choices of studies to be cited nebulous. Quite frequently, the investigator views his or her own research very narrowly, and at first is apt to look only for studies that are directly related—that is, that have been done on exactly the same topic. In this situation, the researcher is oriented to his or her experimental *variables* rather than to the *theory* that is involved. Thus, he or she is likely to search for studies done on bowling, for example, rather than on the theoretical concepts of learning that are involved in the activity. Wider reading helps to form a theoretical framework for the construction of the study. The mere fact that bowling is the activity involved is important to the literature only so far as it contributes to the theoretical concepts of learning. Other studies using bowling may be found, but there is no guarantee that they will be pertinent to the present research. The same might be said of muscular strength variables or other studies that could be mentioned; their relevancy to the research problem must be established on grounds other than their mere similarity of use.

1. *Critical Literature.* As the name would suggest, there are certain published studies that relate directly to the topic under investigation and so are critical to the subject. These studies must be cited for the review of literature to be complete. For example, if the study involves the effect of decreased environmental temperature on muscular endurance for college-aged males, the literature critical to the problem would involve similar studies that have investigated the effects of cold on performance, those that have been concerned with muscular endurance (whether or not temperature has been a variable), and those pertinent studies that have utilized adult males.

2. *Allied Literature.* Allied literature involves those studies that are related to the investigation but are more peripheral than central in nature. They form an important part of the study because they provide the background upon which it rests. In the example just given, the literature allied to the problem might include those studies that have investigated other temperatures (i.e., hot), those concerned with muscular strength or other variables, and perhaps those utilizing the opposite sex or other ages. In essence, each research proposal will require separate analysis to determine just which articles in the literature are critical and which are allied. No formula can be given for this, and opinions might differ on the precise delineation. Obviously, many opportunities for overlapping occur, so at some point a decision must be made as to what to include and what not to include.

Just how far afield one should go in reviewing research for a problem is open to discussion; some feel that only the very critical studies should be cited, whereas others would permit wide latitude. Most research studies, however, probably involve a rather small but select group of articles that really form the nucleus for the current undertaking. When the investigator has completed a search of the literature, he or she will probably have identified certain citations that provide the best means for development of his or her study and statement of the problem. Obviously, the identification of these citations must wait for the review to be completed; when the writing begins they will be mentioned prominently. At the same time, the investigator may decide to eliminate certain of the articles reviewed, as they may be neither critical nor allied. There seems to be little justification for giving space to those studies that cannot fit into either classification.

They may be essential to the student who needs the background reading, but direct inclusion in the study itself may be excessive.

Justification and Understanding of Tests Used. Sometimes, a familiarity with the literature concerning the particular test items to be employed in the study is necessary. This is particularly true for tests that are new or unfamiliar to most readers. Tests that are in continuous use and are well known or that are inherently valid in description may not require much justification. However, if extraordinary use is to be made of the test, such as utilizing grip strength to represent total body strength, then the tests are not satisfactorily justified. Thus, it would appear that the variables, coupled with their use, are the prime determinates of whether or not extensive justification is needed. The best advice might be to include such items in the review of the literature if there is any doubt.

The major point to be made here is that the researcher should know the background of the tools with which he or she is working. The reason is simply that such knowledge gives the theoretical bases and the assumptions underlying the tests he or she plans to use. If the experiment is well conceived, then no difficulty will be experienced; occasionally, however, the review of the literature will reveal inadequacies not anticipated at the outset. The first research effort by a student often results in blind acceptance of any test that has been used previously, especially if it has been published. If there is a basic defect in the original test, the student's results will add another defective study to the literature. Such problems associated with test construction and instrumentation are discussed in detail in Chapter 10, but it should be obvious that two wrongs do not make a right.

DOCUMENTATION OVERVIEW

In the early days of research in physical education, the collection, classification, and dissemination of information were done exclusively at colleges and universities, usually initiated and implemented by a professional person in this field. With the acceleration of scholarly studies in the field and in sports sciences, the sheer volume of information, especially since 1960, made it impossible for individual libraries to keep abreast of this literature. Broekhoff has presented an overview of the historical developments of sports documentation in North America and Europe, with mention of international movements, and has proposed a plan for an international sports information and documentation system.[2] This report was considered at the First World Congress for Sport Information in Bucharest, October 1981. Through various channels, a committee has been appointed to investigate appropriate steps to implement the proposals in the Broekhoff report, which would lead eventually to an international information and documentation system in physical education and sport.

In describing conditions in North America, Broekhoff noted that the United States lacks a national documentation center in physical education and sports. The lack of centralization has resulted in a proliferation of abstracting and indexing services that, in time, will create their own data bases. In Canada, the emergence of the Sport Information Research Center, discussed later, has resulted in one of the largest documentation centers in the world with on-line retrieval capability. Several European countries have national documentation centers, mostly supported by national governments. Such centers are listed and briefly described, and their locations are given in Broekhoff's report. Special recognition is given in two such centers: Deutsche Hochschule für Körperkultur, Leipzig, and Bundesinstitut für Sportwissenschaft, Cologne. The European countries have benefited from their ties with the International Association for Sports Information.

LIBRARY SOURCES

Inasmuch as the range of topics within physical education is wide, source materials are scattered throughout the various library divisions. The researcher, however, will soon discover the sources that are most germane to his or her topic. For example, those involved in exercise physiology will seek reference materials from quite different sources than will those interested in historical or philosophical studies; the same can be said for investigators in motor learning, growth, and biomechanical studies.

Quite often the student will find that his or her institution's library is inadequate for all studies needed. In fact, the growth of the graduate/faculty population often is greater than the increase in library financial support, so that a lag exists between the need for research literature and the resources to provide it. Small schools are notably less endowed than large universities, and some large institutions are far ahead of others of comparable size. If reference is found to material unavailable in the local library, it is incumbent on the investigator to obtain it. This can usually be done by securing the appropriate reference through interlibrary loan, or sometimes a repro-

---

[2]Jan Broekhoff, *Ways and Means of Organizing a System for the Standardized Collection and Documentation in Physical Education and Sport* (Paris: UNESCO, 1980), ED-80/WS/68. (Available free from UNESCO: translated into French and Spanish).

duction or copy of an article can be obtained in the event a journal cannot be sent by mail. In metropolitan areas, however, several libraries within reasonable distance may be available. The saving of time may be considerable, and the advantage in maintaining continuity of effort is well worth the pursuit to secure references locally, if at all possible. For the small, isolated college, sufficient references are often unavailable on campus; thus, great difficulty may be experienced in completing adequately the literature review. Perseverance and willingness to seek further can usually solve most of these problems.

RESEARCH REVIEWS

Several excellent research reviews on various aspects of physical education and sport have been published. If one or more can be found in the area of the student's research, they can be an excellent starting point for a literature search. Such reviews, of course, are secondary sources, abstracted or synthesized by the authors, so relevant original references should be consulted; these references are given in the reviews, so they are easily located. The dates when reviews were terminated should be observed, as, obviously, subsequent references in the subject area are not included. Several collections of research reviews are mentioned next.

1. "Contributions of Physical Activity to Human Well-Being," *Research Quarterly*, 31, No. 2, Pt. II (May 1960). These research reviews were sponsored by the Research Council to commemorate the seventy-fifth anniversary of the American Association for Health, Physical Education, Recreation, and Dance. The reviews present the contributions of physical activity to physical health, social and psychological development, skill learning, growth, and rehabilitation. Chairman: Raymond A. Weiss.
2. "Fiftieth Anniversary Issue," *Research Quarterly for Exercise and Sport*, 51, No. 1 (March 1980). As the title indicates, this issue commemorated the fiftieth anniversary of the *Quarterly*. Two scholars presented separate research reviews in each of the following seven areas of physical education: measurement and research design, psychology of sport, sociology of sport, motor behavior, motor development, kinesiology, and exercise physiology. The first article outlined the history of the *Research Quarterly* since its origin in 1930; notes were also provided in the history of earlier publications of the American Physical Education Association, as it was then known. *Editor*: Margaret J. Safrit.
3. From July 1971 through October 1979, the President's Council on Physical Fitness and Sports published a quarterly *Physical*

Fitness Research Digest. Each of the 34 issues synthesized the research pertaining to a given topic related to physical fitness and drew implications for practice. The types of topics included were: the totality of man, physically, mentally, psychologically, and socially; physical activity and coronary heart disease and related risk factors; understanding and developing the physical fitness components of muscular strength, muscular endurance, and circulatory-respiratory endurance, as well as flexibility, posture, muscular power, fat reduction, aging, menstruation, and pregnancy; exercise related to the knee joint, sit-ups, and arm-shoulder muscles; individual differences, their nature, extent, and significance; physical-motor, mental, and sociopersonal characteristics of athletes; strength development and sports improvement; sport potentials for physical fitness; and utilization of jogging, swimming, bicycling, rope skipping, dancing, walking, golf, and pack carrying in improving various components of physical fitness; and physical and motor sex differences. *Editor and writer*: H. Harrison Clarke.

4. A series of annual volumes, *Exercise and Sports Sciences Reviews*, was initiated in 1973 by the Research Council of the American Association for Health, Physical Education, Recreation, and Dance. In 1978 the series was adopted by the American College of Sports Medicine. The present publisher is The Franklin Institute Press, Philadelphia, Pennsylvania. Editor(s) and editorial board were appointed for each volume. Volume titles are not given; however, each volume contains reviews of the scientific literature pertaining to several selected topics. The research reviews are concerned with physiological, biomechanical, behavioral, sport psychology, and kinesiological aspects of human performance. Topics of special interest that are not typically embraced by these areas are occasionally reviewed. *Editors*: Vol. 1-2, Jack H. Wilmore; Vol. 3, Jack H. Wilmore and Jack Keogh; Vol. 4, Jack Keogh and Robert S. Hutton; Vol. 6-7, Robert S. Hutton; Vol. 8, Robert S. Hutton and Doris I. Miller; Vol. 9, Doris I. Miller; Vol. 10, Robert L. Terjung.

5. Two volumes of *Science and Medicine of Exercise and Sport* have been published by Harper & Row, New York City. The first volume was published in 1960; the second, in 1974. Thirty-five review articles prepared by 42 authorities appeared in the 1960 volume, classified in the following 6 aspects of exercise and sport: structural and mechanical, physiological, maturing and aging, psychological, cultural and historical, and therapeutic. The 1974 edition extended these same topics; some chapters are updated, others are new, and still others are unchanged. *Editors*: 1960,

Warren R. Johnson; 1974, Warren R. Johnson and Elsworth R. Buskirk.

6. An *Encyclopedia of Physical Education, Fitness, and Sport* in five volumes is in preparation. The publisher is Brighton Publishing Company, Salt Lake City, Utah; also available through the American Alliance for Health, Physical Education, Recreation, and Dance. The series editor is Thomas K. Cureton; volume editors are also appointed. Volumes II and III have been printed at the time of this writing. Volume II contains 55 reports classified into 5 categories, as follows: training and conditioning for physical fitness and sports, environmental aspects of physical performance, nutritional aspects of physical performance, youth fitness, and adult fitness. Volume III contains reports on 47 sports, on dancing, and on related activities. *Editors*: Vol. II, G. Alan Stull; Vol. III, Reuben B. Frost.

7. A series of *What Research Tells the Coach* brochures has been published by the American Alliance for Health, Physical Education, Recreation, and Dance in the following six sports and athletic events: tennis, football, swimming, sprinting, soccer, and distance running. These publications were prepared by committees of the Research Council.

8. A series of *NAGWS Research Reports* has been prepared by the National Association for Girls and Women's Sports and published by the American Alliance for Health, Physical Education, Recreation, and Dance. The reports are designed to provide the practitioner with scientific evidence on which to base decisions related to programs of physical activity and athletics for girls and women. Such topics as the following have been covered: endurance training, sports injuries, physical sex differences, sports participation patterns, femininity within social roles, sociological perspectives, swimming movements, and assessment of motor performance.

9. *Exercise and Aging: The Scientific Basis* contains 12 papers presented at the May 1980 meeting of the American College of Sports Medicine, published by Enslow Publishers, Hillside, N.J. Each paper summarizes research pertaining to the normal aging process and the impact of physical exercise upon this process. These papers present aging as related to cardiovascular functioning, skeletal muscle, strength, flexibility, bone mass, and respiration. Editors: Everett L. Smith and Robert C. Sertass.

Physical education researchers can consult research reviews in other disciplines. Examples of such reviews are: *Annual Review of*

Psychology, Annual Review of Physiology, Encyclopedia of Educational Research, Review of Educational Research, and *Handbook of Research on Teaching.* Since 1932 several editions of the *Mental Measurements Yearbook* have been prepared by Oscar K. Buros. These volumes list commercially available educational, psychological, and vocational tests; evaluative statements by selected authorities are presented for most tests. These *Yearbooks* are especially valuable for research in physical education requiring the selection of tests needed to evaluate psychological and social outcomes.

THE CARD CATALOG

The card catalog is an index of all publications in an institution's library, with the exception of serially published periodicals. For convenience in locating relevant materials, most card catalogs provide three listings for each publication: an author card, a subject card, and a title card. Cross-reference cards are inserted which carry a notation to seek elsewhere when the information sought can be located under other subject headings. Library call numbers are given on each card, so that the publication can be easily located on the bookshelves.

Typically also, libraries maintain files of their periodical holdings, including the years each is available. Call numbers are provided for ready location. Libraries may maintain a separate section for periodicals. Back issues are bound and placed on bookshelves; current issues are available as single copies.

INDICES

For the scholar, the periodical literature is the primary and most current source of scientific studies. Typically, and of necessity, books lag two, three, or more years in current information; further, such information is a secondary source, usually selective and synthesized by others. The location of materials relevant to the investigator's research published in periodicals can be a time-consuming undertaking. Fortunately, indices are available that list current materials appearing in a large number of periodicals; in some instances annual volumes and intervening monthly supplements are issued.

Standard Indices

Following is a list of standard indices that may help the physical educator in searching the scientific literature related to his or her research topic: *Bibliographic Index, Education Index, Journals in*

Education, International Index of Periodical Literature, Cumulative Index Medicus, Excerpta Medicus, Reader's Guide to Periodic Literature, Psychological Index, and *Social Science Index.*

Physical Education Indices

1. **Research quarterly indices.** Because the *Research Quarterly* itself is a widely used source of scientific articles in physical education, it is essential to survey these volumes. The reader should be aware of three types of indices available for locating references by subject and author in the *Research Quarterly* (name changed in 1980 to *Research Quarterly for Exercise and Sport*).

   Volume Index. Each year in the December issue of the *Research Quarterly,* an index for the current volume appears with author names and important topics.

   10-Year Indices. The same information has been assembled for 3 10-year periods from 1930 through 1959 and appears as publications of the *Research Quarterly,* as follows:

   1930-39, December, 1952 Supplement
   1940-49, December, 1951 Supplement
   1950-59, December, 1960 Part 2

   47-Year Index. Prepared by George B. Pearson (Miami, Florida: All American Productions and Publications), all issues of the *Research Quarterly* published from 1930 through 1976 have been indexed by author, topic, research design, statistical design, tests and measurements, and instruments. An earlier 30-year index had been prepared by Pearson and Jacqueline K. Whalin.

2. **Physical fitness/sports medicine.** Begun in 1978, this index is published quarterly by the President's Council on Physical Fitness and Sports, in cooperation with the National Library of Medicine. The citations are taken from more than 9,000 periodicals included in the National Library of Medicine's Medical Literature and Retrieval System (MEDLARS). The index is intended for physicians, physical educators, physical therapists, athletic trainers, and others interested in the medical aspects of sports. It contains, but is not limited to, research articles. Subscription is through the Superintendent of Documents, U.S. Government Printing Office, Washington, D.C.

3. **Physical Education Index.** Started in 1978, this index is published quarterly with a bound hard-cover accumulation each year by the BenOak Publishing Company. Citations are from over 170 domestic and foreign publications. Subjects covered are

those deemed important to professionals in physical education, sports, dance, and recreation. The subject matter includes, but is not limited to, scientific articles. The *Index* is edited by Ronald F. Kirby, Southeast Missouri State University, and nine associate editors representing various professional fields.

4. *Physical education/sports index.* This index was first published in 1978 by Marathon Press, Albany, N.Y. There are 3 quarterly issues annually, with the fourth quarter included in hard-bound annual cumulation. Approximately 100 journals are indexed, covering physical education and sports, as well as exercise physiology, sports medicine, and the history, philosophy, psychology, and sociology of sport. Scientific articles are included, but it is not restricted to these.

ABSTRACTS

A number of journals provide an abstracting service that can be very helpful in searching for relevant literature. Among these are the abstracts that appeared for a number of years in issues of the *Research Quarterly*. Prepared by members of the Research Council of the American Association for Health, Physical Education, Recreation and Dance, a large number of journals were examined for appropriate articles of interest to research workers in these fields. The project was abandoned after May 1965.

Under the aegis of the Research Council (now, Research Consortium) of the American Alliance for Health, Physical Education, Recreation, and Dance, an annual volume of *Completed Research in Health, Physical Education, and Recreation* has been published since 1959. Each volume contains an annual compilation of research materials published in over 100 periodicals and abstracts of graduate theses submitted by colleges and universities throughout the country. *Abstracts of Research Papers*, also sponsored by the Research Consortium, contains abstracts of all papers presented at each annual convention of the Alliance; in the 1980 edition, for example, 166 scientific papers were abstracted.

Abstracts outside the discipline of physical education that may contain items pertaining to this field include the following: *Child Development Abstracts and Bibliography, Education Abstracts, Dissertation Abstracts International, Nutritional Abstracts and Reviews, Physiological Reviews, Psychological Abstracts, Sociological Abstracts, Wistor Institute of Anatomy and Biology Abstracts, Exceptional Child Abstracts, Women Studies Abstracts, Mental Retardation and Developmental Disabilities Abstracts,* and *Psychological Abstracts.*

BIBLIOGRAPHIES

A number of bibliographies that are particularly concerned with physical education, sport, and related areas are available. An early series by George B. Affleck appeared annually in the *American Physical Education Review* from 10 March 1910 to June 1929 and then appeared in the *Research Quarterly* in October 1930, May 1931, October 1932, December 1982, and every December thereafter through 1941.[3] Affleck also published a bibliography of Springfield College theses, 1929-1934, in the May 1935 Supplement of the *Research Quarterly*. Also included in this quarterly: T. K. Cureton presented a list of doctoral theses completed from 1930-1946 in March 1949; A. D. Browne provided a list of masters theses in October 1931; C. H. McCloy entered a bibliography in health and physical education, October 1932, and McCloy and Greene on the same topic in December 1936. A number of other bibliographies appear in various issues of the *Research Quarterly* on a wide variety of special subjects, particularly in the earlier years of publication. In recent years, the editorial policy of the *Research Quarterly* has discouraged the presentation of bibliographies as regular articles.

In the late 1940s, several bibliographies not limited to research reports were compiled as master's projects at Springfield College, including the following:

Bruce, Robert M. "An Annotated and Indexed Bibliography of Basketball Publications," 1946.

Conyne, A.M. "Bibliography of Aquatic Courses at Springfield College," 1949.

LoMoglio, A.P. "An Annotated Bibliography of Soccer Publications," 1948.

Robertson, R.R. "An Annotated and Cross-Indexed Bibliography of Physical Reconditioning Material Published in the United States between January 1941 and June 1947," 1949.

Stewart, M.W. "An Indexed Bibliography of Selected Football References," 1948.

Several bibliographies are listed below, published by the American Alliance for Health, Physical Education, Recreation, and Dance; unless otherwise indicated in the title, these are not limited to research.

Compilation of Dance Research, 1964: Graduate theses listed in dance research completed between 1901 and 1963.

[3]All issues of the *American Physical Education Review* (1896-1929) and the *Research Quarterly* from 1930-1979 inclusive are available on microfiche through Microform Publications in Health, Physical Education, and Recreation, University of Oregon, Eugene, Oregon.

Aesthetics for Dancers, 1976: Selected annotated bibliography of books and articles related to dance aesthetics published between ancient and modern times.

Annotated Bibliography on Movement Education, 1977: Collection of selected resources significant to the many aspects of movement education.

Annotated Bibliography on Perceptual Motor Development, 1972: Entries focus on auditory perception, body image, and depth-distance perception as related to body movement.

Annotated Research Bibliography in Physical Education, Recreation, and Psychomotor Function of Mentally Retarded Persons, 1975: Contains 439 studies and biographical citations for 419 additional projects during the period 1888 to 1975.

Bibliography of Research Involving Female Subjects, 1975: Compilation of graduate theses in health, physical education, and recreation involving female subjects; covering such topics as motor learning, psychological and physiological aspects, and physical education for the handicapped.

The Sport Information Research Centre, established in Ottawa by the Coaching Association of Canada, is drawing on its computerized data base, established in 1973, to compile an 8-volume bibliography related to all aspects of sport and physical activity. This project contains over 70,000 citations from more than 1,000 sport and scientific periodicals, newsletters, conference reports, and proceedings. Volumes 1 through 4 index literature pertaining to specific sports; the remaining 4 volumes contain entries related to sport in general. The latter 4 volumes are of special interest to sports scientists because they index the disciplinary aspects of sports, such as sports medicine, exercise physiology, biomechanics, and sports sociology. A simple code indicates whether a reference is basic, intermediate, or advanced (research). At this writing, the Centre had released 7 volumes of the set. The Centre has sold exclusive rights to its data base to Systems Development Corporation, Santa Monica, California. As a result, these data can be accessed from virtually any campus in the United States and Canada.[4]

MICROFICHE REPRODUCTIONS

Microform Publications in Health, Physical Education, Recreation, and Allied Areas, as it is now known, originated at Springfield College in 1948 and has continued since 1953 in the College of Health, Physical

[4]Broekhoff, *Standardized Collection and Documentation*, p. 22.

Education, Recreation, and Dance at the University of Oregon.[5] Until 1972, microform duplications were on microcards. Starting in 1972, all microform publications were placed on microfiche, and all former titles were converted to microfiche.[6] This project originated as a nonprofit service to the professions involved. The emphasis is on unpublished doctoral dissertations and masters's theses and scholarly books and journals that are mostly out of print.

In this project, the complete text of the publications is duplicated on 4" × 6" microfiche. As 96 thesis pages appear on one microfiche, a special machine is necessary to read them. Presently, approximately 5,000 completed references are available; over 200 new titles are added each year. Approximately 150 libraries subscribe to this service, and many more make purchases by individual title. Four Microform Bulletins have been published: Vol. 1, October 1949-March 1965; Vol. 2, October 1965-April 1972; Vol. 3, October 1972-April 1977, Vol. 4, October 1977-April 1982. Supplements are issued each April and October. All titles have proper library catalog headings, including both Dewey Decimal and Library of Congress classification numbers and subject headings.

In each of the four bulletins, the accumulation of titles is listed alphabetically by authors' last names under the following categories: Physical Education, Physiology of Exercise, Recreation and Camping, Health Education, and Psychology. Subject and author indexes are also provided. In the subject index, a code is employed to identify the major research methods used by the investigators and also the statistical techniques utilized in the studies duplicated.

EDUCATIONAL RESOURCES INFORMATION CENTER

An Educational Resources Information Center (ERIC) has been established as a nationwide information system, funded by the National Institute of Education, with support from professional associations, schools, universities, and other groups. There are 16 ERIC clearinghouses, each dealing with a different subject area.[7] The Clearinghouse on Teacher Education processes documents on personnel preparation

---

[5] H. Harrison Clarke, "Microcard Publications," *Journal of the American Alliance for Health, Physical Education, Recreation, and Dance,* 20, No. 7 (September 1949), 440; and H. Harrison Clarke, "Microcards," *Journal of the American Alliance for Health, Physical Education, Recreation and Dance,* 22, No. 5 (May 1951), 34.

[6] L. Richard Geser, "HPER Microcards, 1948-1972; Microfiche, 1973," *Journal of Health, Physical Education, and Recreation,* 44, No. 4 (April 1973), 38.

[7] "ERIC Clearinghouse on Teacher Education," *Journal of Physical Education and Recreation,* 46, No. 8 (October 1975), 49.

and selected aspects of health, physical education, and recreation. Among the 4 sponsoring organizations for the Clearinghouse is the American Alliance for Health, Physical Education, Recreation, and Dance.

The Clearinghouse receives research reports, annotated bibliographies, conference papers, program descriptions, and guides both from established sources, such as schools and professional associations, and from individual researchers, teachers, and project directors. Accepted documents are abstracted and indexed and appear in a monthly issue of ERIC's *Resources in Education*. Documents are made available on microfiche at over 500 locations, including universities, that subscribe to this service. They can also be purchased directly from ERIC in microfiche and xerographic reproduction. Bibliographies have been published separately in physical education, health, and recreation. Further, while users can manually search the ERIC data base, the Clearinghouse is equipped to do this for a price, providing printouts of abstracts of ERIC documents and journal article citations in given areas. A thesaurus is available containing 6,000 index terms for identifying useful and precise search items.

While ERIC documents are not limited to research, such documents are included. Further, as expressed by Burdin: "Importantly and positively, ERIC can nurture decision making, teaching, and research based on conceptually sound, respectable, and scholarly comprehensive ideas and information."[8] Such information may be useful in justifying and formulating problems to be researched.

COMPUTERIZED INFORMATION RETRIEVAL SYSTEMS

Although not confined to physical education, several computerized information retrieval systems are available.[9] Three of these are mentioned here.

Direct Access to Reference Information (DATRIX). This system is employed to manipulate the file of dissertation references at University Microfilms, Ann Arbor, Michigan. The file consists of several hundred thousand references from *Dissertation Abstracts*, dating from 1938, including 77 major and 119 minor subject areas.

[8]Burdin, Joel, "ERIC Can Help," *Journal of Physical Education and Recreation*, 45, No. 4 (April 1974), 89.

[9]John C. Holland, "Computer-Based Storage and Retrieval Systems That Can Be Utilized in Health, Physical Education, and Recreation Research," *Research Quarterly*, 44, No. 2 (May 1973), 227.

Copies of the complete dissertations listed in the DATRIX base are available on 35-mm microfilm roll or as xerographic hard copy.

The Medical Literature Analysis and Retrieval System (MEDLARS). MEDLARS is located in the U.S. National Library of Medicine to provide rapid bibliographical access to the Library's enormous biomedical literature collection. It originated with the publication of the first computer-produced issue of *Index Medicus*, a comprehensive subject-author index of articles from approximately 2,300 of the world's biomedical journals.

Sociology of Leisure and Sport. A pioneer computerized retrieval system for the Sociology of Leisure and Sport was founded by Gerald S. Kenyon at the University of Waterloo in Canada. This system has a collection of some 7,600 documents in the fields of sociology, sociology of leisure, and sociology of sport, culture, and social sciences. The system publishes computer-generated bibliographies in 43 relevant subareas. It also provides user-generated files upon request. The system has complete documents for a high proportion of references, and issues abstracts of most titles. In 1975, the system started experimenting with on-line service; at present, this service is accessible to remote users.

Some scientific journals, such as the *Research Quarterly for Exercise and Sport* and *Medicine and Science in Sports and Exercise*, require a listing of key reference words or terms which are used in indexing. The Medical Literature Analysis and Retrieval System (MEDLARS) of the National Library of Medicine employs a list of technical terms for searching the Library's computer-based citation file. The use of key reference words is essential in utilizing computer-based information and retrieval systems.

SELECTED PERIODICALS

All periodicals that could be listed as containing research reports relevant to various phases of physical education investigation are too numerous to mention here. The list that follows is selective; both journals of primary importance to physical education and those in allied areas are included.

Acta Physiologica Scandinavica
American Anthropologist
American Corrective Therapy
  Journal

American Journal of Cardiology
American Journal of Physical
  Anthropology
American Journal of Physiology

American Journal of Sociology
Arbeitsphysiologie
Archives of Physical Medicine and Rehabilitation
British Journal of Educational Psychology
Canadian Journal of Applied Sport Sciences
Canadian Journal of History of Sport and Physical Education
Canadian Medical Association Journal
Child Development
Circulation
Circulation Research
Ergonomics
European Journal of Applied Physiology
Geriatrics
Growth
Human Biology
International Journal of Sports Medicine
International Journal of Sport Psychology
International Review of Sports Sociology
Journal of Abnormal and Social Psychology
Journal of American Medical Association
Journal of Applied Physiology
Journal of Applied Psychology
Journal of Aviation Medicine
Journal of Biomechanics
Journal of Bone and Joint Surgery
Journal of Chronic Diseases
Journal of Educational Psychology
Journal of Educational Research
Journal of Educational Sociology
Journal of Experimental Education
Journal of Experimental Psychology
Journal of Gerontology
Journal of Health and Human Behavior
Journal of Heredity
Journal of Human Movement Studies
Journal of Motor Behavior
Journal of Orthopaedic Research
Journal of Personal and Social Psychology
Journal of Physical Education, Recreation, and Dance
Journal of the Philosophy of Sport
Journal of Physiology
Journal of Psychology
Journal of Sport History
Journal of Sports Behavior
Journal of Sports Medicine and Physical Fitness
Journal of Sports Psychology
Lancet
Medicine and Science in Sports and Exercise
Mental Hygiene
Monographs of Society for Research in Child Development
Motor Skills: Theory into Practice
Nature
Perceptual and Motor Skills
Physical Education Review (England)
Physical Educator
Physical Therapy Review
Physician and Sports Medicine
Psychological Bulletin
Psychometrica

Psychosomatic Medicine
Quarterly Journal of
  Experimental Physiology
Quarterly Journal of
  Experimental Psychology

Research Quarterly for Exercise
  and Sport
Review of Educational
  Research

LIBRARY READING

A number of suggestions can be made to assist the researcher in making the most effective use of library reading. The researcher may already be aware of specific sources or studies that bear directly on his or her research; in fact, the formulation of the study could hardly have been made without knowing of several such articles. These sources should be examined first for content and then for the bibliography, where additional references can be found.

Working Bibliography

An appropriate way to proceed initially, then, is to begin with the most recent known studies, abstract them, make entries of the studies mentioned, and then trace backward by date. In this way, the researcher will pick up references that gradually lead to the end of the search. Keeping in mind the decision with respect to critical and allied literature, the investigator should proceed first to those studies that by title would seem to be most crucial and then to all others. It may be possible to delay critical reading until the *primary list* has been completed, but eventually the detailed reading will have to be undertaken.

The researcher should realize at this point that his or her efforts have passed the initial stage only and that certainly the first task is to uncover the most obvious and most easily obtained references. However, when these have been exhausted, the *secondary list* should be developed by consulting the appropriate indices and bibliographies under headings that are appropriate to the problem. This in no way implies that references obtained here are secondary in importance or in any way inferior or substandard; actually, the studies uncovered from many publications may be just as appropriate as are those more easily obtained. The most obvious reason is that the abstracting services can observe more journals than any one person could possibly manage; the exposure from carefully combing the indices is greatly enhanced. In other words, the references obtained for the secondary list may be both critical and allied; the decision of where to place them can be made later, after they have been read and analyzed by the investigator.

Card System

The investigator should adopt some system for making appropriate notations. Actually, any method is acceptable, as long as it contains the necessary information that will be needed at a later time. The listing of references on paper, however, is not satisfactory, as they cannot be manipulated later as found desirable. A useful practice is to use $3'' \times 5''$ or $5'' \times 8''$ cards with a single reference on each card. Occasionally, cards with certain prepared headings and places for pertinent information can be purchased commercially, but more often the user will wish to devise an individual style to suit his or her specific needs. Whatever the form, certain factual information that will be needed when the writing phase begins should be recorded.

Several acceptable styles for bibliographical entries exist. The student should find out which ones are favored by his or her institution and then adopt that style in making entries. This procedure will assure consistency and will thoroughly acquaint the researcher with the technicalities of notation, so that no alterations will be necessary when the bibliography is finalized; all pertinent information will have been recorded. Bibliographical and footnote forms are presented in Chapter 16.

The key, of course, is to obtain *all* pertinent information including all nuances of punctuation; if the style adopted somehow results in excessive brevity, a place on the card should be provided for other details. This latter procedure is helpful should additional information be needed for publication at a later time. The following specific information should be recorded in accordance with the style adopted:

1. ***Book.*** Author's name (last name first, followed by first name and initial), title, edition if more than one, city, publisher, and copyright date. It is also helpful for future reference to give the library call number.

2. ***Article.*** Author's name as above (given exactly as it appears on the article), title, periodical, volume number, issue number, month and year, and page number.

Classification

The next task is to classify the references from the titles into various categories, as suggested by the nature of the study and by the references themselves. Quite often, the literature can be divided into more or less discrete entries by titles, although this decision cannot always be made arbitrarily, but must await a more careful reading. Other references sometimes fit more than one category; in such cases, a cross-reference should be made and additional index cards prepared.

As this classification is made primarily on the basis of title, some misplacements will probably occur, as titles are often misleading. With the card system suggested, however, adjustments can be simply made later as needed.

Skimming

The primary need in reading the literature is an ability to bring out the salient features of the material under perusal. At first, the decision must be made as to whether or not the material is actually pertinent and usable. For a book, the table of contents is helpful in giving a rapid overview of the material covered and will point out the most likely sources where specific information is to be found. Ordinarily, the reader would then scan a chapter, to be more specific in the search for pertinent information, and then make appropriate notes. Other key areas yielding information on the type of material to be found are the preface or foreword, the index, and the bibliography. If the information sought is more for the research ideas than for the research results, which would probably be more likely when examining a book, then the reader will quickly skim the selected areas and headings found to be most suggestive and proceed from there. Quite often, introductory and final chapters are helpful in acquainting the reader with the forecast and summation of material to be covered, and thus aid in the summary of results.

A similar process is suggested for articles, although they are organized quite differently, and the material is greatly condensed. If an abstract is available, the reader should peruse it first to decide on the applicability of the findings. When doubts still persist or futher detail is needed at this point, they should be clarified by reading further. When no abstract accompanies the article, the investigator must search for appropriate portions that describe the study: introductory statements, including a statement of the problem (if one exists); summary and conclusions; methodology; results; discussion sections; and so on. In this way, a decision can be made as to the pertinence of the data.

These decision-making processes are important, and as more experience is gained, they become relatively easy. The book or article can be scanned rather quickly to see whether it should be part of the review of literature, whether there is meaningful material presented, or whether ideas are pertinent to the problem. This process is not as quickly accomplished when examining microfiche or microfilm. Due to the mechanical relationship between the material and the reader, more care must be exercised in planning the search. It is suggested for microfiche or microfilm that the table of contents (for theses and dissertations) be consulted first, and then perhaps the abstract or summary and conclusions sections.

Abstracting

The processes of skimming and abstracting should not be arbitrarily separated into discrete categories, as frequently they proceed together. This process is largely a matter of convenience, for once a reference is located it may be easier to read it carefully then than look it up again. However, the mere listing of references does not need to await the reading. There comes a time, though, when the investigator must critically examine the references he has found.

The researcher cannot afford to trust to memory the details of his or her reading. He or she should rely upon abstracting to provide the best information that will be absolutely clear later when collation of the material begins. A number of decisions will have to be made as the writing is anticipated, so that the notes will supply enough of the correct information. In general, the more critical the study, the more material will need to be recorded; those articles that are allied to the study may only require a brief note.

No simplified technique for gleaning the pertinent information from a study is available. Examination of the abstract and the summary gives an overview of what the author has considered pertinent, but this is seldom sufficient; in fact, it is usually so brief as to lack sufficient substance. Pertinent results are so often neglected here that the reader must peruse further in order to understand the study adequately. It is not good scholarship merely to copy down the abstract and then perhaps the conclusions, without examining the content to determine if other important facts are necessary. The same can be said of material located in various abstracting services; these abstracts are not sufficient for the researcher to use in lieu of actually reading the primary source.

Thus, good note-taking is an essential ingredient of the process of reviewing the literature. Keeping in mind the possibilities for later incorporation into the written portion of the thesis, the researcher will make as extensive notes as necessary. An important consideration is the extent of the use of quotations. If the author's exact words are being copied, it is wise to place them in quotes and then make a record of the page number. This does not imply that they be used as quotes in the manuscript, for it is not considered particularly good form to use them too liberally. Occasionally, when the author's words seem the best way to express a thought, quotes can be used, but paraphrasing is usually desirable. In any event, it is imperative to know if the notes are quotations or paraphrasing, so this should be made clear when the notes are taken. Moreover, direct quotations must be entirely accurate— a fact that cannot be stressed too strongly, as any errors made at this stage in note-taking will be perpetuated throughout.

A special problem exists when one source quotes another or paraphrases the results of another study. Reliance cannot be placed upon such secondary accounts, as other authors will bring out only findings that are pertinent to their studies; in such reviews, seldom is the information sufficient. Every effort should be made to find the primary source before accepting the findings. One of the most difficult problems for the researcher in this respect is in literature published in foreign languages. It is suspected that translations are not always performed or obtained and that a secondary source is occasionally used. The reseacher must be sure of the accuracy of the results before utilizing the reference. In the event that it is not possible to find the article or obtain a translation (which is becoming more and more an unacceptable condition), material may be utilized by giving credit to both sources. In this way, it is clear that the investigator did not actually see the original paper.

SUMMARY

Before any research is undertaken, the literature related to the problem area must be searched. The reasons for such a search are to determine if the study has already been completed or is in progress; to discover research allied to the problem; to provide ideas, explanations, or hypotheses valuable in understanding and formulating the problem; to locate comparable material useful in interpreting the results; and to understand the significance of the research.

A discussion of all pertinent sources of information available to investigators in physical education would be tremendously broad, so it was not exhaustive in this chapter. Rather, those sources uniquely appropriate to this field were presented. Library sources considered were research reviews, abstracts, bibliographies, indexes, microform reproductions, computerized information retrieval systems, and selected periodicals. Suggestions related to library reading emphasized working bibliographies, card systems for recording essential materials, reference classifications, and skimming and abstracting.

SELECTED REFERENCES

BEST, JOHN W., *Research in Education* (4th ed.). Englewood Cliffs, N.J.: Prentice-Hall, Inc., 1981, Ch. 3.

BOOKWALTER, CAROLYN W., and KARL W. BOOKWALTER, "Library Techniques," in *Research Methods in Health, Physical Education, Recreation*

(2nd ed.), ed. M. Gladys Scott. Washington, D.C.: American Alliance for Health, Physical Education, Recreation, and Dance, 1959, Ch. 2.

BROEKHOFF, JAN, *Ways and Means of Organizing a System for the Standardized Collection of Documentation in Physical Education and Sport.* Paris: UNESCO, 1980 (ED-80/WS/68).

CRASE, DARRELL, "Selected Periodicals in Sport and Physical Education," *Journal of Physical Education and Recreation*, 50, No. 5 (May 1979), 25.

CRASE, DARRELL, and MICHAEL L. SACHS, "Information Retrieval Systems for Professionals in Physical Education, and Sport," *Journal of Physical Education and Recreation*, 51, No. 2 (February 1980), 65.

HAAG, ENID E., "Literature Searching in Physical Education," *Journal of Physical Education and Recreation*, 50, No. 1 (January 1979), 54.

HOLLAND, JOHN C., "Computer-Based Storage and Retrieval Information Systems That Can Be Utilized in Health, Physical Education, and Recreation Research," *Research Quarterly*, 44, No. 2 (May 1973), 227.

SACHS, MICHAEL L., "Resources in Sport Sciences," *Physical Educator*, 35, No. 3 (October 1978), 119.

Nonlaboratory Studies

4

Methodology in Historical Research

INTRODUCTION TO PART II

In Part II, studies in physical education that do not require laboratory resources are presented. These studies do not usually require the testing of subjects, the conducting of experiments, and the analysis of quantitative data.* A separate chapter is devoted to each of the following research methods: Chapter 4, Methodology in Historical Research; Chapter 5, Philosophical Studies; and Chapter 6, Surveys.

History serves to bring together information about, and to give an accurate account of, past events. Historians strive to understand the various phases of former periods. History is used to understand the past and to try to understand the present in light of past events and developments. The historian employs historical documents, relics, and the like with scholarly care and evaluates them against available criteria. A historian is not just a storyteller who fills in historical gaps with imagination, although today's historian attempts to write an interesting account. The product of history has undergone significant changes in meaning. Woody has expressed this concept well:

*Exceptions will be found in the normative type of survey, in case studies, and in the construction of profiles.

To pre-literate man, history is remembered tradition; in literate societies it may come to be thought of as the written record of things past. To the politically conscious, history is past politics, and politics is history in the making. To philosophers, history is philosophy teaching by example. None of these notions is sufficiently inclusive: things change and have histories as do men. Were there no change, there would be no history. History, the Book of Changes, is the totality of what has transpired: environment, and what it has done to man; man, and what he has done and sought to do with himself and his environment. Whether the totality be known, or knowable, and how precisely, are mooted matters; but historical study aims at the fullest possible knowledge of the past.[1]

Serious historians today espouse an expanded concept of their function: to achieve an interpretation of the past in light of various conceptual frameworks or theories or models of human behavior. Consequently, in a sense, some historians become social scientists. A result of the social science approach to history has been a change from *the* method of historical research to methodology in historical research. Gerber has indicated that this approach creates difficulties when defining the topics to be studied, because concepts are usually interdisciplinary.[2] The concept of sport, for example, has significance in other disciplines, including sociology, history, archaeology, and ethnology.

Historical research should be encouraged because it relates to the heritage of any field. No established profession has depth, traditions, customs, or a present without a history. This heritage should be recorded and preserved for future generations. The origins, growth, and development of the field; the problems faced and solved; the cultural forces exerted; the movements that have waned and persisted; the changes in implements, facilities, and costumes; the thoughts and deeds of the pioneers and leaders who shaped the profession over the years; and many other factors are subjects for historical research.

PROFESSIONAL INTEREST IN HISTORICAL RESEARCH

In recent years, several professionals in physical education and sport have specialized in historical research as their scholarly endeavors. Working with graduate students in universities, they are producing a quantity of quality historical reports. Various organizations have

[1] Thomas Woody, "Of History and Its Method," *Journal of Experimental Education* (March 1947), 175.

[2] Ellen W. Gerber, "Methodology in Historical Research," in *Exercise and Sport Sciences Review*, Vol. 2, ed. Jack H. Wilmore (New York: Academic Press, Inc., 1974), p. 335.

established historians or archivists. As examples: The American Alliance for Health, Physical Education, Recreation, and Dance maintains an Archivists and Records Center; for many years, the American Academy of Physical Education has had an elected historian.

Several extensive bibliographies pertaining to the history of physical education and sport prior to 1971 are contained in a volume edited by Zeigler, Howell, and Trekell.[3] Among the bibliographies are: sports and games in primitive and early societies; history of physical education and sport; history of sports and games in Canada; master's and doctoral studies related to the history of physical education, sport, and athletics in the United States; and biographical theses and related articles, books, and microform publications in physical education and sport.

A positive movement to develop the discipline of sports history has recently become evident. Historians in this field organized the North American Society for Sport History, which held its first meeting in 1973. Starting in 1974, this society has published the *Journal of Sport History*. The main objective of this journal is to present quality but popular articles on sport history topics. This discipline is shared by scholars in history, sociology, and physical education; representatives from all three fields published articles in the first journal.

In 1974 Metcalfe reviewed North American sports historians and their work, particularly during the preceding decade.[4] In the past, "popular" histories of sport and sporting personalities have been published. However, most of these do not adhere to standards of historical scholarship. Actually, according to Metcalfe's analysis, history of sport is in an embryonic state. Most historical work in this field has been done by professional students seeking graduate degrees. Only a small number of these individuals has continued as historians.

Eyler indicated that recent attempts have been made to achieve objectivity in the special field of sport history by use of models emanating from the social sciences.[5] These attempts use such techniques as game theory, theory of conflict resolution, role analysis, and econometrics. However, the heavy use of models has been criticized as a limiting factor in the search for all the facts. It has been intimated that historical research is not being done when models are used, but, rather, sociological research is being accomplished. Eyler suggested

[3]Earle F. Zeigler, Maxwell L. Howell, and Marianna Trekell, eds., *Research in the History, Philosophy, and International Relations of Physical Education and Sport: Bibliographies and Techniques* (Champaign, Ill.: Stipes Publishing Company, 1971).

[4]Alan Metcalfe, "North American Sport History: A Review of North American Sport Historians and Their Work," in *Exercise and Sport Sciences Review*, Vol. 2, ed. Jack H. Wilmore (New York: Academic Press, Inc. 1977), p. 225.

[5]Marvin H. Eyler, "Objectivity and Selectivity in Historical Inquiry," *Journal of Sport History*, 1, No. 1 (Spring 1974), 63.

that the use of models in sport history needs further examination and should be given "its day in court" before being accepted or rejected.[6]

HISTORY IS FUNCTIONAL

History can be functional inasmuch as humanity can profit by past experiences in the solution of present-day problems. Even nations so profit. For example, following World War I, the United States refused to join the League of Nations, believing that great oceans provided sufficient protection against potentially powerful enemies; this country no longer wanted to become involved with international tensions and frictions. World War II demonstrated convincingly that such isolationism by a world power was impossible. Consequently, the United States became a leading exponent and forceful participant in the United Nations; it has worked energetically and aggressively to solve international problems in the interests of world peace.

A fascinating example of the use of historical materials in a very real functional sense is contained in the description of the Sorge spy ring by Major General Charles A. Willoughby, General MacArthur's Chief of Intelligence from 1941 to 1951.[7] As the German armies raced into western Russia, Russian reinforcement from the Siberian border became vital. But the Red Army could not afford to weaken Siberian defenses if the Japanese army intended to attack. Sorge was able to assure his superiors that no attack would be made; Siberian forces were entrained and appeared on the Western Front in time for the successful defense of Moscow. Sorge's decision was based on his extensive and thorough study of Japanese ancient history, ancient political history, and ancient social and economic history. With this background, none of the border disputes between Japan and the U.S.S.R. worried Sorge, as he recognized them as innocuous, but he regarded the various China incidents as the prelude to a great war that would engulf all China. In Sorge's words: "My research also permitted me to evaluate correctly the reliability of information and rumors of vital importance to my secret activities since intelligence in the Far East contains far more rumors and conjectures than in Europe."[8]

The following quotation from the August 1958 *Royal Bank of Canada Monthly Letter* summarizes the functional value of history:

> The vital beliefs and good practices of our western world rest on the fulcrum of historic knowledge. There is no basis of our society save its

[6]Ibid., p. 74.

[7]Charles A. Willoughby, *The Shanghai Conspiracy: The Sorge Spy Ring* (New York: E. P. Dutton, Inc., 1952).

[8]Ibid., p. 226

past. There is no guide to business decisions except that given by business experience. There is no personal maturity that is not built upon reflection of events of yesterday. . . . When we can pluck an example from the past and use it to help us today that is a very practical use of history.[9]

Thomas Vaughn, Executive Director of the Oregon Historical Society, maintained that people are prone to lose their sense of proportion and to become imprisoned in their own time.[10] An understanding of the experiences of other times in which similar situations were encountered is lost. Isolated in the present, unable to profit from previous experiences, people are more likely to make imprudent, one-dimensional decisions when presented with a succession of present problems and pressures, many of which decisions may prove counter to their best interests. Vaughn stated

> It will profit a nation little to possess the most competent accountants, economists, doctors, and electricians if it loses sight of the common heritage which should bind the citizenry together. Police work will then become the most important occupation, because only force can hold together a society that does not rest on voluntary agreement.

An understanding of the history of education is important to professional workers and leaders in this field. It helps to understand the reason for, and the success and failure of, educational movements that have appeared and, in some cases, continue to prevail in the schools. It helps to evaluate not only lasting contributions, but also the fads and "bandwagon" schemes that have appeared on the educational scene only to be discarded.[11] Certainly, physical education has been guilty of the bandwagon syndrome over the years, a syndrome that is still evident today.

Can it be said the physical education has used history in a functional manner? Without being exhaustive, but very general indeed, the historical treatment of physical fitness may be cited. Formal physical education was founded in the United States by refugees from other countries, especially Germany; the Jahn system, so prevalent at the beginning, had the purpose of developing the capabilities and fitness of the body. From 1860 to World War I, physical fitness was the major, and essentially only, objective of physical training as then designated; the doctors of medicine who pioneered physical education during this period employed exercise for its value in preventive

[9]"What Use Is History?" *The Royal Bank of Canada Monthly Letter*, 39, No. 8 (August 1958).

[10]Thomas Vaughn, "Ignorance of Past Mistakes Makes Us Prisoners of Our Own Time," *Sunday Oregonian*, July 2, 1978, p. C1.

[11]John W. Best, *Research in Education*, 3rd ed. (Englewood Cliffs, N.J.: Prentice-Hall, Inc., 1977), p. 342.

medicine. Following World War I, a new urgency to improve the nation's physical fitness became evident, and state laws requiring physical education in the schools became commonplace as a result. Then, in the 1930s, physical education generally repudiated physical fitness, considering it as a concomitant of any activity program conducted with other objectives in mind. The error of this practice was dramatically demonstrated by continued high draft rejections in World War II and by the deplorable physical condition of many draftees reporting for military duty.

Many conscientious physical educators vowed—in retrospect—that this experience would not be repeated. Dynamic support came from a totally unexpected source, the President of the United States, who recognized this situation and intervened by establishing in 1956 the President's Council on Physical Fitness and Sports, as now known. No longer is a physical educator ridiculed for assessing pupils with strength tests, utilizing weight training to strengthen muscles, and employing jogging to develop circulatory-respiratory endurance. The lessons of history become explicit.

THE SCIENCE OF HISTORY

The question of whether or not the historical method is scientific has been debated. Generally, early historians wrote history more as an instrument of propaganda; their purpose was to glorify the cause espoused, whether it be the State, the Church, a given organization or institution, or the perpetuation of the memory of a public servant or professional pioneer. Certainly the historical method so employed was far from scientific. Before the nineteenth century, history as a science was generally unknown.

The contention is made, however, that modern historians exhibit scientific characteristics in that they critically and objectively investigate their source materials; they formulate and evaluate hypotheses; they make explanations, tentatively at least, of the occurrence of events or conditions. But unlike scientists, historians cannot test their hypotheses by direct experimentation; they cannot employ controlled observation. Original conditions cannot be repeated; history cannot be reenacted. The primary function of science is to reconstruct the human scene and judge its meaning—to get at the true facts, or probabilities, as precisely as possible by weighing all the available evidence. Historical evidence can be evaluated. Cause-and-effect relationships and the predictions of outcome, after the manner of other sciences, however, are not so readily realized by historical method.

Actually, the scholar in physical education need not be unduly concerned as to whether the historical method is or is not scientific. It is sufficient to know that certain sources of evidence are available for historical study, that these sources can be appropriately evaluated, that generalizations regarding the past can be made, and that hypotheses relative to the future can be proposed. The method of history must be understood and rigidly followed if historical studies are to be worthy.

BIOGRAPHY

A reconstruction and understanding of the past of physical education can be enhanced by analyses and assessments of the men and women who served as leaders in its development. Thus, biographical studies of teachers and leaders can be a means to a better understanding of these fields. Stressing this view generally, Nevins stated

> Biography may be termed a form of history—a form not applied to nations and groups, but to the single man or woman; history is certainly from one point of view a compound of innumerable biographies. All study of the past, whether for pleasure, instruction, or moral growth, must be based upon a reading of history and biography, and it is a poor literary prescription which demands one at the expense of the other.[12]

Not only do such studies contribute significantly to the history of a discipline, but they preserve for posterity the life, contributions, and thoughts of a leader far beyond the history of a relevant movement. Perhaps for this reason more than any other, a good many biographies have been produced in physical education, especially as master's and doctoral studies. Trekell listed 54 such graduate studies in physical education and sport completed prior to 1971.[13] The earliest subjects of these biographies were Catherine Esther Beecher by Mae Elizabeth Harveson, Ph.D., University of Pennsylvania, 1931; Luther Halsey Gulick by Ethyl J. Dorgon, Ph.D., Columbia University, 1934; William Albin Stecher by Maurice M. Fingels, Ed.M., Temple University, 1935; F.L. Jahn by E.P. Schnepel, M.A., Ohio State University, 1935; and Delphine Hanna by Minnie Lynn, M.S., Pennsylvania State College, 1937.

In a *Time* essay, Gerald Clarke stated that writing biography has always been a demanding discipline. A good biographer should

---

[12]Allan Nevins, *The Gateway to History* (New York: Doubleday & Company, Inc., Anchor Books, 1962), p. 348.

[13]Marianna Trekell, "A Representative Sampling of Biographical Theses and Related Articles, Books, and Microcards in Physical Education and Sport," in *Research in the History. Philosophy, and International Relations of Physical Education and Sport: Bibliographies and Techniques,* eds. Earle F. Zeigler, Maxwell L. Howell, and Marianna Trekell (Champaign, Ill.: Stipes Publishing Company, 1971), p. 162.

combine the skills of the novelist and the detective and add to them the patience and compassion of the priest. Few people want their short-comings exposed and they, or their heirs, often go to considerable trouble to hide them. Somerset Maugham asked his friends to destroy his letters; both Willa Cather and Ernest Hemingway inveighed against posthumous publication of theirs. Charles Dickens burned thousands of letters. Further, besides being given to eradicating much of their past, many people, particularly writers, are prone to fabrication. Mark Twain could not resist a good story about himself, even if he had to make it up; William Butler Yeats dressed his past in colorful myths; and George Bernard Shaw found simple facts insufficiently expressive.[14] Persistent good investigative work is necessary to overcome such situations.

In keeping with this reasoning, Clifford discussed and illustrated problems encountered by the biographer, indicating that a chief task is to evaluate the facts assembled.[15] He asked: How can a serious researcher differentiate what is to be believed and what is incorrect? The necessity for vigorous skepticism is continually to be emphasized. Clifford also indicated that the most difficult problem facing the biographer today is not so much selecting a proper form or validating evidence and estimating its relevance, but deciding how much of all available evidence to use. The term "how much" has different meanings: (1) It can be merely quantitative, referring to the number of details to include about everyday affairs; or (2) it can refer to ethical considerations, involving how deeply to go into another person's private life. Such controversial questions as the following should be considered: What kinds of personal details can be given to the public without offending family and friends? What secrets can be revealed? Are there private matters which must never be told? In physical education, however, biographers have concentrated mostly on the professional careers of their subjects.

According to Lucas, too many physical education biographies are "glossy, laudatory, hymns of praise—romantic novels devoid of dis-interestedness, lacking even a half-hearted effort at 'that elusive thing called truth,'"[16] He stated that sport and physical education scholars who write biography must discipline themselves, learning and practicing the science and art of biography. They must blend the work of the craftsperson and the creative artist. Lucas questioned whether biographies of some sports figures have meaningful value. In most cases, athletes are thrust into national and international prominence

[14]Gerald Clarke, "Biography Comes of Age," *Time*, July 2, 1979, p. 83.

[15]James L. Clifford, *Puzzles to Portraits* (Chapel Hill, N.C.: University of North Carolina Press, 1970).

[16]John A. Lucas, "Sport History through Biography," *Quest*, 31, No. 2 (1979), 216.

exclusively because of their extraordinary physical skills. He asked: Does this uniqueness alone justify biography or did the athlete combine fantastic physical abilities with unusual additional qualities?

SOURCES OF HISTORICAL MATERIALS

As for any investigation, the historian must define the problem and indicate any limitations to be imposed. Hypotheses to be evaluated, issues to be specifically investigated, or special questions to be answered should be included. Such a statement at the start of the project is essential, as it defines the scope of the materials to be assembled.

Two sources of historical materials exist—primary sources and secondary sources. Some materials will be from one or the other of these sources; other materials may be derived from both.

Primary Sources

Primary sources are original materials. As differentiated by some: For a primary source, only one mind comes between the event and the user of the source. The importance of primary sources cannot be overestimated. They compose the solid basis for historical writing and should be utilized whenever possible. In fact, the student should make every effort to study original documents or exhibits no matter how much has been written about them by others.

Common primary sources are given here.

1. *Official records.* Official records are multitudinous. State, district, and national professional associations have minutes of meetings, reports of committees, annual reports, official documents of various kinds, budgets, honors and awards bestowed, attendance records, papers presented, administrative edicts, and the like. State departments have syllabuses, reports of committees and meetings, published materials, laws, court proceedings, and decisions, and so on. Local institutions or schools have courses of study, participation statistics, and many other primary documents.

2. *Personal records.* Especially valuable for biographies are letters, diaries, autobiographies, contracts, lecture notes, honors, diplomas, honorary degrees, and original drafts of speeches, articles, and books.

3. *Oral statements.* Included here are oral traditions, such as

myths, family stories, superstitions, ceremonies, and the like. (At times, these are secondary sources.) Eyewitness accounts of events as told by the beholder are also pertinent. Interviews may be recorded. Speeches may be made.

4. *Pictorial records.* Obvious pictorial records are photographs, movies, drawings, paintings, sculpture, and recorded creative expressions.

5. *Published material.* Some published materials, such as syllabuses and courses of study, have been mentioned. Other such sources are newspaper accounts, pamphlets, yearbooks, magazine stories, and journal articles.

6. *Physical remains.* Classified as physical remains are buildings, facilities, apparatus, equipment, awards, costumes, and various implements.

7. *Printed materials.* Printed materials—other than those mentioned—are textbooks, record blanks, certificates, report cards, newspaper advertisements, and contracts.

8. *Mechanical records.* In today's age of electronics, primary source materials may include tape or video recordings of interviews, meetings, and speeches.

As can be seen, the above categories of primary sources are not mutually exclusive as some overlaps exist. Further, the same source material may be either a document or a relic, depending on its use. For example, a basketball score book is a relic; but, if the score book is used to report the record of a team's season of play, it is a document.

Secondary Sources

Secondary sources are descriptions of primary sources. They are not firsthand reports. They are written by persons who did not live in the period under study or who were not in direct contact with the events reported. More than one mind came between the original happening and its description.

Examples of secondary sources are textbooks, newspaper articles written from interviews with on-the-spot observers, and historical accounts. A source may be secondary or primary depending on its use. For example, a tests and measurements textbook is a secondary source, but it is a primary source for a scholar who is reviewing the contents of such textbooks over a period of years. A citation made to a professional leader is a primary source; its content is very likely a secondary source. Further, in some documents, both primary and secondary materials may appear: A reporter's account of a street riot may describe incidents actually seen as well as those described by other people.

Secondary source materials have definite value for the novice historian. They give acquaintance with work that has already been done in the study area; they provide initial background information relative to the investigation; they usually include a number of key primary sources to be examined. Secondary sources may be useful for investigators who cannot obtain the original sources because of their unavailability.

However, a secondary source is only as good as the person who produced it; its value is proportional to the competency of the author and the extent of primary sources used. Even so, the author of a secondary source has had to select materials germane to his or her purpose from primary documents, and has made his or her own interpretations of their contents. This situation is compounded when the author of a secondary source has used secondary sources in his or her account; actually, some secondary source materials are based on third-, fourth-, and fifth-hand information. If at all possible, an historian should not be dependent upon others for such selections and interpretations, but should make them from primary sources.

EVALUATION OF HISTORICAL MATERIALS

The actual existence of either primary or secondary historical sources does not guarantee their authenticity, accuracy, or validity. The historian must be constantly critical of the historical materials obtained and examined. A remain may not be genuine, a record may not be correct, a photograph may be faked or "doctored," a speech may have been written by a ghostwriter, or a newspaper story may be slanted in support of a cause. Thus, historical materials must be rigorously evaluated. Such evaluations are made by applying two types of criticism: external and internal. These forms of criticism are not always mutually exclusive, but they do serve to explain the types of evaluation that should be applied to historical sources.

External Criticism

Through external criticism, the historian determines whether or not a given source is genuine and admissible as evidence. What is its origin and legality? The answers to a number of questions must be sought.

1. *Who is the author?* Establishing authorship is a common practice performed by historians. Many times—and especially with professional people—authorship is readily determined. Some documents, however, do not carry the name of the writer. The authorship of committee and other reports, no matter by whom they are given, may be uncertain. A writer may use a pseudonym, which could make identification especially difficult. For example, what reader can identify the physical educator who wrote the following: Count Sissicran Etoxinod, "How to Checkmate Certain Vicious Consequences of True-False Examinations," *Education* (December 1940)? This may (or may not) help: The same writer has personally published books and other materials under the publisher's name, The Pleiades Company.

2. *Was the document written by a ghost writer or by another person?* Particularly in political life, the question of who actually wrote a speech may frequently be perplexing. Of course, too, many people in public life employ writers to help with the preparation of the numerous speeches they are called upon to give.

3. *What were the qualifications of the author?* For an author to write with authority on a subject, he or she must be well informed on the subject. For example, for a foreign physical education leader to describe American football after seeing his or her first game would be an inept performance; an understanding of the intricacies of this sport requires a great deal of technical knowledge and appreciation of strategy. An American going abroad for a short time and posing as an authority on foreign physical education upon return is another illustration of unqualified reporting. The ordinary person could describe the mushroom-shaped cloud created by an atomic explosion, but it requires an atomic scientist to describe its composition and physical dimensions—relying on many testing instruments strategically arranged before the blast. Occasionally, authorities in one field pose as authorities on the same level in other fields, where their qualifications do not apply.

4. *Is a particular item of equipment, piece of apparatus, costume, or other professional artifact authentic?* Are the origins of a particular sport correct? Physical education remains should be established as to validity, date of origin, changes and development, and uses to which they were put. This historical effort should be extended to the evolution of games and game rules. At times, initial errors of fact have been perpetuated because subsequent historians accepted original findings without checking. For example, Cooperstown's Baseball Hall of Fame has

projected the "fact" that General Abner Doubleday as a young man invented the name and the game of baseball at a single stroke one afternoon in 1839: Henderson has shown that baseball came from the English game of rounders, which came from stoolball and other old English forms of "baseball."[17] Further, he demonstrates that all these as well as other ball games came from the French medieval game-ritual of *la soule*, which in turn was adapted by the Christian religion from Islamic rites that traced back through pagan rites to the worship of Osiris in Egypt. Any historian want to challenge this research?

Internal Criticism

Internal criticism is concerned with the meaning and accuracy of statements. Evaluation is transferred from the authenticity of the document to the trustworthiness of its contents. A number of questions will serve to clarify this form of criticism.

1. *Is the meaning of words the same?*   The meaning of words may change with time or the same word may have different nuances of meaning for different people. The word "football" is an example: Depending on the country, this sport may be American football, soccer, rugby, or Australian rules football. These games have great differences in playing rules. The word "gymnastics" has had various meanings since early times.

2. *Is the author writing seriously?*   At times, an author may not be writing in a serious vein but, rather, in a humorous, ironic, or symbolic manner. Occasionally, satire is used to emphasize meaning through ridicule and sarcasm. The historian must be able and ready to recognize the difference between serious, straightforward statements of fact and meaning and other forms of expression and to treat them accordingly.

3. *Is the author expressing his or her real beliefs?*   For the most part, beliefs are expressed succinctly and forcefully. On occasion, however, an author may express ideas that an audience wants to hear whether they accord with his or her actual beliefs or not. Political speeches are notorious for this fault.

4. *How soon after the event was the document written?*   Of course, the nearer to an event it is recorded, the more reliable is the account. To ask a person to reminisce back five, ten, fifteen, or more years is to seek the impossible as far as details are

[17]Robert W. Henderson, *Ball, Bat, and Bishop* (New York: Rockport Press, 1947).

concerned. On the other hand, in retrospect the meaning and significance of the happening may be enhanced, as only time can validate these values.

5. *Was the author biased in any way?* Both primary and secondary sources may be biased in numerous ways, almost too many to mention. However, influences stemming from the following may result in prejudice and bias: race, religion, nationality, political party, social or economic group, professional body, period in history, educational philosophy, ideology, special or limited interests within a profession, malice, self-aggrandizement, and need for defensive action. Bias is not always easy to detect, but the historian should be alert to its presence in documents that he reviews.

6. *Are written sources evaluated with an understanding of the times and conditions under which they were produced?* Such data need to be interpreted from an historical rather than a contemporary point of view. For example, health education in the 1920s was subject to the strong influences of the temperance union and was not the broad, practical field it is today. Mores and codes of conduct change with time; therefore, the historian needs to be steeped in the culture of the time when the historical events that he is examining occurred.

General Principles of Criticism

As can be seen from the above, the historian must make judgments relative to the source materials. Woody[18] briefly stated the following principles to be observed in judging and reading historical sources:

1. Do not read into earlier documents the conceptions of later times.
2. Do not judge an author ignorant of certain events necessarily because of failure to mention them (the argument *ex silentio*) or that they did not occur, for the same reason.
3. Underestimating a source is no less an error than overestimating it in the same degree, and there is no more virtue in placing an event too late than in dating it too early by the same number of years or centuries.
4. A single true source may establish the existence of an idea, but other direct, competent, independent witnesses are required to prove the reality of events or objective facts.
5. Identical errors prove the dependence of sources on each other or a common source.

[18]Woody, "History and Its Method," p. 190.

6. If witnesses contradict each other on a certain point, one or the other may be true, but both may be in error.
7. Direct, competent, independent witnesses who report the same central fact and also many peripheral matters in a casual way may be accepted for the points of their agreement.
8. Official testimony, oral or written, must be compared with unofficial testimony whenever possible, for neither one nor the other is alone sufficient.
9. A document may provide competent and dependable evidence on certain points, yet carry no weight in respect to others it mentions.

ORAL HISTORY

In 1948 Nevins conducted the first interview for the Oral History Collection of Columbia University. He believed that a systematic attempt should be made to obtain a fuller record than would otherwise be possible of the participation of living Americans who have contributed significantly to the political, economic, and cultural life of our society. Many such individuals have not written their memoirs or kept diaries or records which would be of value to people today.[19]

An Oral History Research Office in the Graduate Department of Physical Education at the University of Illinois has been described by Trekell.[20] The purpose of this project was to obtain valuable source material through tape-recorded interviews with persons who have made or are making important contributions to physical education and sport. Efforts were directed toward exploring their thinking in relation to persistent and vital professional problems, as well as toward obtaining their memoirs and other biographical data that had not previously been recorded.

The oral historical procedure usually consists of a series of interviews with a subject, conducted via tape recordings. Prior to any interview, the interviewer makes preparations, like any other historian, by reading the primary and secondary sources available pertaining to the subject and should identify historical relationships and problems to be explored. For each session, the subject should be provided in advance with a statement of the pertinent areas to be covered, so that advance preparation by the interviewee is possible. When the tapes are transcribed, the interviewee should be allowed an opportunity to edit them.

[19]Nevins, Gateway to History, preface.

[20]Marianna Trekell, "A Rationale and Organizational Pattern for Oral History," in *Research in the History, Philosophy, and International Aspects of Physical Education and Sport: Bibliographies and Techniques*, eds. Earle F. Zeigler, Maxwell L. Howell, and Marianna Trekell (Champaign, Ill.: Stipes Publishing Company, 1971), p. 31.

As stated by Trekell,[21] the oral history interviewer should adhere to the following procedures:

1. Be prompt.
2. Have all equipment ready.
3. Be relaxed and maintain a confident and easy manner.
4. Conduct the interview in a spirit of scholarly integrity. Guide the discussion by referring to pertinent points which were previously established to be covered during the interview. Remember his or her role as interviewer by limiting remarks to posing and asking questions which will stimulate the subject to respond to the problems under consideration.
5. Never argue with an interviewee (the planned interview is not the place for the interviewer to give views and opinions).
6. Be alert to fatigue and general physical condition of the interviewee.
7. Be alert to closing the interview: one-hour sessions are preferable.

For the historical report prepared following the interviews, the oral sources should be subjected to external and internal criticism, as is essential for any historical study. The autobiographical nature of oral history injects the very real possibility of personal bias. It is only natural that the subject would desire to appear favorably in a personal history. Thus, efforts should be constantly made to maintain objectivity; vigorous applications of the forms of historical criticism should be stressed.

HISTORICAL HYPOTHESES

Historians do not simply collect primary and secondary sources, subject them to external and internal criticisms, and present this mass of facts in some orderly way. To be sure, such procedures add to knowledge about the history of a movement, association, or person being studied. However, scholars of history go beyond the mere accumulation of facts. Rather, they formulate hypotheses to explain the occurrence of events and conditions and then search and apply data to determine whether or not they are tenable.

As in all research, hypotheses are proposed for testing, not for defending. The hypothesis is a tentative assumption that is based on the available facts and best judgments at the time; some elements may be known while others are conceptual. The conceptual elements go beyond known facts to the realm of plausible explanation. Van Dalen

[21] Ibid., p. 33.

states that hypotheses logically relate known facts to intelligent guesses about unknown conditions in an effort to extend and enlarge knowledge.[22] Through conceptualization, investigators can go beyond the known data relating to a problem and suggest possible, theoretical solutions.

The historians may create a synthesis of the actual occurrence of events based upon the use of records, documents, and artifacts, or may explain the present status of and project trends in physical education in light of pertinent antecedents. Contemporary historians endeavor to generalize from their historical findings. Gerber stated

> If generalization cannot be obtained from a study, then it can have no relevance for anything but itself. Since historical studies are by their nature, concerned with out-of-date problems and issues, an inability to generalize from them would place the studies in the category of antiquarianism—suited primarily to the memories of old men and women.[23]

The tyro historian may have, and usually does have, difficulty in locating and clearly defining hypotheses. Possibly, too, hypotheses may not occur or be appropriate in some historical studies. However, the investigator should read widely while considering the meanings and implications derived from these sources; through such critical reading, hypotheses may develop.

PITFALLS IN HISTORICAL RESEARCH

The investigator should guard against various pitfalls—error areas—that are present in historical research. Several of these pitfalls are listed.

1. *Complete misunderstanding of the meaning of historical sources and the ways to evaluate them.* To succumb to this pitfall is to ignore what has been written in this chapter about primary and secondary sources and the external and internal criticisms that should be applied to them. However, the graduate student, especially at the doctoral level, who contemplates an historical dissertation or who wishes to pursue historical research

---

[22]D. B. Van Dalen, "The Function of Hypotheses in Research," *Physical Educator*, 26, No. 1 (March 1957), 21.

[23]Gerber, "Methodology in Historical Research," p. 352.

as a scholarly endeavor in the future should study the historical method intensively. Students would be well advised to take one or more graduate courses on historical methodology, and they should read extensively on this subject. They should also have a strong historical background in their own fields, so as to provide a wide perspective of any historical study undertaken.

2. *Attempt to fill historic gaps with little or no basic evidence and to color narration for the sake of interest, thus sacrificing accuracy and fidelity.*   The good historian will recognize and make every effort to obtain facts that are missing and causing gaps in the account; if unable to do so, he or she will admit to this situation rather than attempt to cover up by use of imagination. If the student wishes to speculate, this can be done, but it should be made clear that this is what is being done. An interesting presentation of history is legitimate but not at the expense of accuracy and validity.

3. *Use of poor logic in handling historical materials and in drawing conclusions from them.*   The historian, as has been repeatedly emphasized, is more than a chronicler of dates and happenings. The historian's real skill and insight are demonstrated by weighing the evidence, characterizing the results, generalizing on the findings, and even predicting future events. The ability to formulate and test historical hypotheses is the epitome of scholarly historical writing.

4. *Bias.*   Bias is one of the greatest dangers in historical writing; it is a dangerous pitfall to be avoided. Bias may rear its ugly head either consciously or unconsciously; its source may be prejudice, self-interest, long-held preconceived notions, or desire to promote a cause or to commemorate an individual. Some years ago there was an historical report on "rehabilitation in World War II" published, in which the author's chief intent was to commend all those who played a leading role in this worthwhile effort. In another instance, a graduate student wrote a biography of his college coach, but, knowing that the coach would read it, he was loath to make even mildly negative comments about him. The historian must strive for the same sort of objectivity that the scientist in a laboratory employs in evaluating data and drawing conclusions.

5. *Carelessness in reporting.*   Very obviously, the historian must employ extreme care in making records of readings, interviews, and other investigative efforts.

ILLUSTRATED STUDIES

In order to illustrate the use of the historical method in physical education, a number of studies that use this method are described in this section.

Research Section AAHPERD

In 1938 Clarke presented an historical sketch of the Research Section of the American Health and Physical Education Association, now known as the American Alliance of Health, Physical Education, Recreation, and Dance.[24] At the time the study was conducted, the Research Section was 10 years old, having been officially accepted as a section of the association in 1928. However, the origins were actually traced back to an organization known as the Athletic Research Society, which held its initial meeting in December 1907. This meeting was attended by men concerned with athletics for boys in elementary schools, secondary schools, colleges, the Young Men's Christian Association, and boys' clubs. In 1911, a Federated Committee was formed to enlarge the research function and effectiveness of the society. With the great expansion of physical education following World War I, the usefulness of the Athletic Research Society waned; it sought affiliation with the American Physical Education Association, as the AAHPERD was then named. Affiliation did not take place immediately; a transition period followed, which culminated in 1928 in formation of the Research Section.

The main historical sources for this study were the following:

1. Reports and minutes of meetings of the Legislative Council of the American Physical Education Association, 1885-1938.
2. Historical articles, official announcements, and news notes that appeared in:
   (a) *Proceedings of the Association for the Advancement of Physical Education*, 1885-1895.
   (b) *American Physical Education Review*, 1896-1929.
   (c) *Proceedings of the Athletic Research Society*, 1907-1921. (Many of these were published in the *American Physical Education Review*.)
   (d) *Journal of Health and Physical Education* and *Research Quarterly*, 1930-1938.
3. Correspondence with past secretaries of the Athletic Research

---

[24]H. Harrison Clarke, "History of the Research Section of the American Association for Health and Physical Education." *Research Quarterly*, 9, No. 3 (October 1938), 25.

Society, national and district chairmen of the Research Section, and the national office of the association.

A difficult problem in completing this historical study was to reconstruct the period from 1920 to 1928, during which the transition occurred from the Athletic Research Society to the Research Section of the Amercian Physical Education Association; considerable correspondence was conducted with the leaders involved during this period. Definite affiliation of the society with the association did not occur until 1925, although its place in the association was not defined at that date. The last meeting of the society was held on December 28, 1927; the year 1928 marked the beginning of the Research Section. The growth of the section was rapid; by 1938, five of the association's six districts had each formed a Research Section.

Cultural Significance
of Colonial Sport

The purpose of a doctoral dissertation by Struna was to examine the cultural significance of sport in the colonial Chesapeake area, which included Maryland and Virginia, and in colonial Massachusetts.[25] In conducting this study, the investigator consulted nearly 600 references. The primary sources consisted of laws, codes, and colony records; county, town, and church records; diaries, journals, and collected papers; letters; travel accounts; treatises, tracts, and histories; sermons; account books, wills, and estate inventories; and newspapers. The secondary sources were books, periodicals, and graduate theses and reports.

The original materials examined in the course of this research were in libraries and historical societies scattered from Williamsburg to Haverill. The Old Colony Historical Society in Taunton, the Ipswich Historical Society, and the Haverhill Public Library provided valuable primary records for eighteenth century Massachusetts. In Maryland, the Hall of Records, the Maryland Historical Society, and the Maryland Room in McKeldin Library at the University of Maryland proved to be nearly limitless in their resources. In Virginia, relevant repositories were found in the State Library and the State Historical Society in Richmond. Especially important, too, were the collections at the Massachusetts Historical Society, the Essex Institute, the Library of Congress, and the Colonial Williamsburg Foundation.

In colonial Chesapeake and Massachusetts, sport was man's attempt to organize play. Both as a result of their English background

---

[25]Nancy L. Struna, "The Cultural Significance of Sport in the Colonial Chesapeake and Massachusetts" (Ph.D. diss., University of Maryland, 1979).

and in response to their new-world environment, the seventeenth- and eighteenth-century sportsmen produced four primary types of sports. Field sports, athletic events, contests with and against animals, and household and tavern games filled a void in men's lives, a gap created by the failure of life's activities to completely provide joy, catharsis, recreation and diversion, physical training and health, prestige and distinction, and a sense of sharing entertaining experiences with others.

To trace changes in colonial perceptions of sport, one begins with England. The earliest colonists were the English who settled in Jamestown, St. Mary's City, and Boston. Only after years of experience, of trial and error, and of modifying goods to fit wilderness conditions did successive generations establish American sporting styles and attitudes. The cultural factors and the contrasting attitudes displayed by first-generation colonists stemmed from the practices and beliefs which prevailed in the mother country. With their countrymen and countrywomen who remained home, the new-world immigrants shared a common, albeit complex and diverse, heritage.

Until the third quarter of the seventeenth century, a survival mentality existed, so the most common sports were those which derived from work, from acquiring food and building homes, and from defensive requirements. Particularly after 1675, men who had learned to control the land practiced sports which were not as utilitarian, which enabled some to develop new social relationships and communities based on common interests and shared perceptions, and which enabled still others to realize their individual satisfactions.

Eighteenth-century sportsmen shared many perceptions and uses of sport. As it had in precolonial England, sport complemented the interests of various occupational and ethnic groups, of those who wanted to be seen and those who were spectators, and of those who were haunted by the past but driven by fulfillment into the future. Yeomen and husbandmen hunted and fished in a land where 90% of the population was rural. Lawyers, merchants, and landed gentry displayed their prowess before constituents and customers or joined with their friends in fashionable games. Laborers played in the streets of towns, those cultural mingling pots where commercial interests and specialization of occupation had encouraged toleration and heterogeneity of thought and action. Young sons of the rich and educated devoted themselves to games and frolics of which their elders sometimes disapproved and which no manner of legislative or religious pronouncement could restrain. Even militia trainings, huskings or harvest festivals, or other communal festivities occurred because people desired to belong to a larger community.

Differences in sport forms and emphasis did occur among colonists of the two regions. In the Chesapeake region, landed gentlemen participated in exclusive forms of sport, which their mercantile and professional counterparts in Massachusetts did not. After 1714, immigrants from northern Europe to the Chesapeake region introduced sports rarely seen in Massachusetts. Gambling appeared to be more prevalent in the Chesapeake region than in Massachusetts. Such differences stemmed primarily from personal preferences and perceptions rather than from organic differences in the respective colonists' conception of sport itself.

Women's Sports Costumes

Doull investigated the evolution of women's costumes in the following eight sports: archery, baseball/softball, basketball, bowling, field hockey, golf, lacrosse, and tennis.[26] The primary sources consulted included books, magazines, periodicals, clothing catalogs, rule books, and photographs. *Ladies' Home Journal* and *Sears* catalogs were useful guides to trends in fashion and sports costumes. *Spalding Sports Guides, DGWS Rule Books,* and magazines such as *Outing, The Sportswoman, Journal of Health, Physical Education, and Recreation, Sports Illustrated,* and *Womensports,* as well as books written by champion sportswomen, provided an overall view of women's sports. Other primary information was obtained through correspondence with the secretaries of national sports associations. Sports and fashion books published since the end of the nineteenth century constituted helpful secondary sources. The data were critically examined for their internal and external validity.

In the thesis, answers were sought to seven questions. These questions, with brief summarizing statements of results, follow.

1. *Who selected costumes for the particular sports?* Replies from five sports associations indicated that only bowling and field hockey were regulated. Dress for other sports followed current fashions.

2. *How have individual sports costumes related to fashion trends in society?* Archers have never deviated from the fashions of the time and have not produced a special archery costume. Bowlers stayed with the fashions of the times until 1940; since then, special bowling dresses have been designed. Golfers continued to wear everyday clothes until the great upsurge of interest in the 1960s; from this time, they designed their own

[26]Judith D. Doull, "The History and Development of Women's Costumes in Selected Team and Individual Sports" (Master's thesis, University of North Carolina at Greensboro, 1976).

special costumes. The first individual sport to produce a special costume was tennis, in the 1920s.

3. *How have team sports costumes related to fashion trends in society?* Baseball/softball followed the fashion trends until the 1940s, when brief skirts and shorts joined the regular knicker-bocker outfits. Basketball players abandoned everyday fashion clothes as early as 1894, when they adopted the current baggy bloomer outfit; since the 1920s, brief skirts and shorts have been the regular costume. Field hockey and lacrosse players stayed with the fashion trends until the early 1920s, when they adopted the English-style tunic as their special uniform.

4. *How have individual sports costumes related to team sports costumes?* All the team sports have retained the same uniforms for many years, while the individual sports have shown different styles at least every 10 years.

5. *Has the nature of the games affected costume selection and development?* The more vigorous games, such as tennis, field hockey, basketball, and lacrosse, produced special outfits much earlier than the more sedate sports.

6. *Has the composition of the internal structure of sports associations affected costume selection and development?* Sports associations conducted entirely by women have not shown any distinctive traits in this regard.

7. *Has the institutional affiliation of a sport affected costume selection and development?* Basketball, field hockey, and lacrosse have been closely associated with schools and colleges. In these institutions, sport uniforms have been very unflattering and bulky until recently, and changes in style and design have taken place over a long evolutionary period.

Biography of Frederick Rand Rogers

An exhaustive, penetrating, and interpretive biography of the life, professional beliefs, and contributions of Frederick Rand Rogers nas been written by Pennington.[27] Rogers was the first physical educator to receive the Ph.D. degree. Actually, however, the degree was earned in educational administration and awarded in 1925 by Teachers College, Columbia University. The major positions held by Dr. Rogers were Director of Health and Physical Education for New York state, 1926-

[27]G. Gary Pennington, "Frederick Rand Rogers: Educational Provocateur" (Ph.D. diss., University of Oregon, 1972).

1931 and Dean of Student Health and Physical Education at Boston University, 1931-1940. After 1940, although only 46 years old at the time, Rogers did not hold a professional position; yet, he continued to exert a national professional influence in physical education through addresses, personal contacts with leaders, letter writing to influential people, and publications. He was widely quoted and his ideas discussed in journal articles, books, and newspapers. Characterized as an "educational provocateur" by Pennington, Rogers was a controversial figure throughout his career, largely because of his somewhat radical beliefs and the often uncompromising manner in which he pursued them.

An immense amount of primary and secondary source materials was employed by Pennington in preparing the biography, including the following:

1. *Visitations and interviews.*   Visitations were made to 16 locations throughout the United States and one in England where Rogers had been professionally active or where individuals who had been associated with him in some way were residing. Library archives, department files, yearbooks, annual reports, and other source material were examined. Interviews were held with 45 individuals, most of which were tape-recorded. Eighteen hours of extended interviews and discussions were held with Rogers himself.

2. *Publications.*   Rogers's publications, 11 books and 137 articles, were reviewed. Morgue files of leading newspapers in New York state; Boston; and Monterey, California, yielded 167 news accounts related to Rogers. Reviews of 28 general bibliographies and 26 historical studies in health, physical education, and recreation were included.

3. *Correspondence.*   Rogers provided numerous letters, statements, pictures, and documents pertaining to his life, professional career, and basic beliefs. Over 5,000 letters were released to Pennington for review by various people who had corresponded with Rogers.

4. *Questionnaires and letters.*   Two questionnaires were developed to collect information concerning Rogers's professional career. One was designed to evaluate his teaching ability, as seen by former students; the other asked for information and opinions concerning various facets of his life and works. A total of 170 detailed responses were received; 156 were from former students.

5. *Expert opinion.*   Leaders in seven national associations were

invited to submit statements concerning Rogers's beliefs and activities.

6. *Other sources.* Additional source materials examined to obtain information regarding Rogers's beliefs and activities included: pictorial materials from library and newspaper files and collections; records from each state association of health, physical education, and recreation in the United States and from the New York State Public High School Athletic Association; academic records from registrars's and alumni offices of pertinent schools and colleges; and naval service records from the United States Naval Academy, where Rogers had undergone training.

The provocative nature of Rogers's beliefs, their development, professional impact, and evaluation, make this biography uniquely significant; it is the one single source in existence that presents and critiques these contributions in historical detail. Among the most notable of these contributions are: creation of the Physical Fitness Index and the individualization of physical fitness programs based on test results; development of objectives of education, characterized by separation of the sexes and recognition of the desirable and undesirable outcomes of education; formulation of Rogers' Law of General Learning Potential with proposed formula based on intelligence and physical fitness; player control of athletic contests whereby contestants run their own contests without the on-going-game direction of coaches; utilization of the Strength Index for the equation of abilities of participants in athletic contests; formulation of the tie-score ideal; and rejection of state championships in schoolboy sports.

WRITING THE REPORT

The writing of an historical account has many of the same characteristics as the writing of any research report. A statement of the problem and any limitations imposed should be made. Questions to be answered may be posed, or hypotheses may be stated. Special care should be exercised in identifying the primary and secondary sources found and utilized. The ways by which events are double-checked, contradictions resolved, and facts sifted from rumor or conjecture should be clear to the reader.

Considerable thought should be given to the organization of the historical report. Such reports are usually lengthy and need to conform to a definite plan to avoid duplication and confusion. Still, they should be concise and to the point; they should be accurate and cohesive. If questions have been asked or hypotheses have been formulated, the organization can center around them. Otherwise, the historian should pattern his or her material in some systematic order, such as chronological, geographical, topical, or a combination of these. Judgments need to be made relative to the amount of emphasis or space given to each phase of the history. Minor points or trivia should be treated as such. Such accounts should be as interesting as the material will permit without sacrificing accuracy or meaning; historians must refrain from embellishing their narrations with dramatic statements that distort the truth. Historical writings should be lucid, lively, logical accounts that are honest and scholarly.

SUMMARY

As mentioned in this chapter, the history of any field is its heritage. Not only is the past recorded for posterity, but many lessons can be learned that may be applied as a guide for and a prediction of the future. Historical research can also be fascinating. Professional vistas unfold before the historian's consciousness; the unexpected is encountered, evaluated, and resolved; doubtful facets of history may be clarified; new acquaintance is gained with great leaders of the past; new respect and understanding of the profession and its pioneers are engendered.

In this chapter, the methodology of conducting historical research was explained. The nature of, and professional interest in, such research were discussed. The fact that history can be functional was considered. Attention was given to the writing of biographies. The nature of primary and secondary sources and the means of evaluating them by external and internal criticisms were presented. The special aspects and procedures in oral research were examined. The use of hypotheses was considered. Some pitfalls in historical research were discussed. Illustrations of completed historical studies were provided. Comments on writing the historical report closed the chapter. More and more historical studies are appearing in physical education. Some professionals in this field are now turning to historical writing as their primary contribution to scholarship.

SELECTED REFERENCES

BEST, JOHN W., *Research in Education* (4th ed.). Englewood Cliffs, N.J. Prentice-Hall, Inc., 1981, Ch. 10.

GERBER, ELLEN W., "Methodology in Historical Research," in *Exercise and Sport Sciences Reviews*, Vol. 2, ed. Jack H. Wilmore. New York: Academic Press, Inc., 1974, pp. 335-355.

GOOD, CARTER, V., *Essentials of Educational Research*. East Norwalk, Conn.: Appleton-Century-Crofts, 1966, Ch. 4.

VAN DALEN, DEOBOLD B., *Understanding Educational Research*, 4th ed. New York: McGraw-Hill, Inc., 1979, Ch. 11.

ZEIGLER, EARLE F., MAXWELL L. HOWELL, and MARIANNA TREKELL, eds., *Research in the History, Philosophy, and International Relations of Physical Education and Sport: Bibliographies and Techniques*, Pt. One. Champaign, Ill.: Stipes Publishing Company, 1971.

5
Philosophical Studies

This chapter considers studies related to philosophy in physical education. As presented here, these studies take two general directions: (1) studies of philosophy per se, in which philosophies are developed, aims and objectives are formulated, and principles are proposed based on existing evidence, astute observation, and forefront thinking; and (2) determination of the philosophical beliefs of leaders and comparison with eminent, broadly based philosophies that are accepted by philosophers on the frontier of educational thought.

This chapter is *not* concerned with philosophical beliefs expressed by leaders in the field, but, rather, is directed toward the process of developing philosophies and applying them to practice. For many years, philosophical expressions have appeared in the literature and have given direction to physical education. For example, Ziegler presented a bibliography of 189 selected books, papers, and theses on the philosophy of physical education and sports between 1922 and 1971; most of these references, however, dated from 1955.[1] The first studies with primarily philosophical approaches in this bibliography

---

[1] Earle F. Zeigler, "A Chronological, Selected Bibliography of the Philosophy of Physical Education and Sport," in *Research in the History, Philosophy, and International Aspects of Physical Education and Sport: Bibliographies and Techniques*, eds. Earle F. Zeigler, Maxwell L. Howell, and Marianna Trekell (Champaign, Ill.: Stipes Publishing Company, 1971), p. 216.

were completed by Larkin[2] in 1936 and by Esslinger[3] in 1938. Zeigler indicated that the first significant philosophical study using the analytical approach was completed by Clark in 1943.[4] Although there were earlier works of a philosophical nature, Harper[5] identified Davis's book[6] in 1961 as the first attempt to make philosophy palatable to the profession of physical education.

Of what use is the philosophical method? Certainly it is utilized for resolving problems, especially problems that currently cannot be solved by other means or that cannot wait on other means for an answer. The philosophical method can be applied to a problem at once without protracted experimentation. Therefore, the philosophical solution is timely: But such a solution is more prone to be wrong than are solutions gleaned by other methods, as subsequent experimentation may reveal.

Vital and far-reaching decisions made in education are philosophically based. The objectives of education, the organization of the curriculum, the content of courses, and the selection of methodology are established more prevalently by philosophical considerations than through scientific means, although the latter are not ignored in reaching decisions. Even before objectives are set, the ideology of a society is determined on a philosophical basis, since education systems planned for democratic and totalitarian states are vastly different. The same considerations apply to religions and the choice of denominations within religions. Today, how are such great human challenges as intergroup and racial relations, poverty, war, and crime being met? Certainly, the decisions have profound influences upon man's way of being and living.

In this time of science, people are prone to rely upon material resources; and, certainly, these have been developed in overwhelming abundance. To meld these resources for the common good may be more vital today than increasing them. But with what means will people accomplish this task? The concepts and methods of instrumental

[2] Richard A. Larkin, "The Influence of John Dewey on Physical Education" (Master's thesis, Ohio State University, 1936).

[3] Arthur A. Esslinger, "A Philosophical Study of Principles for Selected Activities in Physical Education" (Ph.D. diss., University of Iowa, 1938).

[4] Margaret C. Clark, "A Philosophical Interpretation of a Program of Physical Education in a State Teachers College (Ph.D. diss., New York University, 1943).

[5] William Harper, "Philosophy of Physical Education and Sport," in *Exercise and Sport Sciences Review*, Vol. 2, ed. Jack H. Wilmore (New York: Academic Press, Inc. 1974), p. 239.

[6] Edward Craig Davis, *The Philosophical Process in Physical Education* (Philadelphia: W. B. Saunders Company, 1961), p. 240. (Second Edition, 1967, with Donna Mae Miller.)

thinking—a result of unbridled science—cannot enable people to grasp absolute ends that are capable of directing them to use those instruments. "Instrumental thinking will rather be tempted to misrepresent all absolute ends as sheer useful fictions or imaginary satisfactions of human desires."[7]

Philosophical studies are needed in physical education, and they should be dedicated to the task of establishing the vision of ultimate ends. Philosophical solutions should be considered tentative and subject to constant reappraisal. But, then, is this not true of science as well—where today's firmly held truth is modified by tomorrow's fresh discovery? The growing and menacing gap between humanity's technical and scientific capacity and its apparent inability to deal with affairs on a rational basis must be narrowed.

NATURE OF THE
PHILOSOPHICAL METHOD

Although the philosophical method by itself is not scientific, this method is needed to resolve certain kinds of problems. The philosophical method is largely subjective, since the solution of the problem is accomplished through critical thinking. However, this thinking is based upon whatever evidence may be available. Reason is applied to this evidence and is supplemented by astute observation of the passing scene and the historical forces that brought it into being.

In its broadest sense, philosophy is the study of processes that govern thought and conduct, of the principles of laws that regulate the universe and underlie all knowledge and reality. Included in the study of philosophy are aesthetics, logic, ethics, and metaphysics. Philosophy projects the meanings derived from experience and from knowledge in terms of purposes appropriate for the guidance of humanity's choices and conduct.

Philosophical research involves critical thinking on levels of extensive generalization beyond the realm of fact-finding science. Philosophy takes the conclusions of science, uses these facts as raw materials for further reflection, and thereby develops larger and more inclusive points of view. Philosophy constructively criticizes experience as it exists at a given time and thus renders experience more unified, stable, and progressive. The conflicts of experience demand a thorough, critical appraisal of contents and procedures. However, criticism does not end with mere intellectual discrimination; it provides a basis for the projection of values as yet unrealized—values that may

---

[7] Maximillian Beck, "A Plea for Philosophical Research," *School and Society*, 62, No. 1610 (November 3, 1945), 293.

be translated into ends that move people to action. Philosophy, thus conceived, makes the greatest possible use of experience resulting from both empirical and scientific observations.

Zeigler observed that, rather than aim at a solution to a limited number of factors through rigid experimental control, the philosophic method points at including every variable which is either directly or remotely relevant to the problem.[8] In this way, an effort is made to arrive at a synthesis which is not only consistent with the best current data but also with the best experience from the past. He quotes Brubaker as follows: " . . . philosophy itself uncovers no new facts. It processes the facts of other disciplines but owns none of its own." Stated in another way, philosophy is a basic understanding of one's beliefs which can be applied to problematic situations which occur in physical education. Philosophy should serve as a guide in arriving at reasonable and consistent solutions to problems encountered in everyday practice.

THE METHOD OF PHILOSOPHY

When confronted with a problem, people frequently try to recall a personal experience that will help lead to a solution. For example, the football coach may remember a play that worked well against a particular team the previous year, so he uses it again against the same opponent. Although reference to personal experience is a useful and common method of reaching decisions on problems, its uncritical use can lead to erroneous conclusions. Thus, an individual's experience may have been too limited to justify reliance on it; evidence may be omitted that does not agree with the opinion held; significant factors related to a specific situation may be overlooked; only evidence that supports bias or prejudices may be selected; the situation may be sufficiently different so that previous experience does not apply (as in the football illustration, the opponents may also realize the possibility and be ready for it, or the personnel on either or both sides may have changed significantly). To avoid these general pitfalls, the philosophical method must be applied with the same care in weighing the evidence as the scientist applies in weighing results.   One must consider the pros and cons as objectively as possible, raising objections to all suggested solutions until the proper one seems to emerge.

[8] Earle F. Zeigler, "Philosophy of Physical Education and Sport: An Approach to the Research Method and Its Techniques," in *Research in the History, Philosophy, and International Aspects of Physical Education and Sport: Bibliographies and Techniques,* ed., Earle F. Zeigler, Maxwell L. Howell, and Marianna Trekell (Champaign, Ill.: Stipes Publishing Company, 1971), 171.

Various steps in critical thinking have been advocated by eminent scholars. An example is Dewey's five steps presented in Chapter 2.[9] These steps are: (1) recognition of a felt difficulty, (2) its identification and definition, (3) formulation of hypotheses for its solution, (4) expansion and development of the hypotheses through the reasoning process, and (5) acceptance or rejection of the hypotheses as a consequence of formal research. As can be seen, these steps exceed the purely philosophical, since they provide for experimentation. This observation indicates the close association between philosophy and science. Actually, no scientific work can be undertaken without critical thinking, as will be demonstrated.

The first three of Dewey's steps are common to all research. Certainly, the investigator has a "felt difficulty," as from it comes his or her research topic. The difficulty is formulated into a problem with appropriate delimitations that permit solution, and the method of solution is determined, which includes that statement of an hypothesis. If a differentiation may be proposed in the fourth step, the philosopher basically gathers existing evidence to use in appraising his or her hypothesis, whereas the scientist resorts to experimental procedures to produce evidence. Thus, for philosophical studies, Dewey's steps stop short of scientific evaluation.

Philosophical research rests heavily on the formulation of an hypothesis and the application of critical reasoning in its appraisal. The hypothesis is a statement tentatively accepted in light of what is known about a phenomenon at the time; it is employed as a basis for action in the search for new truth. The hypothesis should be in agreement with observed facts; it should not conflict with known truths but may challenge them in light of new evidence or reasoning.

As summarized by Van Dalen, a hypothesis specifies the facts and the relations among them that provide a logical explanation for the conditions that give rise to a problem. Some variables and relations in hypotheses are known while others are speculated in order to provide a solution, at least tentatively, to the problem. "By logically relating known facts to intelligent guesses about unknown variables or relations, hypotheses are able to extend and enlarge our knowledge."[10] Thus, hypotheses are calculated guesses.

The hypothesis is stated for the purpose of evaluating its tenability. At no time should it be considered a statement that must be defended at all costs in order "not to lose face." Actually, rejected hypotheses contribute to knowledge in a negative sort of way; the investigator may not have arrived at a solution to his or her problem,

[9]John Dewey, *How We Think* (Boston: D. C. Heath & Company, 1933), p. 68.

[10]Deobold B. Van Dalen, *Understanding Educational Research: An Introduction*, 4th ed. (New York: McGraw-Hill, Inc. 1979), p. 198.

but he or she does know some possibilities that are not correct. Many highly respected sciences are strewn with rejected hypotheses that lead to the one final solution that is valid.

Thus, in philosophical research, the investigator follows certain specific steps, as follows:

1. Identifies the problem area; the problem is defined and delimited to manageable proportions.
2. Collects available facts related to the problem.
3. Synthesizes and analyzes the facts, working them into patterns that identify relationships among them.
4. From these patterns, derives general principles that describe the relationships inherent in the principles.
5. States these principles in the form of hypotheses or tentative assumptions.
6. Critically tests hypotheses for acceptance, rejection, or modification.

THE CRITICAL-THINKING CONTINUUM

As mentioned, an association exists between philosophy and science; no sharp line of demarcation between the two is identifiable. In actuality, the most scientific study imaginable requires critical thinking—the primary feature of the philosophical method. Thus, in such a scientific study, the problem must be identified, hypotheses must be stated, results must be analyzed and integrated, and conclusions must be drawn.

On the other hand, philosophical studies per se depend more on critical thinking. Instead of the deliberately acquired experimental evidence in the scientific study, existing knowledge is assembled and applied with a heightened utilization of reflective process. Some philosophical studies may have an abundance of available evidence whereas others may need to obtain additional evidence to guide thinking. Thus the degree of reliance upon critical appraisal applied to studies may be considered on a continuum, extending from the minimal amount in scientific studies to the maximal amount where astute observation is dominant, as in proposing a philosophy for physical education. Examples of these extremes—minimal and maximal poles—may help clarify the meaning of this critical-thinking continuum, as well as the definition and concept of philosophical research intended here.

Minimal Pole

The minimal pole of the critical-thinking continuum—the pole with the minimal amount of critical thinking upon which to base results—is illustrated by an investigation of the "memory drum" theory of neuromotor reaction by Henry and Rogers.[11] The theory proposes a nonconscious mechanism that uses stored information (motor memory) to channel existing nervous impulses from brain waves and general afferent stimuli into the appropriate neuromuscular coordination centers, subcenters, and efferent nerves, and thus causing the desired movement.

Hypothesis Formulation. The authors first indicated that the time for the simplest voluntary response to a stimulus (RT) is .15 seconds under the most favorable circumstances, although longer times of .20 to .25 seconds are more typical. When complications are present, such as discrimination between several stimuli and/or choice between several possible movements, the RT increases and may be twice as long as these times.

Basing their actions on current knowledge of the neuromuscular system and its control by cephalic nervous centers, the investigators modified the traditional reflex theories of voluntary response time. The facts cited in the formulation of their theory were: (1) No reflex exists in the modern physiological use of the term, since a reflex must be nonwillful and not voluntary. (2) Not more than a minimal involvement of the cerebral cortex is involved in the RT response, because the neuromuscular coordination centers and pathways are chiefly cerebral or subcortical without cortical termination. (3) As a consequence, perhaps neuroanatomy, neuromotor perception, is extremely poor, although neuromotor coordination or kinesthetic adjustment is well developed in humans.

Next, it was observed that performance of acts of skill may involve neuromuscular memory. Such memory was operationally defined as "improved neuromotor coordination and more effective response, the improvement being the result of experience and practice, possibly accumulated over a period of many years." The implication was made that this neuromotor memory is different from ideational or perceptual memory, since conscious imagery is indefinite and largely excluded.

However, a rich store of unconscious motor memory is available for the performance of neuromotor skill. Added to this are innate motor

---

[11] Franklin M. Henry and Donald E. Rogers, "Increased Response Latency for Complicated Movements and a 'Memory Drum' Theory of Neuromotor Reaction," *Research Quarterly*, 31, No. 3 (October 1960), 448.

coordinations that are important in motor acts. The use of this store of motor responses was thought of broadly by the authors as a "memory drum" phenomenon, using an analogy from the electronic computer.

> The neural pattern for a specific and well-coordinated motor act is controlled by a stored program that is used to direct the neuromotor details of its performance. In the absence of an available stored program, an unlearned complicated task is carried out under conscious control in an awkward, step-by-step, poorly coordinated manner.

The authors indicated that the concepts discussed can lead to a number of testable predictions. One of the implications becomes the hypothesis for this study. This hypothesis was that simple reaction time becomes longer when the response movement required is of greater complexity. It was contended that a longer latent time for the more complicated circulation of neural impulses through the coordination centers is inevitable when more complicated patterns are involved.

Experimentation. The hypothesis that simple reaction time becomes lengthened with increased movement complexity was tested. Data were obtained on 120 subjects—college men and women and 12- and 8-year-old boys. Sixty of the subjects were tested with two experimental procedures in order to improve the adequacy of the control conditions. Three types of movement varying in complexity were used; both reaction time and movement time were measured.

The results were in agreement with the hypothesis. By substituting a very simple finger movement with an arm movement of moderate complexity, the reaction was slowed by about 20%; additional complexity produced a further slowing of reaction of 7%. Other aspects of this study, each of which represented another hypothesis which was investigated in this study, were reported as follows: (1) The speed of an arm movement is considerably faster in college men than in college women or younger boys. (2) The correlation between reaction time and speed of movement is approximately zero. (3) Individual differences in ability to make a fast arm movement are about 70% specific to the particular movement being made; "general ability for arm speed" occurs only to the extent of 30%.

Comments. The study by Henry and Rogers was presented to show the reliance upon critical thinking required even in a highly scientific study. Evidence was marshaled from several sources, especially knowledge of the neuromuscular systems. A "memory drum" theory of neuromotor reaction was evolved. From this theory, a number of hypotheses were stated. Up to this point, the investigators had confined their efforts to the critical evaluation of existing facts and the formulation of implications from them. Obviously, the philosopher does likewise. However, science took over when experimentation began; critical appraisal, however, was again evident when interpretations were made and conclusions were drawn.

Maximal Pole

The maximal pole of the critical-thinking continuum requires the maximal amount of critical thinking and the minimal amount of scientific evidence available to guide that thinking. This pole is illustrated by the charts of "The Objectives and Anathemata of Education" developed by Frederick Rand Rogers and shown in Figures 5.1 for males and 5.2 for females.[12] The aims of this study were prepared with the assistance of scores of men and women in all walks of life and after exhaustive analyses of the aims and objectives of some sixty educational leaders, including state commissioners, college presidents, and deans of schools of education.

A complete exposition of this formalized hierarchy of aims, objectives, and their anathemas would require considerable space, including particular definitions of each word that appears and the logical, psychological, and social justification for its inclusion. In philosophically establishing the charts of aims, such explanations must be made. The investigator draws on observations of the passing scene and interprets them in the light of current knowledge and the pioneering aims of leading educational philosophers. Obviously, the logic must be sound and be supported by an objective approach to the truth where pros and cons for each concept are carefully weighed before being accepted. The following interpretations are made as an aid to understanding the charts:

1. The aims and objectives of boys and girls are separate and different. The logic is: Nature made men and women differently, including different constructions of their bodies and different manifestations of emotions of their spirits; boys were intended to grow into men and girls into women; and the continuance of life itself depends on nurturing the unique qualities of male and female.

2. The aims are listed in heavy print at the top of each chart: Vitality, Justice, and Spirituality for boys; Salvation, Revelation, and

[12]Frederick Rand Rogers, "An Educational Mariner's Portfolio of Basic Charts," 1960; charts reproduced here with his permission. An earlier form of these charts appears in: Frederick Rand Rogers, ed., *Dance: A Basic Educational Technique* (New York: The Macmillian Company, 1941), pp. 7-17. (Reprinted by Dance Horizons, 1980.)

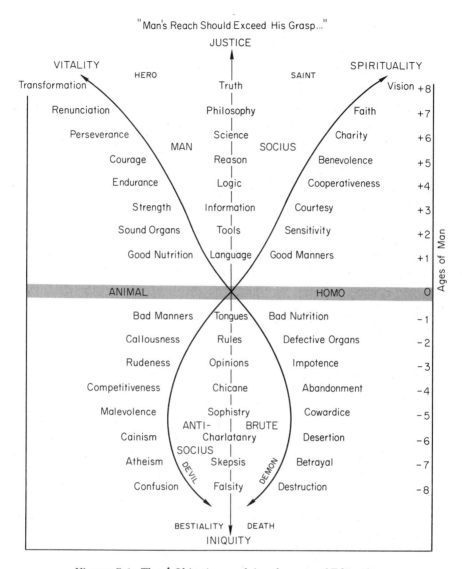

Figure 5.1. The ♂ Objectives and Anathemata of Education.

Grace for girls. These aims are admittedly above mortal man's grasp; they are spiritual rather than secular, indefinitely extended into the future, as expressed by "man's reach should exceed his grasp." However, these aims are only logical extensions of mundane striving for health, culture, and social efficiency. Their religious terminology is appropriate, since one appeals to religion for spiritual terms.

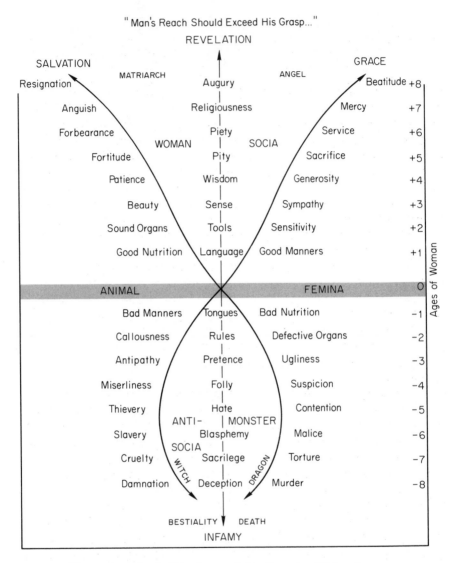

Figure 5.2. The ♀ Objectives and Anathemata of Education

3. Each sex has three kinds of growth represented by three scales that extend upward from the midpoint of its own base. These indicate physical, mental, and social development leading toward ultimate goals. Teachers must be equally concerned with all three kinds of growth. A strong man who is antisocial can be a menace to society. A beautiful girl who lacks sympathy is a perpetual source of anxiety.

4. The qualities, virtues, or kinds of behavior named on each scale represent objectives to be achieved during each stage of growth. Eight stages are indicated by the objectives on each chart.

5. The author did not intend that the order must be maintained in the effort to reach higher levels. For example, boys can persevere before they are strong and courageous, and girls can serve before they are sympathetic, generous, and sacrificial; but they are not as likely to do so. On the other hand, the placing of each virtue gives a clue to its proper definition. Thus, perseverence placed above endurance and courage means the capacity to persevere significantly for the benefit of society. Further, the separation of men's and women's qualities is not intended to convey that boys should have no feminine traits and that girls should have no masculine traits. For example, women must have strength to fulfill their life's functions, and men need some courtesy to be bearable. Nor is it possible for most men and women to move equally up all scales.

6. Knowledge of the anathematic of aims and objectives is almost as necessary as is appreciation of virtues and ultimate goals. This concept recognizes that education can have undesirable as well as desirable results, depending on the educational process. Eight negative stages are indicated from the midpoints on the charts, leading to "iniquity" for men and "infamy" for women.

7. The curvings of the scales away from each midpoint illustrate growing and expanding life. As a boy becomes strong, informed, and courteous, his horizons and influence widen and increase. As a girl becomes beautiful, sensible, and sympathetic, so does her life expand.

8. To illustrate applications of the traits, "strength" *presupposes* sound organs and good nutrition; it *indicates* ability to work, play, and study for long hours without fatigue; it *implies* not great absolute strength (a Sampson) but abundant strength in proportion to sex, age, and weight. Likewise, "beauty" *presupposes* sound organs and good nutrition for girls; it *indicates* clear complexion, general cleanliness, regularity of feature and figure, grace, and poise of body, graciousness of bearing; it *implies* not a pretty face but a sympathetic spirit shining through a healthy body.

Comments. The charts of aims of education developed by Rogers show the results of a philosophical approach in which reliance is primarily placed on critical thinking. The process by which Rogers arrived at his charts of aims is not described in this statement other than to say that assistance was obtained from many nonprofessionals and educators. The author had a broad background of education and experience upon which to draw information; he was familiar with allied professional and scientific literature, which helped to guide his thinking. This process is typical of the establishment of educational aims and objectives whether they be prepared by individuals or by committees or commissions. Their impact on education is great, so they should be approached with true critical appraisal, free of bias, prejudice, or self-interest.

SELECTED EXAMPLES OF PHILOSOPHICAL STUDIES

In order to indicate various approaches to the conduct of philosophical studies, several examples of such studies actually completed will be given. In selecting the studies for review, unique features in each were sought.

Principles of Physical Education

In 1938 Esslinger submitted a philosophical study of principles for selecting activities in physical education.[13] The need expressed for the study and the proposals that resulted should be judged in view of the situation facing physical education in the mid-1930s rather than the present.

Purposes. The purposes of this study were: (1) to establish principles upon which the selection of subject matter could be based, and (2) to develop implications for the physical education program based on the principles established. A principle was conceived of as being a fundamental belief based upon facts available. Drawn from the facts that developed and substantiated the principle. implications were offered as practical suggestions for selecting and adapting the content of the program.

Procedures. The principles and their implications were developed from facts regarding the child in the present and future environment. The specific steps in this process were

1. *Discovering the facts.*
   (a) Facts related to the growth and development and the capacities and interests of children that are of significance for the

[13]Arthur A. Esslinger, "A Philosophical Study of Principles for Selecting Activities in Physical Education" (Ph.D. diss., University of Iowa, 1938). Excerpts reprinted by permission of the author.

physical educator were derived from the study of anatomy, physiology, psychology, and education.

(b) Facts related to the needs of children and adults were found by the study of present-day society and social trends.

2. *Evolving the principles from the facts.*
   (a) From a study of the facts that had been collected, the chief characteristics of the facts were determined. Those that appeared to have some characteristics in common or seemed to be of the same general type were organized under an appropriate head stated in the form of a generalized statement.
   (b) After a generalized statement or principle had been evolved, it was substantiated with all the facts that were applicable to it.

3. *Developing the implications.* By a careful study of each principle and the facts used to substantiate it, practical implications for the program were suggested. Although it was not the purpose of the investigation to construct a course of study, these implications offered concrete suggestions in regard to the definite activities or types of activities that should be included in the program.

Principles established. As an indication of the results of this philosophical study, the principles evolved are given.

1. The physical education program should provide opportunities for a wide range of muscular movements involving large-muscle groups.
2. The activities of the physical education program should be selected and adapted in light of known facts regarding biological growth and development of children.
3. Activities should be selected in the light of psychological age characteristics of the child.
4. Individual differences that exist among children should be considered in the selection of activities.
5. Only activities that are physiologically wholesome should be selected for the physical education program.
6. The physical education program should consist predominantly of activities organized and developed from racial activities.
7. In the selection of the activities, some provision should be made for progression.
8. The curriculum should stress activities that are recreative in nature.

9. Activities should be selected for their contribution to the youth's training for citizenship in a democracy.
10. Activities that are valuable in providing opportunities for training and expressing emotions should receive much emphasis in the physical education curriculum.

Implications. To illustrate the implications of a principle in this study, the second principle above is chosen: "The activities of the physical education program should be selected and adapted in light of known facts regarding biological growth and development of children." The implications developed are:

1. Activities should be selected for the child upon the basis of physiological rather than chronological age.
2. Facts related to the growth and development of the skeleton indicate the need for an early selection of postural activities.
3. The elementary school program should consist of a variety of activities rather than just a few.
4. The elementary school child has a great need for physical education activities that are valuable in developing neuromuscular coordination. Junior high school boys and girls also need coordinating activities.
5. The physical education time allotment in elementary school is far from adequate to meet the needs of children for large-muscle exercise.
6. No differentiation in the program of activities is necessary for boys and girls until the seventh grade.
7. The facts suggest the inadvisability of strenuous exercise during the junior high school period.
8. The lack of arm and shoulder girdle strength of junior and senior high school boys requires the special attention of the physical educator.
9. Activities emphasizing the development of the upper body should be selected for the physical education program in senior high school and college.
10. Various activities should be modified for the girls' physical education program in junior and senior high schools and college.
11. It is generally conceded that active, vigorous sports and games are valuable for girls and that participation in them does not interfere with the special biological functions of women.

Comments. Esslinger's study conforms closely to the classical approach to a philosophical study; his methodology is located toward the maximal pole of the critical-thinking continuum. He utilized a vast resource of available facts and current pioneer thinking to formulate and justify his principles. Then he followed through by making numerous implications for physical education for boys and girls from elementary school through college. New scientific facts were not sought; rather, the resource was a synthesis of existing knowledge.

A critical observation that today's thoughtful, informed reader would make is that some of the implications are no longer valid or nearly so valid. For example, the sixth and seventh implications above would now be challenged in light of current research knowledge. Such a consequence is inevitable in any such philosophical study completed years ago, for human knowledge continues to increase. The appropriateness of the proposals made in Esslinger's study must be judged in relation to the time they were made and the level of thought and knowledge then available.

Another exhaustive philosophical study to establish the principles that are essential for the realization of the objectives of physical education was completed by Price in 1946.[14] In 1949 this study received a Research Citation from the American Academy of Physical Education.

Aesthetics of Sport

Wulk analyzed and synthesized the instrumental and institutional concepts of metacritical aesthetics and utilized these concepts for speculation on the nature of a metacritical aesthetic of sport.[15] The delineation of philosophical theory concerning the nature of an aesthetic of sport was examined for concepts that were consistent with metacritical theory.

The study utilized two complementary types of philosophical research: "theory building" as described by Fraleigh and "analysis of the structure of knowledge" as developed by Gowin. Fraleigh's theory-building elements with application to this study were as follows:

1. Choosing the general phenomenon of interest: sport.
2. Selecting a facet of the phenomenon for extensive study: aesthetic.
3. Selecting, describing, and explaining the source of philosophy: interrelated instrumental and institutional theories by Beardsley and Dickie.

[14]Hartley d'O. Price, "The Establishment of the Principles Which Are Essential for the Realization of the Objectives of Physical Education" (Ph.D. diss., New York University, 1946).

[15]Nancy G. Wulk, "Aesthetics of Sport: A Metacritical Analysis" (Ph.D. diss., University of North Carolina at Greensboro, 1977).

4. Relating the philosophy to the specific phenomenon of interest: sport examined for consistency with the aesthetic-determining factors of the source theories.

Gowin's method for the analysis of the structure of knowledge was applied to collate the phenomenon of sport and the philosophical positions of Beardsley and Dickie. This analysis consists of the use of a series of telling and connecting questions to explore a philosophical concept. The questions utilized in this study were focused on the central concepts of aesthetics, sport, and their interrelationships. This process is illustrated next.

Telling Question: Is there an aesthetic of sport?

Connecting Questions: What is aesthetics? What factors designate an object as a candidate for appreciation?

Aesthetics is an axiological subdivision of philosophy which is concerned with the nature and significance of art, with the evaluation and value assessment of art objects, and with beauty. Aesthetic discourse attempts to clarify the basic concepts utilized in thinking and talking about the objects of aesthetic experience. Metacritical criticism indicated that aesthetic experiences are distinctive and can be described utilizing the three aesthetic-designating factors of unity, intensity, and complexity as a basis for explanation. The categorizing of these three factors objectifies the explanation of the aesthetic experience.

Connecting Question: What is sport?

The following definition of sport was derived from a synthesis of critically derived sport definitions proposed by various theorists: "Sport is physical, playful, bounded, rule-governed, and competitive/ challenging activity. It offers opportunities for social interaction and for pursuit of personal and group excellence. It is dynamic, tense, absorbing, and potentially fulfilling. Sport is related to play and athletics. Differentiation among these four concepts is not readily apparent, but the degree and institutionalization of organizations offers a means of discrimination."

Telling Question: Can an aesthetic of sport be defined?

Connecting Question: What aesthetic-designating factors are exhibited by sport?

Applications were made to the three aesthetic-designating factors of unity, intensity, and complexity. *Unity*: Sport provides unity through total coordination of body and movement parts, which are fundamental to skilled execution and basic to aesthetic appreciation. Well-executed movements, which display balance, rhythm, and economy of effort, provide great pleasure to the viewer. *Intensity*: Sport requires the total involvement of both participants and spectators, thereby encompassing the whole range of human emotions. *Complexity*: By its nature, the sport situation is constantly shifting and changing; this necessitates strategy, invention, improvisation, and experimentation by the participant.

Connecting Question: Is the exhibition of these factors central or peripheral to sport?

If the achievement of the sport goal is considered independently from the manner in which the goal is achieved, the aesthetic is peripheral and of secondary importance. When the manner of performance is intrinsic to the achievement of the sport goal, the aesthetic is primary and central.

Telling Question: Can sport be classified relative to the aesthetic?

Connecting Questions: Is there variability in the exhibition of aesthetic-designating factors? Is there variability in the visibility of these factors?

Variability in the exhibition and visibility of the aesthetic-designating factors of unity, intensity, and complexity is found from sport to sport and from contest to contest in the same sport. Variability seems to be a function of the structure and aims of particular sports, the style and level of play of particular contests, and the integration of the aesthetic factors into the evaluation procedures of particular sports.

Telling Question: Can a paradigm be formulated for aesthetic sport?

The author carved a synoptically viewed model from basswood, which was designed to clarify and symbolize the interaction of sport and the metacritical aesthetic-designating factors of unity, intensity, and complexity. Characteristics of the model were: (1) Curvilinear paths suggesting the flow and flexibility of interaction of the three factors. (2) Sport symbolized as an ellipsoid to show flow, flexibility, and energy in the model. (3) The three aesthetic-designating factors presented as curved channels: each channel intersects with other channels at a variety of angles; the intersections were designed to reflect the unpredictable interactional effects of the factors; variability in channel length, size, and intersecting angles suggests the range and diversity in the possible interaction of the factors. (4) Holes in the model representing the threefold metacritical aesthetic of sport and alllowing access to aesthetic pathways. Shaped to suggest the flow of energy within sport, variations in their shapes showed potential variability among the three factors. (5) Interactions among the factor pathways occurring toward the center of the model to indicate the centrality of aesthetics to sport.

The nature of this philosophical study places it near or at the upper end of the critical-thinking continuum. Guidance was provided by the work of other theorists: the theory-building elements proposed by Fraleigh, the structure of knowledge process developed by Gowin, and the application of instrumental and institutional theories by Beardsley and Dickie. A voluminous literature was consulted in developing the metacritical analysis of the aesthetics of sport.

Leaders in American Physical Education

Morland examined the philosophical veiws held by selected leaders in American physical education.[16] This philosophical study is quite different from the ones previously described. The views of the selected leaders were identified from their writings and then related to systematic schools of educational philosophy. Seven leaders were selected who were considered influential in determining the direction of physical education during the period following World War I, when the field was striving for educational status and recognition. These leaders were Thomas D. Wood, Clark W. Hetherington, Jesse Feiring Williams, Jay B. Nash, Charles H. McCloy, Mabel Lee, and Elmer D. Mitchell.

A comparative approach to philosophy was adopted. After reviewing several different classifications, four schools of thought were identified; progressivism, reconstructionism, essentialism, and perennialism. A broad frame of reference consisting of 20 subareas was constructed as a basis for the comparative analysis. These areas centered on specific aspects of the educational process and its theoretical foundations. Included were the general philosophical orientation, the nature and factors involved in learning, the curriculum and the role of the teacher, administration and administrative practices, school and community relations, and educational aims. Quotations were gathered from the works of 96 different educators and philos-

---

[16] Richard B. Morland, "A Philosophical Interpretation of the Educational Views Held by Leaders in American Physical Education" (Ph.D. diss., New York University, 1958). Excerpts reprinted by permission of the author.

ophers who were chosen as exponents of the four schools of thought. A basic approach toward each of the subareas of the general frame of reference was formulated from the themes of each of these competing philosophies.

Using the same topical headings, quotations were collected from the writings of the seven physical education leaders; a synopsis of their beliefs about each of these four philosophies, whether expressed explicitly or implicitly, was set forth. By comparing the views expressed by the physical educators with the general position as determined from the expositions of the representatives of the four schools of educational philosophy, the physical educators were classified in accordance with the consistency with which they followed the line of thought of one of the four schools. Upon this basis, Wood, Hetherington, Williams, Nash, and Mitchell were classified primarily as progressivists; McCloy and Lee supported essentialism.

Bair also completed a study of the philosophical beliefs of American physical education leaders.[17] This investigator, however, employed a different approach from Morland's. He surveyed by checklist 51 contemporary leaders in the field. The purpose of the study was to determine with what eminent philosophies these leaders were identified and from such identification to consider the philosophical directions that seemed to be indicated for American physical education.

The checklist was composed of twelve categories selected from background reading that indicated these to be areas where philosophical beliefs were manifest. The following categories were included: the universe, the nature of man, values, education, program building, program content, the administrator, the teacher, the learner, learning, teaching methods, and evaluation. Each category contained statements representative of four eminent philosophical positions—idealism, realism, pragmatism, and aritomism.

The study was approached through an examination of numerous publications that describe the philosophical systems underlying present-day education and the forces that have shaped American physical education. The philosophical comparisons were with naturalism and spiritualism. The investigator's definitions of these philosophies were as follows: Naturalistic philosophy includes realism and holds that the universe requires no supernatural explanation; the universe is self-directing and constitutes the whole of reality; nature is dynamic and characterized by change. The spiritualistic philosophy is a general doctrine that includes idealism and aritomism; the ultimate

---

[17]Donn E. Bair, "An Identification of Some Philosophical Beliefs Held by Influential Professional Leaders in American Physical Education" (Ph.D. diss., University of Soutern California, 1956). Excerpts reprinted by permission of the author.

reality in the universe is spirit; the universe is changeless and is composed of primary, stable factors that stem from a supernatural source.

On the basis of the beliefs revealed, most of the physical education leaders appeared to be providing a predominantly naturalistic direction to American physical education. However, the study revealed some evidence of strong spiritualistic beliefs, which suggested a dual influence and lack of general agreement in some areas.

Comments. The studies reported in this section are not philosophical per se, but, rather, deal with comparative philosophies in which the beliefs of physical education leaders are compared with eminent philosophies broadly developed and accepted by educators on the frontier of educational thought. The study by Morland has historical connotations, as he studied the philosophical views of a small group of seven leaders who dynamically influenced physical education during the critical period following World War I. The author, himself, suggested that additional research is needed to determine if the favorable ratio to progressivism which he found holds as well for other leaders in the profession and whether or not the philosophy of progressivism is the most representative of practicing teachers. The study by Bair provides a statement of the then current beliefs, as beliefs change with time as do leaders.

PITFALLS IN PHILOSOPHICAL RESEARCH

VanderZwaag has presented seven pitfalls that must be avoided in doing philosophical research.[18] The following pitfalls are patterned after, but are not exclusively, his suggestions.

Confusing science with philosophy. As pointed out earlier in this chapter, the philosopher should utilize the findings of the scientist insofar as they are available and applicable. Conversely, the scientist can find new frontiers for research through the vistas opened by the philosopher. The philosopher is on shaky ground when setting forth judgments which are in apparent contradiction to established facts; on the other hand, he or she should not refrain from challenging such facts when the challenge can be reasonably justified. In any event, the

---

[18]Harold J. VanderZwaag, "Pitfalls in Philosophical Research," in *Research in the History, Philosophy, and International Aspects of Physical Education and Sport: Bibliographies and Techniques*, eds., Earle F. Zeigler, Maxwell L. Howell, and Marianna Trekell (Champaign, Ill.: Stipes Publishing Company, 1971), p. 182.

philosopher should carefully distinguish between scientific conclusions and value judgments.

Lacking a definite methodology.   Philosophical research should follow a sequential methodology, as discussed in this chapter. Vander-Zwaag stressed that this is a crucial point for the philosopher who is faced with the fact that he or she does not have a definite methodology such as is found in many other fields of inquiry.

Assuming philosophy is not practical.   The philosopher in physical education should apply, when applicable, the results of his or her deliberations to issues that bear on practices in the field.

Failing to distinguish between a survey and a philosophy.   A survey is not philosophical, but a survey may be employed as a means of collecting relative data. The philospher may utilize such data in normative and analytic processes.

Trying to provide answers to all questions.   Like the scientist, the philosopher must adhere to the available "data" and not extend them beyond their validity in answering posed questions.

Being influenced by bias.   Bias is a pitfall of considerable magnitude in philosophical writing. The marshaling of facts just to support a preconceived, perhaps long-held, belief must be avoided. A belief, or hypothesis, should be stated only for the purpose of testing its validity; both pro and con evidence should be impartially evaluated and applied. "Let the chips fall where they may."

Lacking adequate training to conduct philosophical research. An individual should not attempt philosophical research without an adequate background in philosophy generally and the philosophy of his or her field specifically. Zeigler contends that graduate students without proper training should not be encouraged or allowed to select master's or doctor's thesis philosophical problems.[19]

In 1971 Osterhoudt descriptively analyzed the body of research concerning the philosophy of physical education and sport as it developed in the twentieth century. This examination was based on taxonomy, adopted and developed so as to organize this literature systematically.[20] During the early decades of the century, he observed,

[19] Earle F. Zeigler, "Philosophy of Physical Education and Sport: An Approach to the Research Method and Its Techniques," in *History, Philosophy, and International Aspects of Physical Education and Sport*, p. 172.

[20] Robert G. Osterhoudt, "A Descriptive Analysis of Research Concerning the Philosophy of Physical Education and Sport" (Ph.D. diss., University of Illinois, 1971), p. 237.

a number of physical educators produced largely dogmatic accounts of the nature and significance of physical education and sport. After that, a greater number of treatments of a genuine philosophic stature appeared, until at the time he wrote several sophisticated works were available. He contended that the production of still more revealing philosophical treatises in this field will depend on the emergence of more professional scholars educated in and dedicated to the ways and ideals both of philosophy per se and of the philosophy of physical education and sport. As did Zeigler, Osterhoudt urged that a more abiding consultation with the mother discipline, philosophy proper, be required so as to avoid the dogmatic espousals with which the philosophy of physical education and sports has been preoccupied. What must be sought are more informed and comprehensively and systematically argued views.

SUMMARY

In this chapter, the philosophical approach to the resolution of educational problems has been presented. Although the philosophical method by itself is not scientific, it is needed for dealing with certain kinds of problems. The method of philosophy is the application of critical thinking, but the thought processes are guided by available facts and current pioneer thinking. A critical-thinking continuum was proposed, extending from the minimal amount in scientific studies to the maximal amount where astute observation is dominant. Examples of these extremes were provided. Examples of philosophical studies, each selected to illustrate different and unique approaches, were presented. Pitfalls in conducting philosophical research were examined.

SELECTED REFERENCES

DEWEY, JOHN, *How We Think.* Boston: D. C. Heath & Company, 1933.

FRALEIGH, WARREN P., "Theory and Design of Philosophical Research in Physical Education, *Proceedings of Annual Meeting of National College Physical Education Association for Men*, 1970, p. 28.

HARPER, WILLIAM, "Philosophy of Physical Education and Sport," in *Exercise and Sport Sciences Review*, Vol. 2, ed. Jack H. Wilmore. New York: Academic Press, Inc., 1974, pp. 239-263.

MORLAND, RICHARD B., "The Philosophic Method of Research," in *Research Methods in Health, Physical Education, and Recreation* (3rd ed.), ed. Alfred W. Hubbard. Washington: American Alliance for Health, Physical Education, Recreation, and Dance, 1973, Ch. 13.

VAN DALEN, DEOBOLD B., *Understanding Educational Research: An Introduction* (4th ed). New York: McGraw-Hill, Inc. 1979, Ch. 8.

ZEIGLER, EARLE F., MAXWELL L. HOWELL, and MARIANNA TREKELL, eds., *Research in the History, Philosophy, and International Aspects of Physical Education and Sport: Bibliographies and Techniques*, Pt. Two. Champaign, Ill.: Stipes Publishing Company, 1971.

6
Surveys

This chapter considers various types of surveys. It focuses on questionnaire and interview procedures, normative surveys, and the uses of case studies and profiles. Surveys are primarily descriptive in nature. Typically, data are gathered from a sample of a large population at a given point in time. Thus the value of the survey is transitory, as it indicates current status only in regard to a particular phenomenon, so may only be relevant at later times for comparative purposes. Further, past surveys may have historical significance.

The determination of present status through analytical surveys is often an essential first step in proposing changes that lead to improved services for children and adults through appropriate programs and processes in physical education. Proper survey data in the hands of an astute investigator can be used for forward-looking purposes. In today's society, surveys are utilized extensively to determine people's views, as in opinion polls conducted by Gallup, Roper, Harris, and others; the continuing polls taken of the television-viewing public by the A.C. Nielson Company determine the ratings and the fate of TV shows.

SURVEY BY QUESTIONNAIRE

By use of the questionnaire, information can be obtained from a sample of an extensive population in regard to a variety of specific topics; samples may be national, regional, state, or local in scope. In general, the main justification for its use rests on the need for information that cannot be reasonably obtained in any other way. However, the questionnaire should be used sparingly in research and then only after careful preparation, so that responses can be accurate and valid. The use of questionnaires has received strong criticism. Many times unfavorable reactions are intensified when questionnaires are unduly long, the subjects are trivial, the questions are vaguely or ambiguously stated, or the forms are poorly structured. The indictment of the questionnaire frequently centers less on method than on the way it is applied.

Questionnaires may be presented to potential respondents by direct contact or through the mail. By direct contact, they are administered to individuals or to groups in face-to-face situations. The individual contact may be too restrictive in sample size and location and may be excessively costly and time-consuming; this method may approach the interview process, to be discussed later. Direct application of questionnaires to groups is feasible when logical groups are readily available in local situations. For example: canvassing the leisure activities of adolescent boys and girls in an underprivileged area of a large city through school classes; determining health misconceptions of students at the start of health education classes; surveying the attitudes of high school girls toward physical education programs through randomly selected classes. The direct-contact method has distinct advantages in that the investigator can establish rapport with the respondents, explain the purposes of the study, clarify points, answer questions, and motivate respondents to answer all questions.

The mailed questionnaire, of course, can reach more people over a wide geographical area quickly and at a relatively low cost. This survey approach is the more common one, so it will be the main concern of this chapter. The construction of this instrument must be meticulous, since questions should be understood correctly without the aid of an interpreter; the procedures employed to obtain an acceptable number of responses are vital.

Types of Information

Several types of information can be secured by the questionnaire and can be categorized generally as follows:

Status Studies.   The most frequent use of the questionnaire is to secure information of status or of current practice of individuals, groups, or institutions. Status studies seek to determine events or practices as they are, which in physical education have often meant the status of professional preparation, finances, facilities, or some other aspect of operation. This type of questionnaire may be the simplest to construct; it relies heavily on factual information rather than on opinion and seeks information about aspects that are often contained in operational records.

Status studies of the attitudes and opinions of individuals may also be part of the research design and can be incorporated as items in the questionnaire. Questions such as those concerning the advisability of interschool athletics for young children, for example, call for the opinion of the respondent. The term "opinionnaire" has been used to designate such instruments; in format, they may resemble those tests used in some psychological studies.

A further use of status studies is found in those testing knowledge. Used extensively in health education, they seek to sample the extent of factual information on the part of some population or group. For example, the knowledge of nutrition, sex education, or health misconceptions may be of interest to those concerned with curricular matters. Such devices resemble typical examinations of subject matter but are more difficult to construct since they are intended to reach a group with varied background, experience, and education.

Authoritative Opinion. Another type of information that can be obtained from the questionnaire is the opinion of authorities. In the present context, authorities are individuals with outstanding qualifications in the area under study. They may qualify as such by virtue of their specific training, positions held, professional contributions, honors received, or other facts that give them authoritative status. Deans and department heads, presidents of associations, recognized authors of scientific and professional publications, head coaches, are examples of people who possess backgrounds that give their responses added weight when judgments are sought within their range of expertise. Each authority chosen should be justified as such in the study report.

Construction of the Questionnaire

It has been said, hopefully in jest, that a person who knows little about a subject prepares a questionnaire and sends it to others who also know little about it, and from their pooled ignorance they produce research. *Let it not be so—nor need it be.* A proper questionnaire is difficult to construct. Obviously, the survey conducted cannot be better than the instrument utilized in gathering the essential data. Therefore the investigator should take great care in developing a questionnaire that will assure accurate and valid responses, that will produce meaningful data. This can only be done when the investigator has a thorough background in the field to be surveyed. He or she must have sufficient experience to be able to outline thorough, appropriate questions, not only the salient features to be covered but the necessary detail of such features that will provide a valid picture of the situation as it exists.

The investigator should be cognizant of the limitations of the questionnaire approach and carefully weigh the various factors involved. The most important problem concerns the accuracy of responses. Thus: Will respondents give truthful and complete answers to questions? If questions involve controversial or sensitive matters, will honest answers be given? The tendency for self-protection is strong, so individuals will often slant responses to produce a favorable impression. Furthermore, a real danger is that respondents whose program practices are contrary to current standards in the field may not return the questionnaire, which results in biased returns. The following suggestions are offered to assist in the construction of questionnaires:

1. *The purpose of the survey should be clearly identified.* A statement should define the scope of the study undertaken, and the questionnaire itself should conform to this scope.

2. *The investigator should outline the field of study.* Broad categories of information should be identified so that overlapping can be avoided, and the questions should be developed in an orderly fashion. A hierarchy of interrogatives should be established based upon categories of questions. In this manner, the investigator will gain insight into the task of writing questions, and it will also assure that nothing of importance is omitted. Without organization of the task, the omission of essential information is likely, the sequence of questions will appear disjointed, and the reader may justifiably conclude that the study has been ill conceived.

3. *The questions should be arranged in logical order.* Once the decision is made on the organizational pattern, the questions themselves should be presented. They should follow the theme of the study, adhering to some adopted pattern—such as proceeding from the simple to the complex or the easy to the difficult or building each succeeding question upon the one that came before. The respondent, particularly if he or she received the instrument in the mail and does not know the investigator personally, must be made to feel that the study has been carefully prepared. Otherwise his or her attitude and care in answering the questions may be affected.

4. *Each question in the survey must be absolutely clear.* In fact, the success or failure of the whole project may rest upon the care and precision that is taken in stating the questions so that no

statement contains ambiguities or grammatical errors or is misleading. The use of words must be clear. For example, such words as "extracurricular," "intramural," and "recreation" must be defined so that all respondents know exactly how they are being used. If the respondent does not understand what is being asked, he or she cannot respond validly. Unfortunately, the investigator may never know if this has occurred, but must be able to assume that the response is accurate.

5. *Pictures or diagrams in the questionnaire may prove helpful in clarifying particular situations.* For example, the investigator wishes to study special exercise equipment utilized in adapted and remedial physical education programs in colleges. Illustrations of the pieces of equipment under consideration, perhaps obtained from the manufacturers, would ensure their identification, especially when different trade names are used for basically the same item. Thus nomenclature would not be a problem.

6. *Formulation of the questions should take into consideration the following suggestions:*
   (a) Define or qualify terms that can easily be misunderstood or misinterpreted. For example, the term "physical fitness" can be ambiguous and may need definition. Further, it may be desirable to break it down into its basic components.
   (b) Avoid questions with double implications. For example: Do you believe that handicapped children should be placed in special groups for instructional purposes and assigned to special schools? This is a very poor question, as some people may feel that some, but not all, handicapped children should be "mainstreamed" (and this term needs definition). Others may feel that special classes are best but might be opposed to special schools, and there are other combinations of beliefs. Also, what is meant by "handicapped" children?
   (c) Avoid leading questions. For example: Do you agree that physical fitness is the primary objective of physical education? It would be best to provide choices as to which one, if any, is the primary objective of physical education.
   (d) Beware of double negatives, as their positive assumptions may be missed by respondents.

7. *The questions should be stated in a manner that elicits short answers.* If the questions require extensive answers, respondents may become discouraged and rightly feel that they do not have the time to write essay responses to a number of questions. Further, understanding the meaning of questions

becomes difficult. The best questions are those that are well stated and clear and that require short answers.

8. *The investigator should remember the need for responses that can be easily and completely summarized.* When long essay responses are obtained, it is very difficult for the investigator to group the data in convenient form for analysis. Thus, some scheme should be worked out that will yield objective answers, preferably countable answers. If possible, simply checking a category is best for the respondent's reply.

9. *Precoding of the items for future data processing should be considered.* An examination, such as is used in knowledge studies, may have responses keyed in such a manner that the scoring is accomplished by automated methods. If this is feasible in surveys with a questionnaire, the investigator should explore procedures that would implement this technique. Evaluative questions may also be coded for computer tabulation and statistical treatment, especially if the answers can be given a quantitative value.

Appearance of the Questionnaire

A most important consideration in this type of survey research is the appearance of the questionnaire. Although not involved with content per se and not affecting the quality of research, it may be a determining factor in the overall acceptance of the study by the respondent. Anything that deters a prompt and accurate response influences the research results by default. Other things being equal, the more attractive the format, the more likely the return of the questionnaire. The following features of the questionnaire must be considered for effective presentation:

1. The questionnaire should be as short as feasible, only long enough for essential data. Long questionnaires frequently are consigned by recipients to the wastebasket. However, this admonition does not signify that the questions should be jammed together in an unsightly mass or that significant questions should be deleted.

2. The selection of paper size is ordinarily $8\frac{1}{2} \times 11$ inches, a size that conveniently folds into standard-size envelopes. The paper need not be white, as attractive colors are available. One device that has been successfully employed is the coding of different groups of subjects by color so that upon receipt of the completed questionnaire they may be quickly separated by color. For example, if both sexes are queried and their replies are to be distinguished, one color of paper can be used for girls and another color for boys.

Considerable time will be saved, for, unless some other scheme is used, the investigator must search through the questionnaires one by one to sort them into appropriate categories for analysis.

3. Consideration should be given to the neatness and proper spatial arrangement of the questionnaire. A questionnaire that is hastily constructed shows it. Special care is required to arrange the headings symmetrically, to make major headings larger than subheadings, to assure proper alignment, and to effect a host of other details that may not bear on the subject matter itself but that may affect the number of returns. If the investigator can afford the expense, a printed questionnaire is preferable; it usually gets more returns than other kinds and so may be more profitable in the long run. The ditto questionnaire should be avoided; mimeographing is more satisfactory; and, better yet, lithographing is an excellent possibility. The use of cheap paper, ineptness in typing, crowding, and other factors detract from the appearance of a study that otherwise may be entirely satisfactory.

4. Provide adequate space for answers. A common error made on many questionnaires is that of providing too little space for answers. Nothing is more exasperating than being asked to respond to a question only to find that the space for the answer is inadequate. The requirement of adequate space begins with the heading where the name and address of the respondent will go, and extends to all questions thereafter. If open-ended questions are included on the questionnaire, sufficient space should be allowed for each answer.

5. The place for all answers should be clear. Failure to offer some easy-to-follow scheme invites inaccurate replies. For an objective response, parentheses ( ), a block □, or other scheme may be used. When factual information is requested, such as the number of children in physical education classes, a short dotted or solid line may be provided. The same question should not be split between two pages, in order to preserve continuity.

6. At the top of the first page, the questionnaire should contain the following items:
   (a) Complete name and address of the investigator, so that the respondent knows where the questionnaire originated.
   (b) A statement concerning the purpose of the questionnaire and asking for support. If a covering letter is used, to be considered below, this statement can be shorter than would otherwise be the case.
   (c) Complete instructions for filling out the questionnaire. These instructions should be clear, concise, and explicit. Do not assume that the respondent will understand simply by look-

ing at the format. For example, if it is necessary for the best single answer to be selected in all cases, this must be explicitly stated in the instructions. Even then, several unanswered questions may remain, which must be dealt with in some manner in tabulating or scoring. No response does not necessarily constitute an incorrect answer; such responses must be placed in a separate category. Occasionally, a category may be offered on the questionnaire for a "no opinion" or "do not know" in order to care for situations in which the respondent has no basis for an answer.

(d) Instructions for returning the questionnaire to its source.
(e) A place for the name, address, and position of the person replying. Other data relative to this individual may be considered essential, but only those items should be requested that actually bear directly on the study. Very little is gained by requesting superfluous information that will not be used. This is particularly true of sensitive matters concerning race, religion, salary, and other things that may be considered personal. If such items are necessary, it should be so stated; and then it may be helpful to make assurances that the information will be kept confidential.

Questionnaire Development

It is not a simple matter to phrase questions properly so that no ambiguities exist and so that the terminology is precise and to the point. Yet, if this is not accomplished, the responses may be inadequate or incorrect. The following procedures apply to questionnaire development:

Initial Writing. The first attempt at writing the questions and organizing the progression will require several revisions before the final draft is ready. The writer must be prepared to change and rephrase statements when desirable so that the meaning is clear to the reader, the sequence is proper, and the directions are appropriate. The directions should be simply stated, clear, and concise so that the reader will not misunderstand the manner in which to respond. Occasionally, the sequence of questions will depend upon the answer to one main question (e.g., "If you conduct an interscholastic athletic program for either grades 4, 5, or 6, please answer the following questions"); this must be clarified, and at the same time respondents who do not have such a program must be instructed to move on to another section.

In writing questionnaire items, some problems occur that serve to make questions unacceptable, which, if corrected, may assure valid responses. Some of the more prominent difficulties will be mentioned.

1. *Using specialized terminology.* Investigators are expected to examine the literature of their subject matter and in doing so will come upon terms that may not be generally known to teachers or administrators in the field. The answer to such a question as "all schools should employ tests of aerobic capacity in examining the physical fitness of their students" may well depend upon the respondent's understanding of the term "aerobic capacity"; such terms should be defined or simpler ones used.

2. *Questions obviously biased.* Occasionally, questions are phrased in such a way that the bias involved precludes subdivision into categories. For example, the question "athletics are harmful to children" would leave little room for argument, and it would be unusual for a repondent to answer in any way but "strongly disagree." The respondent might feel differently if he or she knew what type of athletics, what was considered harmful (inducing psychological as well as physical aspects), and what category of children was involved.

3. *Words to avoid.* The words "always" and "never" should be avoided, as they immediately raise the possibilities of exceptions. It might be better in this situation to use a scale of some sort so that respondents can express varying degrees of approval and disapproval.

4. *Questions not complete.* When a question such as "isometric exercises contribute most" is used, the reader is completely at a loss as to what to answer (contribute most to what or compared with what?).

5. *Question too long.* Sometimes a lengthy question is necessary so that the meaning is clear and the terms are carefully described. The danger in employing long and complicated questions, however, is that the reader may miss a key phrase, or, if it is too complex, may give up entirely. Worse yet, the respondent may just guess at the answer. If the question is essential, it would be best to break it up into more than one question or state the meaning in other ways.

6. *Question too difficult or time consuming.* In questionnaire surveys, the respondent may be reluctant to reply if asked to locate information that is unusual. Asking him or her to calculate the percentage of freshmen girls that play tennis in intramurals may be quite time consuming if the information is not already available. However, it may not be too difficult to check categories such as "not offered," "below 25%," "25-49%," "50-74%," "75-99%," or "100%."

Trial Run. After the questionnaire has been written to the satisfaction of the researcher—to include all items considered essential and with the sequence organized in a logical and orderly manner—the next step is to submit it to a trial run. The purpose of the trial run is to discover if the meanings of all statements on the questionnaire are clear and if the questions are adequate to obtain the information desired. Preliminary to the trial run, graduate students may seek reviews of their instrument from their respective advisers, from other staff members, and from fellow graduate students who are knowledgeable in the study area. For the trial run, send the initial questionnaire, as revised, to a number of individuals corresponding in category to those who will receive the final instrument. These individuals should answer the questionnaire in the same manner as will be required when it is actually used for data collection. Trial-run respondents should be asked to criticize the questionnaire in terms of the adequacy and clarity of the questions. The investigator should seek out ambiguities, incomplete or misunderstood questions, insufficiently defined technical or other terms, defects in the instructions, inadequacies of space for answers, and the like.

Tabulation. Also as a trial, tabulate the results of the trial run. Quite possibly, some additional modification of the question or rearrangement of the answer locations may be found that will permit easier tabulation when the final questionnaire responses are analyzed.

Rewriting. Based upon the information obtained from the trial run, again revise the questionnaire. If extensive revisions are necessary, a second trial run, using different respondents, may be indicated.

Aids to Responses

A primary difficulty in questionnaire surveys is to obtain an adequate response. Obviously, if the investigator could personally administer the questionnaire to the respondent or enlist the support of colleagues for personal approaches, then he or she could be assured of a high return. However, for mail surveys, the investigator should adopt procedures that will encourage the greatest possible return. The following aids are presented for this purpose:

1. Enclose in the mailing a self-addressed and stamped envelope. This provides a tangible means whereby the respondent may get the questionnaire off his or her desk and at no cost. Further, this procedure insures that the correct return address is used. For those employing a large sample, the appropriate return address can be printed on the envelopes when they are ordered, or a rubber stamp can be made to facilitate this process.

2. The initial appeal in the form of a covering letter to the recipient will be an important procedure in securing a good return of the questionnaire. This letter should not be an emotional appeal or a "hat-in-the-hand" approach, but it should be a carefully worded and thoughtful statement that presents the reasons and purposes of the study and a compelling picture of the contribution to knowledge anticipated. If the respondent can be made to feel an important part of a worthwhile project, he or she will be more inclined to participate wholeheartedly. On the other hand, a poorly worded statement or one that relies primarily on the plea that "it is in partial fulfillment of a degree" may not personally involve the reader. As a result, the reader may feel that his or her time is too valuable to spend in answering the questionnaire. Other things being equal, the timeliness and scholarship exhibited by the study will do more to gain its acceptance than any other single factor. If the study is properly conceived in the first place, then this should be conveyed to the recipient in the most effective manner possible.

3. Frequently, support of the survey by a sponsor aids materially in securing a greater return of questionnaires. Such a sponsor may be an individual or an organization that has status in the population to be sampled. For example, the state superintendent of schools might influence teachers in the state; the commissioner of athletics could well affect the response of coaches; the executive secretary of an association would be expected to carry weight among the membership. The investigator may indicate the sponsor's interest in the survey in a covering letter; better yet, the sponsor may be persuaded to provide the covering letter on his or her letterhead, setting forth strong endorsement of the project and urging all recipients of the questionnaire to reply.

4. Another aid to increase the number of responses is to agree to send respondents a summary of the results. If the project is timely and appropriate, the recipients of the questionnaire may be eager to know the results. However, if this plan is adopted, space should be provided for the respondent to check whether or not a copy is wanted; this procedure may increase the number of returns, as certainly the respondent would not be likely to check "yes" unless he or she filled out the questionnaire. The investigator should recognize, of course, that this agreement constitutes an obligation to provide the summaries when the survey is completed.

5. Occasionally, survey research deals with subject matter or asks questions that are personal or sensitive in nature, such as amounts of salaries, personnel practices, rating of teachers, and other matters. In such instances, it may be best to indicate that the

replies will be kept confidential, that the questionnaires will be secured, and that there will be no identification of the individual or school in the final report. Thus, apprehensions may be allayed that the information might be used to embarass the respondent or his or her institution, and this may help in obtaining a greater number of returns. It is incumbent that the investigator keep the information confidential if this has been so stated. The broad survey distributed by mail that attempts to delve into highly personal matters is almost certainly doomed to failure. If recipients reply at all, quite likely the information may be inaccurate, incomplete, or biased. Under this circumstance the interview technique is indicated, as it provides time to develop rapport with the respondent and to establish confidence in the integrity of the research.

6. Anonymous questionnaires are sometimes utilized in an attempt to secure a greater return. They are based upon the premise that if respondents cannot be identified they will be more likely to cooperate. No doubt, situations exist in which this is helpful as a technique, but there is no guarantee that the responses will be more accurate, that greater care will be taken, or that fidelity of response will result. One could argue that the reverse may occur on occasion, simply because the respondent assumes that anonymity gives impunity. From the point of view of recipients, they may be disappointed to realize that they will not be identified after spending some time in answering the questionnaire; and, of course, the investigator loses any opportunity to follow-up the study or to ask the subject for additional information in cases where it is desirable. In using the anonymous questionnaire, however, the following considerations are pertinent:

   (a) Do not use it unless it is absolutely necessary. The use of anonymity may cause certain suspicions on the part of recipients, who may be more guarded than might otherwise be the case. Many times merely assuring that the results will be kept confidential is enough.

   (b) If it is decided to keep the questionnaire responses anonymous, then this procedure must be followed. It would be ill-advised to claim that no one will know who has completed the instrument and then to set up an elaborate scheme to do just that.

   (c) Sometimes, little can be done to conceal the identity of the respondent, especially when he or she is "one of the few selected national leaders." The postmark on the return envelope is certain to reflect the source of the sender, and thus the anonymity is destroyed.

7. The questionnaire should be sent at an appropriate time, when it

will have the best chance of being answered. Educators are frequently especially busy and may be absent at certain times of the year, so it may be helpful to consider the academic calendar and avoid such times as holidays, vacations, registration and examination periods, and the like. Questionnaires sent to coaches during their sports season may not be returned.

8. A technique that has been successful on occasion is that of sending out an advance letter and self-addressed card and asking about willingness to participate in the study. This practice has the advantage of providing a willing group of respondents. A similar device is simply to send out an advance notice announcing that in a few days the individual will receive a questionnaire and appealing for support. This tends to soften the impact of a questionnaire being received without prior knowledge.

9. An effective procedure that should be utilized to obtain a maximum number of responses to a questionnaire is the follow-up. If the study is well conceived and the questionnaire is properly developed, the surveyor may expect to receive a 50-75% return from the initial mailing. The ultimate return may be improved through the use of follow-up procedures, which is usually the only way high returns of 90-100% can be realized. A limit need not be imposed on the number of follow-up efforts. However, the following attempts are possibilities, although the actual number applied should be judged as the response to each follow-up is observed.

First Follow-up. At the end of the second week, send a courteously worded postcard to those who have not replied, indicating that the completed questionnaire has not been received and its return would be most helpful in realizing the purposes of the survey.

Second Follow-up. At the end of the fourth week, send a copy of the original covering letter and another questionnaire to those who have not yet responded, with a note again indicating the importance of their response.

Nonrespondents

Critical decisions are frequently based on survey results, so valid representations from samples of large populations are vital. When mail surveys are conducted, those who do not return questionnaires may pose a problem: Would their responses have differed significantly from those who did respond? If they would have, results based on data from the actual respondents would not be a true picture of the situation under investigation. Unfortunately, unless a special study of the nonrespondents is undertaken, it will not be known how they would have answered the questions. Of course, when over a 90% return is achieved, this problem is not serious. When well-conceived and well-constructed questionnaires are sent to professionals in the investigative field, returns are usually high, especially when follow-ups are employed. However, when they are sent to the general public, return percentages are usually lower, unless interest in the problem under study is high.

Some studies have been conducted on the differences in responses to questionnaires by respondents and nonrespondents. In these studies, nonrespondents were contacted by phone or visitation, and their replies were compared with replies on the questionnaires. Statistical tests of significance were applied to responses by the two groups. For example, the significance of the difference between means was tested when the data were numerical, as for the amount of salaries; chi-square was applied to responses to practices in various geographical locations.

Surveys by questionnaire have been utilized to determine practices or needs within a community or state. In reviewing responses to mailed questionnaire surveys appearing in psychology, sociology, and marketing research, Igo found generally that respondents had better education, higher incomes, and greater interest in the problem under study than did nonrespondents.[1] However, such results did not occur in all surveys. Thus, he was unable to make a definitive statement that applied to all disciplines. In his own study, Igo found no significant differences between the education, family income, geographical location, and amount of participation of respondents and nonrespondents in studies of boating and snowmobiling demands among adults in Michigan.

INTERVIEW SURVEY

The interview, or visit, is a better method of obtaining survey information than the broad survey in which a mailed questionnaire is utilized. Rather than rely on the impersonal approach inherent in the latter technique, the interviewer gathers data directly from individuals in face-to-face contact. The interview has been likened to an oral questionnaire. It has the obvious advantage of insuring a greater return. Occasionally, the investigator will be unable to interview an individual for one reason or another, but this will occur far less frequently than with the survey by mail.

[1]Allison J. C. Igo, "Recreation Research Mail Survey Techniques: Effects of Self-administration and Non-response" (Master's thesis, Michigan State University, 1971).

Characteristics of the Interview

The interview is marked by several unique characteristics that make it a useful adjunct to the researcher. These are as follows:

1. The interview may permit obtaining confidential information. Whereas recipients of a questionnaire by mail may be reluctant to divulge information that is confidential or that they may think reflects adversely on their policies or practices, the interview may make it possible to obtain such data. The investigator must show insight and gain rapport with interviewees and assure them that the information will be kept confidential. This procedure has been notably successful in medicine and health education, where personal health information or sexual practices have been under investigation.

2. The personal contact has the advantage of drawing out informants by on-the-spot follow-up questions, which is not possible through a formal questionnaire. For example, methods of administration, operation of the budget, practices in athletics, and so forth frequently are handled in different ways; the interview allows considerable adaptation to different situation.

3. The interview permits the interpretation of the meaning of questions. No matter how carefully phrased is the questionnaire, the likelihood is present that some questions may still be misunderstood or certain concepts misinterpreted; in the interview, the investigator can make sure that the intent is clear and thereby obtain more adequate responses.

4. The interview permits the follow-up leads, which can then be explored with questions designed to elicit additional information. The more insight obtained in investigating a problem, the stronger the study.

5. The investigator can form some judgment of the adequacy of replies. A prevalent problem in surveys is to obtain valid responses. This is not to suggest that dishonesty prevails in survey research, but occasionally accuracy may be strained in the interest of self-enhancement. However, such responses may be due to misunderstanding questions, so are unintentional. For example, a positive response to the question "do you have an intramural program" may be based wholly on the fact that in physical education classes the students frequently compete against each other. The interview would provide a means for clarifying this situation.

6. The interview survey affords an opportunity for the interviewer to *give* information and to develop rapport with the respondent. This

aspect of the interview is seen to permeate the whole atmosphere, where the respondent can make clear the intent of the research, perhaps bring out the salient facts that preceded the study, and develop the confidence of the interviewee. If this is done properly, the response will be much better, and therefore the information that is needed will be given more readily. Obviously, if the interviewer antagonizes the respondent, the reverse would hold true.

The Interview

The investigator should carefully prepare for the interview. It is a mistake to think that this survey method consists merely of making an appointment and sitting down and asking a series of questions. If the study warrants an interview, then the researcher must develop the method of presentation as precisely as possible. This does not mean making the same statement to each person in exactly the same manner, as this may provide very little flexibility. Informality in the interview may well enhance the rapport between interviewer and interviewee.

The well-prepared investigator who has carefully researched his or her study should have no trouble in the interview. It should be conducted in a businesslike manner, with courtesy and friendliness, and with the questions directed along the lines that have been prepared. Not all interviewees will have an unlimited amount of time available, so it is important not to waste it with extended small talk or to permit the discussion to digress for long periods. The successful interviewer will adroitly maneuver the conversation so that all areas of the study are covered. Because time is a factor, the respondent should be told in advance approximately how long the interview should be expected to last.

The questioning must be performed in such a manner as not to introduce an aspect of bias; thus, an impersonal but professional attitude should be maintained. The examiner should avoid leading the respondent. Questions beginning with "you don't . . ." would imply that "you shouldn't . . ." and this would very likely put the individual on the defensive. After all, if someone thinks he or she should not, he or she may agree that he or she does not. Also, voice influence may imply the direction an answer should go, which, of course, would bias the response. It is human nature to wish to agree with others, so if a note of approval or disapproval can be sensed, the response may be influenced in that direction.

In planning for the interview, attention should be given to the classification of responses which should be similar to those employed in the questionnaire survey. Once again, open-ended questions are difficult to handle objectively, and, because the type of response may vary from very short replies to lengthy and detailed commentaries, it may be difficult to make proper notations. The investigator should not hesitate to make whatever record is necessary at the time, even though it may detract somewhat from the interview; if he or she waits until later, he or she must rely on memory, which may introduce inaccuracies into the interview record.

A tape recorder is a convenient and effective method of recording the interview, provided the interviewee is agreeable to its use. It eliminates the necessity for writing during the interview, which may be a distraction for both the interviewer and the respondent. Interviews recorded on tape can be replayed as often as desired for complete and objective analysis at a later time; thus, inadequate recall of interview statements or inaccurate written notes at the time of the interview are eliminated as potential errors in the survey. Also, in addition to the words spoken, the tone of voice and emotional impacts of responses are preserved on tape.

Immediately after the interview, the investigator should review all materials, organize his or her notes, and fill in any details while they are still fresh in mind. All notes and data should be kept with the interview questionnaire for future reference.

OPINION ASSESSMENT

When questionnaire or interview surveys call for opinions or preferences, some means of assessing the strength of respondents' beliefs may be helpful. Two such evaluative instruments are presented here.

Likert Scale. In the Likert Scale, each relevant statement allows for five degrees of response from most to least favorable.[2] Thus, the statement "Interscholastic athletics are harmful to children in elementary school" may be followed by five degrees of agreement or disagreement, such as (1) strongly approve, (2) approve, (3) undecided, (4) disapprove, and (5) strongly disapprove. If the investigator assigns a score of 5 to strongly approve, 1 to strongly disapprove, and the remaining values to the intervening responses, then there is a basis for later statistical analysis. In such attitude studies, care must be taken in phrasing the questions and assigning the numerical values so that the

---

[2]R. Likert, "A Technique for the Measurement of Attitudes," *Archives of Psychology*, No. 140, 1983.

high score always reflects the best attitude. Thus, a score of 5 may accompany strongly approve in some cases and strongly disapprove in others.

Q-sort. The Q-sort is a technique for scaling objects or statements, especially when the items to be ranked are numerous.[3] The process consists of sorting slips, or cards, differentiating statements or items into numbered piles. Usually, nine to eleven piles are established on a continuum from least to most favorable. Continua may be based on such designations as least-most important, least-most preferred, least-most desirable, least-most admired, and the like. The number of slips to be placed per pile is predetermined, usually corresponding roughly to positions on a scale based on the normal probability curve.

Following is a distribution of statements sorted into nine piles from least to most desirable; this distribution consists of stanine-scale percentages for the different piles.[4] The numbers in the top line are the scale values; the numbers in the bottom line are the percentage of slips to be placed in each scale category.

	Least Desired							*Most Desired*	
Scale	1	2	3	4	5	6	7	8	9
% of Slips	4	7	12	17	20	17	12	7	4

The Q-sort can be used to assess attitudes, values, artistic judgments, interests of subjects, or relative merits of various concepts or practices. For example, qualified observers may be requested to respond to the following question: What importance should be attached to activities employed in the development of physical fitness? A large number of slips should be prepared, each carrying the name of a different activity, such as various games, sports, and contests; activities for developing the strength and endurance of different muscle groups; circulatory-respiratory endurance items; and exercise for improving flexibility around various joints of the body. For analysis, the numerical values for the many activities can coincide with their corresponding scales.

The Q-sort can also be used to study the characteristics of one individual or group of individuals. It can be used to assess the effects of programs in physical education by applying the sort before and after a given program. And it can be utilized to identify subjects within a group with similar responses, in order to study differences among the subgroups.

[3] William Stephenson, *The Study of Behavior* (Chicago: University of Chicago Press, 1953).

[4] See Chapter 7 for a description of the stanine scale.

Normative Survey

A normative survey uses an established test to assess the status of a given population in regard to some trait. It has been utilized in physical education to compare a population sample with available norms on a variety of achievement tests. The results have been utilized to determine the status of a designated population, to determine changes in status over a period of time, and to compare the status of different populations in regard to traits under investigation.

A well-known normative survey was reported by Kraus and Hirschland, who compared eastern United States schoolchildren with European (Swiss, Austrian, and Italian) children, utilizing the Kraus-Weber tests of minimum muscular fitness.[5] The results showed that the American sample was greatly inferior to the European sample. These results subsequently led to the establishment of the President's Council on Physical Fitness and Sports, as now known, by President Dwight D. Eisenhower. Subsequently, surveys using this test were conducted in Iowa, Indiana, Oregon, and elsewhere around the United States and in other countries.

In 1957 the AAHPER Youth Fitness Test was proposed and percentile norms were established from a national sample of schoolchildren in grades four through twelve. Normative samples from other countries were subsequently used for comparisons with the United States children. In 1965 and in 1976 American samples were again tested, and normative comparisons for the different years were made. The results showed that United States children made substantial improvement in motor fitness between 1957 and 1965, but remained essentially the same between 1965 and 1976.[6]

Testing Techniques If comparisons on the basis of test scores are to be made between groups, states, or nations, the testing techniques must be precisely the same in all instances. It can be demonstrated easily that a test as simple as chinning the bar can be given differently with considerable variance in results. Such things as placement of the hands, permitting body sway or kipping movements, or not requiring that the elbows straighten completely may permit spurious scores to occur. Comparable differences in testing techniques could easily be found in giving many of the tests commonly used in physical education. In any research project, whether it be a normative survey or a

[5] Hans Kraus and Ruth P. Hirschland, "Minimum Muscular Fitness Tests in School Children," *Research Quarterly*, 25, No. 2 (May 1954), 178.

[6] *AAHPER Youth Fitness Test Manual*, new ed. (Washington: American Alliance for Health, Physical Education, Recreation, and Dance, 1976.)

laboratory experiment, extreme care should be taken to qualify testers before data are obtained.

Subject Motivation. Motivation plays an important role in the performance of certain types of physical activities. In experimental situations, researchers routinely attempt to invoke a common motivational pattern in test administration in order to equalize this factor. In applying subject motivation to normative surveys, the necessity for using a common motivational approach can be seen. However, it will always be possible for boys and girls of other countries to compete against American standards. Just how much motivation this provides cannot be calculated, but it could conceivably contribute significantly to increased test performances. Only when both groups are knowingly or unknowingly competing against each other can intergroup comparisons be valid.

Data Analysis. Various statistical applications can be made to normative survey data. In the Kraus-Weber and AAHPER test comparisons, percentages for passing or reaching certain standards were commonly employed. The comparison of test results with norms has been done by use of chi-square.

CASE STUDIES

The limitation of studies to single individuals, or at most to a very limited number, in research has received rather wide condemnation in physical education. However, the practice is employed effectively in medicine and in social work. Single cases, of course, can claim little validity as a sample representing a population; more and more, as a greater understanding of sampling procedures and probability is obtained, the need for samples of some size is recognized.

However, certain kinds of problems do not lend themselves to the usual statistical treatment—where a population as such cannot be defined, where the number of individuals is limited, or where the interrelation of several factors in the same individual is desired. For example, the study of cerebral palsy children with varying degrees of involvement, of the mentally retarded, of champion athletes, or of physically unfit boys and girls may require an individual approach. Such studies permit analysis of the total individual.

The case study approach has been successfully employed in developmental physical education classes for those students who are subpar in basic physical fitness elements, especially those who do not improve through exercise.[7] The causes of poor physical fitness are many and vary from individual to individual; case studies reveal a variety of patterns to account for this condition. The following three objectives typify the extent to which case studies may be employed:

1. *To conduct intensive studies of individuals within a defined group.* This is the most obvious objective of the case study procedure; the primary justification rests on the assumption that the individuals are unique in some way and that an examination of them as individuals should be carried out in some depth. Cursory testing or trivial examination procedures would not suffice to make this process acceptable research. The number of such subjects that must be employed cannot be stated, as it would depend upon a number of factors; conceivably, a small number might be studied if the data gathered were extensive and quite unique. (The case study approach is not a substitute for a small sample size if, in fact, a larger sample could be obtained and the appropriate statistical treatment applied.

2. *To attempt to generalize from a synthesis of the individuals in the group.* The ultimate aim of most research is to be able to draw generalizations from an examination of members of a particular population. For example, from a study of certain champion athletes has come a greater understanding of a number of essential qualities that help make championship performances possible. At the other end of the scale, with the assessment of the individual with exceptionally inadequate physical ability, has come an appreciation of some of the causes of poor fitness. In the latter instance, case studies have sometimes led to the identification of a medical rather than a physical genesis for the difficulty, and they point up the possibility for the use of case study techniques in adapted physical education. One would suppose that a synthesis of enough subjects within a group would eventually lead to satisfactory generalizations.

3. *To contrast groups.* The objective of much experimental research is to contrast groups on various traits; a similar possibility exists with case studies. A synthesis of information from one group may be contrasted with similar data from another group. Although the comparison may not be statistical, other descriptive methods may be employed.

---

[7] H. Harrison Clarke and David H. Clarke, *Developmental and Adapted Physical Education*, 2nd ed. (Englewood Cliffs, N.J.: Prentice-Hall, Inc., 1978), Ch. 6.

Applications. The individual who wishes to employ the case study approach may get suggestions and guidance from collections of case studies of boys with low Physical Fitness Indices by Coefield and McCollum,[8] Popp,[9] and Wilson,[10] all of which are available on microfiche from Health, Physical Education, and Recreation Microform Publications at the University of Oregon. A description of the study by Popp follows.

Case studies were conducted on the 20 lowest and the 20 highest sophomore high school boys on Rogers' Physical Fitness Index, a test battery consisting of muscular strength and endurance relative to age and body weight. The following information was obtained for each student in both groups: medical records from school examinations by physicians, nutritional status from the Baldwin-Wood age-height-weight tables, living habits from the Clarke Health-Habit Questionnaire, personal problems from the Mooney Problem Check List, social adjustment from the Washburne Social Adjustment Inventory, and mental aptitude and achievement from intelligence quotient and grade-point average. Each student was interviewed for other possible factors involved in his high or low fitness status. Additional data were recorded three years later following the boy's expected high school graduation year.

Contrasted with the low-fitness group, the high-fitness group had a higher mean intelligence quotient and a higher mean grade-point average. Only one boy in the high group failed to graduate from high school, as contrasted with 8 in the low group. Ten of the low PFI boys were 15% or more overweight, while none of the high PFI boys were in this category. The boys in the low group checked twice as many fatigue problems on the Health-Habit Questionnaire than did boys in the high group. These problems pertained to insufficient sleep; tiredness in the morning; sleepiness during the day, in class, and from studying; and undue fatigue after work and play. From an alphabetical list of all 40 of these boys (so as to obscure their fitness status), 5 teachers and administrators independently chose 10 boys they would most and would least like to have for sons. Sixty-nine percent of the boys chosen as sons they would *most* like to have were from the high PFI group and

[8]John R. Coefield and Robert H. McCollum, "A Case Study Report of 78 University Freshmen with Low Physical Fitness Indices" (Master's thesis, University of Oregon, 1955).

[9]James C. Popp, "Comparison of Sophomore High School Boys Who Have High and Low Physical Fitness Indices through Case Study Procedures" (Master's thesis, University of Oregon, 1959).

[10]Peter G. Wilson, "Personality Traits, Academic Achievement, and Health Status of University Freshmen with High and Low Physical Fitness Scores" (Master's thesis, University of Oregon, 1967).

75% of those they would *least* like to have for sons appeared in the low PFI group.

PROFILES

Profile studies have been employed in order to show various trait patterns. Essentially, they involve placement of the individual on test scales for a number of characteristics. Thus, the individual's strengths and weaknesses may be noted from his or her position on a common scale for all traits. The scale may be from norms already available or may be constructed from a sample of the population to which the subjects belong. The *T* scale, described in Chapter 7, is a convenient scale for this purpose, although other scales have also been used.

Three profile studies are cited as examples of this procedure. Behnke employed profiles based upon a number of anthropometric variables to assess the relative size and proportions of the body.[11] Shelley presented Hull scale profiles of 38 outstanding elementary and junior high school athletes on 22 maturity, structural, strength, motor ability, and intelligence tests.[12] Howe contrasted *T* scales of 20 outstanding 12- and 15-year-old athletes on maturity, body size, strength, motor ability, and scholastic aptitude and achievement when they were 9, 12, and 15 years of age.[13]

The study by Shelley demonstrated that, although successful athletes generally have common characteristics, the patterns of these characteristics vary from athlete to athlete; where a successful athlete is low in one or more such traits, he or she compensates by strengths in others. One example of a 14-year-old junior high school athlete is given. This athlete was outstanding in three sports; football, quarterback and defensive halfback; basketball, guard and playmaker; and track, hurdler. He also played summer baseball, leading in batting average and base stealing. This athlete's profile showed that, for his age group, he was physically immature (skeletal age) and about average in body size; thus these factors were not advantages in his athletic competition. However, his speed and agility, muscular power, muscular endurance, and relative strength were superior; he was well above average on most

[11]Albert R. Behnke, "Anthropometric Estimate of Body Size, Shape and Fat Content," *Postgraduate Medicine*, 34, No. 2 (August 1963), 190.

[12]Morgan E. Shelley, "Maturity, Structure, Strength, Motor Ability, and Intelligence Test Profiles of Outstanding Elementary School and Junior High School Athletes" (Master thesis, University of Oregon, 1960).

[13]Bruce L. Howe, "Test Profiles of Outstanding Twelve-Year-Old Elementary School Athletes at Nine, Twelve, and Fifteen Years of Age" (Master's thesis, University of Oregon, 1966).

muscular strength tests; his physique was strongly mesomorphic; and he possessed high intelligence. A further discussion, with illustrations of profiles of outstanding schoolboy athletes in the Medford Boys' Growth Study, has been presented by Clarke.[14]

SAMPLING

Surveys are usually conducted with samples drawn from the particular population under study. A given study identifies the population, such as elementary school pupils in a community, or in a state, or in the United States.[15] A sample only approximates the population from which it is drawn, and repeated samples from the same population differ from each other within the limits of normal probability. However, if randomly drawn, the differences between such samples do not differ significantly when statistical tests of variances are applied. Thus, if two samples do differ significantly, at least two reasons could account for it: either the populations are definitely different, or the samples were not drawn in a comparable manner. It is this latter situation that could account, unconsciously or carelessly, for a difference in results between two groups under comparison.

In any event, samples are only justified when drawn entirely at random, where every entity in the population has an equal chance of being chosen. Great care should be exercised in all surveys to describe precisely how samples are obtained. If comparisons between groups are to be made, all samples must be drawn in an identical manner.

Random samples may be drawn in different ways. A good method is by use of a table of random numbers; in such a table, the numbers have been scrambled by lottery procedure. By this method, consecutive numbers are assigned to the subjects in the population; starting at any point on the table, consecutive numbers are drawn in any direction (vertically, horizontally, or diagonally) until the number of subjects needed for the sample is reached.

The random-number method of choosing samples is feasible when populations are reasonably well confined, such as students in local schools, residents in a local community, or schools of a given size range in a state. When a very large population is involved, other means of securing a random sample are desirable. The process of drawing the United States sample of public school students in grades five through

---

[14] H. Harrison Clarke, *Physical and Motor Tests in the Medford Boys' Growth Study* (Englewood Cliffs, N.J.: Prentice-Hall, Inc., 1971), pp. 255-63.

[15] Sampling is treated in much greater detail in Chapter 8, where theory is discussed and the effect of sample size is considered.

twelve for the AAHPER Youth Fitness Test by the University of Michigan Research Center illustrates such a procedure.[16] For economic reasons, the sample size was limited to 8,000 pupils, composed of 1,000 per grade, 500 girls and 500 boys. From 62 nonmetropolitan primary sampling areas, 12 were randomly selected; 12 major metropolitan areas were also included. Subsamples of school districts with probability proportionate to size were drawn. Sampling was continued in order to choose schools within the areas and to select pupils within the schools, thus identified as the individuals to be tested.

At times, stratified sampling may be desirable, by which proportionate numbers of subjects are drawn from units of unequal size. As an illustration; from a total of 6,000 elementary school students at the time in Eugene, Oregon, Kirchner and Glines[17] wanted 100 boys and 100 girls from each grade in order to conduct a normative survey of their muscular fitness. They determined the number of children in each school in the city: Proportionate numbers of subjects were taken from the several schools. The subjects actually tested in each grade in each school were drawn from a table of random numbers. Thus, chance was operational in the selection of children in this survey; each child in the Eugene elementary schools had an equal chance of being chosen.

If randomizing is needed for purposes of mailing, for example, consideration should be given to the possibility of utilizing computer facilities. If names and addresses can be put on data processing cards, the computer can be programmed to select a randomized sample, print out the list, and at the same time print out several sets of address labels that can be placed on envelopes. This process saves a great deal of time that otherwise might be spent typing separate envelopes for the initial mailing and any follow-up procedures utilized.

SUMMARY

Various types of survey procedures were considered in this chapter. The mailed questionnaire was presented as a means of gathering data from a large number of individuals, frequently broadly distributed geographically. Although the use of the questionnaire has limitations, it is justified when data can be obtained that would otherwise be impossible in a reasonable length of time and with reasonable expense. The construction of the questionnaire, its ap-

[16]Paul A. Hunsicker and Guy G. Reiff, *A Survey and Comparison of Youth Fitness 1958-1965* (Ann Arbor, Michigan: University of Michigan, 1965), pp. 17-20.

[17]Glenn Kirchner and Don Glines, "Comparative Analysis of Eugene, Oregon. Elementary School Children Using the Kraus-Weber Test of Minimum Muscular Fitness," *Research Quarterly*, 30, No. 1 (March 1959), 75.

pearance, its development, its sponsorship, and follow-up procedures were described. The sequence followed includes initial writing, trial run, tabulation of preliminary results, and rewriting of unclear or ambiguous questions. Various aids that may be employed to obtain a high percentage of responses to the questionnaire were discussed, including vigorous follow-up procedures. Methods of assessing opinions were presented. Sampling processes were explained.

Another type of survey is by interview, in which the investigator visits the subject in person rather than through a questionnaire. The personal contact helps to insure a more adequate and thorough response. Even though the interview is more informal, it is nevertheless rather highly structured. This survey method insures that no information is omitted and permits greater study in depth.

Normative surveys have been employed in research in physical education to compare subjects on various tests with established norms. In such instances, certain precautions that include attention to the sampling process, the testing techniques, and subject motivation, are indicated. In addition, the study of individual subjects may occasionally be desirable through case study and profile techniques.

SELECTED REFERENCES

GOOD, CARTER V., *Essentials of Educational Research: Methodology and Design* (2nd ed.). East Norwalk, Conn.: Appleton-Century-Crofts, 1972, Ch. 8.

VAN DALEN, DEOBOLD B., *Understanding Educational Research* (4th ed.). New York: McGraw-Hill Company, 1979, Ch. 6.

Statistical Applications

7

Central Tendency, Variability, Normal Probability

INTRODUCTION TO PART III

A knowledge of statistics is essential for the physical educator who aspires to scientific competency, either as an evaluator or as a producer of research studies. In laboratory research and other scientific studies, the application of statistics is essential. The investigator typically administers tests to a sample of subjects in order to measure various elements that are essential to the research design. The analysis and interpretation of the test results can be accomplished only through appropriate statistical applications.

The statistical methods presented are restricted to those found most appropriate in the analysis of physical education research data. Some of these computations, such as measures of central tendency and variability and the coefficient of correlation, can be made from both raw (ungrouped) and grouped scores. The universal procedure today is to compute statistics from the individual scores, accomplished through the use of electronic computers and calculators. However, this procedure does not provide an understanding of statistical processes and appropriate interpretations of statistical results: Scores are merely fed into a computer in accordance with a given program and the end result is spewed out as a single figure. Grouped data computations are valuable for instructional purposes, as they show data distributions and they demonstrate computational processes.

Both grouped and ungrouped methods of computation are presented.

It is assumed that the graduate student will have had some exposure to statistics, probably in a prior course. Therefore, computations of elementary statistics are sketchy, serving as a review and permitting a continuous and coordinated account of statistics throughout. Emphasis is on the interpretation of the various statistics presented and on their application to physical education research problems.

Five types of statistical processes are generally recognized: descriptive, comparative, relationship, inferential, and predictive. In descriptive statistics, the characteristics of a single group are described in various ways. In comparative statistics, the characteristics of two or more groups are contrasted. In relationship statistics, the correlations between numerous human traits as possessed by the same population are determined. In inferential statistics, observed data from a sample are used as a basis for generalizing to the total population from which the sample was drawn. In predictive statistics, unknown facts about the individual are predicted or inferred from known measurable qualities.

Although the purpose of this text is to prepare physical educators to conduct research, other values are cited for the study of statistics, as follows:

1. ***To understand, interpret, and evaluate scientific literature.*** This value alone justifies the study of statistics, since the use of statistical terms is commonplace in research journals. For example, seldom has the *Research Quarterly for Exercise and Sport* of the American Alliance for Health, Physical Education, Recreation, and Dance published an article in which quantitative data were not analyzed in some way.

2. ***To determine the scientific worth of tests.*** Although the construction of tests is a phase of research, the evaluation of tests should be a concern of all educators who use them. Statistical procedures are utilized widely in this process: to validate, to establish accuracy, and to prepare norms. The ability, therefore, to determine the scientific worth of tests is dependent upon a knowledge of statistics.

3. ***To prepare reports based on test results.*** The preparation of annual or more frequent reports of progress made in school programs is a common responsibility of educators. An effective aspect of such reports is the inclusion of test results that show progress made by pupils. The utilization of graphs and some of the common, easily understood statistics—such as frequency distri-

butions, percentages, medians, and quartiles—is of value for this purpose.

4. *To discriminate between satisfactory and unsatisfactory evidence in reports containing statistical analysis.* In today's society, people are bombarded from every side with statistical reports, ranging from some nauseating TV and radio commercials to dignified and searching presentations by respected investigators. A knowledge of statistics makes the student critical of these reports and prone to evaluate them, to look behind the figures to the manner in which they were derived. All too frequently, statistics have been misused to misrepresent.

QUANTITATIVE DATA

The term *quantitative data* refers to a collection of numerical values that are usually expressed as scores on a test. Some characteristics of quantitative data of significance for research understanding follow.

Attributes. An attribute (also known as a nominal scale) has a nongradient classification, that is, there is no numerical basis of grouping. Attributes may be in two or more classes. Examples of two-class attributes are teachers as men and women and pupils as boys and girls. Illustrations of more than two-class attributes are color of hair or eyes, various nationalities or races, and different major fields of study.

Variables. A variable has a gradient classification, that is, there is a numerical basis of grouping. Variables are of two types—continuous and discontinuous (or discrete). A *continuous variable* is capable of any degree of subdivision. The fineness of measurement is usually limited to some convenient number. Most of the quantitative data used in physical education are of a continuous nature. Examples of continuous variables are muscular strength, anthropometric dimensions, personality traits, and motor ability elements.

A *discontinuous variable* cannot be, or is not generally, subdivided by less than whole numbers or units. Illustrations are basketball scores, number of pupils in a classroom or children in a family, and salary scales. Thus, a basketball team could not score $47\frac{1}{2}$ points; the number of children in a family cannot be $2\frac{1}{3}$; and, although salary scales can be theoretically reduced to dollars and cents, in practice, they are not. However, although fractions of such scores are unrealistic, discontinuous data are frequently treated statistically as though they were continuous in order to provide significant differentiations. For example, to state that the average number of children in families of two nationalities is 2.5 and 3.4 is to state the impossible; yet, no other comparison would indicate the difference of nearly one child, since to recognize only whole numbers would round off the number of children to 3.0 for both nationalities.

Parametric Data. Data of this type typically consist of measurement scores. Parametric statistical tests assume that the data are essentially normally distributed.

Nonparametric Data. Data of this type are typically counted or ranked. Nonparametric tests, also known as distribution-free tests, do not require the more stringent assumption of normally distributed data.

FREQUENCY DISTRIBUTION

A frequency distribution consists of arranging the scores into groups, or intervals. A frequency table consists of intervals, each of which is of the same size, over the range of scores. To illustrate the construction of a frequency table, the skeletal ages of 67 boys 13 years of age in the Medford Boys' Growth Study are utilized. Skeletal age is a measure of physiological maturity. It is obtained from an X-ray of the wrist and hand as assessed by use of the Greulich-Pyle atlas.[1] Normally, skeletal age corresponds to chronological age until maturity (age 19 years) is reached. Thus, a skeletal age of 13 years means that a boy has the maturity of a boy who is 13 years old. In obtaining the data used here, each boy was tested within two months of his birthday; thus, the chronological ages of the subjects did not vary in any instance by more than four months. The skeletal ages of the 67 boys are given in months.

149	162	158	144	154	161	177	132
150	146	155	147	148	151	156	169
157	149	148	168	135	154	154	136
153	144	154	163	154	156	162	140
136	164	168	144	134	136	162	157
168	139	140	158	128*	154	148	151
144	182*	151	168	156	135	156	171
158	147	140	154	171	169	153	138
154	162	156					

Looking at these data, little sense can be made of them, as just a hodgepodge of scores appears. Once they are organized into a fre-

---

[1] W. W. Greulich and S. I. Pyle, *Radiographic Atlas of Skeletal Development of the Hand and Wrist*, 2nd ed. (Palo Alto, Calif.: Stanford University Press, 1959).

**TABLE 7.1   Frequency Distribution for Skeletal
Ages of Boys 13 Years of Age (months)**

Intervals	Tallies	f
180-184	/	1
175-179	/	1
170-174	//	2
165-169	/HH/ /	6
160-164	/HH/ //	7
155-159	/HH/ /HH/ /	11
150-154	/HH/ /HH/ ////	14
145-149	/HH/ ///	8
140-144	/HH/ //	7
135-139	/HH/ //	7
130-134	//	2
125-129	/	1
		$N = 67$

quency table, as in Table 7.1, a definite pattern emerges. Briefly, the process of constructing a frequency table, as applied to Table 7.1, follows.

Range of scores.   The range of scores is found in order to determine the distance over which the scores are spread. To determine the range, the high and low scores are located and subtracted. For the skeletal ages, these scores are 182* and 128* months, identified by asterisks in the tabulation. Subtracting these scores, the range is 54 months.

Number of intervals.   A general rule to follow is to utilize between 10 and 20 intervals. With a small number of scores, the number should be nearer 10; whereas with many scores, the number should be nearer 20. A limited range would set this guideline aside, so fewer than 10 intervals would be justified. For the skeletal ages in this problem, the number of 67 is relatively small, so the number of intervals should be near 10.

Size of Interval.   Some interval sizes are preferable, as they are more convenient in the tabulation of scores. One such size is 5, which was chosen for this problem, predicated on a skeletal age range of 54 months and the decision to use somewhere near 10 intervals. This resulted in 12 intervals, as shown in Table 7.1.

Tabulation.   The intervals should next be arranged in tabular form with the largest scores at the top. For convenience in tabulation, the lower limits of each interval should be a multiple of the size of the interval. Thus, the highest interval in this problem is 180-184 (scores of 180, 181, 182, 183, 184), which permits tabulation of the highest skeletal age of 182 months. All 67 scores are then tabulated into their intervals. The number of scores in each interval is then designated with the appropriate figures; this column is known as the "frequency column" and is designated by the letter f. The total of the frequency column, indicated by the letter N, should equal 67, the original number of skeletal ages.

Assumptions

Two assumptions are made when statistics are calculated from a frequency table.

1. The scores are evenly distributed within the interval. This assumption is made when computing the median and other percentiles. In these instances, as will be shown later, the calculations are made by interpolating within the step intervals, that is, taking a definite proportion of the size of the interval. Thus, the process demands a linear scale.

2. The average of the scores within each interval is equal to the midpoint of the interval. This assumption is necessary when calculating the mean and standard deviation, as it is necessary to represent the scores within an interval by a single score. The individual scores within the various intervals are not identifiable from the frequency table, so the only consistent way to represent them is to utilize the midpoints of the intervals. Further, although the midpoints may not average out when the actual scores in the intervals are averaged, they balance out quite well throughout the distribution. The greatest violation of this assumption may occur at the tails of the distribution, where the f's are small. In symmetrical distributions, which generally occur with a large number of randomly selected subjects, all midpoints represent their respective intervals with considerable fidelity.

An inspection of the frequency distribution of skeletal ages of the 67 boys in Table 7.1 gives a much better idea of the data in this problem than was obtained from the hodgepodge of individual scores on which the tabulation was based. The frequencies show the shape of the distribution: a concentration of scores in the center and a sloping away above and below the center. This symmetrical distribution is typical of most random samples of subjects tested with a variety of measures.

MEASURES OF CENTRAL TENDENCY

A measure of central tendency is a single score that represents all the scores in a distribution. If one asked the accomplishment of a class on an examination, the answer would not be that David received 85; Nancy, 75; Louise, 90; Stanley, 71; and so on until all the individual scores had been enumerated. Such a response would be both meaningless and confusing; one would still wonder how well the class had performed. Instead, the answer would probably be "The average of the class was 75," or whatever the average may have been. The answer, thus, in terms of central tendency—a single score that represents all the scores.

The measures of central tendency presented are the *median*, and the *mean*. A third measure, the *mode*, shows the score that appears mostly frequently, but has little, if any, use in physical education research.

Median

The median is the midpoint in a distribution, that point above which and below which lie 50% of the scores. It may or may not be an actual score, as central tendency is considered to be a central position.

Ungrouped Data.   When scores are ungrouped but arranged in order from high to low, it is quite easy to find the center, or middle score, by counting. Thus for an uneven number of scores, 18, 17, 15, 11, 9, the middle score, or median, is 15. For an even number of scores, 18, 17, 15, 11, 9, 8, the middle falls between 15 and 11, so the median is halfway between these scores, or 13.

Grouped data.   With grouped data, or scores in a frequency table, the median is found by counting frequencies to the interval that contains the middle point and interpolating to determine its location. The process for computing the median is shown in Table 7.2, which contains the frequency table of the 67 skeletal ages of 13-year-old boys tabulated earlier. The formula is as follows:

$$Mdn = l + \left(\frac{\frac{N}{2} - F}{f_m} \right) i \quad \text{or} \quad l + \left(\frac{.5N - F}{f_m} \right) i \qquad (7.1)$$

With 67 scores, the middle score is located at $33.5 \left(\frac{N}{2} \right)$. Counting

TABLE 7.2   Calculation of the Median, Mean, and Mode from Skeletal Age Data Grouped into a Frequency Table

Intervals Scores in months	f	d	fd	
180-184	1	6	6	
175-179	1	5	5	
170-174	2	4	8	
165-169	6	3	18	
160-164	7	2	14	
155-159	11(28)	1	11	+62
150-154	14	0	0	
145-149	8(25)	−1	−8	
140-144	7	−2	−14	
135-139	7	−3	−21	
130-134	2	−4	−8	
125-129	1	−5	−5	−54
	$N = 67$			+6

$$(1)\ Median = l + \left(\frac{\frac{N}{2} - F}{f_m} \right) i$$

$$= 149.5 + \frac{(^{67}/_2 - 25)}{14} 5 = 152.54$$

$$(2)\ Mean = AM + \left(\frac{\Sigma fd}{N} \right) i$$

$$= 152.0 + (^{6}/_{67}) 5 = 152.45$$

up from the lower end of the frequency (f) column, there are 25 scores below the interval 150-154. If scores have been rounded off to the lowest whole number, as in this situation, the lower limit of the interval is 149.5.[2] The 33.5 score, then, is somewhere in this interval, so a proportion of it is added to the lower limit. With 25 scores counted out, 8.5 more are needed to reach the middle: 33.5 − 25 = 8.5. As there are 14 scores in the step interval, 8.5/14 of it should be taken, or 8.5/14 of 5, the size of the interval. This amount is 3.04.

$$\frac{8.5}{14} \times 5 \quad \text{or} \quad \frac{8.5 \times 5}{14} = 3.04$$

Adding this amount to the lower limit gives the median.

[2] If the rounding off had been to the next whole number, the lower limit of the interval would have been 150.

$$149.5 + 3.04 = 152.54 \text{ months}$$

Mean

The mean expresses the central massing of scores according to the distance scores fall from the center of the distribution. Therefore, each score in the distribution is weighted by its distance from central tendency.

The terms *mean* and *average* may be used interchangeably. The average, of course, is universally known and used. In common utilization, it is calculated by the arithmetic method of adding the scores and dividing by the number. Thus:

$$Ave \text{ (or } M) = \frac{\Sigma X}{N} \tag{7.2}$$

in which Σ means the summation of scores and N is the total number of scores. When the large X is used in a formula, it refers to raw or observed scores.

In computing the mean from the frequency table, the midpoint of an interval is selected, to be called an assumed mean (AM), and a correction is applied. Any midpoint in the distribution may be selected and will produce the same answer. However, the amount of arithmetic involved is less when the assumed mean is a midpoint near the center of the distribution.

Once the assumed mean is selected, the correction is in terms of the deviations of the scores from this midpoint. Initially, the deviations are in terms of the number of intervals from the assumed mean to be designated as d. The formula is developed as follows:

$$M = AM + C$$

$$C = c \times i$$

$$c = \frac{\Sigma fd}{N}$$

thus $\quad M = AM + \left(\frac{\Sigma fd}{N}\right)i \tag{7.3}$

In the sample problem of the 67 skeletal ages of 13-year-old boys given in Table 7.2, the assumed mean is selected at the 150-154 interval; as the midpoint of the interval is used, the AM is 152.0.[3] The step interval deviations of the scores from AM are shown in the column d.

---

[3] The midpoint is obtained by adding one-half the size of the interval to the lower limit of the interval. In this problem one-half of 5 is 2.5; adding 2.5 to 149.5 gives the midpoint of 152.0.

Each interval above the *AM* interval is 1 point farther removed, so the deviations are 1, 2, 3, 4, 5, and 6. These are positive deviations, as they represent numerically higher values than the assumed mean. Below the assumed mean, the same situation exists, except that the deviations are negative, as the values are numerically lower than the assumed mean. If the assumed mean selected is low in the distribution, a predominance of positive values will result; if high, the predominance will be negative. This situation is the reason the same answer will result no matter which assumed mean is selected, as long as only the midpoints are utilized.

Since the number of subjects varies from interval to interval, this fact must be taken into consideration. To do so, the number of scores in each interval (*f* column) is multiplied by the step-interval deviation (*d* column). Thus, $f \times d = fd$. The scores in this final column are then added. As there are positive and negative values in the column, they must be added separately and their difference determined. In the problem, the sum of the positive values is 62 and the sum of the negative values is −56. Thus, the sum of the columns is 6. Substitution in the formula may now be completed.

$$M = AM + \left(\frac{\Sigma fd}{N} \right) i$$

$$= 152.0 + (\text{\%}_{67})5 = 152.45$$

Characteristics and Uses

In the sample problem, the two measures of central tendency vary only slightly: median, 152.54 months; mean, 152.45 months. When the raw scores are added and divided by the number of scores, the average is also close, 152.82 months. These results are typical of symmetrical distributions that peak in the center and taper off about equally on either side. In an exactly symmetrical distribution, these three measures of central tendency are identical. In this instance, obviously, any one of the measures will represent central tendency equally well.

However, for various reasons to be considered, frequency distributions are not always so symmetrical as this one. Therefore, further explanation of the characteristics and uses of the two measures of central tendency will be made.

Median.   The median is not affected by extreme scores or when the equality of a measurement unit is uncertain. The following uses are indicated for this measure of central tendency:

1. When the influence of extremely high or extremely low scores on the measure of central tendency is to be avoided. The actual size of

scores within the distribution does not affect the median, as the scores are merely counted in making the calculation. For example, in Table 7.2, all 25 scores below the interval containing the median could have been in the interval 145-149 without changing the answer; they could also be spread out for any distance below. The mean would be drastically affected by these changes but not the median.

2. When the distribution is truncated—cut off at the top or bottom. A truncated distribution would occur as a result of using a strength-testing instrument with a capacity less than the strongest subjects. Truncation would also occur in some physical education tests, especially when zeros are possible or even probable, as in chinning.

3. When the equality of the unit of measurement is uncertain. The uncertainty of measurement equality occurs when performers are arranged in rank order; the actual difference between those with high and low ranks may well be greater than between those with middle ranks. Judges' ratings may sometimes have a truncation effect at the top and bottom of the scale used by them. Also, the median is useful when numerical measurement is impossible, as in an arrangement of silhouettes depicting poor to good posture.

Mean.   The mean is the most reliable of the measures of central tendency; there is less fluctuation from sample to sample of the same population than is true for the median. The mean should be used when distributions are reasonably symmetrical, when they are not skewed, or when they do not contain extremes at one end of the distribution; extremes at both ends balance each other. Actually, the mean should be used unless the median is more appropriate, as indicated above. Further, the mean should be the measure of central tendency when advanced statistics are to be employed in analyses.

Each score in the distribution carries a weight equal to its distance from the mean when the mean is calculated. This distance from the mean for each score is sometimes called a *moment*, although it is more commonly indicated as *distance from the mean*, designated by the symbol, x. Thus

$$x = X - M \quad \text{and} \quad \Sigma x = \Sigma (X - M)$$

The mean is the only measure of central tendency from which the deviations from central tendency always add algebraically to zero. Also, in some statistical calculations, deviations of scores from central tendency must be squared; therefore, the moments are squared. An important property of the mean is that the sum of the squared deviations around it is smaller than the sum of squared deviations around the median, except when both measures of central tendency are identical.

PERCENTILES

The use of percentiles is valuable in making test scores meaningful; a table of percentiles is one way of presenting norms for a given test. It is impossible to know how well one has done on a test unless his or her score is shown in relationship to others taking or having taken the same test. For example, merely giving a score of 150 on an examination is meaningless. However, if the 30th percentile score is 150, it is immediately known that the pupil has exceeded 30% of those taking the test but is below scores achieved by 70%. Percentiles can also be used in comparing the standing of different individuals in a number of tests. To illustrate, how does a score of 11 seconds in the 100-yard dash compare with a score of 16 feet in the long jump? If 11 seconds is at the 75th percentile and 16 feet is at the 65th percentile, the comparison becomes clear.

The percentile scale extends from P_0 to P_{100}. For ungrouped data, the method of calculating the percentiles is similar to that used for finding the median except different points are sought; in fact, the median is a percentile, the 50th. For example, the 10th percentile is found by counting off one-tenth; the 20th is found by counting off two-tenths (one-fifth) from the low end of the distribution, rather than one-half, as is true for the median.

Table 7.3 illustrates the method used in computing the deciles (each 10th percentile) for the distribution of 67 skeletal ages utilized in the calculation of the measures of central tendency. A cumulative frequency column (cf) appears in the table; those scores were obtained by adding the frequencies cumulatively, beginning with the lowest interval and continuing to the highest. This column is of assistance in locating the desired interval when counting for any particular percentile.

To explain the procedure, the 10th percentile (P_{10}) is located by finding $\frac{1}{10}$ of 67 ($.1N$), or 6.7. From the cf column, 3 scores are below the interval 135-139, so the lower limit of this interval, 134.5, has been reached; 3.7 more scores are needed ($6.7 - 3 = 3.7$). Interpolating into the interval, as was done for the median, P_{10} is computed as 137.14 skeletal age months. The percentiles between the decile points are obtained in a similar manner. Thus for P_{37}:

$$P_{37} = .37N = .37 \times 67 = 24.79$$

$$144.5 + \frac{7.79 \times 5}{8} = 149.37$$

TABLE 7.3   Calculation of Deciles and Quartiles from Skeletal Age Data Grouped into a Frequency Table

Scores (Months)	f	cf		
				Quartiles
180-184	1	67		$Q_1 = 144$
175-179	1	66		$Q_3 = 160$
170-174	2	65		Percentiles at
165-169	6	63		decile points
160-164	7	57		P_{100} 182
155-159	11	50		P_{90} 167
150-154	14	39		P_{80} 162
145-149	8	25		P_{70} 158
140-144	7	17		P_{60} 155
135-139	7	10		P_{50} 153
130-134	2	3		P_{40} 150
125-129	1	1		P_{30} 146
	$N = 67$			P_{20} 142
				P_{10} 137
				P_{0} 128

Calculation of deciles

$$P_{10} = .1N = 6.7 \quad 134.5 + \frac{3.7 \times 5}{7} = 137.14$$

$$P_{20} = .2N = 13.4 \quad 139.5 + \frac{3.4 \times 5}{7} = 141.93$$

$$P_{30} = .3N = 20.1 \quad 144.5 + \frac{3.1 \times 5}{8} = 146.44$$

$$P_{40} = .4N = 26.8 \quad 149.5 + \frac{1.8 \times 5}{14} = 150.14$$

$$P_{50} = .5N = 33.5 \quad 149.5 + \frac{8.5 \times 5}{14} = 152.54 \ (Mdn)$$

$$P_{60} = .6N = 40.3 \quad 154.5 + \frac{1.2 \times 5}{11} = 155.05$$

$$P_{70} = .7N = 46.9 \quad 154.5 + \frac{7.9 \times 5}{11} = 158.09$$

$$P_{80} = .8N = 53.6 \quad 159.5 + \frac{3.6 \times 5}{7} = 162.07$$

$$P_{90} = .9N = 60.3 \quad 164.5 + \frac{3.3 \times 5}{6} = 167.25$$

Calculation of quartiles

$$Q_1 = .25N = 16.75$$

$$139.5 + \frac{6.75 \times 5}{7} = 144.32$$

$$Q_3 = .75N = 50.25$$

$$159.5 + \frac{.25 \times 5}{7} = 159.68$$

The 0 and 100th percentiles may be designated in different ways. The method adopted for Table 7.3 is to designate the lowest score in the distribution as P_0 and the highest score as P_{100}. In the problem, these scores were 128 and 182 months, respectively. Another method is simply to use the lower and upper limits of the frequency distribution. Had this been done in the problem, P_0 would equal 125, and P_{100} would be 185. These two values indicate the boundaries of the percentile scale; they are regulated by two single individuals tested in the sample from which the scale was developed, so are subject to considerable chance in their random selection. Consequently, the latter method of designating P_0 and P_{100} would usually provide some leeway in future testing should more extreme scores be encountered than in the original sample; thus, there is less likelihood that individuals who fell either above or below the values provided on the percentile scale would be subsequently tested.

In test construction, when a percentile scale is presented, the percentile values are frequently given in whole numbers, as in the upper right part of Table 7.3. The decision as to whether or not this should be done is dependent upon the range of scores and the importance of fractions. For example, in the problem a fraction of a month would probably not be important for practical purposes in scoring a boy's skeletal age. However, if a percentile scale were constructed for standing height, where the range of scores is small for any given age, fractions of an inch could well be used.

The percentile scale favors mediocre or "average" performance. As seen in Table 7.3, the values cluster closely in the center of the scale and spread out at the ends. The differences between deciles in the central area is small, only 2 points—for example, between P_{50} and P_{60} (153 to 155 months); at the extremes, the differences are much larger—15 points between P_{90} and P_{100} (167 to 182 months). For this reason, it is comparatively easy for an individual to improve his percentile position in the middle of the distribution but very difficult to do at the ends. To equal the 15 months required to go from P_{90} to P_{100}, a boy could go from P_{30} almost to P_{80} (162 to 146 = 16), which is one-half the scale. Further, due to the inequalities in scale values, percentiles may not be properly summed or averaged. Because of these characteristics of the percentile scale, other scaling methods have been sought, as will be explained later.

MEASURES OF VARIABILITY

In the preceding presentation, measures of central tendency were discussed. Test scores were described in terms of typical performance; the point of greatest concentration of scores was indicated. However, central tendency alone does not adequately give the total picture of the sample measured. For example, 2 groups of sophomore high school girls (groups A and B) have the same Physical Fitness Index mean of 100. From this information, the 2 groups seem alike in so far as the quality being measured is concerned. Suppose, however, that the highest PFI in group A is 150, and the lowest is 50; in group B, the highest is 125, and the lowest is 75. The 2 groups are no longer alike: group A has a range of 100, and group B has a range of 50. The group A range is twice the group B range. Although central tendency is the same, the internal arrangement of the scores is not.

In the above illustration, a measure of variability—the range was applied. For a definition: A measure of variability indicates the spread of the scores in a distribution, usually around a measure of central tendency. In this instance, a distance on a scale is expressed by a single measure, as a range of 100 and a range of 50 in the illustration. This measure is never a point on a scale, as was true for measures of central tendency.

Range

The range indicates the spread of all the scores in the distribution; in use, therefore, it is not related to a measure of central tendency. As explained and illustrated in the preceding chapter, the range is obtained by finding the difference between the highest and lowest scores. Its use as a measure of variability is unreliable when extreme scores occur in the distribution, for it takes into account only the two scores at the ends of the distribution. In order to avoid this situation, the other measures of variability consider only the spread of scores in the center of the distribution.

Quartile Deviation

The quartile deviation, or Q, indicates the spread of the middle 50% of the scores taken from the median. Thus, in an effort to eliminate the effect of extreme scores on the measure of variability, this measure cuts 25% from each end. The formula for calculating Q is as follows:

$$Q = \frac{Q_3 - Q_1}{2} \qquad (7.4)$$

Both Q_3 and Q_1 were calculated in Table 7.3 for the skeletal ages of the 67 13-year-old boys; these values were 159.68 and 144.32 months respectively. The distance between the two quartiles is 15.36 months. One-half this distance, or Q, is 7.68 months. This calculation is shown in Table 7.5.

The meaning of Q is illustrated in Figure 7.1 using the quartiles,

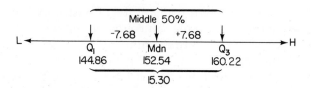

Figure 7.1. Quartile Deviation Relationships: Skeletal Ages in Months.

median, and quartile deviation found in the problem presented. In interpreting Q, this value is marked off in plus and minus distances from the median. In a completely symmetrical distribution, adding and subtracting Q from the median will equal the calculated Q_3 and Q_1. In the illustrated problem, the results are nearly so. Thus, 152.54 months, the median, plus and minus 7.68 months, equal 160.22 and 144.86 months, while the calculated Q_3 and Q_1 are 159.68 and 144.32 months.

Standard Deviation

The standard deviation, or sigma, is the most important of the measures of variability. It is designated either by SD or the Greek sigma sign, σ, although with small samples the lowercase s may be used. This variability measure indicates the spread of the middle 68.26% of the scores taken from the mean. The percentage value of 68.26% will not be seen from the calculation, as the middle 50% for the quartile deviation was seen. The percentage applies when distributions are normal, and it is obtained from the properties of the normal probability curve, as explained later in this chapter.

Ungrouped Data

Basically, the standard deviation is calculated as the square root of the average of the squared deviations from the mean. As expressed in formula,

$$\sigma = \sqrt{\frac{\Sigma x^2}{N}} \tag{7.5}$$

The calculation of SD by this formula is illustrated in Table 7.4, Method A. The column headed X contains 10 scores from which the computation is made; the mean of these scores is 13.2. The second column, x, gives the deviations of the scores from the mean. Thus: $x = X - M$. To illustrate with the first two x scores of 13 and 17:

$$13 - 13.2 = -.2$$

$$17 - 13.2 = 3.8$$

TABLE 7.4   Calculation of the Standard Deviation from Raw Data

Method A: From the mean				*Method B:* From raw scores directly		
X	x	x^2		X	X^2	
13	−.2	.04	$M = \dfrac{132}{10} = 13.2$	13	169	$\sigma = \dfrac{\sqrt{N\Sigma X^2 - (\Sigma X)^2}}{N}$
17	3.8	14.44	$\sigma = \sqrt{\dfrac{\Sigma x^2}{N}}$	17	289	
15	1.8	3.24		15	225	$= \dfrac{\sqrt{10(1794) - (132)^2}}{10}$
11	−2.2	4.84		11	121	
13	−.2	.04	$= \sqrt{\dfrac{51.60}{10}}$	13	169	$= \dfrac{\sqrt{17,940 - 17,424}}{10}$
17	3.8	14.44		17	289	$= \dfrac{\sqrt{516}}{10}$
11	−2.2	4.84	$= \sqrt{5.16}$	11	121	
13	−.2	.04	$= 2.27$	13	169	$= \dfrac{22.7}{10}$
11	−2.2	4.84		11	121	
11	−2.2	4.84		11	121	$= 2.27$
$\Sigma 132$		51.60		$\Sigma 132$	1794	

In the third column, each of the x values is squared. This column is added, and the amount is 51.60. The formula is then applied; the *SD* equals 2.27.

A second method of calculating *SD* from ungrouped data is to work directly from raw scores. It has special usefulness since it can be programmed easily for electronic computer calculation. The formula is as follows:

$$\sigma = \frac{\sqrt{N\Sigma X^2 - (\Sigma X^2)}}{N} \tag{7.6}$$

The calculation of sigma by this formula is illustrated in Table 7.4, Method B. The same 10 scores utilized in the first method are given in the first column; the sum of this column (ΣX) equals 132. In the second column, the first column scores are squared and added (ΣX^2). With these 2 values, the formula is applied. The *SD* is again 2.27.

Grouped Data

The formula for calculating the standard deviation from grouped data—that is, calculating it from an assumed mean in a frequency table rather than from the actual mean—is

$$\sigma = i \sqrt{\frac{\Sigma fd^2}{N} - \left(\frac{\Sigma fd}{N}\right)^2} \qquad (7.7)$$

As for the calculation of the mean via the frequency table, the use of an assumed mean (AM) in determining the standard deviation requires a correction, which in this instance is squared.

It will readily be seen from the formula and from Table 7.5, where the standard deviation is computed, that the only computation that is

TABLE 7.5 Calculation of Measures of Variability from Data Grouped into a Frequency Table (Data from Table 2)

Step intervals Scores in months	f	d	fd	fd^2
180-184	1	6	6	36
175-179	1	5	5	25
170-174	2	4	8	32
165-169	6	3	18	54
160-164	7	2	14	28
155-159	11	1	11 (+62)	11
150-154	14	0	0	
145-149	8	−1	−8	8
140-144	7	−2	−14	28
135-139	7	−3	−21	63
130-134	2	−4	−8	32
125-129	1	−5	−5 (−56)	25
	$N = 67$		+6	342

Quartile deviation

$$Q = \frac{Q_3 - Q_1}{2}$$

$Q_3 = 159.68$ (Table 5)
$Q_1 = 144.32$ (Table 5)

$$Q = \frac{159.68 - 144.32}{2}$$

$$= \frac{15.36}{2}$$

$$= 7.68 \text{ months}$$

Standard deviation

$$\sigma = i \sqrt{\frac{\Sigma fd^2}{N} - \left(\frac{\Sigma fd}{N}\right)^2}$$

$$\frac{\Sigma fd^2}{N} = \frac{342}{67} = 5.10$$

$$\left(\frac{\Sigma fd}{N}\right)^2 = \left(\frac{6}{67}\right)^2 = (.09)^2 = .01$$

$$= 5\sqrt{5.10 - .01}$$
$$= 5 \times 2.26$$

$$= 11.30 \text{ months}$$

new at this point is Σfd^2. The steps to be followed in finding SD are as follows:

1. Calculate the fd column, as previously described in the presentation of the mean in Table 7.2.
2. Add another column, fd^2, which is calculated by multiplying each figure in column d by the corresponding figure in column fd. It should be noted that only d is squared. Thus: $d \times fd = fd^2$. Add this column serially, since all the signs are positive. This will be Σfd^2. In this problem: $\Sigma fd^2 = 342$. In the formula, this sum is divided by N; the quotient is 5.10.
3. Compute the correction required when computations are made from an assumed mean. In this instance: $(\Sigma fd/N)^2 = .01$.
4. Substitute in the formula and complete the computations. The SD for the skeletal ages of the 67 13-year-old boys is 11.30 months.

Characteristics

Variability measures provide a common unit for specifying the distance from central tendency to any individual score or point on the scale of scores. For example, a score of 15 points above the mean is meaningless. However, if 15 points is 1.5σ above the mean, the performance becomes understandable.

Measures of variability can be used as "yardsticks" on the scale of scores, regardless of differences in distribution ranges. Given the following, for example

Height: $M = 65$ inches; $\sigma = 2$ inches

Weight: $M = 135$ pounds; $\sigma = 15$ pounds

An individual whose height is 67 inches (2 inches above the mean for height) and whose weight is 150 pounds (15 pounds above the mean for weight) is 1σ above the mean on both tests. Thus, his or her positions on the scale for both tests are the same.

In considering the uses of the various measures of variability, ease and quickness of computation are in the following order: range, quartile deviation, and standard deviation. When the reliability of the measures is compared, the reverse is true. Thus, standard deviations from repeated random samples cluster closer together than do other variability measures. As will be explained later, quartile deviations from repeated samples range about 25% more than do standard deviations. Specific uses of the variability measures follow.

Range   In random sampling, the range is subject to the greatest fluctuation as compared with the other measures of variability. As a consequence, it is the most unreliable of these measures; only 2 scores determine it, the lowest and the highest. An extreme score at either end will distort this variability indicator. For example, for 2 groups of 100 subjects each, 98 subjects in both groups may have scores between 75 and 125, a range of 50. But, if group A had an extreme score of 140, while group B did not, the group A range would be 65. The 1 extreme score in this illustration carries far too much weight in describing variability of the scores in group A that 1 score in 100 should.

However, the range does have an important use when a knowledge of the total spread of scores is wanted. In physical education and athletics, extreme scores are frequently of great interest in the news media: the tall and the short basketball player, the heavy football lineman, the speedy back, the youngest female world champion swimmer, and the like.

Quartile Deviation.   According to the definition given, the quartile deviation is used to indicate variability when the median is the measure of central tendency. Both of these measures are obtained by counting scores. Therefore, both have comparable characteristics, which accounts for their close association in descriptive statistics.

The quartile deviation is uninfluenced by the upper and lower 25% of the scores. These scores may be located anywhere below the first quartile and above the third quartile without affecting the amount. Thus, a fault of the range is avoided by cutting off the extremes in the distribution. Inasmuch as one-half of the distribution is cut off at the two ends combined, great importance is placed on the center mass of scores when the quartile deviation is used to describe the variability of a distribution of scores. Other situations in which the median is the appropriate measure of central tendency also apply to the quartile deviation as the appropriate measure of variability.

Standard Deviation.   By definition given, the standard deviation is used as the measure of variability when the mean is the measure of central tendency. Both these measures are obtained from the actual distance of scores in the distribution rather than from their order. So both have common characteristics, which is the reason for their close association in describing the performance of a group. Whenever the mean is the appropriate indicator of central tendency, the standard deviation is appropriate to describe variability.

The standard deviation is utilized when coefficients of correlation and other statistics are to be computed. It is the only measure of variability encountered in advanced statistics. The standard deviation is also used extensively in the construction of various test scales, as presented later.

Research Uses

Two illustrations of the use of variability measures in research will be presented here. These uses are related (1) to the equating of groups for experimentation or for study in other ways, and (2) to the presentation of growth data.

Equating Groups.   In experimental research, it may be desirable to equate two or more groups on the basis of test scores. This is usually done by a process of matching—that is, of placing individuals with like scores (approximately) in separate groups. When the matching process is completed, the similarity of the groups should be shown statistically in so far as the test scores are concerned. This similarity is usually indicated by giving the mean and the standard deviation of the test scores for each group. If these are nearly alike, equation is accepted. Thus it is demonstrated that not only are the central values the same but that the spread of scores in the different groups is also comparable.

To illustrate this procedure, the equating of groups by Clarke and Jarman in a study of the scholastic achievement of boys 9, 12, and 15 years of age as related to 5 strength and growth measures is cited.[4] The strength and growth measures were Rogers' Strength Index, Rogers' Physical Fitness Index, Rogers' Arm Strength Score, McCloy's Classification Index, and Wetzel's Developmental Level. For each strength and growth measure at each age, 2 groups of 20 boys were formed in the following manner. Two subjects were selected at a time; these subjects had intelligence quotients (IQ) as nearly equal as possible, but one had a high score and the other had a low score on a given growth variable. Thus in each instance, high and low scoring groups on the strength and growth measures were established, with the groups having comparable IQs.

The equating process was repeated 15 times, once at each of the 3 ages for each of the 5 experimental variables. To show the degree the groups were equated by IQs, the means and standard deviations for each equational operation were computed. In Table 7.6 the results of the equations for the 9-year-old boys are presented. The differences between the IQ means ranged from .01 to .50 IQ points; the differences between the standard deviations varied from .00 to 1.35 IQ points. Although tests of significance for the differences between the means and standard deviations are not given here, such differences were found to be slight.

---

[4] H. Harrison Clarke and Boyd O. Jarman, "Scholastic Achievement of Boys 9, 12, and 15 Years of Age as Related to Various Strength and Growth Measures," *Research Quarterly*, 32, No. 2 (May 1961), 155.

TABLE 7.6   Intelligence Quotient Means and Standard Deviations
for Nine-Year-Old Boys in Five Equated Groups

Test Groups	IQ Means			IQ Standard Deviations		
	High group	Low group	Diff.	High group	Low group	Diff.
Strength Index	106.52	106.53	.01	8.15	9.50	1.35
Physical Fitness Index	107.50	108.00	.50	7.25	7.50	.25
Arm Strength Score	105.75	105.50	.25	9.45	8.83	.62
Classification Index	108.75	109.25	.50	8.85	8.60	.25
Development Level	109.00	109.50	.50	9.00	9.00	.00

Growth Study Results.   Growth studies encompass a diversity of detectable and measurable changes in size, shape, and function that occur in living organisms with the passing of time; and the degree of individual differences is defined by measures of variability. Common statistics utilized are mean, standard deviation, coefficient of variation, and range.

In the Medford Boy's Growth Study, Clarke and Wickens presented maturity, structural, muscular strength, and motor ability growth curves of boys 9 through 15 years of age.[5] Cross-sectional samples of 40 boys at each age served as subjects. Table 7.7 presents results from this study of skeletal age; tests were given within 2 months of each boy's birthday.

A number of observations may be made from this table, among which are the following:

1. In a normal population, chronological age and skeletal age would be expected to coincide. However, for the Medford boys, the 10-year-olds were 5.6 months retarded; and the 15-, 13-, and 14-year-old boys were advanced by 4.3, 4.5, and 5.6 months, respectively.

2. The standard deviations did not change appreciably between ages 9 and 14 years inclusive; for these years, the largest standard deviation was 13.2 months at 11 years of age and the smallest was 11.2 months at 14 years of age, a difference of 1.97 months.

3. The greatest range of scores was 62 months (5 years, 2 months) at 13 years of age. All but the oldest 2 ages had ranges that equaled or exceeded 48 months, or 4 years.

4. The lower variability at age 15 years was thought at first to be due to a truncation effect of some of the boys reaching full maturity at

[5] H. Harrison Clarke and J. Stuart Wickens, "Maturity, Structural Strength, and Motor Ability Growth Curves of Boys 9 to 15 Years of Age," *Research Quarterly*, 33, No. 1 (March 1962), 26.

TABLE 7.7   Skeletal Age (Months): Central Tendency
and Variability of Boys Nine to Fifteen Years of Age

Chronological Age		Mean	Standard deviation	Range
Years	Months			
9	108	106.1	11.6	51
10	120	114.4	11.8	48
11	132	131.8	13.2	54
12	144	146.3	12.1	52
13	156	160.5	12.5	62
14	168	173.6	11.2	42
15	180	184.3	7.7	32

this age. However, subsequent testing with larger samples revealed as great a variability at 15 years as at the other ages. As
a consequence, this occurrence must be considered a sampling
circumstance.

NORMAL PROBABILITY CURVE

An understanding of the normal probability curve is essential for the
student of research. Upon it is based an understanding of reliability,
that important phase of statistics dealing with the interpretation of
statistical results. It is only through measures of reliability that the
true value of such obtained measures as means, standard deviations,
and coefficients of correlation can be understood and that tests of
significance can be made.

The normal curve is bilaterally symmetrical, with a high concentration of scores in the center and a sloping off toward the ends. The
frequency distribution of the 67 skeletal ages of 13-year-old boys (Table
7.1) resembles the normal curve. As is typical of small samples,
irregularities usually appear largely due to sampling error. However, it
may be *guessed* that this curve does not depart significantly from the
normal probability curve; whether or not this guess is tenable will be
tested in the next chapter. Such curves are typical of many sample
distributions based upon physical, mental, and psychological test
scores.

Principle of the Normal Curve

The principle of the normal curve is based upon the probable
occurrence of an event when the probability depends upon chance—
when each event has an equal chance of occurring. Thus, the occur-

rence of the event must be equally likely and must be mutually independent. By "mutually independent" is meant that one event has no effect on any other event. To illustrate: If a coin is flipped to determine heads or tails, each flip is unaffected—is independent—of flips made before and after; the chance remains 1 out of 2 that a head will fall.

The customary way of introducing the statistics of probability is to refer to various games of chance such as tossing coins, rolling dice, or drawing cards. In each instance, there is a specified event, and this event can occur in more than one way. A tossed coin has 2 possibilities, a head or a tail; a die has 6 possible results; and drawing from a playing deck of cards permits 52 different outcomes. As can be seen, the chance occurrences of the events vary. However, all can be expressed as *probability ratios*, with the number of times a given event can occur as the numerator and the total number of possible outcomes as the denominator. Thus, the probability ratios for the above examples are: $\frac{1}{2}$, 1 chance in 2 to toss a head; $\frac{1}{6}$, 1 chance in 6 to roll a given number on a die, say a 5; $\frac{1}{52}$, to draw a given card, such as the ace of spades.

As shown in flipping a coin, the chances are even, or 1 in 2, that it will come down heads, and there is the same probability that it will come down tails. These probabilities add to 1.00, or certainty of occurrence: $\frac{1}{2} + \frac{1}{2} = 1.00$. If two coins are flipped, there are four possibilities, as follows:

a	b	a	b	a	b	a	b
H	H	H	T	T	H	T	T

Thus, the chances of both coins falling heads is 1 in 4; 1 head and 1 tail, 1 chance in 2; and of both tails, 1 chance in 4. The ratios are: $\frac{1}{4} + \frac{1}{2} + \frac{1}{4} = 100$. If this process were to be carried still further, it would be found that there is 1 chance in 8 of getting all heads when 3 coins are flipped, and 1 chance in 1024 when 10 coins are tossed.

The same ratio of chance probabilities in flipping coins is found in the binomial expansion theorem. To illustrate the above examples:

2 coins: $(H + T)^2 = H^3 + 2HT + T^2$

3 coins: $(H + T)^3 = H^3 + 3H^2T + 3HT^2 + T^3$

10 coins: $(H + T)^{10} = H^{10} + 10H^9T + 45H^8T^2 + 120H^7T^3$

$+ 210H^6T^4 + 252H^5T^5 + 210H^4T^6 + 120H^3T^7$

$+ 45H^2T^8 + 10HT^9 + T^{10}$

The normal distribution closely resembles the binomial distribution. With limited binomial expansion, even to $(H + T)^{10}$, the plotted graph would show a series of distinct bars, each bar erected at one of

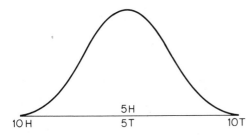

5H

10 H   5T   10 T

Figure 7.2. Theoretical Curve for Coin Tossing

the number of heads and tails. When an infinitely large number of coins is tossed, these bars merge, provided that the width of the graph is unchanged. Then the normal and binomial graphs become as one. Generally speaking, then, the two curves can be considered identical. A smoothed polygon representing the chance possibilities when 10 coins are tossed is shown in Figure 7.2.

This theory of normal distribution as applied to the chance occurrence of heads and tails in coin tossing is also applied to the chance occurrence of human characteristics. Heredity, environment, and training are the factors that influence the amount of any human attribute: biological, anthropometrical, motor, psychological, and sociological. These factors are a matter of chance, and the scores of these various factors will cluster about the middle and will be distributed in much the same way as in coin tossing.

The occurrence of the normal curve, however, whether it be in coin tossing or in the presence of human traits, depends upon two very important factors.

1. The occurrence of the event must depend upon *chance*. If skill in coin tossing, which influences the results, is present, the requisite of chance is not satisfied; the results are biased and a normal distribution will not result. The same situation prevails when loaded dice are rolled. Also, the strength of athletes would not logically be normally distributed since their scores tend toward the upper end of the distribution of strength for the population as a whole.

2. A *large number* of observations must be made. An even distribution of heads and tails would not be expected from only a few tosses; with a small number of flips, runs of heads would not be compensated for by opposite runs of tails, or vice versa, over many trials. But, with a large number of trials, the distribution would begin to take on a normal aspect. The same rule applies to human traits. For example, a teacher would not be justified in grading on a normal curve if the class were small, and so, would have only a few observations upon which to base grades. It would be possible

for the entire class to be exceptionally good, exceptionally poor, or quite a normal group.

Actually, the normal curve is a mathematical model—a theoretical curve as utilized in statistics. It should not be considered an actual and exact curve found in physical, motor, and psychological assessments. However, this model describes the distribution of human traits so well that its properties can be used to make inferences and predictions about them.

Properties of the Normal Curve

Although the normal curve is bilaterally symmetrical, not all symmetrical curves are normal, as will be demonstrated later in this chapter. Actually, there is only one normal curve as conceived as a mathematical model. The binomial expansion explanation above gives definiteness to the description of the normal curve. In addition, this curve has a general equation that constructs it mathematically.

Other characteristics of the normal curve are: (1) It is asymptotic to the base line—extends out at each end indefinitely without touching the base line. (2) The points of inflection—where the curve changes direction—are each one standard deviation from the ordinate at the mean. (3) The height of an ordinate at any given standard deviation distance from the mean ordinate is an exact proportion of the height of the mean ordinate. Thus, the area under the curve included between the mean ordinate and an ordinate at any given standard deviation from the mean will be an exact proportion of the total area under the curve.

Measures of central tendency and variability have definite statis-

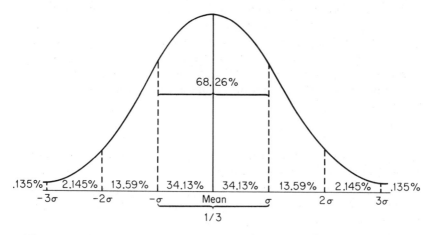

Figure 7.3. Properties of the Normal Curve in Terms of Standard Deviation

tical relationships to the normal curve, and as shown in Figure 7.3 as follows:

Central Tendency.   In the normal curve, the mean, the median, and the mode are all exactly in the center of the distribution and hence are numerically equal. This must be true, as it has been shown that the normal curve is perfectly bilaterally symmetrical; as a consequence, all the measures must fall in the exact middle of the curve.

Variability.   In the normal curve, measures of variability include fractional amounts of the total area of the curve, as expressed from central tendency. For example, a standard deviation is laid off in plus and minus distances from the mean on the base line of the normal curve. It will include the middle 68.26% of the scores, 34.13% either side of the mean; also, for all practical purposes, it will take up the middle third of the base line. Thus, as shown in Figure 7.3, 6 standard deviations encompass nearly the complete distribution; within these limits lie 99.73% of the scores, as will be seen next.

A most important factor related to the normal curve is the division of the curve into percentage areas. Knowing the mean and the standard deviation and knowing that the distribution is normal, the percentage of scores falling between the mean and any given standard deviation distance above or below the mean can be obtained from a standard table. Table 7.8 shows the fractional parts of the total area under the normal curve that correspond to distances on the base line and successive points from the mean in standard deviation units.

To illustrate the use of Table 7.8, go down the left margin, x/σ to 1.0; the next column headed .00 indicates 1.00σ from the mean. The percentage is 34.13; doubling this amount, $\pm\sigma = 68.26$. This is where the percentage spread for standard deviation, the middle 68.26% from the mean, came from in the definition for standard deviation. The percentages for other sigma distances from the mean may also be read from the table. Thus: $2\sigma = 47.71$, or 95.44 for $\pm 2\sigma$; $3\sigma = 49.865$, or 99.73 for $\pm 3\sigma$. To use the body of the table: $1.47\sigma = 42.92\%$; go down the left margin to 1.4 and over to column .07.

Divergence from Normality

Most physical, mental, and psychological traits are distributed normally in nature. Thus, test data usually result in a normal curve, provided a sufficiently large number of subjects is tested and a representative sample of the total population is obtained. This phenomenon is so well established that it is seldom challenged. However, there are traits that are not normally distributed. Further, some

TABLE 7.8   **Percentage Parts of the Total Area under the Normal Probability Curve Corresponding to Distances on the Base Line between the Mean and Successive Points from the Mean in Units of Standard Deviation**[a]

Example: Between the mean and a point 1.57 sigma is found 44.18 per cent of the entire area under the curve.

(x/σ)	.00	.01	.02	.03	.04	.05	.06	.07	.08	.09
.0	.00	.40	.80	1.20	1.60	1.99	2.39	2.79	3.19	3.59
.1	3.98	4.38	4.78	5.17	5.57	5.96	6.36	6.75	7.14	7.53
.2	7.93	8.32	8.71	9.10	9.48	9.87	10.26	10.64	11.03	11.41
.3	11.79	12.17	12.55	12.93	13.31	13.68	14.06	14.43	14.80	15.17
.4	15.54	15.91	16.28	16.64	17.00	17.36	17.72	18.08	18.44	18.79
.5	19.15	19.50	19.85	20.19	20.54	20.88	21.23	21.57	21.90	22.24
.6	22.57	22.91	23.24	23.57	23.89	24.22	24.54	24.86	25.17	25.49
.7	25.80	26.11	26.42	26.73	27.04	27.34	27.64	27.94	28.23	28.52
.8	28.81	29.10	29.39	29.67	29.95	30.23	30.51	30.78	31.06	31.33
.9	31.59	31.86	32.12	32.38	32.64	3.290	33.15	33.40	33.65	33.89
1.0	34.13	34.38	34.61	34.85	35.08	35.31	35.54	35.77	35.99	36.21
1.1	36.43	36.65	36.86	37.08	37.29	37.49	37.70	37.90	38.10	38.30
1.2	38.49	38.69	38.88	39.07	39.25	39.44	39.62	39.80	39.97	40.15
1.3	40.32	40.49	40.66	40.82	40.99	41.15	41.31	41.47	41.62	41.77
1.4	41.92	42.07	42.22	42.36	42.51	42.65	42.79	42.92	43.06	43.19
1.5	43.32	43.45	43.57	43.70	43.83	43.94	44.06	44.18	44.29	44.41
1.6	44.52	44.63	44.74	44.84	44.95	45.05	45.15	45.25	45.35	45.45
1.7	45.54	45.64	45.74	45.82	45.91	45.99	46.08	46.16	46.25	46.33
1.8	46.41	46.49	46.56	46.64	46.71	46.78	46.86	46.93	46.99	47.06
1.9	47.13	47.19	47.26	47.32	47.38	47.44	47.50	47.56	47.61	47.67
2.0	47.72	47.78	47.83	47.88	47.93	47.98	48.03	48.08	48.12	48.17
2.1	48.21	48.26	48.30	48.34	48.38	48.42	48.46	48.50	48.54	48.57
2.2	48.61	48.64	48.68	48.71	48.75	48.78	48.81	48.84	48.87	48.90
2.3	48.93	48.96	48.98	49.01	49.04	49.06	49.09	49.11	49.13	49.16
2.4	49.18	49.20	49.22	49.25	49.27	49.29	49.31	49.32	49.34	49.36
2.5	49.38	49.40	49.41	49.43	49.45	49.46	49.48	49.49	49.51	49.52
2.6	49.53	49.55	49.56	49.57	49.59	49.60	49.61	49.62	49.63	49.64
2.7	49.65	49.66	49.67	49.68	49.69	49.70	49.71	49.72	49.73	49.74
2.8	49.74	49.75	49.76	49.77	49.77	49.78	49.79	49.79	49.80	49.81
2.9	49.81	49.82	49.82	49.83	49.84	49.84	49.85	49.85	49.86	49.86
3.0	49.865									
3.1	49.903									
3.2	49.93129									
3.3	49.95166									
3.4	49.96631									
3.5	49.97674									
3.6	49.98409									
3.7	49.98922									
3.8	49.99277									
3.9	49.99519									

[a] An adaptation from Karl Pearson, *Tables for Statisticians and Biometricians* (Cambridge: Cambridge University Press, 1924).

distributions obtained may deviate from normality for various reasons even though the trait may be normal in the total population.

Some illustrations of traits that do not distribute normally are: The incidence of infectious diseases is greater during childhood than during middle and later years; the opposite is true for degenerative diseases. The curve of forgetting shows greatest decrease during a short time after learning. Mean learning curves may exhibit plateaus.

Illustrations of divergence from normality for test data obtained from testing traits normally distributed in nature are: (1) The test utilized to measure the trait is too hard or too easy, creating concentrations of scores at the lower and upper ends of the distribution, respectively. (2) The utilization of a biased, or nonrepresentative, sample could result in a skewed distribution; an illustration of such a biased sample would be obtaining strength test scores from athletes. (3) Tests from a small, homogeneous group would be likely to result in a narrow, peaked distribution, whereas a large, heterogeneous group would be likely to produce a broad, flat distribution. Rolling loaded dice would also result in a nonnormal distribution, as would coin tossing if a biased coin were used or the tosser could apply skill to this performance. Because of the value and utility of the normal curve, it may be desirable to test a given distribution for normality. If a nonnormal distribution is suspected from inspection, a chi-square test can be applied to determine generally whether or not the divergence is significant. This test, however, does not indicate the ways by which a given distribution departs from normality. For more specificity, other tests are available, especially for skewness and kurtosis.

Skewness. When the concentration of scores is significantly above or below the center, the distribution is skewed. Skewness may be positive or negative; the direction is designated after the "tail" rather than the "hump" of the curve. Therefore, in positive skewness the concentration of scores is below the center, and it tails off toward the right; in negative skewness, the opposite is true. The mean is lower than the median in negative skewness and higher than the median in positive skewness. Thus the mean is pulled toward the tail of the distribution, where more extreme scores exist.

A useful formula for determining skewness is based upon the location of the median (P_{50}) between the 10th and 90th percentiles. If the median is exactly between these percentiles, no skewness is present by this method. If the median is nearer the 10th percentile, the hump of the curve is toward the low end, so skewness is positive in direction; negative skewness is indicated when the median is nearer the 90th percentile. The formula is

$$Sk = \frac{P_{90} + P_{10}}{2} - P_{50} \qquad (7.8)$$

The percentiles for the 67 skeletal ages of 13-year-old boys used to illustrate statistical computations so far in this book were computed in Table 7.3. Substituting these values in the formula,

$$Sk = \frac{167.25 + 137.14}{2} - 152.54$$

$$= 152.20 - 152.54$$

$$= -.34$$

Thus, the skewness indicated is negative by $-.34$ months. The median is closer to P_{90} than to P_{10}. Whether or not the amount of $-.34$ months is a significant departure from normality remains to be seen; a test of significance will be presented later. This method of determining skewness is not the strongest measure. However, for most problems in physical education, it is considered adequate, as only rough approximations of skewness are needed.

Kurtosis.   Kurtosis refers to the height of the curve. The curve may be bilaterally symmetrical but still be a height different from the normal curve. Three terms designate the general height of a curve, as follows: *mesokurtic*, comparable to the normal curve; *leptokurtic*, higher or more peaked than the normal curve; and *platykurtic*, lower or flatter than the normal curve. Thus, a symmetrical, nonskewed curve may have the same mean as a normal curve distribution, but the standard deviations would differ: smaller for the leptokurtic and larger for the platykurtic distribution.

The formula for kurtosis is based on the ratio of scores between the middle 50% and middle 80% of the distribution. A Ku of .263 is the ratio for the normal curve. A smaller ratio indicates a leptokurtic tendency; a larger ratio indicates a platykurtic trend. The formula is

$$Ku = \frac{Q}{P_{90} - P_{10}} \qquad (7.8)$$

The skeletal ages of the 13-year-old boys will illustrate this computation. The values for P_{90} and P_{10} are given above in the skewness problem. Q is 7.68 months, as calculated in Table 7.5. Substituting in the formula,

$$Ku = \frac{7.68}{167.25 - 137.14} = .255$$

Thus, the distribution of skeletal ages has a leptokurtic tendency, as Ku

is smaller than the .263 necessary for a mesokurtic, or normal, distribution. The amount of leptokurtic trend is: .255 − .263 = −.008. It should be noted that calculated kurtosis is not interpreted as a deviation from zero but from .263.

As for the skewness measure given above, this method of determining kurtosis is not a strong one, but it does have usefulness in obtaining a rough approximation. Computation based on the moments of the distribution should be employed if a more exact result is wanted.

SCORING SCALES

The construction of scoring scales may be desirable in some physical education research, especially when tests are constructed. Percentiles were presented earlier in this chapter as one means of scaling test scores. It was shown, however, that percentiles bunch together in the middle of the distribution—68% within $\pm\sigma$ from the mean in a normal curve. Inequalities in scale values are also prevalent, especially marked at the tails of the distribution.

In order to avoid shortcomings of the percentile scale, a number of scoring scales based on the properties of the normal curve have been proposed and are in general use. These scales differ mostly in divisions made of the base line of the normal curve. Several of these scales are presented below. The data utilized, again, are from the 67 skeletal ages of 13-year-old boys: $M = 152.45$ months; $\sigma = 11.30$ months.

Z Scale

The Z scale consists of standard deviation distances of scores from the mean. Consequently, the mean has a Z score of 0; those scores above the mean have plus scale values and those scores below the mean have negative scale values. The formula for computing Z scores is

$$Z = \frac{X - M}{\sigma} \qquad (7.10)$$

To illustrate the use of this formula, given a boy's skeletal age of 165 months,

$$Z = \frac{165 - 152.45}{11.30} = \frac{12.55}{11.30} = 1.11$$

Also, given a skeletal age of 147 months,

$$Z = \frac{147 - 152.45}{11.30} = \frac{-5.45}{11.30} = -.48$$

Inasmuch as a Z score of 0 equals the mean and the scale has positive and negative values from 0, this scale is awkward to use. Other normal-curve scales convert M and σ into distributions in which all scores are positive and reasonably easy to handle.

T Scale

The concept of the T scale was originated by William A. McCall in the construction of a series of elementary school reading tests.[6] Zero in the T scale is located 5σ below the mean, with 100 at 5σ above the mean. The unit for the scale, or one "T" is $.1\sigma$ of the distribution. The mean T score, therefore, is 50; each 10 points above and below this point represent one standard deviation. Thus, the percentile equivalents of T scores of 40 and 60 are respectively 16 and 84 in a normal curve, inasmuch as 34% lies 1σ from the mean.

By mean and standard deviation. When the data are normally distributed, the T scale may be satisfactorily constructed from the mean and standard deviation. The process followed is to enter the mean as T_{50}; then add $.1\sigma$ for each T above the mean and subtract $.1\sigma$ for each T below the mean. To illustrate: For the 67 skeletal ages of 13-year-old boys, the mean was 152.45 months and the standard deviation was 11.30 months.

$$.1\sigma = .1(11.30) = 1.13 \text{ months}$$

Subtracting and adding 1.13 months for each T above and below the mean, we obtain the following results:

M and above		M and below	
T_{50}	152.45	T_{50}	152.45
T_{51}	153.58	T_{49}	151.32
T_{52}	154.71	T_{48}	150.19

and so on to the ends of the distribution. Each decile point on the T scale will be 1σ farther from the mean. Thus, by subtracting and adding 11.30 months from the mean of 152.45 months

M and above		M and below	
T_{50}	152.45	T_{50}	152.45
T_{60}	163.75	T_{40}	141.15
T_{70}	175.05	T_{30}	129.85
T_{80}	186.35	T_{20}	118.55

[6] William A. McCall, *Measurement* (New York: The Macmillan Company, 1939), Ch. 22.

When the frequency table for these data was constructed, the low score was 128 months and the high score was 182 months. It will be observed in the above explanation that T_{20} and T_{80} exceeded these extreme scores. However, this situation is typical of the T scale, since scores beyond $\pm 3\sigma$ are rare in a normal distribution. The situation here is further aggravated by the small number of scores (67) upon which to construct the T scale.

On the credit side, this method of constructing the T scale has advantages: The scale is simple to construct once the mean and standard deviation are known; irregularities within the distribution are ignored, thus are smoothed out; all scores in the distribution are awarded scale values when gaps exist in the original data, as in the illustration (i.e., all scores from 125 to 182 months are not found); and the scale may be extended to provide for extreme scores if desired.

By percentage amounts. As indicated, construction of the T scale from the mean and standard deviation is suggested when the data upon which the scale is based are normal. However, when the test data are not symmetrical, the method is not appropriate. When data are significantly skewed, the T scale should be constructed by normalizing standard scores. This normalizing process is accomplished by using percentage amounts from the mean for standard deviation equivalents. For example, 34.13% above the mean is the percentage equivalent of 1σ in a normal curve; thus, the T score is 60, whether or not the distance is exactly 1σ.

Construction of the T scale by percentage amounts can be accomplished from the individual scores arranged in order of a frequency table with an interval of 1. However, this process will be explained here utilizing the frequency table contructed in Table 7.1 for the skeletal ages of the 67 boys 13 years of age. As shown in Table 7.9, the following steps are necessary:

1. Construct a frequency table from the individual scores in the usual manner; the step intervals and frequencies from Table 7.1 appear in columns 1 and 2.
2. Cumulative frequencies are given in column 3. The frequencies in column 2 are added cumulatively from the bottom.
3. In column 4, add the *cum f* below each interval to ½ the scores in the interval. For example, take the interval, 140-144: Add the 10 scores below the interval (*cum f*) to one-half the scores in the interval (½ of 7 = 3.5); 10 + 3.5 = 13.5. A second illustration for interval, 165-169: 57 scores from the *cum f* column added to ½ of 6, the scores in the interval; 57 + 3 = 60.

TABLE 7.9 Calculation of *T* Scores by Percentage Amounts Method (Data from Table 7.1)

(1) Skeletal age Months Intervals	(2) f	(3) cum f	(4) cum f below score + ½ f for given score	(5) Column 4 in percents	(6) T scores	(7) T Score Values: Midpoints
180-184	1	67	66.5	99.75	78	182
175-179	1	66	65.5	98.25	71	177
170-174	2	65	64.0	96.00	68	172
165-169	6	63	60.0	90.00	63	167
160-164	7	57	53.5	80.25	59	162
155-159	11	50	44.5	66.75	54	157
150-154	14	39	31.0	46.50	49	152
145-149	8	24	21.0	31.50	45	147
140-144	7	17	13.5	20.25	42	142
135-139	7	10	6.5	9.75	37	137
130-134	2	3	2.0	3.0	31	132
125-129	1	1	.5	.75	26	127
	N = 67					

4. Column 4 is changed to percentages in column 5. To do this, first obtain a percentage rate—the percentage value of a single score. In this problem, the rate is: $1/67 = 1.5$ (1.49 is slightly more accurate). This rate is multiplied by each *cum f* in column 4. For example, again take the interval 140-144: The column 4 amount is 13.5; $13.5 \times 1.5 = 20.25$.

5. The T score for the column 5 percentages may be read directly from Table 7.10 and listed in column 6. To illustrate with the 160-164 interval: The column 5 value is 80.25; entering the percentage from Table 7.10, the nearest T score is 59.

6. As developed from a frequency table with intervals greater than 1, the T score values are the midpoints of the various intervals; these are given in column 7. Thus, 147 months, midpoint of the interval 145-149, has a T score of 45.

7. In constructing a T scale, however, T scores for all scale values within the distribution should be provided; therefore, interpolations should be performed.

TABLE 7.10   Percentage T-Scores Equivalents

The per cents refer to the percentage of the total frequency below a given score $+\frac{1}{2}$ of the frequency on that score. T scores are read directly from the given percentages.*

Per cent	T score	Per cent	T score	Per cent	T score	Per cent	T score
.0032	10	2.87	31	53.98	51	98.21	71
.0048	11	3.59	32	57.93	52	98.61	72
.007	12	4.46	33	61.79	53	98.93	73
.011	13	5.48	34	65.54	54	99.18	74
.016	14	6.68	35	69.15	55	99.38	75
.023	15	8.08	36	72.57	56	99.53	76
.034	16	9.68	37	75.80	57	99.65	77
.048	17	11.51	38	78.81	58	99.74	78
.069	18	13.57	39	81.59	59	99.81	79
.097	19	15.87	40	84.13	60	99.865	80
.13	20	18.41	41	86.43	61	99.903	81
.19	21	21.19	42	88.49	62	99.931	82
.26	22	24.20	43	90.32	63	99.952	83
.35	23	27.43	44	91.92	64	99.966	84
.47	24	30.85	45	93.32	65	99.977	85
.62	25	34.46	46	94.52	66	99.984	86
.82	26	38.21	47	95.54	67	99.9890	87
1.07	27	42.07	48	96.41	68	99.9928	88
1.39	28	46.02	49	97.13	69	99.9952	89
1.79	29	50.00	50	97.72	70	99.9968	90
2.28	30						

*T scores under 10 or above 90 differ slightly so are not included here.

For the data in this problem, the T scales by both methods coincide quite well. For example, the values at T_{60} by the two methods are 164 months by the mean standard deviation process and 163 months by the percentage amounts procedure. These results would be expected from data that are as bilaterally symmetrical as those in this problem; no appreciable skewness is present. If the data had been significantly skewed, however, larger differences between the scales by the two methods would have occurred.

Although the T scale is the most commonly used of the standard-score scales, a common fault of the scale is that its ends are never or seldom utilized. As shown before (Table 7.8), 99.73% of the scores in a normal distribution fall between $\pm 3\sigma$; T_{20} and T_{80} are at these points. Table 7.10 also demonstrates this fact; T scores on this table extend only between 10 and 90. T scores under 10 and above 90 differ so slightly in percentage amounts that they cannot be read as two-place numbers. As a consequence of this characteristic of the T scale, other scales have been proposed based upon standard scores but placing 0 and 100 on the scales nearer to the mean in order to utilize all the scale.

6-Sigma Scale

A 6-sigma scale has been utilized by a number of investigators in physical education measurement. Zero for this scale is located 3 sigmas below the mean, and 100 is 3 sigmas above the mean. The scale can be constructed by the same two methods as for the T scale. These procedures are explained below, again utilizing the 67 skeletal ages of boys 13 years of age.

By mean and standard deviation.   The steps in constructing the 6-sigma scale are as follows:

1. *Locate the zero scale value.*   The zero scale value is three sigmas below the mean. Multiplying the σ of 11.30 months by 3 and subtracting from the mean,

$$11.30 \text{ months} \times 3 = 33.90 \text{ months}$$

$$152.45 \text{ months} - 33.90 \text{ months} = 118.55 \text{ months.}$$

Thus, the 6-sigma scale value of zero is 118.55 months.

2. *Determine the rate of increase for each scale value.*   The 6-sigma scale of 100 points is spread over 6 sigmas, $\pm 3\sigma$ from M. The distance, then, is: 6×11.30 months $= 67.80$ months. Each scale point will be $1/100$ of this distance, or $(67.80/100) = .68$ months.

3. ***Assign scale values.*** Starting with the zero value of 118.55 months, add .68 months for each point on the scale. For each decile position on the scale, this amount is .68 × 10 = 6.80 months. The assignment of scale values for each decile position is shown in Table 7.11. In the actual construction of a 6-sigma scale, of course, values for all scale points would be given. The decision of whether or not to use fractions in the scale depends on the range. For a large range, fractions would not be used; for a small range, they would be used.

By percentage amounts. Without a special table, as prepared for the T scale, the construction of the 6-sigma scale by use of percentage amounts when the data are significantly skewed is more complicated; so it will not be described in detail here. The process requires the use of Table 7.8. From this table, percentages of scores for the sigma equivalents of the scale values, 0 to 100, must be determined; the values on the scale are then derived in terms of percentages from the mean rather than from standard deviation distances.

Neilson, Cozens, and associates resolved the problem of skewness in a simple way when they encountered significant skewness in constructing a large number of 6-sigma achievement scales in physical education activities.[7] They estimated the size of the standard deviation

TABLE 7.11   **Calculation of 6-Sigma Scale by Mean Standard Deviation Process in Deciles**

Mean = 152.45 Months
Standard Deviation = 11.30 Months
Decile Scale Value = 6.80 Months

6-σ Position	Calculation	6-σ Decile table	
		6-σ Scale	Score
0	118.55		
10	118.55 + 6.80 = 125.35	100	187
20	125.35 + 6.80 = 132.15	90	180
30	132.15 + 6.80 = 138.95	80	173
40	138.95 + 6.80 = 145.75	70	166
50	145.75 + 6.80 = 152.55	60	159
60	152.55 + 6.80 = 159.35	50	153
70	159.35 + 6.80 = 166.15	40	146
80	166.15 + 6.80 = 172.95	30	139
90	172.95 + 6.80 = 179.75	20	132
100	179.75 + 6.80 = 186.55	10	125
		0	119

[7]One reference among several is Frederick W. Cozens and N. P. Neilson, *Achievement Scales in Physical Education Activities for Boys and Girls in Elementary and Junior High Schools* (New York: A. S. Barnes & Company, Inc., 1934), p. 169.

above the mean and below the mean. These estimates were obtained by dividing by three the range of scores above the mean and the range of scores below the mean. The quotients thus obtained were used in place of the standard deviation values; scales on either side of the mean had different values as reflected by the two "standard deviation equivalents."

Other Standard-Score Scales

A fourth type of scoring table based upon standard deviation distances is the Hull scale, which extends 3½ sigmas either side of the mean. It goes beyond the somewhat narrow limits of the 6-sigma scale, but it does not leave the ends of the scale so generally unused as does the T scale.

The stanine is a fifth scoring scale based upon the properties of the normal curve. In this instance, a 9-point scale is used. The standard deviation distances for points on the scale are: 1, below -1.75; 2, between -1.75 and -1.25; 3, between -1.25 and $-.75$; 4, between $-.75$ and $-.25$; 5, between $-.25$ and $+.25$; 6, between $+.25$ and $+.75$; 7, between $+.75$ and $+1.25$; 8, between $+1.25$ and $+1.75$; 9, above $+1.75$.

The standard score scale for the Graduate Record Examination is a variation of the T scale: The mean equals 500 instead of 50; the standard deviation for scale points is 100 instead of 10; and the scale extends only to three standard deviations instead of five. Thus, GRE scores of 200 and 800 are respectively three sigmas below and above the GRE mean of 500.

Comparison of Various Scales

Figure 7.4 is presented to compare the various scoring scales as related to the normal curve. The percentile scale is the only one that does not divide the base line into equal segments. As discussed above, the percentile scale bunches in the middle, as that is where the bulk of the scores are located; 68.26% are within ±1σ of the mean, which represents about one-third of the range of scores. The test-score increments between percentiles is not constant but varies, especially toward the tails of the distribution.

The decision as to which scale, other than the percentile, the investigator will use is largely pragmatic—the scale that best fits the data or that is liked the best after evaluating their characteristics. Selection of the T scale will mean under normal circumstances that the parts of the scale below 20 and above 80 will be seldom utilized, as these points are located ±3σ from the mean. Psychologically, too, T_{20} does not seem too low, but it is; and T_{80} does not seem too high, but it is exceptional. However, this scale can be extended by the mean standard deviation construction method to ±5σ if desired in order to accommodate extreme scores.

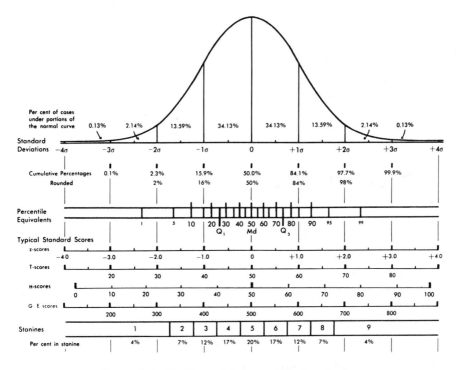

Figure 7.4. The Normal Curve and Various Scales

With the 6-sigma scale, the entire scale from 0 to 100 will be utilized. However, occasional scores may fall beyond these points. This is not a serious matter, as the number that do so will be very small if normal probability prevails.

The Hull scale, which extends to $\pm3.5\sigma$, may be considered a compromise between the T scale and the 6-sigma scale, and the occurrence of an extreme score falling outside the scale is more remote than for the 6-sigma scale. However, an exceptional score can fall outside this scale. In constructing Hull scales for Medford Boys' Growth Study data, a check was run on the number of scores that were sufficiently extreme as to extend above 100 points and below 1 point in the distribution. In one study, a total of 412 boys were tested at six ages, 9 to 14 years inclusive, with eight anthropometric tests; thus, for the eight scales, 3,296 entries were made (412 boys × 8 scales = 3,296). For all scales, only seven entries (.02%) were above 100, and only one entry was below 1.[8]

[8]Charles J. Becker, "The Construction of Maturity and Anthropometric Test Norms for Boys Nine Through Fourteen Years of Age" (Master's thesis, University of Oregon, 1960).

8
Inferential Statistics

Chapter 7 presented descriptive statistics, including measures of central tendency, percentiles, measures of variability, and normal probability. In this chapter, inferential statistics are explained. This form of statistics is vital for statistical interpretations and for the application of tests of significance.

MEANING OF RELIABILITY

In research, the actual or true measure of any quality in a total population is seldom, if ever, obtained. For example, in the development of norms, it is impractical, if not impossible, to test all individuals in the population for which the test is intended. Fortunately, such a practice is unnecessary; a sample, when properly drawn, closely resembles all individuals in the population.

The term *population* means all individuals in a defined group. A statistic, such as the mean or standard deviation, computed from all individuals in a population for a given variable is known as a *parameter*. Population parameters are seldom, if ever, computed, especially when populations are extensive; rather, samples are drawn from large populations, and sample statistics are computed from which corresponding parameters are inferred. Population parameters for the mean and standard deviation are symbolized by $\overline{M}$ and $\overline{\sigma}$, each with a bar over it; the symbols for samples will remain herein as M and σ, without the bar.[1]

A population is designated in terms of the research problem, as is the specific variable or trait under investigation. To illustrate: If the investigator were to study the weights of 12-year-old boys in a state, then all 12-year-old boys in the state would constitute the population. Thus, to determine the parameter mean weight of 12-year-old boys, all boys of this age in the state must be tested. To do so, however, would place a great and unnecessary hardship on the investigator. However, a sample can be drawn from this population. It is the usual procedure to depend upon sampling and to assume that the sample represents the whole, which it does within definable limits to be considered later.

Sampling is a common practice in society today, being employed in such diverse fields as business, politics, science, agriculture, medicine, psychology, education, and recreation. The various opinion polls are examples. Around the time of national elections, these polls predict from samples how the American public will vote. Such samples actually are minute compared with the millions of citizens who actually cast ballots; yet, they are surprisingly close in anticipating election results. When one buys a packet of seeds to plant, the germination rate is given. How does the grower know this rate? Certainly, those particular seeds had not been planted to make the determination. Rather, a sample had been drawn from the huge number of seeds from which those in the packet came. Much useful information can be inferred from observation secured from a few experimental animals, a handful of corn, a small section of human tissue, a pinprick of blood, or a group of schoolchildren.

The United States government hires thousands of men and women to gather and compile and draw conclusions from statistical facts that help keep the nation functioning. Eliminate from any government department, or any business, those who specialize in sampling data, and management is soon in trouble. The gathering and classifying of basic facts from samples provide the foundation for logical, inductive reasoning. From these samples, general truths are inferred.

After a sample is obtained, a measure of reliability can be applied to any statistic computed from it, say the mean. The reliability measure indicates by inference how closely the sample corresponds to the parameter mean—the unknown mean of the entire population. Thus the reliability of the mean provides the limits within which a sample mean approximates the corresponding parameter mean. What is true for the reliability of the mean is equally true for other statistics

[1]In some statistics books, M and σ are reserved for parameter mean and standard deviation, and $\overline{X}$ and S for sample mean and standard deviation.

computed from a sample. Consequently, statistical methods are available for determining the reliability of the mean, median, standard deviation, skewness, percentage, coefficient of correlation, and so forth.

SAMPLING

Processes

If the inferences concerning facts or characteristics of a population obtained from a sample are to be valid, obviously the sample must adequately represent the population. By the very nature of sampling, complete agreement between sample and population will not be achieved, except by coincidence. However, great uniformity between the two does result when a proper sampling process is applied. Yet a sampling error does occur; the nature and amount of this sampling error will receive attention later in this chapter.

Sampling procedures were discussed in the conduct of surveys in Chapter 6, indicating that a sample is representative, or random as it is frequently called, when each person in the population from which the sample is obtained has an equal chance of being chosen. A good method of drawing a random sample is to use a table of random numbers, such as those prepared by Fisher and Yates.[2]

Samples, of course, can be biased. Bias occurs when the members of a sample are selected in a manner that favors one result over another. For example, a random sample of college athletes may be drawn; generalization from this sample to the characteristics of athletes could be properly made. But, if generalizations to all college students were made, the sample would be considered biased, for if physical and motor traits were being studied, the athletes would be a select group.

The investigator should be alert to the possibility of biased sampling. Conditions should be controlled to prevent this occurrence or, if uncontrolled, to discover their effects. When bias is known or suspected, a more detailed than usual description of the samples should be made, and generalizations from the results should be restricted to the nature of the sample. For example, in pack-carrying studies, the subjects were male college students, most of whom were majoring in physical education.[3] Anticipating that a bias had been introduced by

[2]Ronald A. Fisher and Frank Yates, *Statistical Tables for Biological, Agricultural, and Medical Research* (New York: Hefner Publishing Company, Inc. 1953).

[3]H. Harrison Clarke, Clayton T. Shay, and Donald K. Mathews, "Strength Decrements from Carrying Various Army Packs on Military Marches," *Research Quarterly*, 26, No. 3 (October 1955), 253.

using physical education majors, the sample was further described in terms of the heights, weights, Strength and Physical Fitness Indices, and somatotypes of the subjects.

Sampling Theory

The statistics of sampling are of utmost importance to research in physical education. In most, if not all, scientific studies, the investigator will use a sample and will wish to infer from the results to the total population from which the sample was taken. An investigator is not content with a statement that the findings are limited only to the particular subjects tested.

An understanding of the elementary principles of sampling may be gained from an illustration. Kirchner and Glines surveyed the muscular fitness of Eugene, Oregon, elementary school children utilizing the Kraus-Webber test; 1,200 boys and girls composed a random sample from a much larger population.[4] The investigators found that 38.1% of the sample failed one or more of the tests. This sample percentage may *not* be accepted unconditionally but should be considered only an *approximation* of the true value of the population. In other words, the true failure percentage of all elementary school boys and girls may well be some other value than that of the sample percentage. However, since the sample was part of the population, the deviation from this totality is in small amounts, and since the members of the sample were drawn at random from a table of random numbers, chance dictates the amount of the sampling error for the percentage obtained from samples of a given size. What is said here about the percentage of failures on the test can be repeated for other statistics, such as the mean and standard deviation.

Statistical methods are available that provide a definitive statement of the fidelity with which a sample represents its population. Such statements are made in terms of normal probability; the inferences made are related to the characteristics of the normal curve. The reason this can be done is that the distribution of means from repeated samples of the same size from the same population corresponds to a normal curve. Theoretically, the correspondence is identical; in practice, nonsignificant deviations would be found between an exact normal curve and an actual distribution of means obtained from repeated samples of a given population.

To illustrate this effect, one of the authors had 80 members of his statistics classes twice toss 7 coins 50 times; these combined tosses provided 1 series of 100 times tossed. The mean number of heads was

---

[4]Glenn Kirchner and Don Glines, "Comparative Analysis of Eugene, Oregon, Elementary School Children Using the Kraus-Weber Test of Minimum Muscular Fitness," *Research Quarterly*, 30, No. 1 (March 1959), 75.

computed for each of the 50 and 100 tosses. These 50 and 100 trials constituted samples from an infinite number of tosses that could be made. The means of these tosses provided sample means that could be incorporated into a distribution of sample means. The distribution of sample means for the 50 and 100 tosses formed appear in Table 8.1.

The distributions of coin-tossing means resemble the normal curve; the concentration of means in the center and the tailing off toward the ends is obvious. With 8 possibilities for heads (0 to 7 inclusive) for the 7 coins, the middle—or theoretical—mean is 3.50. The coin-tossing means for the 2 distributions are close to this theoretical mean, 3.53 for the 50 tosses and 3.51 for the 100 tosses. The overall number of tosses was 8,000. According to the tabulations, if a single sample had been drawn, the mean would most likely have been around 3.50. For the 50 tosses, the chances of drawing a sample with a mean between 2.96 and 3.03 is only 1 in 160, as only one of the 160 means fell in that interval; for 100 tosses, no chance is indicated that the sample mean would fall that low.

The distribution of sample means was more extensive for the tosses of 50 than for the tosses of 100. In Table 8.1, the upper and lower 2 intervals do not have sample means for the tosses of 100. This situation is further reflected in the standard deviations of the 2 distributions. The standard deviation of .20 for the 50 tosses is 25% greater than the

TABLE 8.1 Distributions of Sample Means from Coin Tossing Mean Number of Heads from 50 and 100 Tosses

Mean intervals	Frequencies	
	50 Tosses	100 Tosses
4.00-4.07	2	
3.92-3.99	3	
3.84-3.91	5	2
3.76-3.83	14	4
3.68-3.75	16	8
3.60-3.67	26	10
3.52-3.59	24	12
3.44-3.51	27	16
3.36-3.43	17	13
3.28-3.35	14	8
3.20-3.27	3	6
3.12-3.19	6	1
3.04-3.11	2	
2.96-3.03	1	
N	160	80
M	3.53	3.51
σ	.20	.16

standard deviation of .16 for the 100 tosses. These results are typical and illustrate a sampling truth: The larger the samples taken from the same population, the closer together the repeated sample means.

The standard deviation of a distribution of sample means, of course, is not the same as the standard deviation of a single sample. In the former instance, the standard deviation will be several times smaller, depending on the size of the samples. The standard deviation of a distribution of sample means reflects its sampling error; the smaller the standard deviation, the smaller the error. The term *sampling error* does not intimate that a mistake has been made in sampling. Rather, it refers to the amount of difference that would logically be expected between samples as a consequence of the fact that they were independently drawn from a large population and so will probably differ from each other.

In research, the investigator does not draw repeated samples in order to establish a sampling error. Instead, one sample is drawn and related to the population mean by use of a statistic known as the *standard error*. The standard error of the mean of a given random sample is comparable to the standard deviation of a distribution of sample means of the same size as the given sample. The reference to the population mean is made by inference that applies normal probability concepts. Inference is necessary because investigators seldom, if ever, know their population means, as all subjects in the population are not tested. This situation is unlike the coin-tossing illustration, where a theoretical "population mean" exists.

The above comments about the sampling error of the mean can be applied to other statistics. Thus, comparable results would occur if distributions of other sample statistics were obtained. Standard error formulas to indicate sampling reliability are available for the standard deviation, percentages, coefficients of correlation, and other statistics of use to the investigator.

Statistical Power

Baumgartner criticized sampling practices employed in studies published in the 1971 *Research Quarterly*, especially as related to small sample size and faulty random selection methods.[5] Christensen and Christensen supported this criticism by presenting the statistical power of samples of various sizes, basing their observations on 1975 *Research Quarterly* articles.[6] It is obvious, and is demonstrated in this

[5]Ted A. Baumgartner, "Remarks Concerning Sampling Used in the *Research Quarterly*," *Research Quarterly*, 45, No. 2 (May 1974), 215.

[6]James C. Christensen and Carlene E. Christensen, "Statistical Power Analysis of Health, Physical Edcation, and Recreation Research," *Research Quarterly*, 48, No. 1 (March 1977), 204.

chapter, that the larger the samples the less the sampling error. In other words, a large sample more closely represents the total population than does a small sample; thus, it has greater statistical power. When a small sample is employed in a study, the investigator must accept the possibility that results may be insignificant because of the inevitable large sampling error. Only large differences or effects can be detected from small samples.

STANDARD ERROR OF LARGE SAMPLES

The *standard error* is the principal reliability measure in current use. In the statistics and research of 40 years ago, another such measure, the *probable error*, was also in common use. Thus, the scientific literature of this earlier time contains frequent reference to probable error. However, in this book, attention will be given to standard error only.

Factors Affecting Reliability

Three major factors affect the reliability of a statistic or, to express it differently, show how nearly a sample statistic approximates the same statistic for the total population. These three factors are presented below, using the mean as the statistic for purposes of illustration.

Representativeness of Sample. This factor does not need further explanation here, as it has been stressed in some detail that if the investigator wishes to infer from the results of a sample to the population from which is was drawn, as invariably happens—the sample must be random, or representative. As has been shown, normal probability is definitely lacking if the factor of selection or bias enters into the process.

Size of Sample. The second factor that influences the reliability of the mean is the number of subjects contained in the sample. It can be readily demonstrated that a sample mean may be changed by the addition of one new subject to the sample and that this new subject will affect the mean much more when it is based on a few scores than when a large number is involved. For example, the addition of one extreme score to a sample of 10 subjects will cause a greater change in the mean than the addition of a similar score to a sample of 1,000 subjects, as the score counts for less in the larger group ($1/10$ as contrasted with $1/1000$).

Further, the reliability of the mean increases not in direct proportion to the number of subjects upon which it is based but in proportion to the square root of the number. Thus, the reliability of the mean obtained from 50 subjects is not twice that from 25; 100 cases would be needed to obtain twice the reliability. To illustrate:

$$\sqrt{25} = 5; \qquad \sqrt{100} = 10.$$

Variability.   The third factor that affects the reliability of a statistic is the variability of the sample. The more variable the distribution, the farther scores can be from the mean. The farther scores are removed from the mean, the greater the fluctuation of scores that affect the sample mean. This phenomenon can also be noted by the effect of extreme scores on a sample mean. To illustrate: An extreme weight of 225 pounds will have a greater effect on a sample mean of 150 pounds than will an extreme height of 76 inches on a sample mean of 65 inches.

The factor of variability is dependent upon the nature of the variable being considered. For example, the variability of weight is much greater than the variability of height for any given sample. This is an unavoidable situation, since heights simply do not vary to the same extent as weights. For the investigator to control variability would be either to change the nature of the sample or to introduce unwarranted bias into it.

Thus the reliability of the mean, or any other statistic, depends first upon the representativeness of the sample itself. When this condition has been met, the other two factors—the number of subjects and the variability of the distribution—can be accounted for in a formula.

Standard Error of the Mean

The reliability of the mean is directly proportional to the standard deviation of the population and inversely proportional to the square root of the size of the sample. The standard deviation of the population is not known; therefore, the standard deviation of the sample is used. This practice is satisfactory when samples are large; when samples are small, adjustments must be made, as explained later in this chapter. At this point, the large-sample application is made, even though the sample is not large. Thus, the standard error of the mean is

$$\sigma_M = \frac{\sigma}{\sqrt{N}}. \tag{8.1}$$

Taking skeletal age data in months from Tables 7.2 and 7.5: $M = 152.45$; $\sigma = 11.30$; $N = 67$. Substituting in the formula

$$\sigma_M = \frac{11.30}{\sqrt{67}} = \frac{11.30}{8.19} = 1.38$$

It will be noted in the standard error of the mean that the larger the number of cases and the smaller the deviation of the scores, or the greater the reliability of the sample mean, the less will be this measure. This fact was further demonstrated in Table 8.1, when the distribution of sample means for 100 coin tosses varied less than for 50 coin tosses.

As indicated earlier, the σ_M can be thought of as the σ of a distribution of sample means of the same size as the given sample. Not knowing the population mean but knowing the standard error of the sample mean, inferences can be made relative to the probable location of the population mean in relation to the sample mean. The chances of the population mean being close to the sample mean are much greater than that of being farther away. The validity of this assumption was demonstrated in the coin-tossing experiment when the distribution of sample means resembled a normal curve.

Therefore, using the sample mean and its standard error and applying normal probability proportions from Table 7.8, the inference can be made that the chances are 68.26 in 100 that the population mean is within one standard error either side of the sample mean. The 68.26 proportion is taken from the table in the same manner that standard deviation percentages were obtained in the preceding chapter. This same process can be extended to $\pm 3\sigma_M$.

Utilizing the skeletal age data, the following definitive statements may be made relative to the reliability of the sample of 67 12-year-old boys:

1. Chances are 68.26 in 100 that the population mean lies between 151.07 and 153.83 months: 152.45 ± 1.38.
2. Chances are 95.44 in 100 that the population mean lies between 149.69 and 155.21 months: $152.45 \pm 2 \times 1.38$.
3. Chances are 99.73 in 100 that the population mean lies between 148.31 and 156.59 months: $152.45 \pm 3 \times 1.38$.

If the investigator feels that the amount of the standard error is too large and wishes to obtain a smaller amount, the only recourse is to increase the size of the sample. As already indicated, the effect of sample size on reliability is in proportion to the square root of the number. This situation can be demonstrated with the following illustration of samples of 25 and 100, in which the standard deviation has been maintained as a constant, although in practice it would be expected to change somewhat with the addition of new cases to the sample:

$$\sigma_M = \frac{\sigma}{\sqrt{N}} = \frac{10}{\sqrt{25}} = 2.0$$

$$= \frac{10}{\sqrt{100}} = 1.0$$

Thus, the standard error for a sample of 25 is twice as large as for a sample of 100 subjects; the 100 sample has twice the reliability of the 25 sample.

This question is frequently asked: "How large a sample do I need?" There is no satisfactory answer to this question, except in terms of the amount of a predetermined standard error. Knowing the standard deviation and the standard error desired, the investigator can compute the number of subjects needed. In the above problem, if the standard error wanted were around 1.0 and the standard deviation were 10, the sample size would need to be 100.

Levels of Confidence

In considering the probable location of the population mean from the sample mean, the concept of levels of confidence has been developed. Two such levels of confidence have come into common use. The 2 levels are the .05 and .01, also stated as 5% and 1%. Other levels of confidence may be used if desired by the investigator, such as the .10, .02, and .001. This presentation will be limited to the .05 and .01 levels.

A level of confidence indicates the chances that the population mean falls outside the limits expressed. Thus, for the .05 level, the chances are 5 in 100 that the population mean is beyond the expressed limits and 95 in 100 that it is between. These limits are located in the following manner: The middle 95% of the normal probability curve is involved, or 47.5% either side of the mean. Entering the body of Table 7.8, 47.5% is $1.96\sigma_M$ from the mean. Therefore, the chances are 95 in 100 that the population mean lies between the sample mean and $\pm 1.96\sigma_M$; this middle 95% is known as the *confidence interval*. And, the chances are 5 in 100 that the population mean lies beyond the sample mean by $\pm 1.96\sigma_M$. To illustrate with the skeletal age problem,

$$M \pm 1.96\sigma_M$$

$$152.45 \pm 1.96 \times 1.38$$

$$152.45 \pm 2.70$$

By this level of confidence, the chances are 5 in 100 that the population mean lies beyond the limits of 149.75 and 155.15 months; there are 2½ chances that it lies below 149.75 and 2½ chances that it lies above 155.15 months.

At the .01 level of confidence, the chances are 1 in 100 that the population mean lies outside the limits expressed. These limits are located in the same manner as before, except for the .01 level. The middle 99% of the normal probability curve is involved; from Table 7.8, $\pm 2.58\sigma_M$ will encompass 49.5%. Again illustrating with the skeletal age problem,

$$M \pm 2.58\sigma_M$$

$$152.45 \pm 2.58 \times 1.38$$

$$152.45 \pm 3.56$$

Thus, the chances are 1 in 100 that the population mean lies beyond the limits of 148.89 and 156.01 months; there is one chance in 200 that it is below 148.89 and one chance in 200 that it is above 156.01.

Other Statistics

Standard errors are also available for other statistics presented so far. The formulas differ, but interpretation remains the same as for the mean. Each statistic is obtained from a sample; the purpose is to infer from it to the population statistic. Inferences can be made by application of normal probability, since the distribution of a given statistic from repeated samples resembles a normal curve, as was true for the mean.

Median. The standard error of the median may be computed from either the standard or quartile deviations as the measure of variability. The formulas are

$$\sigma_{Mdn} = \frac{1.25\sigma}{\sqrt{N}} \tag{8.2}$$

$$\sigma_{Mdn} = \frac{1.86Q}{\sqrt{N}} \tag{8.3}$$

The formula with Q (8.3) is the preferred one when the median is the appropriate measure of central tendency; for a normal distribution, either formula is satisfactory. Applying this formula to the skeletal age sample of 67 12-year-old boys ($Q = 7.65$ months),

$$\sigma_{Mdn} = \frac{1.86Q}{\sqrt{N}} = \frac{1.86 \times 7.65}{\sqrt{67}} = 1.74 \text{ months}$$

The standard error of the median is approximately 25% greater than the standard error of the mean. For this problem, the standard error of the mean, as computed above, was 1.38 months; the difference between the 2 standard errors (1.74 − 1.38) is .36, which is 25% higher. This demonstrates that the reliability of the mean is greater—is less subject to sampling fluctuations—than is the median.

Since its sampling error is greater, a larger sample is needed when the median is the measure of central tendency to produce a standard error of the same size as when the mean represents central tendency. In order to reduce the standard error of the median to the same magnitude as the mean, 57% more subjects are needed in the sample. To illustrate with the skeletal age problem: For the N of 67, a 57% increase in sample size equals 105. Using 105 in the formula and maintaining the same Q as before,

$$\sigma_{Mdn} = \frac{1.86\,Q}{\sqrt{N}} = \frac{1.86 \times 7.65}{\sqrt{105}} = 1.39 \text{ months}$$

It is, therefore, poor research economy to use the median instead of the mean if the reason is ease of computation. The median should only be used as central tendency when the mean is inappropriate because of extreme scores, skewness, and the like, as discussed in Chapter 7.

Standard Deviation.   A formula for computing the standard error of the standard deviation is as follows:

$$\sigma_\sigma = \frac{\sigma}{\sqrt{2N}} \tag{8.4}$$

Applying this formula to the skeletal age sample ($\sigma = 11.30$ months),

$$\sigma_\sigma = \frac{\sigma}{\sqrt{2N}} = \frac{11.30}{\sqrt{2 \times 67}} = .98 \text{ months.}$$

As for the other statistics considered, the standard deviation of 11.30 months was obtained from a sample; and, again, the purpose is to infer from the sample standard deviation to the parameter standard deviation. Levels of confidence can be applied in the same manner as before. Thus, at the .05 level, the chances are 5 in 100 that the population standard deviation lies outside the limits expressed by

$$11{:}30 \pm 1.96 \times .98 \text{ months}$$

or, below 9.38 or above 13.22 months.

Quartile Deviation.   The standard error of the quartile deviation can be obtained from the following formula:

$$\sigma_Q = \frac{1.17\,Q}{\sqrt{N}} \tag{8.5}$$

Applying this formula to the skeletal age data ($Q = 7.65$ months),

$$\sigma_Q = \frac{1.17\,Q}{\sqrt{N}} = \frac{1.17 \times 7.65}{\sqrt{62}} = 1.10 \text{ months}$$

As for the median compared to the mean, the sampling error of the quartile deviation is greater as contrasted with the standard deviation. The usual levels of confidence can be applied to the sample quartile deviation of 7.65 months by use of its standard error of 1.10 months.

Percentage.   Research problems may be involved in the percentage of a given sample that manifests certain characteristics or that reveals different attitudes toward problems in physical education. The reliability of a percentage can be determined through its standard error. The formula is

$$\sigma_P = \sqrt{\frac{PQ}{N}} \tag{8.6}$$

in which:

$$P = \text{percentage occurrence}$$
$$Q = 100 - P$$

To illustrate the use of this formula, an example will be given. Borcher interviewed a sample of 202 men and women drawn from the registration lists of 40,324 voters in 4 Willamette Valley, Oregon, communities in order to determine their opinions toward physical education.[7] As one phase of the study, each respondent indicated the 5 physical education activities in schools they considered most important for young people. For secondary schools, swimming was checked by the largest number; the percentage was 71.8. The question should now be asked: How well does the sample of 202 reflect the opinions of the population of 40,324? Applying the standard error formula and interpreting,

$$\sigma_P = \sqrt{\frac{PQ}{N}} = \sqrt{\frac{(71.8)(28.2)}{202}} = 3.2$$

To interpret at the .05 level in the usual way: The chances are 95 in 100 that the population percentage lies inside the limits and 5 in 100 that it lies outside the limits expressed by

$$71.8\% \pm 1.96 \times 3.2$$

or the limits of 65.5 and 78.1%. The .01 and other levels of confidence, of course, may be used.

[7]William J. Borcher, "An Analysis of Public Opinion in Regard to Physical Education," (Ed.D. diss., University of Oregon, 1964).

STANDARD ERROR OF SMALL SAMPLES

The preceding presentations of the normal probability curve in Chapter 7 and of reliability so far in this chapter assume large samples. As was shown, a normal probability distribution occurs when many chance observations are made, either in coin tossing or in drawing random subjects from a huge population. Further, a distribution of sample means will resemble the normal curve only when a large number of samples have been drawn. For example, in the coin-tossing experiment (Table 8.1), the distribution of 160 means from tossing 7 coins 50 times approached, but was not precisely, a normal curve. A small number of sample tosses would have produced an erratic and ill-defined distribution. With small samples, various deviations from the reliability theory for large samples discussed above occur. A discussion of these deviations and the statistical adjustments for them are considered here.

Effect of Standard Deviation

With a small sample, the standard deviation will underestimate (that is, be smaller than) the standard deviation of the population from which it is drawn. Extreme deviations in the population are rare and so are likely to be missed in small samples; the total range of scores is more and more curtailed as samples reduce in size. This fact reduces the amounts of the standard deviations as compared with this deviation for a large sample.

Because of this situation, a change in the formula for standard deviation should be made for small samples so as to increase its amount. This change is made by using $N - 1$ in the formula rather than N. Instead of the symbol σ, s is utilized to designate the standard deviation of a small sample. Thus, the formula is

$$s = \sqrt{\frac{\Sigma x^2}{N - 1}} \qquad (8.7)$$

The standard error for the mean becomes

$$\sigma_M = \frac{s}{\sqrt{N}} \qquad (8.8)$$

The use of s instead of σ is suggested when N is 30 or less. Any larger number would have little effect on the computation and is generally disregarded.

Degrees of Freedom

In the formula for s, a new statistical concept known as degrees of freedom (df) was employed; reference is made to $N - 1$. Degrees of freedom refer to the scores that are free to move in the computation of a given statistic. The degrees of freedom vary for some statistics. However, when computing a single statistic from a single distribution, df equal $N - 1$.

To explain degrees of freedom by use of the mean, a single statistic from a single distribution demonstrates: All scores are free to move except 1, hence $N - 1$. Take the five scores of 10, 9, 8, 7, and 6, the mean of which is 8. All scores but the last one can be different, that is, free to move; the last one, however, makes the final determination of the mean. In the illustration, any last number other than 6 would have produced a different mean.

Distribution of t

A phenomenon of distributions of sample means is that a normal curve results only when a large number of samples are drawn. Under this circumstance, the use of the normal probability table (Table 7.8) is appropriate. In its use above, the standard error distances from the mean at the .05 and .01 levels of confidence were determined as 1.96 and 2.58. However, these are *not* the proper distances when samples are small.

When samples are small, distributions of sample means lie mostly under the normal curve, except that the tails or ends of the curves are higher than the corresponding parts of the normal curve; the smaller the samples, the higher they will be. As the levels of confidence involve the tails of the distribution, adjustments of standard error distances are necessary for the various levels of confidence. Such adjustments are done by use of a statistic known as t.

A t is a standard error distance from the mean. In the earlier discussion, two t's have actually been used. These are: At the .05 level, $t = 1.96$; at the .01 level, $t = 2.58$. For small samples, a larger t is necessary for the same level of confidence, depending upon the degrees of freedom; such t's are found in Table 8.2.

In Table 8.2, df's appear in the left-hand column; the other columns give the t's for the four levels of confidence—.10, .05, .02, and .01—identified as probability (P) at the heads of the columns. The t's in Table 8.2 at the .05 and .01 levels for df's of infinity and 1,000 are 1.96 and 2.58, the same t's obtained from Table 7.8. However, for the rest of the table, the t's increase in magnitude as the df's decrease in amount. For the sample of 67 skeletal ages of 12-year-old boys: $df = N - 1 = 67 - 1 = 66$. Entering Table 8.2 with 70 df, the nearest df on the table,

TABLE 8.2 Table of t for Levels of Significance

Degrees of freedom	Probability (P) .10	.05	.02	.01
1	$t = 6.34$	$t = 12.71$	$t = 31.82$	$t = 63.66$
2	2.92	4.30	6.96	9.92
3	2.35	3.18	4.54	5.84
4	2.13	2.78	3.75	4.60
5	2.02	2.57	3.36	4.03
6	1.94	2.45	3.14	3.71
7	1.90	2.36	3.00	3.50
8	1.86	2.31	2.90	3.36
9	1.83	2.26	2.82	3.25
10	1.81	2.23	2.76	3.17
11	1.80	2.20	2.72	3.11
12	1.78	2.18	2.68	3.06
13	1.77	2.16	2.65	3.01
14	1.76	2.14	2.62	2.98
15	1.75	2.13	2.60	2.95
16	1.75	2.12	2.58	2.92
17	1.74	2.11	2.57	2.90
18	1.73	2.10	2.55	2.88
19	1.73	2.09	2.54	2.86
20	1.72	2.09	2.53	2.84
21	1.72	2.08	2.52	2.83
22	1.72	2.07	2.51	2.82
23	1.71	2.07	2.50	2.81
24	1.71	2.06	2.49	2.80
25	1.71	2.06	2.48	2.79
26	1.71	2.06	2.48	2.78
27	1.70	2.05	2.47	2.77
28	1.70	2.05	2.47	2.76
29	1.70	2.04	2.46	2.76
30	1.70	2.04	2.46	2.75
35	1.69	2.03	2.44	2.72
40	1.68	2.02	2.42	2.71
45	1.68	2.02	2.41	2.69
50	1.68	2.01	2.40	2.68
60	1.67	2.00	2.39	2.66
70	1.67	2.00	2.38	2.65
80	1.66	1.99	2.38	2.64
90	1.66	1.99	2.37	2.63
100	1.66	1.98	2.36	2.63
125	1.66	1.98	2.36	2.62
150	1.66	1.98	2.35	2.61
200	1.65	1.97	2.35	2.60
300	1.65	1.97	2.34	2.59
400	1.65	1.97	2.34	2.59
500	1.65	1.96	2.33	2.59
1000	1.65	1.96	2.33	2.58
∞	1.65	1.96	2.33	2.58

the t's at the .05 and .01 levels are 2.00 and 2.65, respectively. These t's should be used in indicating the reliability of the mean rather than the former t's of 1.96 and 2.58. Thus for the mean of 152.45 months and the σ_M of 1.38 months at the .05 level: $M = 152.45 \pm 2.00 \times 1.38$. The differences between the t's for the large sample and the sample of 67 boys is small. However, such is not the case for df of 10, where the t's are 2.23 and 31.7 at the two levels of confidence.

Other Statistics

The adjustments indicated for interpreting the reliability of a mean obtained from a small sample apply to such other statistics as the median, quartile deviation, standard deviation, and percentage when they are likewise obtained from small samples. The degrees of freedom for these statistics are the same as for the mean: $df = N - 1$.

DIFFERENCES BETWEEN MEANS

A most important point, which deals with the significance of a difference between statistics, has now been reached. From what has been explained before, the means of 2 or more random samples drawn from the same large population will be expected to vary from each other because of sampling error, that is, due to the act of obtaining random samples. Thus, a difference found between 2 such means may not be a real difference at all. For example, say the same strength test is given to random samples of 10-year-old boys in two neighboring communities. Assume that the mean strength score in community A is 110 pounds and in community B is 115 pounds; the difference between the means is 5 pounds. May this difference be attributed to the chance error arising from the random selection of the sample members, or is it evidence of a real superiority in strength for the 10-year-old boys in community B? A test of the significance between these means is needed.

Null Hypothesis

The null hypothesis, as applied here, is a *statistical* hypothesis to the effect that no real difference exists between the means of two samples—that any difference found may be attributed to sampling error. This form of hypothesis should not be confused with an experimental hypothesis, which has been reached by critical evaluation. The null hypothesis is merely a convenient way to express a statistical concept.

The null hypothesis is stated for the purpose of testing; it is either accepted or rejected. To accept the hypothesis is to conclude that a given difference between means may be due to sampling error; at least, under the conditions of the study, no other conclusion is tenable. To reject the null hypothesis is to conclude that a difference between means of the magnitude obtained cannot be attributed to sampling error—that a real or definite difference exists.

The null hypothesis is accepted or rejected at a level of significance. Levels of significance are comparable to the levels of confidence discussed above. For this purpose, however, level of significance is the proper terminology. The common significance levels are the .05 and .01 as explained earlier.

Another common way of expressing the significance of a difference between means is merely to state that the difference is or is not significant at the level of significance accepted. To state that a difference between means is not significant is the same as accepting the null hypothesis; to state that a difference is significant is synonymous with rejecting the null hypothesis.

Uncorrelated Data

When 2 samples are independently drawn, they are uncorrelated; the means computed from the samples are known as uncorrelated means. Only the standard errors of the 2 sample means are considered in computing a standard error of the difference between these means (σ_{DM}). The formula is

$$\sigma_{DM} = \sqrt{\sigma_{M_1}^2 + \sigma_{M_2}^2} \tag{8.9}$$

To illustrate with a study by Whittle[8] that compared 2 samples of 81 12-year-old boys each: The boys in 1 sample had participated for three years in a "good" elementary school physical education program; the boys in the other sample had had no physical education or had participated in a "poor" program. The Rogers' Physical Fitness Index (PFI) was one of the tests utilized in making comparisons between the samples. The PFI means in the good and poor programs were 120.79 and 103.02, respectively; the difference between the means (DM) was 17.77. The questions now aries: May this difference be attributed to sampling errors? Or is there a real difference due to participation in physical education?

Utilizing formula 8.9,

$$\sigma_{M_1} = 2.21; \qquad \sigma_{M_2} = 2.25$$

$$\sigma_{DM} = \sqrt{\sigma_{M_1}^2 + \sigma_{M_2}^2}$$

$$= \sqrt{2.21^2 + 2.25^2} = \sqrt{9.94} = 3.15$$

[8]H. Douglas Whittle, "Effects of Elementary School Physical Education upon Some Aspects of Physical, Motor, and Personality Development of Boys Twelve Years of Age," (Ph.D. diss., University of Oregon, 1956).

Thus, $DM = 17.77 \pm 3.15$. To explain, the chances are 50-50 that a difference between the means due to sampling error would favor either program. The chances are 68.26 in 100 (Table 7.8) that a difference as great as 3.15, the σ_{DM} could favor either group by sampling error. To extend the chance occurrences to the .01 level of significance, the standard error obtained for the difference between means is multiplied by the t for this level:

$$\sigma_{DM} \times t = 3.15 \times 2.58 = 8.13$$

Thus, a difference between means as great as 8.13 could occur by chance at the .01 level of significance. To state it differently: There is only 1 chance in 100 that a difference between the means as great as 8.13 could occur by sampling procedure. Inasmuch as the difference between means, 17.77, exceeds this amount, the null hypothesis is rejected at this significance level. The null hypothesis may be applied at other levels of significance in the same manner by utilizing appropriate t's.

A simpler way of applying tests of significance to the differences between means, and the one generally utilized, is by use of the t ratio. The t ratio is the ratio of the difference between means and the standard error of the difference. For the problem under consideration,

$$t = \frac{DM}{\sigma_{DM}} = \frac{17.77}{3.15} = 5.69$$

The t ratio necessary for a given level of significance is obtained from Table 8.2. For uncorrelated groups, the N's are combined and one degree of freedom is lost for each mean. Therefore, the df necessary for entering the table are

$$df = N_1 + N_2 - 2$$

$$81 + 81 - 2 = 160$$

Entering Table 8.2 with df of 160, the t ratio necessary at the .01 level of significance is 2.61. Inasmuch as the t ratio obtained in this study was 5.69, much greater than 2.61, the investigator rejected the null hypothesis above the stated level.

The t ratios for other levels of significance and for other df's may also be obtained from the table. For example, a t ratio of 2.09 is necessary for significance at the .05 level for df 20.

Correlated Data

In the preceding section, the difference between the means of uncorrelated groups was considered; two samples were independently drawn. In this section, the difference between correlated means will be presented. Here only one sample is independently drawn from the population; the data for the second mean are obtained in some manner that produces a high correlation with the sample randomly drawn.

There are various ways by which correlated means can be obtained. A common occurrence is found in the one-group experiment. Typically, two means are computed from the same sample: a pretest mean before and a posttest mean after application of an experimental factor. Another such situation is encountered when two equivalent groups are formed through an equating process. Here, one sample is randomly drawn; the subjects in the other group are paired with the individuals in the random sample on the basis of a factor or factors significant to the experiment, in order to control it or them by experimental design.

The statistical treatment of the difference between correlated means differs from the treatment for uncorrelated means in the formula used to compute the standard error. The formula for correlated means is

$$\sigma_{DM} = \sqrt{\sigma_{M_1}^2 + \sigma_{M_2}^2 - 2r_{12}\sigma_{M_1}\sigma_{M_2}} \qquad (8.10)$$

The r in the formula designates a coefficient of correlation. The meaning, computation, and interpretation of r will be explained in the next chapter.

To illustrate: Kurimoto longitudinally studied the growth changes of the same boys 15 through 18 years of age on many maturity, body size, physique type, strength, and motor measures.[9] Most of his tests naturally improve with age during these years. However, the Physical Fitness Index normally does not, as it is derived from norms based on age and weight. Therefore, this test could be used to determine changes that result from developmental activity. The means of 66 boys at 15 and 16 years of age were 113.17 and 117.21, respectively; the difference between the means was 4.04, showing an increase at the older age. The standard errors of the means were 2.48 at 15 years and 2.63 at 16 years; the interage correlation was .73. Utilizing formula 10.13,

$$\sigma_{DM} = \sqrt{\sigma_{M_1}^2 + \sigma_{M_2}^2 - 2r\sigma_{M_1}\sigma_{M_2}}$$
$$= \sqrt{2.48^2 + 2.63^2 - 2(.73)(2.48)(2.63)}$$
$$= \sqrt{12.95 - 9.65} = 1.52$$

A t ratio is computed:

$$t = \frac{DM}{\sigma_{DM}} = \frac{4.04}{1.52} = 2.66$$

[9] Etsuo Kurimoto, "Longitudinal Analysis of Maturity, Structural, Strength, and Motor Development of Boys Fifteen through Eighteen Years of Age," (Ph.D. diss., University of Oregon, 1963).

The degrees of freedom for the difference between correlated means: $N - 1$, or $66 - 1 = 65$. Entering Table 8.2 with 65 df, t's of 2.00 and 2.66 are necessary at the .05 and .01 levels of significance, respectively. In this problem, the t ratio exactly equals the 2.66 for significance at the .01 level.

An alternative method, the differences method, can be used to test the significance of a difference between correlated means without the necessity of computing a correlation coefficient. This method is usually perferred when the number of subjects is small. The computational process consists of obtaining the difference between each pair of scores, the standard deviation of the differences, the standard error of the differences mean, and a t ratio.

To illustrate: The same 15 boys were tested on bar pushups (pushups from one end of parallel bars) at the ages of 13 and 14 years. The question to be answered: Did the mean number of pushups increase significantly over the one-year period? The test results and computations are shown in Table 8.3. The procedures are as follows:

1. The numbers of bar pushups for each boy are listed in pairs in the first 2 columns of the table.
2. The differences between these scores are given in column 3; in each instance, the 13-year old score is subtracted from the 14-year-old score. The sum of this difference column is 30; divided by the N of 15, the mean of the differences is 2.0. This difference, of course, is the same as the difference between the means obtained from averaging columns 1 and 2.
3. In order to obtain the standard deviation of the differences, columns x and x^2 are needed. For the x column, each of the differences in the third column is subtracted from the differences mean (2.0). A computational check on this column is possible by adding the scores; the sum should be zero. In the final column, the values in the fourth column are squared and added ($\Sigma = 62$).
4. The standard deviation formula for small samples (s) is logically used in this problem because of the small N (formula 8.7). This computation is shown in the lower part of the table.

With 14 df ($15 - 1$), a t ratio of 2.98 is needed for a significant difference between these correlated means at the .01 level. Therefore, the null hypothesis is rejected at this level, since the t ratio obtaineu for this problem was 3.70.

When equivalent, or equated, groups are utilized, the correlation in the formula is computed from the scores of the paired subjects. These paired scores would be placed opposite each other in columns 1 and 2 if the differences method were used.

TABLE 8.3 Computation of Mean Differences for Correlated Groups Bar Pushups of Boys 13 and 14 Years of Age

Ages		Differences		
13 Years	14 Years	(14-13)	x	x^2
2	4	2	0	0
4	7	3	1	1
3	7	4	2	4
1	2	1	−1	1
4	5	1	−1	1
8	11	3	1	1
5	9	4	2	4
6	9	3	1	1
7	4	−3	−5	25
5	7	2	0	0
7	10	3	1	1
8	11	3	1	1
5	5	0	−2	4
3	2	−1	−3	9
5	10	5	3	9
73	103	$\frac{30}{15} = 2.0$		62

M 4.87 6.87

$$D_M = 2.0$$

$$s = \sqrt{\frac{\Sigma x^2}{N-1}} = \sqrt{\frac{62}{15-1}} = 2.10$$

$$\sigma_{DM} = \frac{s}{\sqrt{N}} = \frac{2.10}{3.88} = .54$$

$$t = \frac{2.0}{.54} = 3.70$$

Matched Groups

For equivalent groups, two groups are formed by equating individuals on the basis of a crucial test. Thus, the number of subjects in both groups is identical, and the means and standard deviations will be comparable.

When it is not feasible to equate groups, an alternative method is to form the two groups by obtaining matching means and standard deviations. In this instance, the N's may or may not be the same, and the order of the scores is not regulated as in pairing. For this method, the formula for standard error of the mean is

$$\sigma_{DM} = \sqrt{(\sigma^2_{M_1} + \sigma^2_{M_2})(1 - r^2_{12})} \qquad (8.11)$$

The r_{12} in the formula is the correlation between the matching variable and the experimental variable when these are not the same. If the two variables are the same, the reliability (test-retest) coefficient (r_{xx}) is used; however, in this case, the r is not squared.

Comparison with Norm

An occasion may arise when the investigator wishes to compare a mean obtained from a sample with a mean representing a norm for a large population. For example, in the study by Whittle mentioned above, 81 12-year-old boys, who had participated for three years in a "good" physical education program, had a mean Physical Fitness Index of 120.79. Is this mean significantly higher than the PFI of 100, which is the mean amount in accordance with the norms?

With a standard deviation of 19.89, the standard error of the mean is computed: $\sigma / \sqrt{N} = 19.89 / \sqrt{81} = 2.21$. The difference between the means is 20.79 (120.79 − 100). A t ratio is obtained: 20.79/2.21 = 9.41. This t ratio is so large that reference to Table 8.2 is not necessary, although the investigator may still wish to know that a t ratio of 2.64 meets the requirement for significance at the .01 level. Thus, these boys were far superior to the mean performance expected from the population from which the norms were obtained.

Significance Level

In deciding on the significance level, it should be stressed that acceptance of the null hypothesis does not prove that no difference between means exists. Rather, in the given problem, for the number of subjects especially, the difference in the total population could be zero, and the amount obtained could be attributed to sampling error. Further, if the null hypothesis is rejected, say exactly at the .05 level, there are still 5 chances in 100 that the difference between means could be due to sampling error.

The investigator, therefore, is faced with a balancing of risks at which level to accept or reject the null hypothesis. As can be seen, two distinct types of errors are possible in making this decision—known and defined, as follows:

Type I: *rejecting the null hypothesis when in fact it is true.*

Type II: *accepting the null hypothesis when in fact it is false.*

At the .05 level, there are 5 chances in 100 of being wrong in the rejecting null hypothesis when it is true (Type I error): at the .01 level, there is only 1 chance in 100 of being wrong. As the level of significance is decreased the chances of making a Type II error are increased; the chances of making a Type I error are decreased as the level of significance is increased.

In the adoption of levels of significance, various practices have been followed. Strict statisticians maintain that the decision should be made as part of the experimental design, before the data are collected and analyzed. Some investigators have utilized both the .05 and .01 levels coincidentally, a process that permits reference to either level in accordance with the magnitude of the differences obtained between means. A flexible plan of accepting the null hypothesis at the .10 level, rejecting it at the .01 level, and reserving judgment in between has been proposed. A practical consideration of which level to adopt is to use higher levels (.01 and .001) when the application of the research results necessitates expensive equipment or extensive curricular reorganization and to use lower levels (.10 and .05) when the adoption of new practices is simple and uninvolved.

Two- and One-Tailed Tests

In the presentation of tests of significance so far, the assumption has been made that chance differences between sample means could favor either group equally. For example: If the same strength test were given to 2 random samples from the same population, there is no reason to believe that the results would favor one group over the other. Still, a difference between means would be expected by sampling error; however, the chances of a higher mean for either sample are equal. The test of significance applied is a two-tailed test. The two-tailed test only has been considered to this point, and it is the common one employed in research. The tables utilized thus far are also constructed for two-tailed tests. At the .05 level, for example, one-half of this amount (.025 or 2.5%) is placed at either end of the normal curve of sampling probability.

In some experiments, the scientific hypothesis being tested is concerned with the results obtained in one direction only. In such situations, all chances of a significant difference between means are at one end of the normal curve of sampling reliability; thus, a one-tailed test is appropriate. Instances where one-tailed tests are proper follow.

1. *When a difference, if it exists at all, would necessarily be in one direction.* For example, if a skill is taught, teaching and practice do not make children worse in performing the skill; they may not get better, but, if anything happens, they should improve. Another example can be taken from studies of muscle fatigue from exercise. Fatiguing exercise interferes with the contractile power of muscles (as one chins the bar, it becomes harder and harder

until it is no longer possible). In both illustrations, the differences move in one direction only: in the former, to improve performance; in the latter, to hinder it.

2. **When results in the opposite direction to the one predicted are not to be used to decide upon a course of action that is different from the course of action if no difference is found.**   In this instance, the experimenter is only interested in results in one direction. Examples are intimated by the following questions: Is a new type of gymnasium shoe better than one now on the market? Are boys stronger than girls? In these situations, the investigator is not concerned with which product is better or which sex is stronger (two-tailed tests), but, rather, whether one is better or stronger than the other (one-tailed tests). Some danger exists here of the researcher taking advantage of smaller differences between means as being significant by stating experimental hypotheses only in order to produce one-tailed tests.

The statistical procedure in applying a one-tailed test is to use the *t* ratios in the .10 column of Table 8.2 for the .05 level and the *t* ratios in the .02 column for the .01 level. When the .10 level of the table is utilized, one-half this amount (.05) is at each end of the normal curve of sampling probability; for the .02 level, also, one-half the amount (.01) is at each end. These amounts are correct for one-tailed tests.

DIFFERENCES BETWEEN OTHER STATISTICS

In presenting tests of significance above, attention has been confined to the difference between means. The same approach is made for the differences between other statistics. The standard error and the *t* ratio for a given statistic are computed; Table 8.2 is utilized to determine the *t* ratio needed for the various levels of significance; the degrees of freedom are the same as for the difference between means. The only change is in the formulas used, so what has been said before for the difference between means can be repeated for each of the other statistics. The differences between statistics considered so far in this text will be explained here.

Medians

When the proper measure of central tendency is the median, the formula for computing the standard error of the difference between uncorrelated medians is

$$\sigma_{DMdn} = \sqrt{\sigma^2_{Mdn1} + \sigma^2_{Mdn2}} \tag{8.12}$$

A t ratio is obtained:

$$t \frac{DMdn}{\sigma_{DMdn}}$$

When medians are correlated, the computation of r does not meet basic assumptions for correlation and so cannot be accurately determined.

Standard Deviations

When N is reasonably large, say 30 and above, the standard errors for uncorrelated and correlated standard deviations can be obtained from the following formulas:

Uncorrelated: $\quad \sigma_{D\sigma} = \sqrt{\sigma^2_{\sigma1} + \sigma^2_{\sigma2}}$ $\hspace{2cm}$ (8.13)

Correlated: $\quad \sigma_{D\sigma} = \sqrt{\sigma^2_{\sigma1} + \sigma^2_{\sigma2} - 2r\sigma_{\sigma1}\sigma_{\sigma2}}$ $\hspace{1.5cm}$ (8.14)

A t ratio is obtained:

$$t = \frac{D\sigma}{\sigma_{D\sigma}}$$

When samples are small and uncorrelated, the t ratio is inappropriate for testing the difference between standard deviations. The reason is that a distribution of standard deviations from repeated samples of the sample population is skewed rather than normal. In this situation, an F test should be applied. The F test is not presented here.

Percentages

The significance of the differences between percentages for uncorrelated and correlated samples can be determined through use of the appropriate formula for the standard error of the difference. The formulas are

Uncorrelated: $\quad \sigma_{DP} = \sqrt{\sigma^2_{P_1} + \sigma^2_{P_2}}$ $\hspace{2cm}$ (8.15)

or: $\quad = \sqrt{PQ\left(\frac{1}{N_1} + \frac{1}{N_2}\right)}$ $\hspace{1.8cm}$ (8.16)

Correlated: $\quad \sigma_{DP} = \sqrt{\sigma^2_{P_1} + \sigma^2_{P_2} - 2r\sigma_{P_1}\sigma_{P_2}}$ $\hspace{1cm}$ (8.17)

In the formulas, P_1 and P_2 represent the percentages being tested for significance; their computations are made by use of formula 8.6. A t ratio is obtained:

$$t = \frac{DP}{\sigma_{DP}}$$

In Borcher's study mentioned earlier, a sample of 202 Willamette Valley, Oregon, voters were asked if they favored a physical education requirement in the elementary schools of the state. Of this number, 23 had completed only 2 years of high school, and 24 had had only a grade school education. The favorable responses of these voters were 92% for the two-year high school (P_1) group and 63% for the grade school (P_2) group. The question to be resolved: Is this difference of 29% (DP) between these groups significant? The statistical computations are as follows:

$$\sigma_{P_1} = \sqrt{\frac{PQ}{N-1}} = \sqrt{\frac{(92)(8)}{23-1}} = 5.79$$

$$\sigma_{P_2} = \sqrt{\frac{PQ}{N-1}} = \sqrt{\frac{(63)(37)}{24-1}} = 10.06$$

$$\sigma_{DP} = \sqrt{\sigma_{P_1}^2 + \sigma_{P_2}^2} = \sqrt{5.79^2 + 10.06^2} = 11.56$$

$$t = \frac{DP}{\sigma_{DP}} = \frac{29.0}{11.56} = 2.51$$

$$df = N_1 + N_2 - 2 = 23 + 24 - 2 = 45$$

Entering Table 8.2 with 45 df, t ratios of 2.02 and 2.41 are needed for significance at the .05 and .02 levels, respectively. The t ratio of 2.51 in Borcher's study was sufficiently high to reject the null hypothesis at the .02 level. He was able to conclude, therefore, that the differences in the voters' education were an influential factor in their acceptance of physical education at the elementary school level (only 2 chances in 100 that this was not so.)

Skewness

In Chapter 7, skewness was presented as a form of deviation from normal probability distributions, and the process of computing skewness was explained. After skewness is computed, a test of significance is necessary in order to determine if any amount of skewness obtained can be attributed to sampling error. In order to make this test of significance, the standard error of skewness and a t ratio are needed. The formulas will be given in the example to follow.

In the Medford Boys' Growth Study, 112 boys 12 years of age were given bar pushups (pushups from one end of parallel bars). Skewness was found to be 2.49. The standard errors of skewness and t ratio were

$$\sigma_{Sk} = \frac{.5185D}{\sqrt{N}} \tag{8.18}$$

in which $D = P_{90} - P_{10}$. In this problem, these percentiles were: $P_{90} = 11.26$ times; $P_{10} = .90$ times. Substituting in the formula:

$$\sigma_{Sk} = \frac{.5185(11.26 - .90)}{\sqrt{112}} = .51$$

$$t = \frac{Sk}{\sigma_{Sk}} = \frac{2.49}{.51} = 4.88$$

Entering Table 8.2 with $df = N - 1$, or $112 - 1 = 111$, a t ratio of 2.63 indicates significant skewness at the .01 level. With a t ratio of 4.88 for these 12-year-old boys on the bar pushups test, the null hypothesis is rejected beyond this level. It is most unlikely that this amount of skewness could have occurred by sampling error.

Kurtosis

Kurtosis, as related to the height of a given distribution curve, was presented in Chapter 7. When a curve is mesokurtic, it corresponds to the height of a normal curve; in this case, kurtosis equals .263. If kurtosis is less than .263, the distribution is leptokurtic; if greater than .263, it is platykurtic. However, a deviation from normal for a given sample needs to be tested for significance in the usual manner.

Kurtosis was computed for the bar pushup performances of the 112 12-year-old boys in the skewness problem above. $Ku = .239$, which is lower than .263: $.239 - .263 = -.024$, a leptokurtic distribution. The standard error of kurtosis is

$$\sigma_{Ku} = \frac{.28}{\sqrt{N}} \tag{8.19}$$

For this problem:

$$\sigma_{Ku} = \frac{.28}{\sqrt{112}} = .026$$

$$t = \frac{Ku}{\sigma_{Ku}} = \frac{-.024}{.026} = -.96$$

Entering Table 8.2 with $df = N - 1$, or $112 - 1 = 111$, a t ratio of 1.98 indicates significance at the .05 level. As the t ratio for the bar pushup distribution does not reach this amount, the null hypothesis is accepted.

CONDITIONS FOR USE OF
STANDARD ERROR FORMULAS

The application of sampling statistics depends upon certain conditions of sampling. If these are not satisfied, standard errors may give incorrect impressions. After making this assertion, it must also be said that the investigator can hardly draw any conclusions from his or her research without such errors. However, in planning studies, the conditions for proper use of standard errors should be understood and recognized. The consideration of such basic conditions follows.

1. As developed in this chapter, standard error inferences may be made relative to the location of the population mean from a sample mean by application of normal probability. Justification for this practice emanates from the fact that a distribution of sample means of the same size resembles a normal curve. Even when samples exhibit skewness, the means of repeated samples will tend to be normally distributed, especially if N is large. What is said about the distribution of sample means applies equally well to repeated samples for other statistics.

2. In using standard error, the sample should be randomly obtained so that chance operates, thus permitting application of normal probability. Situations that tend to interfere with randomness of selection will produce improper standard errors, leading to inaccurate and misleading conclusions. Some such situations lead to standard errors that are too small to describe the actual distribution of sample means, and others lead to standard errors that are too large; these would result in overconfidence and underconfidence, respectively, in the reliability of a sample mean.

3. Random sampling implies independence of observation. If certain restricting conditions tie subjects together, observations are not independent. This situation may occur when samples are obtained from subgroups of the population.

4. When sample sizes are small, the null hypothesis is apt to be accepted too often for the reason that a difference between means must be sizeable before it is rejected. On the other hand, if a real difference is so small that its statistical demonstration requires very large samples that run into the thousands, its practical or scientific importance may be questioned.

ANALYSIS OF VARIANCE

Analysis of variance is an extension of the significance of differences between means. The t ratio is used when the significance of the difference between the means of 2 independent samples is tested

However, it is not appropriate when more than 2 means are compared, each with all others. When more than 2 groups are involved, the means are no longer completely independent, as each sample serves more than once in the significance tests. Analysis of variance compensates for this situation and is the proper test of significance to use under this circumstance.

In analysis of variance, an F ratio is obtained. The t and F ratios are equivalent when only 2 independent samples are involved. The F required for testing the significance between 2 means is the square of t: $F = t^2$ and $t = \sqrt{F}$. For example, the t ratio required for significance of the difference between 2 means for large samples ($N = 1,000$) at the .05 level is 1.96; the corresponding F ratio is 3.84.

If an F test is insignificant, the null hypothesis is automatically accepted at the level stated for the differences between all sets of paired means. If the F ratio is significant, the null hypothesis is rejected. However, it does not indicate which of several differences between paired means are significant. To make this determination, *post hoc* tests must be applied for all differences between paired means.

One-way and multivariant analysis of variances may be performed. In a one-way analysis, significance between the means of several groups is determined. For example, with four samples, A, B, C, and D, 6 differences between means are involved: A vs. B, A vs. C, A vs. D, B vs. C, B vs. D, and C vs. D. The round-robin formula provides the number: $N(N-1)/2 = 4(4-1)/2 = 6$. The F ratio is obtained from 2 variances, as follows:

$$F = \frac{\text{variances between groups}}{\text{variance within groups}}$$

The between-groups variance represents the differences between the means; when it is sufficiently greater than the within-groups variance, the F ratio is significant. An F table is consulted to indicate the F ratio necessary to reject the null hypothesis at a given level of significance.

In 1-way analysis of variance, only 1 experimental factor is involved. In 2-way analysis, 2 factors or treatments operate together; 3 F ratios are computed. To illustrate: Badgley studied the effects on ankle flexibility (range of motion) of administering whirlpool baths under varying conditions.[10] Four water temperatures and 4 lengths of time in the water were systematically changed. Thus 16 treatments were involved; 24 means were compared, 4 temperatures, 4 times, and 16 combinations of temperature and time. The 3 F ratios were for differences in water temperature, differences in length of time in the water, and combinations of temperature and time (known as inter-

[10] Marion E. Badgley, "A Study of the Effect of the Whirlpool Bath on Range of Motion of the Right Ankle under Selected Conditions" (Master's thesis, University of Oregon, 1957).

action). Conceivably, this investigation could have been extended to a 3-way analysis of variance by also varying the force with which the water circulated, as a third experimental factor.

A number of proposals have been made for making *post hoc* comparisons between paired means following significant F tests. Winer contrasted the power of five such methods.[11] He concluded that: The Scheffe method has the greatest power and is most conservative with respect to Type I error; the Tukey honestly significant difference method is also a stringent test of significance; the Duncan multiple range, the Newman-Keuls, and the Tukey least significant difference methods are the least powerful tests.

ANALYSIS OF COVARIANCE

For a random-group experiment, as has been explained, the means of groups will be different, except by merest chance, as a consequence of drawing random samples from the same population. The fact that the initial means will differ from each other, even though the difference is not significant—and therefore can be attributed to sampling error—may well affect the significance of the differences between postexperiment means for example,

	Group A	Group B	Difference
Initial Means	32	35	3
Final Means	41	38	3
Mean Gains	9	3	6

Assuming that the difference of three each between the initial means and the final means is not significant, the investigator would erroneously conclude that the effects of the experiment would be nonsignificant if a t test were applied to the final means. However, on the average, group A gained nine points whereas group B increased only three points, a mean difference of six points. Quite probably, the difference between mean gains is significant, since group A made three times the increase of group B.

One way to treat these experimental data is to test the difference in mean gains for significance. A more acceptable way, however, is to apply analysis of covariance. In covariance analysis, the final means in an experiment are adjusted for differences in initial means, and the adjusted means are tested for significance. A further advantage of this method is that analysis of variance is first computed for differences

---

[11]B. J. Winer, *Statistical Principles in Experimental Design* (New York: McGraw-Hill, Inc., 1962), p. 88.

between initial means. In this instance, a nonsignificant F ratio will provide confidence that the initial samples came from the same population and are devoid of sampling bias. When more than two experimental groups are involved, the same *post hoc* methods of testing the significance of the differences between paired means following a significant analysis of variance F ratio can be applied to the differences between paired adjusted final means after a significant covariance F ratio.[12]

NONPARAMETRIC STATISTICS

The tests of significance discussed so far in this chapter are applied to parametric data obtained from test scores; the assumption is made that the distribution of population scores conforms to the normal curve. When this requirement is not met, the data are nonparametric, so require other tests of significance. Nonparametric tests may also be applied in two other situations: when the variables are expressed in nominal form (classified in categories by frequency count) and when the variables are expressed in ordinal form (ranked in order). Nonparametric tests are less precise, have less power, than parametric tests, and they are not as likely to reject the null hypothesis when it is false.

Many statisticians suggest that parametric tests be used if possible and that nonparametric tests by used only when parametric assumptions cannot be met. Some argue that nonparametric tests have greater merit than generally acknowledged because their validity is not based upon assumptions about the nature of the populations, assumptions that may be ignored or violated by researchers employing parametric tests.[13]

Several nonparametric tests have been proposed. Siegel has devoted a complete text to this subject.[14] Some of these tests are chi-square, Mann-Whitney U test, median test, Kolmogorav-Smirnov tests, and sign tests. Other such statistics are correlational in nature so will be considered in Chapter 9. The only nonparametric test presented here is chi-square.

---

[12] For a presentation of analysis of variance and analysis of covariance, see H. Harrison Clarke and David H. Clarke, *Advanced Statistics with Application to Physical Education* (Englewood Cliffs, N.J.: Prentice-Hall, Inc., 1972), Chaps. 1 and 2.

[13] John W. Best, *Research in Education*, 4th ed. (Englewood Cliffs, N.J.: Prentice-Hall, Inc., 1981), p. 289.

[14] Sidney Siegel, *Nonparametric Statistics for the Behavioral Sciences* (New York: McGraw-Hill, Inc.), 1956.

CHI-SQUARE

Chi-square (X^2) is a versatile statistic since it may be used to test various hypotheses and is applicable to a variety of situations. Chi-square constitutes a test of significance, used primarily with nominal scales. It is a generalized expression between an actual and a theoretical distribution. The chi-square formula is

$$X^2 = \Sigma\left[\frac{(fo - f_2)^2}{fe}\right] \tag{8.20}$$

In this formula

fo = frequency of occurrence as obtained

fe = frequency of occurrence by some hypothesis

Two illustrations are provided.

Equal Occurrence Hypothesis

A random sample of 150 adults in a community was surveyed to determine hobby interests in order to develop a schedule of classes. The preferences were: 56, art; 45, music; and 49, drama. On the basis of these responses, it might be assumed that art groups should be scheduled with greater frequency than the other 2, and music groups with least frequency. However, realizing the role that chance plays in the selection of a random sample, the differences in choices might well be due to sampling, that is, there might actually be no preference in the choice of hobby groups in the total community from which the sample was drawn. The equal occurence hypothesis, that theoretically equal numbers would choose each hobby ($fe = 50$), would be tested. To apply the chi-quare test (formula 8.20):

	Art	Music	Drama	Total
fo	56	45	49	150
fe	50	50	50	150
fo-fe	6	5	1	
(fo-fe)²	36	25	1	
$\dfrac{(fo-fe)^2}{fe}$	.72	.50	.02	$X^2 = 1.24$

The degrees of freedom are: $df = (r = 1)(c - 1)$, in which r and c refer to the number of rows and columns. In this case: $df = (2 - 1)(3 - 1) = 2$. Enter Table 8.4, which is much abridged to cover the two chi-square problems presented here, with $2df$. The columns in this table refer to levels of significance; for example, the .05 column gives the X^2

TABLE 8.4 Partial Chi-Square Table

df	0.20	0.10	0.05	0.02	0.01
1	1.652	2.706	3.841	5.412	6.635
2	3.219	4.605	5.991	7.824	9.210
3	4.642	6.251	7.815	9.837	11.345
4	5.989	7.779	9.488	11.668	13.277
5	7.289	9.236	11.071	13.388	15.086
6	8.558	10.645	12.592	15.033	16.812
7	9.803	12.017	14.067	16.622	18.475
8	11.030	13.362	15.507	18.168	20.090
9	12.242	14.684	16.919	19.679	21.666
10	13.442	15.987	18.307	21.161	23.209
11	14.631	17.275	19.675	22.618	24.725
12	15.812	18.549	21.026	24.054	26.217
13	16.985	19.812	22.362	25.472	27.688
14	18.151	21.064	23.685	26.873	29.141
15	19.311	22.307	24.996	28.259	30.578
16	20.465	23.542	26.296	29.633	32.000
17	21.615	24.769	27.587	30.995	33.409
18	22.760	25.989	28.869	32.346	34.805
19	23.900	27.204	30.144	33.687	36.191
20	25.038	28.412	31.410	35.020	37.566

Source: Table 8 in E. S. Pearson and H. O. Harley, eds., *Biometrika Tables for Statisticians*, vol. 1, 3rd ed. (Cambridge: Cambridge University Press, 1966); reprinted and abridged by permission of the editors and the trustees of *Biometrika*.

necessary for significance for various degrees of freedom. With $2df$, the X^2 needed for significance at this level is 5.99. Inasmuch as X^2 in this illustration is 1.24, the null hypothesis is accepted. From the results of the survey, then, the equal-scheduling of the three hobbies would be justified.

Contingency Table

School authorities investigated whether or not flavored milk would increase consumption of milk in school cafeteria. The choice and consumption of milk was checked for a period of time with four flavors made available: plain, chocolate, strawberry, and orange. The results are shown in Table 8.5.

The independence values that compose fe in the contingency table are obtained by multiplying the total frequencies of the rows and columns for a given cell and dividing by the amount of N. For example, in the upper left-hand cell containing an fo of 30, the column and row frequencies are 162 and 70 respectively and $N = 300$. Thus: $(162)(70)/300 = 37.8$. The X^2 for each cell is then computed in the usual manner from formula D.20 (part B of the table).

TABLE 8.5 Chi-Square Table by Contingency Table for Flavor and Milk Consumption

		Flavor Reaction		
Flavor	Consumed	Partially Consumed	Not Consumed	Total
Plain	30 (37.8)	18 (15.4)	22 (16.8)	70
Chocolate	45 (40.5)	15 (16.5)	15 (18.0)	75
Strawberry	48 (43.7)	16 (17.8)	17 (19.4)	81
Orange	39 (40.0)	17 (16.3)	18 (17.8)	74
Totals	162	66	72	300

A. *Calculation of Independence Values (f_e):*

$$\frac{162 \times 70}{300} = 37.8 \qquad \frac{66 \times 70}{300} = 15.4 \qquad \frac{72 \times 70}{300} = 16.8$$

$$\frac{162 \times 75}{300} = 40.5 \qquad \frac{66 \times 75}{300} = 16.5 \qquad \frac{72 \times 75}{300} = 18.0$$

$$\frac{162 \times 81}{300} = 43.7 \qquad \frac{66 \times 81}{300} = 17.8 \qquad \frac{72 \times 81}{300} = 19.4$$

$$\frac{162 \times 74}{300} = 40.0 \qquad \frac{66 \times 74}{300} = 16.3 \qquad \frac{72 \times 74}{300} = 17.8$$

B. *Calculation of χ^2:*

The regular formula (4.1) is applied to each of the twelve cells in the above frequency tabulation:

$$\frac{(30 - 37.8)^2}{37.8} = 1.61 \qquad \frac{(18 - 15.4)^2}{15.4} = .44 \qquad \frac{(22 - 16.8)^2}{16.8} = 1.61$$

$$\frac{(45 - 40.5)^2}{40.5} = .50 \qquad \frac{(15 - 16.5)^2}{16.5} = .14 \qquad \frac{(15 - 18.0)^2}{18.0} = .50$$

$$\frac{(48 - 43.7)^2}{43.7} = .42 \qquad \frac{(16 - 17.8)^2}{17.8} = .18 \qquad \frac{(17 - 19.4)^2}{19.4} = .30$$

$$\frac{(39 - 40.0)^2}{40.0} = .03 \qquad \frac{(17 - 16.3)^2}{16.3} = .05 \qquad \frac{(18 - 17.8)^2}{17.8} = .00$$

These values added: $\chi^2 = 5.78$

The chi-square for this problem is 5.78. To determine significance between the obtained and expected frequencies, enter Table 8.4 with the degrees of freedom of 6: $(c - 1)(r - 1) = (4 - 1)(3 - 1) = 6$. The chi-square needed for significance at the .05 level is 12.59. Thus, in this situation, the flavor of milk did not affect consumption, so the null hypothesis is accepted.

Comment

The fundamental concept of chi-square can be explained in its relation to Z, the standard score (or standard deviation distance of a score from its mean). For example, in a normal distribution, Z at the .05 level is 1.96: $Z^2 = 3.84$, which is the amount for the .05 level in Table 8.4. This relationship holds true only for $1df$. Distributions of chi-square are not normal. Of course, the distribution of Z is normal, but squaring Z to obtain chi-square (with $1df$) results in all values being positive and in changing the shape of the distribution.

9

Correlation

Up to this point in presenting statistics, only one variable has been treated at a time. This chapter considers the degree of relationship between two variables, that is, correlation. There are various methods of computing correlation, but the method most commonly used is the *product-moment* method, which is signified by the symbol r. This method is appropriate when data are linear (to be explained later), as is the case for the bulk of research data analyzed in physical education.

MEANING OF CORRELATION

Correlation simply refers to the relationship between pairs of measures. Usually, each pair of measures is obtained from the same individual. Thus, if the heights and weights of 100 boys are to be correlated, the heights and weights of these boys are used, and the heights and weights must be kept in pairs. Although not so frequent a practice, measures of the same trait from 2 individuals who have been paired on some basis are correlated, for instance, correlating personality traits of husbands and wives or equated pairs in an equivalent group experiment.

The coefficient of correlation is a single figure that indicates the extent to which traits are related: to indicate the extent that variations in 1 trait go with variations in another. A different way of expressing this meaning is the closeness with which traits together vary from their respective means. The range of possible magnitude of correlations extends from +1.00 through .00 to −1.00, all divisions of the scale being used such as .90, .13, −.35, and so forth. The sign does not have mathematical meaning, but, rather, it indicates the direction of the correlation—the plus sign for a positive correlation and the minus sign for a negative correlation.

A +1.00 indicates a perfect positive correlation: A large amount of 1 variable is found with a large amount of the other; a small amount of 1 with a small amount of the other. These are in direct proportion throughout the ranges of their distributions. An illustration of a +1.00 correlation is of that between the circumference of a circle and its diameter; this relationship is always *pi* (3.1416) regardless of the size of the circle. A −1.00 is just as significant a correlation as is a +1.00, but the proportions are in reverse: A large amount of one variable is found with a small amount of the other. An illustration of a −1.00 correlation is of that between the circumference of a wheel and the number of times it revolves for a given distance: the larger the wheel, the fewer times it revolves.

In some instances, negative correlations have positive connotations. This is true when a high score on one of the traits represents a good performance, whereas a low score on the other trait is best. An example is the correlation between distance in the long jump and time for the 50-yard dash. In computing correlations, the magnitude of the scores rather than their value is considered.

For a .00 correlation, no relationship exists: An individual with a high score in one variable may appear anywhere on the scale for the opposite variable. With high positive and negative correlations, one can predict with considerable accuracy an individual's score in one variable by merely knowing his or her score in the other. With zero or near-zero correlations, such prediction would be worthless—in fact, would be entirely a matter of guessing.

To explain the meaning of the term *product-moment*: "Moment" is the sum of the deviations of scores from their mean raised to some power and divided by N; "product-moment" is when pairs of deviations in x and y are multiplied, summed, and divided by N. In correlation, x and y have the same meaning, except x represents one of the variables, and y represents the other. Thus: $x = X - Mx; y = Y - My$.

CORRELATION WITH UNGROUPED DATA

There are many variations of the formula for computing product-moment correlations from ungrouped data, all of which yield the same answer. The basic formula from which the others are derived is

$$r_{xy} = \frac{\Sigma xy}{N\sigma x \sigma y} \tag{9.1}$$

in which:

r_{xy} = correlation between variables X and Y

x and $y = X - Mx$; $Y - My$

Σxy = sum of products of x and y deviations

σx and σy = standard deviations of the X and Y distributions.

This formula illustrates the definition of correlation given earlier as the "closeness with which traits together vary from their respective means." Inasmuch as the magnitude of the traits may differ, the variances from the means are relative to the amounts of the standard deviations.

Only one correlational method for ungrouped data will be described here. The one chosen can be applied directly to the raw scores (original measurements) rather than relating each score to its mean (formula 9.1). An advantage is that the formula can be simply programmed for electronic computer operation. The formula may appear formidable but is actually easy to apply.

$$r_{xy} = \frac{N\Sigma XY - (\Sigma X)(\Sigma Y)}{\sqrt{[N\Sigma X^2 - (\Sigma X)^2][N\Sigma Y^2 - (\Sigma Y)^2]}} \tag{9.2}$$

where X and Y are the raw scores for the two variables.

The computation of a coefficient of correlation using formula 9.2 is shown in Table 9.1. The data are the heights and weights of 15 boys 15 years of age. These boys were tested within 2 months of their birthdays so that they would not vary in chronological age by more than 4 months. The steps in making the computations are

1. Enter X and Y scores by pairs in columns 1 and 2.
2. Square X and Y scores, columns 3 and 4.
3. Obtain the XY products $(X \times Y)$, column 5.
4. Apply formula 9.2 as shown in the table.

CORRELATION WITH GROUPED DATA

The coefficient of correlation may also be computed from grouped data, which necessitates the construction of a scattergram. In today's extensive use of computers in making this computation, it seems unlikely that this method will be generally employed in making such

TABLE 9.1   Computation of a Product-Moment Correlation by the Raw Data Method Data: Heights and Weights of 15-Year-Old Boys

Height X	Weight Y	X^2	Y^2	XY
62.2	135	3,869	18,225	8,397
70.0	129	4,900	16,641	9,030
67.6	164	4,570	26,896	11,086
61.9	104	3,832	10,816	6,438
67.9	138	4,610	19,044	9,370
67.0	193	4,489	37,249	12,931
64.3	112	4,135	12,544	7,202
67.5	152	4,556	23,104	10,260
66.1	114	4,369	12,996	7,535
67.2	121	4,516	14,641	8,131
70.9	149	5,027	22,201	10,564
67.8	158	4,597	24,964	10,712
64.9	119	4,202	14,161	7,723
67.0	138	4,489	19,044	9,246
66.3	116	4,397	13,456	7,691
Σ998.6	2,042	66,557	285,982	136,316

$$r_{xy} = \frac{N\Sigma XY - (\Sigma X)(\Sigma Y)}{\sqrt{[N\Sigma X^2 - (\Sigma X)^2][N\Sigma Y^2 - (\Sigma Y)^2]}}$$

$$= \frac{(15)(136{,}316) - (998.6)(2{,}042)}{\sqrt{[(15)(66{,}557) - (998.6)^2][(15)(285{,}982) - (2{,}042)^2]}}$$

$$= \frac{5{,}611}{\sqrt{[1{,}134][119{,}966]}}$$

$$= \frac{5{,}611}{11{,}666}$$

$$= .48$$

calculations. Nevertheless, the scattergram method does have some advantages, especially for the neophyte researcher, as follows: (1) If a large sample and only a single or small number of correlations are to be computed, recourse can be had to the scattergram. (2) Means and standard deviations of each pair of variables can be readily computed. (3) In the event of a high correlation, regression lines can be drawn on the scattergram for predictive purposes.[1] Perhaps most important, the scattergram itself serves as a graph of the data; the investigator can see the relationship pattern, which is not possible with ungrouped scores.

The procedures for calculating a product-moment coefficient of

[1] H. Harrison Clarke and David H. Clarke, *Advanced Statistics with Application to Physical Education* (Englewood Cliffs, N.J.: Prentice-Hall, Inc., 1972), p. 70.

TABLE 9.2   Pairs of Scores for Correlation Problem
Skeletal Age Versus Standing Height

SA	Ht	SA	Ht	SA	Ht	SA	Ht	SA	Ht
149	58	162	64	154	59	162	59	160	64
150	59	146	64	134	58	162	65	164	64
157	64	149	59	135	55	148	60	161	63
153	64	144	59	156	64	156	59	154	66
182^H	65	164	64	161	67	153	60	150	57
136	56	135	54	151	62	132^L	56	151	60
168	62	147	60	154	62	169	61	164	67
173	62	158	61	136	60	136	56	133	57
144	60	155	58	156	61	140	61	169	63
158	60	130	52	154	58	157	60	154	61
144	60	148	60	135	59	173	61	149	59
147	59	154	58	154	62	151	60	148	57
168	66	168	69^H	162	61	171	67	146	62
163	63	140	60	156	60	138	61	156	63
144	59	171	64	154	59	154	61	149	64
155	61	151	56	171	65	167	64	166	64
158	60	140	57	169	67	158	64	154	56
172	67	154	62	176	64	159	63	149	61
170	62	149	58	156	60	166	68	178	65
168	63	135	51^L	154	62	157	60	158	63

SA = Skeletal age in months
Ht = Standing height in inches
H = High score
L = Low score

correlation by the scattergram (grouped-data) method are best described by showing the actual computations involved. To illustrate this method, the skeletal ages and standing heights of 100 13-year-old boys will be used. These scores are listed in Table 9.2. The problem is to determine the correlation between the skeletal ages and the standing heights of the 13-year-old boys. The steps are illustrated in Figure 9.1.

1. Construct a scattergram by preparing a double-entry table as follows:
   (a) Decide upon the step intervals to be used for each variable. This is done in the same manner described in Chapter 7 for setting up a frequency table. Care should be taken to obtain approximately the same number of intervals for each variable; the size of the intervals will not be the same unless the ranges of the 2 variables are comparable. In the illustration, the interval sizes are 2 inches for standing height and 5 months for skeletal age; the number of intervals are 10 and 11, respectively.

(b) List the intervals for one variable on the left (Y variable) and the other variable on the top (X variable). For the Y variable (skeletal age), the intervals run from high at the top to low at the bottom, in the accepted manner for frequency tables, and for the X variable (standing height), from low at the left to high at the right. (Actually, there is no mathematical reason for this procedure, but it is common practice.)

(c) Starting with the first pair of scores in the tabulation, 149 for skeletal age and 58 for standing height, make a tally in the proper square. The proper square is where intervals 145-149 and 58-59 meet on the scattergram; as can be seen, eventually 5 pairs of scores fall in this square. Continue until all 100 pairs of scores are entered. The tallies are placed across the top of the various squares.

(d) Complete the scattergram with frequency columns by counting the scores tallied in rows and columns: fy at the right for skeletal age and fx at the bottom for standing height. In effect, 2 frequency tables now exist with the scattergram intervening; the intervals are on left side and top and the frequencies are at right side and bottom, respectively.

2. Select as assumed mean (AM) for each variable the midpoint of an interval approximately in the middle of each distribution. Rule off with heavy lines the squares in the row and column in which these assumed means lie, as shown in the table: 155-159 for the Y variable and 60-61 for the X variable. Then compute c and σ' for each variable; these procedures were described earlier in the computations of the mean and standard deviation and are shown at the right side of the table. In making these computations, the following columns are necessarily adjacent to the scattergram: fy, dy, fdy, and fd^2y at the right side, and fx, dx, fdx, and fd^2x at the bottom. In the computations of r from the scattergram, the size of the step interval is not considered; the amounts of variance of the 2 variables were compressed into approximately the same space in constructing the scattergram by differences in the size of the intervals (2 and 5 in this problem). So far in calculating r, with the exception of construction of the scattergram, no new statistical work has been required.

3. The next step in the problem is to compute $\Sigma x'y'$. This computation is made by multiplying the deviation of the scores from one assumed mean by the deviation from the other, in terms of deviation units (that is, without considering the size of the interval). This procedure is explained as follows:

(a) The lines representing the 2 assumed means divide the scattergram into four quadrants: upper right, upper left, lower

X – Variable: Standing Height

Y – Variable: Skeletal Age

	50-51	52-53	54-55	56-57	58-59	60-61	62-63	64-65	66-67	68-69	f_y	d_y	fd_y	fd^2_y	$x'y'$ −	$x'y'$ +
180-184								I 10 / 10			1	5	5	25		10
175-179								II 16 / 8			2	4	8	32		16
170-174						I	II 6 / 3	II 12 / 6	II 18 / 9		7	3	21	63		36
165-69						I	III 6 / 2	II 8 / 4	II 12 / 6	II 16* / 8	10	2	20	40		42
160-164					I -1 / -1	I	II 2 / 1	卌 10 / 2	II 6 / 3		11	1	11	11	1	18
155-159					II	卌 IIII	III	III			17	0	65			
150-154				III 6 / 2	卌 5 / 1	卌	卌 -5 / -1	I -2 / -2	I -3 / -3		20	-1	-20	20	10	11
145-149				I 4 / 4	卌 10 / 2	IIII	I -2 / -2	II -8 / -4			13	-2	-26	52	10	14
140-144				I 6 / 6	II 6 / 3	IIII					7	-3	-21	63		12
135-139	I 20 / 20		II 24 / 12	II 16 / 8	I 4 / 4	II					8	-4	-32	128		64
130 134		I 20 / 20		II 20 / 10	I 5 / 5						4	-5	-20	100		45
f_x	1	1	2	9	17	27	16	18	7	2	100		-119 / 65 / -54	534	-21	268 / -21 / 247
d_x	-5	-4	-3	-2	-1	0	1	2	3	4						
fd_x	-5	-4	-6	-18	-17	-50	16	36	21	8	81 / -50 / 31					
fd^2_x	25	16	18	36	17		16	72	63	32	295					

$$c_y = \frac{\sum fd_y}{N} = \frac{-54}{100} = -.54$$

$$c_x = \frac{\sum fd_x}{N} = \frac{31}{100} = .31$$

$$\sigma'_y = \sqrt{\frac{\sum fd^2_y}{N} - c^2_y} = \sqrt{\frac{534}{100} - (-.54)^2} = 2.247$$

$$\sigma'_x = \sqrt{\frac{\sum fd^2_x}{N} - c^2_x} = \sqrt{\frac{295}{100} - .31^2} = 1.689$$

$$r = \frac{\frac{\sum x'y'}{N} - c_x c_y}{\sigma'_x \sigma'_y}$$

$$= \frac{\frac{247}{100} - (-.54)(.31)}{(2.247)(1.689)}$$

$$= \frac{2.47 - (-.167)}{3.795}$$

$$= \frac{2.637}{3.795}$$

$$= .695$$

$$M_y = AM_y + (c_y \times i)$$
$$= 157.0 + (-.54 \times 5) = 154.30$$

$$\sigma_y = \sigma'_y \times i = 2.25 \times 5 = 11.25$$

$$M_x = AM_x + (c_x \times i) =$$
$$= 60.5 + (.31 \times 2) = 61.12$$

$$\sigma_x = \sigma'_x \times i = 1.69 \times 2 = 3.38$$

Figure 9.1. Calculation of the Coefficient of Correlation by Product-Moment Method Utilizing a Scattergram.

right, lower left. Scores in the upper right quadrant are above both assumed means, so the values for both variables are plus; this quadrant, therefore, is a positive quadrant since plus times plus equals plus. Scores in the lower left quadrant are below both assumed means, so the values for both variables are negative; this quadrant, then, is also positive since negative times negative equals plus. In the upper left and lower right quadrants, the values are above one assumed mean but below the other; consequently, the values in these quadrants are negative, since plus times minus equals minus.

(b) Each of the squares containing frequencies on the scatter-gram is given a value indicating its interval deviation from the two AM's. This value is determined by multiplying the interval deviation from one AM by the interval deviation from the other AM. On the scattergram, these values appear in the lower right corners of each square. For example, take the square with 2 frequencies formed by the step intervals 165-169 and 68-69 (an asterisk appears in the upper right corner). This square deviates +2 from AMy and +4 from AMx; thus: $2 \times 4 = 8$. The values of all squares are determined in like manner; these values are placed in the lower right-hand corner of each square.

(c) As there are more scores in some squares than in others, this fact must be taken into account. To do so, the frequencies in each square are multiplied by the square value just deter-mined. Thus, for the illustration above (square with the asterisk), $2 \times 8 = 16$. These values appear in the centers of the squares throughout the scattergram.

(d) When the products of all the squares have been computed, with due regard for plus and minus signs, the entries for the $x'y'$ column can be made. Add the products for each step interval of the Y variable, placing the sum of the positive values in the column under the plus sign and the sum of the negative values in the column under the negative sign. The algebraic sum of this column, then, is the difference between positive and negative values, 247 for this problem. This procedure may be duplicated for the X variable columns to check the work; the 2 answers should agree.

4. Compute the coefficient of correlation, r, by means of the formula

$$r = \frac{\dfrac{\Sigma x'y'}{N} - cxcy}{\sigma'_x \sigma'_y} \tag{9.3}$$

This computation is shown in Figure 9.1: $r = .695$.

In the lower right corner of Figure 9.1, calculations of the means and standard deviations for the two variables are made. As seen, most of the necessary computations for these statistics had been made in the correlation computation.

INTERPRETATION
OF PRODUCT—MOMENT
CORRELATION

In the presentation of sampling reliability, it was explained that the distribution of means of repeated samples of the same size drawn from the same population (as well as other statistics) takes on the form of a normal distribution. The whole concept of statistical reliability was then based on this assumption of normality. In a distribution of sample r's, however, such normality exists only when the population r is .00 and the sample size is large. With a high population correlation, say of .80, the distribution of sample r's is negatively skewed (positively skewed if $-.80$) and leptokurtic; Figure 9.2 illustrates this situation. As a consequence of this fact, a special problem exists in applying tests of significance, in determining the probable limits of the true relationships, and in making other correlational applications. Several of these situations will be considered below.

Significance

Invariably, the investigator will want to know if any obtained r is significant, that is, whether or not an obtained coefficient can be attributed to sampling error. A standard error of a coefficient of correlation (σ_r) may be computed and a t ratio obtained.

$$\sigma_r = \frac{1 - r^2}{\sqrt{N}}$$

$$t = \frac{r}{\sigma_r}$$

(9.4)

However, this formula is based on the assumption that the sampling distribution of r is normal. Thus, to use the formula when the population r is substantial violates the validity of reliability statistics.

When only the significance of the correlation is wanted, the null hypothesis can be applied. In this case, the null hypothesis states that the population r is in fact zero, and any correlation obtained is due to sampling error. In applying the null hypothesis, the amount of correlation necessary to reject at a given level of significance is determined. In doing so, the standard error for $r = .00$ is first computed.

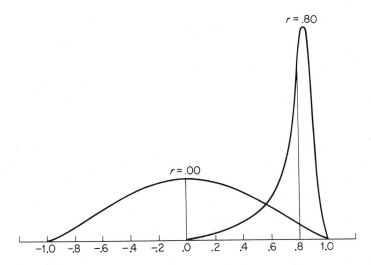

Figure 9.2. Distribution of Sample r's around Population r's of .0 and .8.

If $r = .00$, formula 9.4 becomes

$$\sigma_{r.00} = \frac{1}{\sqrt{N}} \tag{9.5}$$

$(N - 2)$ should be used in the denominator when N is small, 30 and below.) This amount is multiplied by the appropriate t for the df of the problem. Inasmuch as two variables are involved in a product-moment correlation, one df is lost for each variable; therefore, $df = N - 2$. This t is multiplied by $\sigma_{r.00}$.

An example will clarify this process. For the correlation between skeletal age and standing height, r is .695 and N is 100. Utilizing formula 9.5,

$$\sigma_{r.00} = \frac{1}{\sqrt{N}} = \frac{1}{\sqrt{100}} = .10$$

Entering Table 8.2 with $df = N - 2$, or $100 - 2 = 98$, $t = 2.63$ at the .01 level, then

$$\sigma_{r.00} \times t = .10 \times 2.63 = .263$$

Thus, a correlation as high as .263 should occur only 1 in 100 times by sampling error. Inasmuch as the r of .695 is much higher than .263, the null hypothesis can be rejected with assurance.

The above process was explained in order to demonstrate the meaning and application of the null hypothesis to a coefficient of correlation. However, a simple way is available to obtain the r's needed

TABLE 9.3 Correlation Coefficients at the
.05 and .01 Levels of Significance

Degrees of freedom ($N-2$)	.05	.01	Degrees of freedom ($N-2$)	.05	.01
1	.997	1.000	24	.388	.496
2	.950	.990	25	.381	.487
3	.878	.959	26	.374	.478
4	.811	.917	27	.367	.470
5	.754	.874	28	.361	.463
6	.707	.834	29	.355	.456
7	.666	.798	30	.349	.449
8	.632	.765	35	.325	.418
9	.602	.735	40	.304	.393
10	.576	.708	45	.288	.372
11	.553	.684	50	.273	.354
12	.532	.661	60	.250	.325
13	.514	.641	70	.232	.302
14	.497	.623	80	.217	.283
15	.482	.606	90	.205	.267
16	.468	.590	100	.195	.254
17	.456	.575	125	.174	.228
18	.444	.561	150	.159	.208
19	.433	.549	200	.138	.181
20	.423	.537	300	.113	.148
21	.413	.526	400	.098	.128
22	.404	.515	500	.088	.115
23	.396	.505	1,000	.062	.081

to reject the null hypothesis at the .05 and .01 levels. In Table 9.3 the r's are given for various degrees of freedom.

For the illustrated problem, enter this table with df of 98. By interpolation between df's of 90 and 100, the r's necessary to reject the null hypothesis at the .05 and .01 levels are .197 and .259. These r's are not quite the same as for the computational method above, where the r at the .01 was .263. The differences are in rounding off; the table is considered the more accurate.

An examination of the r's in Table 9.3 shows the great importance of sample size in the significance of correlation coefficients. With df of 10, a correlation of .708 is necessary for significance at the .01 level; and, for df of 1,000, the significant r is .081. Therefore, descriptions of correlation coefficients as being high or low are meaningless without reference to the correlation needed for the number of subjects upon which the correlation is based.

Fisher's z Coefficient

As explained above, the sampling distribution of r is not normal except when the population r is .00; and, when r is high, the sampling distribution is skewed and leptokurtic. Thus, the standard error of r is invalidated. Yet the investigator frequently wishes to make statistical inferences from high correlations.

Fisher developed a useful technique for handling sampling errors for high values of r, although it can be used with low r's as well.[2] The technique consists of converting the obtained r into a Fisher z coefficient equivalent. The distribution of sample z's is nearly normally distributed, so it is safe to apply to a standard error of z in the same manner as for the mean and other statistics previously considered. The sampling distribution of z's is shown in Figure 9.3. Compare this sampling distribution representing r's with the sampling distribution of r's in Figure 9.2.

The mathematical convergence of r to z requires logarithmic computations. However, a direct convergence table is available and appears in Table 9.4. The z coefficient equivalent of the r of .695 in the illustrated problem is .86, when interpolated. Situations in which the Fisher z coefficient is utilized follow.

Reliability limits.   Levels of confidence can be applied to correlation coefficients through z coefficients. A standard error of z is needed (σ_z):

$$\sigma_z = \frac{1}{\sqrt{N-3}} \tag{9.6}$$

In this instance, $df = N - 3$. Two degrees of freedom are lost for the two variables in the correlation and one is lost for the conversion from r to z.

[2]R. A. Fisher, *Statistical Methods for Research Workers*, 10th ed. (London: Oliver and Boyd, 1946), p. 200.

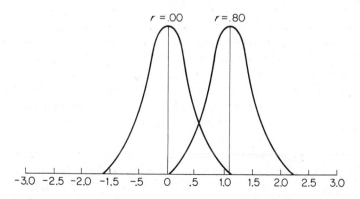

Figure 9.3. Distribution of Sample z-Coefficient Equivalents of Population r's of .00 and .80.

TABLE 9.4 Conversion of Product-Moment Correlation
to Fisher's z Coefficient Equivalent*

r	z	r	z	r	z	r	z	r	z	r	z
.25	.26	.40	.42	.55	.62	.70	.87	.85	1.26	.950	1.83
.26	.27	.41	.44	.56	.63	.71	.89	.86	1.29	.955	1.89
.27	.28	.42	.45	.57	.65	.72	.91	.87	1.33	.960	1.95
.28	.29	.43	.46	.58	.66	.73	.93	.88	1.38	.965	2.01
.29	.30	.44	.47	.59	.68	.74	.95	.89	1.42	.970	2.09
.30	.31	.45	.48	.60	.69	.75	.97	.90	1.47	.975	2.18
.31	.32	.46	.50	.61	.71	.76	1.00	.905	1.50	.980	2.30
.32	.33	.47	.51	.62	.73	.77	1.02	.910	1.53	.985	2.44
.33	.34	.48	.52	.63	.74	.78	1.05	.915	1.56	.990	2.65
.34	.35	.49	.54	.64	.76	.79	1.07	.920	1.59	.995	2.99
.35	.37	.50	.55	.65	.78	.80	1.10	.925	1.62		
.36	.38	.51	.56	.66	.79	.81	1.13	.930	1.66		
.37	.39	.52	.58	.67	.81	.82	1.16	.935	1.70		
.38	.40	.53	.59	.68	.83	.83	1.19	.940	1.74		
.39	.41	.54	.60	.69	.85	.84	1.22	.945	1.78		

*r's under .25 may be taken as equivalent to z's.

In the illustrated problem: $r = .695$; $z = .860$; $N = 100$. Applying formula 9.6,

$$\sigma_z = \frac{1}{\sqrt{N-3}} = \frac{1}{\sqrt{100-3}} = .102$$

Entering Table 8.2, the t at the .05 level for df of 97 is 1.98. Thus

$$\sigma_z + t = .102 \times 1.98 = .202$$

Adding and subtracting this amount from the z of .860:

$$.860 + .202 = 1.062$$

$$.860 - .202 = .658$$

Returning to Table 9.4, the r's for these z's are determined; the amounts are .580 and .785. Interpreting, the chances are 95 in 100 that the population r lies between .580 and .785, and 5 in 100 that is lies outside these limits.

The reliability limits for the .01 level of confidence can be determined in the same manner as for the .05 level by substituting the t of 2.63 for the 1.98 at the .05 level, as shown in Table 8.2.

Difference between uncorrelated r's. The investigator may encounter a situation where he or she wishes to determine the significance between two coefficients of correlation. When the coefficients are uncorrelated (i.e., the correlations are from independent random samples), the difference between z coefficient equivalents of the r's is tested for significance by application of the t ratio. A standard error of the difference between z's (σ_{Dz}) is needed. The formula is

$$\sigma_{Dz} = \sqrt{\frac{1}{N-3} + \frac{1}{N-3}} \qquad (9.7)$$

An illustration will explain the procedure for making this test of significance. In a study by Carter, the body weights and upper arm girths were correlated separately for 120 junior high school and 120 upper elementary school boys; the r's were .89 and .79, respectively.[3] If these correlations are to be compared, the possibility that the difference of .10 correlational points may be due to sampling errors must be determined. In other words, should the null hypothesis be accepted or rejected? The procedures for testing the null hypothesis in this problem follow.

1. Determine the difference between z coefficient equivalents for the 2 r's; the equivalents are obtained from Table 9.4.

School levels	r	z
Junior High School	.89	1.42
Upper Elementary School	.79	1.07
D_z		.35

2. Compute the standard error of the difference between z's by use of formula 9.7 and the t ratio.

$$\sigma_{Dz} = \sqrt{\frac{1}{N-3} + \frac{1}{N-3}} = \sqrt{\frac{1}{120-3} + \frac{1}{120-3}} = .134$$

$$t = \frac{D_z}{\sigma_{Dz}} = \frac{.35}{.134} = 2.68$$

3. Enter Table 8.2 with $df = N_1 + N_2 - 6$, or $120 + 120 - 6 = 234$. A t ratio of 2.60 is needed for significance at the .01 level. Inasmuch as the t ratio obtained for this problem was 2.68, the null hypothesis is rejected at this level. Thus, there is only 1 chance in 100 that the correlation difference of .10 between body weight-arm girth correlations of the junior high and elementary school boys could have occurred as a consequence of random sampling.

Averaging correlations. On occasion, the investigator may have several r's that he wishes to combine. One example is when correla-

---

[3] Gavin H. Carter, "Reconstruction of the Rogers' Strength and Physical Fitness Indices for Upper Elementary, Junior High, and Senior High School Boys" (Ph.D. diss., University of Oregon, 1957).

tions are computed for the same two variables for several samples from the same population. Another example is when the correlations have been obtained from samples drawn at successive years. Of course, a new correlation could be computed from the raw data for all samples. However, a much simpler way is to average the correlations.

If the sample r's are about the same value and are not large, a simple arithmetic average is satisfactory. However, if the r's differ considerably in size and are large, the Fisher z coefficient equivalents should be averaged, inasmuch as the value of correlation coefficients does not vary along a linear scale. If N differs for the various samples, a weighted mean should be computed, using df $(N - 3)$ rather than N in the computations. The hypothetical correlations given below will serve to illustrate this process; Table 9.4 is used to obtain the z coefficients.

r	z	N	$(N - 3)$	Weighted $z(N - 3)$
.74	.95	78	75	71.25
.82	1.16	103	100	116.00
.60	.69	63	60	41.40
			235	228.65

$$M_z = \frac{228.65}{235} = .97$$

Returning to Table 9.4, the r for the z of .97 is .75. Had the r's been averaged directly, using $df = N - 2$, the weighted r would be .738.

Actually, the difference between averaging r's and z equivalents is not great unless the differences in r's are considerable. However, when such is the case, a serious question can be raised as to whether or not r's that differ greatly come from the same population by random sampling.

Difference between Correlated r's

A situation is encountered occasionally when the investigator wants to determine the significance of the difference between two correlated r's. A correlated situation occurs when two variables X_2 and X_3 are correlated with the same third variable X_1 utilizing the same subjects. Thus, there are two correlations, r_{12} and r_{13}, and the significance of their difference is to be tested. An illustration of this situation is when several test items are correlated against some performance criterion of, say, academic achievement or athletic ability.

For this kind of problem, Hotelling developed a t ratio.[4] The

---

[4] Harold Hotelling, "The Selection of Variates for Use in Prediction, with Some Comments on the General Problem of Nuisance Parameters," *Annals of Mathematical Statistics*, II (1940), 271.

Hotelling formula is

$$t_{d_r} = (r_{12} - r_{13})\sqrt{\frac{(N-3)(1+r_{23})}{2(1 - r_{23}^2 - r_{12}^2 - r_{13}^2 - 2r_{23}r_{12}r_{13})}} \qquad (9.8)$$

FACTORS AFFECTING CORRELATION

The major assumption that must be met when using the product-moment method of correlation is that the data are linear. By linear it is meant that the plotted pairs of scores, as in the scattergram in Figure 9.1, are best represented by a straight line. If the correlation in Figure 9.1 had been +1.00, all pairs of scores would have fallen on a straight line from the lower left to the upper right corner of the scattergram. If the correlation had been −1.00, the straight line would have been from the upper left to the lower right corner. When correlations are less than ±1.00, which is almost always the case, the drift of scores across the scattergram should be linear.

The product-moment correlation follows a straight line only. Therefore, if the pairs of scores show a definite curve of some sort, a curvilinear relationship may be present. The presence of curvilinearity should be tested for significance. If present, the product-moment method should not be used; the proper method is the correlation ratio, or *eta*. The *r* will always be too low in designating the relationship when applied to curvilinear data.

At one time, an assumption for use of the product-moment correlation was that the data for the two variables were normally distributed. This assumption is no longer valid, unless the nonnormality of the data causes a curvilinear relationship. This may happen when one or both distributions are markedly skewed. In this event, the curvilinearity can be avoided by *T* scaling the two distributions, utilizing the normalizing process, and correlating the *T* scale equivalents. If the data are still curvilinear, then use *eta* as the correlational method. Otherwise, the forms of distributions may vary, so long as they are reasonably symmetrical.

Errors of measurement, if accidental or random, distribute normally they are "hit or miss" in their effects. Such random errors reduce the size of correlations. Two completely inaccurate tests, where chance determines the score, will produce a zero correlation. The same situation does not prevail for systematic errors, where the errors are in one direction only. An illustration of a systematic error is the use of an improperly calibrated testing instrument.

Another factor affecting the magnitude of product-moment correlations is the range of scores for the variables. A narrow range tends to reduce r, as slight changes anywhere in a distribution result in much greater variations in distribution positions. It becomes almost essential to pinpoint testing when the range of scores is small, without introducing considerable random testing error into the correlation.

PREDICTION VALUE OF CORRELATION

The real importance of r is not in terms of its magnitude per se but in terms of its predictive value. The predictive value of r increases in a curvilinear manner from .00 to 1.00. Thus, whereas an r of .80 is twice an r of .40 in magnitude, its predictive value is more than twice as great. A number of statistical procedures have been proposed to reveal the predictive value of the correlation coefficient. Three ways by which this value can be expressed are the coefficient of alienation, the coefficient of forecasting efficiency, and the coefficient of determination. All these coefficients are based on r^2.

Coefficient of alienation.   The coefficient of alienation (k) is the absence of predictive value between two variables. The formula is

$$k = \sqrt{1 - r^2} \qquad (9.9)$$

For the correlation of .695 between the skeletal ages and the heights of the 13-year-old boys:

$$k = \sqrt{1 - .695^2} = .72$$

Thus, the absence of predictive value for a correlation of .695 is .72. The larger the coefficient of alienation, the less its predictive value. When $r = .99$, $k = .14$. It is not until $r = 1.00$ that $k = .00$.

Coefficient of forecasting efficiency.   The coefficient of forecasting efficiency (E), also known as the predictive index (PI), expresses the presence of predictive value. The formula is

$$E = I - \sqrt{1 - r^2} \qquad (\text{or, } E = 1 - k) \qquad (9.10)$$

For the skeletal age-height correlation of .695:

$$E = 1 - \sqrt{1 - .695^2} = .28$$

This coefficient may be interpreted as percentage of predictive value better than a "best guess." In the illustration, the prediction of skeletal age from height for 13-year-old boys is 28% better than "guessing."

When $r = 1.00$, $E = 1.00$, or 100% predictive accuracy;

when $r = .00$, $E = .00$, or no predictive accuracy.

As indicated earlier, the predictive value of r increases in a curvilinear manner. This curvilinearity may be shown by plotting the coefficients of forecasting efficiency, as shown in Figure 9.4. As demonstrated in the graph and as computed by E, an r of .80 has five times the predictive value of an r of .40:

$$E = 1 - \sqrt{1 - .80^2} = .40$$

$$E = 1 - \sqrt{1 - .40^2} = .08$$

The E of .40 is five times greater than the E of .08.

Coefficient of determination. The coefficient of determination (d) is simply

$$d = r^2 \qquad (9.11)$$

When multiplied by 100, this coefficient gives the percentage of variance in Y that is associated with, determined by, or accounted for by variance in X. For the skeletal age-height correlation of .695:

$$d = .695^2 = .48.$$

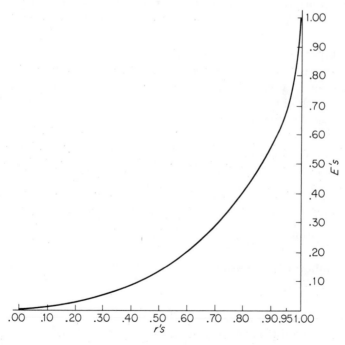

Figure 9.4. Predictive Value of r in Terms of the Coefficient of Forecasting Efficiency (E).

Thus, 48% of the variance in Y is accounted for by the variance in X (or vice versa, as this relationship is reversible). To account for one-half the variance of any set of measurements, the r between variables would have to be .707.

OTHER CORRELATIONAL METHODS

Various methods of computing correlations have been devised, many of these for special conditions. Several of the more commonly used ones are mentioned below.

Multiple Correlation. The coefficient of multiple correlation indicates the degree to which values of one variable correlate with values of two or more other variables. For example, how well does broad jumping ability correlate with sprinting ability and leg strength?

Partial Correlation. The coefficient of partial correlation determines the net relationships between two variables when the influence of one or more other factors is excluded. For example, how well do weight and strength correlate when skeletal age is held constant?

Rank-Difference Method. The rank-difference method, designated as rho, is designed to correlate two variables when the scores are arranged as ranks. For example, if football players were ranked according to their tackling and blocking abilities, these two traits could be correlated by this method.

Biserial Correlation. This correlation method is used when one variable is in a continuum and the other is a dichotomy (classified into two categories). This method was utilized by McCurdy and Larson when they correlated the results of their "Organic Efficiency Test" with a criterion consisting of two groups, infirmary patients and varsity swimmers.

Tetrachoric Correlation. This method is used when both variables are dichotomies.

Contingency Coefficient. The contingency coefficient is used when both variables are classified into the same number of categories from two or more.

PREDICTION

In prediction, results are anticipated beforehand. Usually the anticipated results are not chance guesses, but are based upon some known facts or relationships or are carefully conceived beliefs. As examples: the Gallop poll may predict the winner of a national presidential election; the prediction is based on the voting intentions of the American people. A football coach names the starting lineup for a game; the selections are based upon opinions of players' abilities formed from many observations of their performances in practice and during competition. Colleges and universities predict probable academic success when they admit freshmen to their institutions; typically, their predictions are based upon high school grades and results from admissions tests.

The statistical approach to prediction is through the use of "regression" equations, which are based upon correlations among the variables involved. If the correlation is ±1.00, which seldom if ever occurs, prediction can be made with absolute certainty. If the correlation is .00, prediction is worthless, the same as random selection. Thus, the higher the correlation, the more confidence can be placed in predicting from it. Inasmuch as the predictive value of a correlation increases on a curvilinear rather than a linear scale (Figure 9.4), a very high correlation is needed before prediction can be made with reasonable assurance.

The four available regression equations are regression lines drawn on a scattergram, regression equation in deviation form, regression equation in score form, and regression equation in standard score form. Regression lines are restricted to two-variable correlations; the other three equations may be applied to both two-variable and multivariable correlations. A standard error of estimate (Gest.) is necessary to indicate the amount of potential error in making individual predictions. An illustration of one study using multiple regression equation is next.

The Rogers' Strength Index for boys from which the Physical Fitness Index is derived requires administration of 7 tests: lung capacity, right and left grips, back and leg strengths, and arm strength obtained from pull-ups and bar push-ups. Hoping to reduce testing equipment and testing time, Clarke and Carter undertook research to seek simplifications of this battery at each of 3 school levels: upper elementary, junior high, and senior high.[5] At each of the 3 school levels, multiple correlations were completed; in each instance, the Strength

[5]H. Harrison Clarke and Gavin H. Carter, "Oregon Simplifications of the Strength and Physical Fitness Indices," *Research Quarterly*, 30, No. 1 (March 1959), 3.

Index was the criterion (dependent) variable and the test items composing the battery were the experimental (independent) variables. The multiple correlations reached and exceeded .977. In order to use the Strength Index norms to predict the Physical Fitness Index, score-form multiple regression equations were computed. These equations were

Upper elementary school: SI = 1.05 (leg lift) + 1.35 (back lift)
+ 10.92 (push-ups) + 133 (Gest. = 43).

Junior High School: SI = 1.33 (leg lift)
+ 1.20 (arm strength) + 286. (Gest. = 76)

Senior High School: SI = 1.22 (leg lift)
+ 1.23 (arm strength) + 499. (Gest. = 86)

In this illustration, high multiple correlations were expected, since spuriousness was present in that the test items correlated composed the criterion measure. Further, by a third test to the multiple correlations at the junior and senior high school levels, the respective correlations were increased and the standard error of estimates were reduced by more than one-half.

Laboratory Research

10
Laboratory and Experimental Research

INTRODUCTION TO PART IV

Laboratory resources may be in a formally established laboratory, or they may be a gymnasium, athletic field, track, or swimming pool when utilized for conducting scientific investigations. Such scientific studies involve the adoption of a study design with appropriate hypotheses, the use of proper tests to measure the essential elements under investigation, and the appropriate statistical analyses of these data.

The first chapter in Part IV, Chapter 10, is "Laboratory and Experimental Research." The methods presented are common to the various types of studies considered in subsequent chapters. This practice was adopted in order to avoid unnecessary duplication of methodology; cross-references to this chapter should suffice. The other chapters are devoted to five broad investigative areas, as follows: Chapter 11, Physiology of Exercise; Chapter 12, Motor Learning/Motor Control; Chapter 13, Psychological Studes; Chapter 14, Biomechanical Research; and Chapter 15, Growth and Development.

The reader should be aware that the intention in Chapters 11–15 is to present the most relevant processes and procedures for conducting experimental research, with examples of relevant studies employing these techniques. This should serve to direct the student to sources of literature from which more formal analyses can be made. Substantive knowledge of the state of the literature in each of these major areas should be approached from the appropriate subject matter, which normally is found in formal course work or independent study at the graduate level. In this way, the student can be assured of remaining up to date in the several fields. The use of various techniques, it will be noticed, changes less dramatically with the passing of time.

A number of experimental methods may be employed in research; the acceptability of any one will depend entirely on the experiment to be conducted. There are advantages and disadvantages to each, and the student of research must be reasonably knowledgeable in all the more common ones so as to know when they are to be used. Failure to use the proper experimental design can render the results invalid. This chapter deals with such factors, as well as general considerations that concern instrumentation, precision of testing, tester competency, and the establishment of a research laboratory.

EXPERIMENTAL METHODS

The primary responsibility of the investigator is to adopt the appropriate experimental methodology before proceeding with data collection. The essence of the experimental method is to attempt to control all the essential factors except one variable which is manipulated in such a manner that the effect of its operation can be determined and measured. Thus, if a single factor is to be studied, and it is determined later that either of two factors could account for the measured change, serious doubt may be cast on the validity of the research. It is incumbent upon the investigator to assess correctly those factors that must be controlled and then control them in the study.

One of the forces behind experimental research originally was the desire to be able to set up a cause-and-effect relationship. In fact, early experimenters were of the belief that all factors must be held constant, except one which was manipulated in such a way that it would lead to a specific effect. The modern researcher has a wide variety of procedures available for conducting experimental research.

Frequently, a misunderstanding exists of what is entailed when one attempts to control experimental variables. Actually, the term is a misnomer, because operationally one seldom controls variable factors; rather, one measures their basic properties to determine the directional change that could be expected under normal conditions. In experiments dealing with human performance, it is sometimes essential to know the normal reactions of subjects tested under conditions identical to those of the experimental group. Therefore, one variable is allowed to operate in the experimental group but not in a control group; if the two groups eventually differ, the investigator should be able to claim that the difference was due to the main effects involved.

Simple research designs are presented in this section, with brief references to more sophisticated plans. They were chosen to meet the needs of graduate students who are mostly neophytes in research. Campbell and Stanley have presented 16 experimental designs, classified as preexperimental, true experimental, and quasi-experimental.[1] The validities of these designs are examined against 12 common threats to valid inference. The designs are also discussed by Good.[2] These references should be helpful to the investigator when an experimental design not presented in this text is needed.

The simple experimental designs are so called because they are relatively uncomplicated and lead to problem solution in a direct manner. One or the other of the techniques described next is employed in much of published research in physical education and, therefore, can be considered potentially more functional for the beginner researcher.

Single-Group Design

The single-group design involves one group of subjects in the following manner: They are first given an initial test, the experimental factor is applied, and a final test follows. This is particularly well adapted to studies of physical conditioning, where changes in physical fitness are known not to occur unless systematic exercise is given.

The strength of this design is that it does not require the equation or rotation of groups, and it is particularly well adapted to classroom use. The weaknesses encountered begin with the lack of a control group, but this is a deficiency only if a control group is needed and cannot be considered a blanket indictment. However, if the changes that result from conditioning can be attributed in part to maturation—the subjects grew larger, became more mature, and consequently stronger, and so on—then the full impact of the main effects cannot be ascertained. This is true, similarly, if learning of the criterion variables can be said to exist; it could then be argued that the full effects of the conditioning program are unknown because of the ameliorating influence of this factor.

An example of the one-group experiment is a study by Davis, in which a group of subjects was conditioned for 5 weeks to middle

[1]Donald T. Campbell and Julian C. Stanley, "Experimental and Quasi-Experimental Designs for Research in Teaching," in *Handbook of Research in Teaching*, ed. N.L. Gage (Chicago: Rand McNally & Company, 1963), Ch. 5.

[2]Carter V. Good, *Essentials of Educational Research* (East Norwalk, Conn.: Appleton-Century-Crofts, 1966), Ch. 8.

distance swimming.[3] They were measured before and after the program on a number of muscular strength, endurance, and motor fitness variables. The results of the study showed a statistically significant decrease of 23.7 seconds in mean swimming time ($t = 6.47$). Significant conditioning effects were realized, as shown from improved gross and relative muscular strength, strength of muscles primarily involved in swimming the crawl stroke, Rogers' and McCloy's arm-shoulder endurance measures, and all items on the World War II Navy Standard Physical Fitness Test. Of interest was the finding that the amount of strength decrement from the first and last 200-yard swim at maximal speed was the same, even though the mean time decreased by 23.7 seconds during the training period. Apparently, the subjects swam faster for the same degree of muscular fatigue.

A variation of the single-group design is the *reverse* design, in which an initial test is given, and factor *A* is applied. Then the subjects are retested, and factor *B* is applied, to be followed by the final test. Unless the cumulative effect of factors *A* and *B* are sought, this design would seem to have little advantage to offer. Fewer subjects are required, to be sure, but there are a number of weaknesses that make this design particularly suceptible to artifacts. For example, in learning studies, gains may be greater as a result of factor *A*, since the typical curve of learning shows more rapid acceleration in earlier stages of practice with the additional possibility of plateaus occurring. The practice effect of taking a series of measurements may be more pronounced for factor *B* than for factor *A*, which would cause spuriously large differences. Related to this is the possibility of a carry-over of attitude or method of attack by the subject from one experimental task to another, which in fatigue or endurance studies may result in learning to endure pain or discomfort. Differential maturation and other factors may also impinge upon the acceptability of this method of experimental design.

Repeated-Measures Design

A variation of the single-group design is the repeated-measures design, in which all subjects in a group receive all treatments. If several experimental treatments are to be investigated, it may be desirable for all subjects to be exposed to each treatment. This process serves to control intersubject variability, which is sometimes a problem when

---

[3]Jack F. Davis, "Effects of Training and Conditioning for Middle Distance Swimming upon Measures of Cardiovascular Condition, General Physical Fitness, Gross Strength, Motor Fitness, and Strength of Involved Muscles" (Ed.D. diss., University of Oregon, 1955).

different subjects are employed. In fact, the subject serves as his or her own control in this design. Such a design is not normally utilized in situations that involve physical conditioning or learning, for example, because a basic assumption is that each subject must be susceptible to the main effects. Once conditioning or learning has occurred, it is not possible to return to the previous level for another treatment.

It should be pointed out that some performance variables themselves contain a rather large amount of learning, but as long as the learning per se is not examined, other ways of ameliorating the mitigating influence of this factor may be applied. For example, one method is to give a sufficient number of trials of the criterion task to all subjects at the outset of the experiment in a deliberate attempt to cause learning to occur at an approximately equal extent. The number of trials needed for learning to occur should be determined by preliminary investigation during the preparatory experimental stages. This point should be given careful consideration if novel or unfamiliar tasks are to be employed, because, as shown in Chapter 12, large amounts of learning may occur that, if not anticipated, could cause difficulties with data analysis and interpretation.

The small amount of learning (or conditioning) that may occur during the experiment can be tolerated by rotating the order of treatment administration—employing a randomized order—or by a systematic method, such as a Latin-square arrangement, which will be discussed later in this chapter. The intent is to balance the effect of individual differences and the progressive influence that the same order of experimental treatment might have on the results.

The repeated-measures design is illustrated in a study of the effect of muscular tension on reaction time.[4] Forty-one subjects were given a simple reaction time measure that consisted of responding to an auditory signal and giving a maximal contraction of the handgripping muscles. However, each test was preceded by a preparatory submaximal muscular contraction, amounting to 0 (control condition), 10, 15, 20, 25, and 30 kg. Each subject undertook all conditions, but the order of testing was balanced to offset possible learning of the task. Reaction time did improve significantly, but the differences were entirely between control and 10 kg pretension, both of which were slower than all other conditions. Thus, the concept that increased muscular tension, in the form of preparatory set, resulted in faster reaction time was supported. While it is clear that some experiments will require use of the repeated-measures design, the reader should be aware of certain

[4]David H. Clarke, "Effect of Preliminary Muscular Tension on Reaction Latency," *Research Quarterly*, 39, No. 1 (March 1968), 60.

statistical risks involved that may not be inherent in the random-groups design.[5]

Static-Group Comparison Design

This design compares the status of a given group that had experienced an experimental variable with a group that had not. Actually, no experimentation takes place; no attempt is made to establish any equivalence of the groups. An example of such a study is the comparison of high school football athletes and nonathletes on various physical and motor measures. Significant differences will readily be found. However, to infer that such differences are due to participation in football could be faulty and unjustified, since predisposition to superior athletic performances may be inherent in such natural selective factors as advanced maturity, physique type, and muscular strength of the athletes. Reports of such studies have been presented by Clarke.[6]

Random-Groups Design

For this experimental design, two or more groups are formed of subjects selected by random means. The experimental procedures to be evaluated should also be randomly assigned to the various groups. If a control group is desired, one of the groups may be used for this purpose. In the simplest form of this design, the subjects, assigned randomly to groups A and B, would be given a preliminary test. Group A would undergo the experimental treatment; group B would serve as a control, so would not receive the treatment; both groups would be retested on the criterion task at the conclusion of the treatment period. When more than one treatment is desired, other groups would be included.

The advantages of employing a random-groups design are similar to those of the repeated-measures design; that is, the difficulties of the single-group experiment can be avoided. A control group may be used, and any number of treatment groups may be established so that the simultaneous observation of several factors may be made. By this method, it is logical to expect that the groups selected will have different means, due to the sampling process.[7] The differences in initial means may affect the corresponding differences in final means. Analysis of covariance is a statistic that may be used in analyzing the

[5] Harold H. Morris, "Analysis of Repeated Measures," in *Symposium Papers*, eds. Richard H. Cox and Robert C. Serfass (Reston, Va.: American Alliance for Health, Physical Education, Recreation, and Dance, 1981), pp. 5-60.

[6] H. Harrison Clarke, *Physical and Motor Tests in the Medford Boys' Growth Study* (Englewood Cliffs, N.J.: Prentice-Hall, Inc., 1971), pp. 236-64.

[7] See Chapter 8.

results of such a study, as final means adjusted for differences between initial means are tested for significance.

A study employing this technique divided 62 college men into 2 groups:[8] One group was given 10 weeks of weight training exercises; the other remained inactive in order to serve as a control group. At the outset of the experiment, all subjects were measured for arm strength, effective arm mass, and speed in a lateral adductive arm movement. The experimental group improved significantly in speed, strength, and strength-mass ratio, whereas the control group declined. However, individual differences in the amount of change in the strength-mass ratio correlated low but significantly with individual changes in maximal speed of movement.

Posttest only Random-Groups Design

This design is similar to the preceding random-groups design, except no pretests are given. Experimental and control groups are formed by random assignment. At the close of the experiment, the difference between the means of the groups is tested for statistical significance. In applying this design, it is assumed that the groups are from the same population, so their means should only differ in accordance with normal probability. This assumption might well be fallacious if, for the sake of convenience, each group were from a different class within the school, where actual differences could exist unknown to the investigator. In such instances, some means of justifying equivalence seems indicated.

To illustrate: 40 subjects are drawn by random means, none of whom has had experience in gymnastics. From those subjects, 2 groups of 20 each are formed, also by random. One group is taught a gymnastic skill by the whole method and the other group by the part method. In this insance, the assumption seems sound that the 2 groups are comparable at the start of the experiment; further a pretest of the gymnastic skill would be meaningless since all subjects are unfamiliar with it. Shay conducted such a study utilizing the upstart on the horizontal bar with college freshmen as subjects.[9] The subjects in each group were randomly selected but were in a different class. Consequently, he did equate the groups for other factors: general motor ability by the Brace Test and gross strength by Rogers' Strength Index.

[8]David H. Clarke and Franklin M. Henry, "Neuromotor Specificity and Increased Speed from Strength Development," *Research Quarterly*, 32, No. 3 (October 1961), 315.

[9]Clayton T. Shay, "The Progressive-Part Vs. the Whole Method of Learning Motor Skills," *Research Quarterly*, 5, No. 4 (December 1934), 62.

Related-Groups Design

This procedure involves dividing a sample into two or more groups, primarily on the basis of some initial trait, so that the groups are equated (as described in Chapter 7). The equating may be done by pairing and then randomly assigning the pairs to groups or by simply adjusting various groups so that both means and standard deviations are equivalent. Thus, the groups are formed, the treatment is administered to the experimental group—perhaps while the control group does nothing—and then the posttest is administered to all groups.

For some experiments, experimental and control groups need not be equal on the initial test; the control group may be wanted simply to assure that a practice effect, or some other influence, did not cause a significant change from initial to final test; thus, only a finding of no difference is required. Equating on the basis of some initial factor may not assure equal vulnerability to change; randomizing subjects, rather than equating, offers this assurance. The student should approach the design and analysis of the experiment with great care if control groups are not similar to experimental groups.

To illustrate the related-groups design: Two groups of male subjects were equated by Brumbach on the basis of serum cholesterol, a physical fitness test, deviations from normal weight, and chronological age in order to study the effect of exercise on serum cholesterol.[10] One group, designated control, participated in no organized physical activity for 10 weeks; the experimental group engaged in a formal exercise program consisting of vigorous exercise, running, and weight lifting. The exercise group improved more in physical fitness than the control group, but the difference between the means in final serum cholesterol was not significant.

A variation of this design was utilized by Clarke and Jarman in studying the academic achievement of boys 9, 12, and 15 years of age.[11] At each age, high and low groups were formed separately based on Rogers' Strength Index and Physical Fitness Index and other tests. In each instance, paired subjects were matched by intelligence quotients; the differences between the means and between the standard deviations were not significant. Generally, the high groups had significantly higher grade-point averages in their class work and significantly higher means on standard academic achievement tests.

[10] Wayne B. Brumbach, "Changes in Serum Cholesterol Levels of Male College Students Who Participated in a Special Exercise Program," *Research Quarterly*, 32, No. 2 (May 1961), 147.

[11] H. Harrison Clarke and Boyd O. Jarman, "Scholastic Achievement of Boys 9, 12, and 15 Years of Age as Related to Various Strength and Growth Measures," *Research Quarterly*, 32, No. 2 (May 1961), 155.

TABLE 10.1 Scheme of Experimental Factors for Treatment
Groups in $2 \times 2 \times 2$ Factorial Design

	Sedentary		Spontaneous	
Light	Nonstroke	Stroke	Nonstroke	Stroke
Dark	Nonstroke	Stroke	Nonstroke	Stroke

Factorial Designs

Factorial designs permit simultaneous examination of the effects of 2 or more experimental variables, as well as their interaction. Thus, the term 2×2 indicates that 2 variations each of 2 factors are being investigated; $2 \times 2 \times 2$ would indicate that 2 variations each of 3 factors are examined. In an example of the latter design, Hanson, Clarke, and Kelley[12] studied the effects of 3 sets of factors on the ability of the laboratory rat to run on a motor-driven belt treadmill: running in light areas vs. running in dark areas; a comparison of those housed in spontaneous cages vs. those in sedentary cages; and posttrial stroking versus nonstroking. Table 10.1 illustrates the arrangement of experimental factors, with an equal number of subjects assigned randomly to each of the 8 cells ($2 \times 2 \times 2 = 8$).

Another example of a factorial design is provided in Badgley's study of the effects on ankle flexibility of various conditions for administering whirlpool baths.[13] Four water temperatures and four lengths of time in the water were systematically varied (4×4 design). The range of motion of the ankle joint was measured before and after each bath; the difference between these tests indicated the treatment effect. The significance of the differences between means was determined by 2-way analysis of variance. Three F ratios were obtained for differences in water temperature, length of time in water, and combinations of water and time (interaction).

TEST CONSTRUCTION

The construction of tests has been commonplace in physical education research for well over a century; special textbooks are replete with tests germane to this field. Typically, such texts present tests of muscular

[12]Dale Hanson, David Clarke, and David Kelley, "Effect of Selected Treatments upon the Treadmill Running Success of Male Rats," *Research Quarterly*, 40, No. 1 (March 1969).

[13]Marion E. Badgley, "A Study of the Effect of Whirlpool Baths on Range of Motion of the Right Ankle under Selected Conditions" (Master's thesis, University of Oregon, 1957).

strength, muscular endurance, circulatory-respiratory endurance, physique type, nutritional status, posture, general motor ability and capacity, skills in many sports, physical education and sports knowledge, personal-social effectiveness, and attitudes. A great variety of procedures has been employed in the process of test construction. Typically, graduate students in physical education will have had a course in tests and measurements, so will have some familiarity with test construction. Tests are vital to laboratory research since a matter, thing, or phenomenon cannot be scientifically studied unless it can be measured. Three primary functions are fulfilled in the construction of tests, as briefly described here.

Validation

A valid test is one that measures what it purports to measure. Consequently, in constructing tests, the researcher presents evidence to support stated contentions regarding the elements or traits that the test measures. In order to do so, a criterion is established of the element being measured, and the test is compared with this criterion. If the two have a high relationship, it may be logically concluded that the test measures the same quality as does the criterion. In general, the following types of criteria have been utilized in physical education test construction:

Critical Appraisal. This process consists of analyzing the activity in terms of its fundamental components and selecting a test item to represent each. An example of this procedure was employed in constructing the original Youth Fitness Test for the American Association for Health, Physical Education, and Recreation. A committee of qualified personnel, through critical appraisal, designated the following seven components of motor fitness: arm-shoulder muscular endurance, abdominal muscular endurance, agility, speed, muscular leg power, muscular arm-shoulder power, and circulatory-respiratory endurance. Then, based on their extensive knowledge of tests, they selected one test item to represent each of the seven components. The same situation prevailed for the newly created AAHPER Health Related Physical Fitness Test.

Established Test. A simple criterion is to utilize a test of the same quality, the validity of which has already been established, if such a criterion test exists. If the relationship between the old and the new tests is close, they measure essentially the same thing. Validation then rests on the validation of the old test. This practice has not been followed to any extent in the validation of physical education tests. However, several established tests have been revised or simplified in this manner, as was done for the Iowa Revision of the Brace Test, the Metheny-Johnson Test of Motor Educability, and the Oregon Simplification of the Rogers Strength Index.

Subjective Judgments. In the utilization of this criterion, ratings of the relative ability of the subjects in an activity to be measured are made by experts. This criterion has been used in constructing tests in team sports, such as basketball, soccer, field hockey, and volleyball. In such activities, it is otherwise difficult to isolate the quality of the individual's performance from that of a teammate's.

Composite Score. The composite score is the sum (or average) of all the scores made by each individual on all tests included in the experimental situation. These scores are usually expressed in standard score form, as, otherwise, such values as distance in the standing broad jump, number of chins, and speed in the 50-yard dash could not be added. This criterion has been in common use in the evaluation of motor ability and motor fitness tests.

Functional Evidence. This criterion consists of functional evidence of the performance for which the test is constructed. As examples of the application of this criterion, the following may be mentioned: Dryer used round-robin play to validate her tennis test; Cureton used a manikin as a criterion of posture; and Rogers utilized major sports lettermen, captains, and "best players" as representing superior athletic ability.

Precision

A test is precise when essentially the same scores are obtained on repeated tests of the same subjects under similar conditions. Procedures for determining the precision of tests follow.

Test-Retest Consistency. A common practice for determining the precision of physical, motor, and skill tests has been to repeat the test with the same subjects under similar conditions and correlate the results. The two tests should be given by different testers, so that testing consistency between testers is determined; this result is more important than just self-agreement, which occurs when the researcher administers both tests. In physical education, the resultant correlation when different testers are involved has been known as an *objectivity coefficient*, also, called a reliability coefficient, especially when both tests are given by the same tester.

As a general rule, objectivity coefficients of .90 and above should be obtained before satisfactory test precision is realized. Lower correlations may be considered as rough approximations; they may be useful when more precise tests are not available. Guides for securing adequate objectivity in measurement are: (1) provide accurately phrased and fully detailed instructions of testing procedures; (2) keep testing procedures as simple as possible without loss of validity; (3) when possible, use mechanical instruments of measurement; (4) reduce results to mathematical scores; and (5) use trained testers.

It is possible for the test-retest correlation to be high, and yet the subjects have different scores on the two tests. Such a situation would happen if the subjects had consistently higher scores on the second test than they did on the first, while still maintaining their relative positions in the distribution; conceivably, this could occur if maturation or learning took place between the tests. For example, strength could increase scores on a strength test and learning could do likewise on a skill test. Also, motivation may be involved, with the subjects exerting more or less effort on the second test; consistency of tester motivation is essential.

Maturation can be reasonably controlled by administering the two tests within days of each other. To control learning, at least in part, provide practice of the test prior to giving it the first time. These conditions will not affect the test's objectivity coefficients if the effects are even for all subjects throughout the distribution of scores, that is, if all subjects maintain their relative portion in the distribution on both tests. However, the means, and possibly the standard deviations, would differ; a check on these statistics would indicate whether this effect was present.

Split-half Method.   In knowledge tests where a large number of questions are asked, the test-retest method of determining test consistency could be seriously affected by learning taking place between the tests. To relieve this situation, the split-half method has been employed. By this method, all questions are administered once and then divided evenly into two parts, usually odd-numbered and even-numbered items. The scores made on the two halves are then correlated. As can be seen, dividing the questions into halves reduces the length of the test by one-half. As a consequence, the correlation obtained is lower than for the total test, since, generally, the longer the knowledge test the greater its consistency. To correct for this situation, the Spearman-Brown prophecy can be applied; this formula provides an estimate of the correlation for the test at its full length, twice as long as the split half. In the following example, the split-half correlation is .80, the estimated reliability for the whole test compiled from the formula is .89.

S-B Formula: $\dfrac{2 \times \text{r for halves test}}{1 + \text{r for halves test}} = \dfrac{2 \times .80}{1 + .80} = \dfrac{1.60}{1.80} = .89$

Equivalent-forms Method.   Another method of estimating the precision of knowledge tests is by applying equivalent forms of the test to the same subjects and correlating the results (also called parallel or alternate forms). The problem here, of course, is to form the equivalent groups. To do so, a large number of questions are administered to appropriate subjects and arranged on a scale according to their order of difficulty from easiest to hardest. Equivalent forms are obtained by matching questions of approximately equal difficulty for each form evenly throughout this scale.

Norms

Generally, in the construction of tests, norms are prepared from testing large random samples of subjects for whom the test is intended. Thus, norms represent the status quo of a specified population. They provide a means for interpreting a person's score in relation to scores made by individuals in the population at large. In physical education, norms have been based upon various combinations of age, height, and weight. For example, norms for Rogers' Strength Index, in order to obtain a Physical Fitness Index, are based on age and weight for each sex separately. Scales based upon percentiles or upon standard deviation values of normal distribution have been used extensively. To illustrate, percentiles are the basis of norms for both the AAHPERD Youth Fitness and the AAHPERD Health-Related tests. Random procedures for obtaining representative samples appear in Chapter 8; the construction of scales based on percentiles and on standard deviations is presented in Chapter 7.

RELATIONSHIP STUDIES

A perusal of the literature in physical education will reveal many studies designed to examine the relationships among variables. The relationship study is not experimental, but it does require that at least two different measures be obtained on the same subjects. Thus, the process represents a single-group design. Relationship studies are typically based upon zero-order, partial, multiple, and canonical correlations.

Any significant relationship may have importance for the investigator. However, the ultimate goal for such studies is the ability to predict a criterion measure from one or more test variables. If the correlation coefficient is sufficiently high to warrant it, regression equations provide the means for making such predictions.[14]

Some relationship studies are continued into a factor analysis, since this analysis is based on the intercorrelation of all variables involved. A general factor is sought from the matrix of correlations as well as other factors that may load together. Principal and rotated factors are obtained in carrying out the computations. As an example, Phillips conducted a factor analysis for the same boys at each age, 9 through 12, inclusive; each subject was given 50 tests of physique type, anthropometry, muscular strength and endurance, and motor ability elements.[15] A total of 12 rotated factors appeared during the 8 ages of the subjects. However, only 3 factors appeared at all ages; these factors were identified as body bulk-physique, body linearity, and arm-shoulder endurance. As another example, a series of factor analysis of 25 cable-tension strength tests for boys and girls at the various school levels from upper elementary through college failed to reveal a general strength factor.[16] When rotations were applied, the highest loadings were scattered across many factors; mostly, only 1 strength test loaded moderately high on a single factor. These results support the concept of strength specificity.

COMPARATIVE STUDIES

The comparison of various traits exhibited by different identifiable (intact) groups is another prevalent type of study in physical education. The typical procedure is to test the significance between the means for each trait involved for the various groups in the study. The usual tests of significance for the mean differences are the t ratio for two means and the F ratio by analysis of variance for more than two means.[17] An example of a comparative study is the determination between the maturity, physique type, body size, muscular strength and endurance, and motor traits of athletes and nonparticipants in the Medford Boys' Growth Study.[18] Other possibilites are differences between the sexes,

[14]See Chapter 9 for statistical applications.

[15]Dean Allen Phillips, "Annual Factor Analysis of Potential Maturity Indicators of the Same Boys from Nine through Sixteen Years of Age" (Ed.D. diss. University of Oregon, 1965).

[16]H. Harrison Clarke and Richard A. Munroe, *Test Manual: Oregon Cable-Tension Strength Test Batteries for Boys and Girls from Fourth Grade through College* (Eugene, Oreg.: Microcard Form Publications in Health, Physical Education, and Recreation, 1970).

[17]See Chapter 8.

[18]H. Harrison Clarke, *Physical and Motor Tests in the Medford Boys' Growth Study* (Englewood Cliffs, N.J.: Prentice-Hall, Inc., 1971), Ch. 6.

between races, between cultures, between socioeconomic groups, and between urban-rural populations. Such studies need not be confined to physical and motor traits, but may be involved with behavioral patterns, personality traits, and attitudes toward physical education and sports.

CONTROL OF EXPERIMENTAL FACTORS

In this chapter it has been pointed out that the investigator must do everything possible to control the experimental factors, the need for a control group was indicated for certain research designs. In addition, other methods are at the disposal of the experimenter to make testing more valid, to reduce the error that is inevitably involved in testing human subjects, and to make the data collection as rigorous as possible. Problems of instrumentation will be discussed subsequently, but, first, a number of other matters must be mentioned.

Subjects

In experimental research in physical education, the investigator uses mostly human subjects and to a lesser extent small animals such as laboratory rats, as will be discussed in Chapter 11. Too often the choice of subjects is made carelessly, considering availability without serious thought to type needed. Frequently, samples have consisted of students enrolled in college or university classes, high school students, athletes, and the like simply because they were conveniently available for testing. This statement is not intended to criticize the use of such subjects categorically, for in many experiments they are entirely satisfactory. However, selection of a sample should be made on considerations other than just convenience. The following matters are pertinent:

1. *Randomization.* The concepts of population samples and reliability are discussed in Chapter 8, so only brief mention of this aspect will be made here. The point to be stressed is that a sample, to be representative of the population from which it is drawn, must be obtained at random; further, each individual in the population should have an equal chance of being chosen. This process permits application of the principles of normal probability. When sampling procedures violate the assumptions of normality, then the sample may be biased. In a practical way, the investigator should exert care in obtaining subjects, in regard to both type and number; for example, if adult males are desired, then they should

be of the same sex, old enough to be considered adult, and restricted somewhat in range of age. The selection of actual subjects to form the same population may be accomplished by using a table of random numbers.[19]

2. *Age.* In some studies, the age of the subjects need only be specified in broad categories, such as junior high school girls or adult men; in other situations, stricter control of age is necessary. The control of age is especially important in growth studies where the variables are affected by age. Thus, a single age may be restricted to testing the subjects within a few days to a month or more from their birthdays. On the other end of the scale, the study of the aging process may mean that subjects must be recruited from the ranks of the elderly. Whether or not old men or women can be tested on vigorous physical activities is a question of their health; thus, the sample at these ages may indeed be biased, as those who are infirm will not be available, so the sample will reflect only healthy adults. In determining procedures, subjects of widely divergent ages should not be mixed when the research calls for homogeneity. The reader should remember that once the appropriate age of subjects has been determined, the specific subjects are still randomly selected.

3. *Sex.* The traditional approach to physical education research is to restrict each study to one of the sexes. Definite differences between the sexes exist in such measures as physique type, body size, strength, and motor ability. As a consequence, the sexes should not be combined in the same sample. Such sex differences have been presented by Clarke.[20]

4. *Physical ability.* The research design that seeks to understand the nature of human performance should use subjects randomly selected from the population, as outlined above. When a sample is thus drawn, it will inevitably include those individuals of high and low physical ability; the majority will be centered about the middle of the distribution, according to the dictates of normal probability. A bias may be introduced should the investigator select as subjects either those of extremely low or extremely high physical ability. The best random sample would span the range, avoiding too much concentration at the extremes, either inten-

[19] R. A. Fisher and F. Yates, *Statistical Tables for Biological, Agricultural, and Medical Research*, 5th ed. (New York: Hafner Publishing Co., 1957).

[20] H. Harrison Clarke, ed., "Physical and Motor Sex Differences," *Physical Fitness Research Digest*, 9, No. 4 (October 1979). (President's Council on Physical Fitness and Sports, Washington, D.C.)

tionally or unintentionally. The danger of using all athletes or physical education majors should be clear, except in such instances where they are the subject of the investigation (e.g., athletes versus nonathletes). On the other hand, some studies require subjects who possess unique physical attributes that make their use in experiments imperative. For example, analysis of the pole vault, springboard dive, and others can only be accomplished with subjects who are skilled in such activities.

5. *Motivation and interest.*   Experimental control will also extend to subject motivation and interest. All subjects may not be equally interested in the experiment nor motivated to participate wholly, yet, in most situations, they are usually willing to follow directions and do their best. In the administration of tests that require maximum human effort, which is true for many physical and motor sports events, such as chinning the bar, lifting on a dynamometer, and running 600 yards for time, testee motivation should be constant for all subjects. The same is true for a psychological test, since subject cooperation is essential to obtaining valid answers to the questions.

Experienced researchers know the frustration that occurs when subjects refuse or are unable to give a maximum effort when one is called for or when they continually miss appointments. Still, some subjects may be lost from a study for one reason or another, so frequently the investigator will find that the sample size has shrunk during the course of the study. The repeated-measures design in which the subjects must return to the laboratory several times is particularly frustrating, especially toward the end of the experiment when subject loss is most serious.

One technique that helps to assure adequate interest and motivation is to recruit subjects from a population known to the investigator. Although this practice may violate the assumptions of randomization, certain kinds of experiments demand excessive time and energy, and one simply must have the full cooperation of the individuals serving as subjects. Anything less than total cooperation may result in the collection of inconsistent and unreliable data.

Methodology

The manner of handling the various details of experiments is extremely important to the success of the research; many of these details can be foreseen by careful preparation before data collection. As will be emphasized repeatedly in the chapters to follow, the haphazard rush into the mainstream of testing frequently results in inadequate and inappropriate data collection. Some experiments are difficult to perform, some require rather technical background, and most require considerable precision. Several general factors related to methodology that bear on the control of experimental protocol are discussed here.

1. *Randomization.* Not only should the subjects be selected randomly and assigned to treatment groups by random means, but the order in which the various treatments are applied should also be arranged so as not to affect results. Especially important in repeated-measures designs, randomizing helps hold constant any learning or conditioning that may occur or other factors that could have a cumulative effect on the outcome.

For example, in a single-group experiment, the subjects carried army packs of different types and amounts on 7.5-mile military marches. Muscular fatigue from marching and carrying the packs was studied.[21] Over a period of several such marches, the strength and motor fitness of the subjects improved significantly. Thus, the subjects were in much better condition for pack carrying on the final march than on the first. Consequently, less muscular fatigue from carrying the final packs could be logically expected as a consequence of the conditioning; the real differences due to the main effect studied (muscular fatigue from pack carrying) is obscured. Although conditioning from repeated marches cannot be avoided, the effect of such conditioning can be equalized by distributing it evenly over the various carries. This distribution can be accomplished by a Latin-square arrangement.[22] One such Latin-square is as follows:

Order of Treatments

Groups I	A	B	C	D
II	B	A	D	C
III	C	D	B	A
IV	D	C	A	B

By way of explanation, suppose that 4 packs are to be carried by 24 subjects, each subject carrying each pack on a different march. Placement of the subjects into 4 groups of 6 each (I, II, III, IV) gives the sequence in which they are to proceed during the experiment. Therefore, subjects in group III, for example, would carry packs *C*, *D*, *B*, *A* in that order for the 4 marches. Thus, all

[21] H. Harrison Clarke, Clayton T. Shay, and Donald K. Mathews, "Strength Decrements from Carrying Various Army Packs on Military Marches," *Research Quarterly*, 26, No. 3 (October 1955), 253.

[22] See Fisher and Yates, *Statistical Tables*, for a series of Latin-square arrangements.

packs are carried on the first march and all are likewise carried on the last march.

2. *Statistical control.* Occasionally in experimental research, extraneous factors may occlude the true findings, which either could not be controlled or were not taken into account during the planning of the study. The age of the subjects is a pertinent example of the distortion of a correlational analysis that could result if subjects of varying ages during the period of rapid growth were combined in the same sample. The correlation between two strength tests would be higher than would be true if homogeneous ages were employed. Because maturation results in an increase in size and muscle tissue, this results in greater strength, which tends to inflate the real correlation. The way to cope with such a situation is to use partial correlation, whereby the effect of such tertiary factors may be statistically partialled out of the correlation.

Investigator

Investigators must possess the technical qualifications to handle the detailed phases of data collection. The necessary qualifications are dependent upon the type of experiment conducted and so are specific. On the other hand, some things are more general in nature, which tend to permeate a number of experimental designs and seek to add some control to the gathering of data.

1. *Personal characteristics of the investigator.* Much of experimental research involves direct contact of the investigator and the subjects, so the personal characteristics of the investigator become essential factors in data collection. Obviously, if volunteer subjects are employed and if they receive no remuneration for their efforts, the researcher is asking them to devote time and expend energy in his or her work. The extent to which the investigator makes them welcome and treats them considerately during arduous periods will largely determine how well they perform. It is something of an art to drive subjects, sometimes to exhausting efforts, and yet at the same time maintain their full cooperation. The zeal, enthusiasm, and personality of the investigator are essential characteristics for ensuring full subject participation. Moreover, when the testing phase lasts several weeks, it is also difficult for the investigator to maintain proper subject decorum and still be pleasant and interested after many hours of repetitious and technical work. In order to counteract any such situations, the systematic rotation of testing sequence (Latin-

square) may be desirable to prevent the investigator from exerting undue influences on one group and not on the others.

2. *Hawthorne effect.* A number of years ago reports emerged from the study of factory workers in General Electric Company's Hawthorne plant, where variables were introduced which were presumed to affect productivity. It was found, however, that it did not matter whether the variables were present or absent; the productivity of the subjects continued to rise over the two-year period the experiment was conducted. The reason for this ("Hawthorne") effect was attributed to group solidarity and motivation engendered by the special attention these workers received. Apparently, this attention resulted in the development of an informal social cohesiveness among the worker subjects, which increased their motivation; as a consequence, productivity actually increased. As suggested by Hanson,[23] the manner of dealing with experimental subjects over a period of time may develop the type of esprit de corps on the part of those in the group that alone may enhance performance. On the other hand, control subjects who are tested before and after the experimental period and who are not seen during the interim time would not be expected to exhibit this trait. The investigator should be alert to the presence of this phenomenon.

3. *Double-Blind experiments.* Some types of research investigations require naïveté on the part of both the subject and the investigator in order to intentionally remove any contamination that might result from prior knowledge of the conditions of treatment. One of the largest areas of application is in medicine or in exercise physiology where the effects of drugs are studied.[24] In fact, it is mandatory to use a double-blind design in such instances if at all possible. This means that neither the subject nor the investigator has knowledge of the drug dosage. Of course, the nature of such an experiment must be revealed to the subject as a matter of informed consent, but the order of drugs and placebo may still be masked.

INSTRUMENTATION

Scientific research carries the impression that a formal laboratory is required; in many disciplines, this is correct. In physical education, however, a number of settings may be employed, including a formal

[23] Dale L. Hanson, "Influence on the Hawthorne Effect Upon Physical Education Research," *Research Quarterly*, 38, No. 4 (December 1967), 723.

[24] Melvin H. Williams, *Drugs and Athletic Performance* (Springfield, Ill: Charles C. Thomas, Publisher, 1974).

laboratory to be sure, but it should not be so limited; the playing field, track, gymnasium, pool, or other facility may be just as functional, if not essential, for the needs of many experiments.

Regardless of locale, however, the need is apparent for kinds of instruments that are specific to the research anticipated. Such instruments will be considered in succeeding chapters that deal with study areas available to physical education. In discussing instrumentation here, attention is given to the individual who uses instruments. A differentiation is made between what the instrument *can* do and what the operator is *able* to do when testing human subjects.

Precision

A major concern of the investigator in deciding on the feasibility of a study is whether or not the measurement tools are available. If not, either the study will need to be abandoned or proper instruments must first be designed and constructed. However, the availability of an instrument is not enough, as the investigator must be qualified to use it properly and must be able to use it with *precision*. Just how precise must the measurement be to secure valid data? This has been a perplexing problem with investigators; at first, many have been inclined to say "as precise as possible." However, this is not true; the decision must be based upon logical and statistical grounds and upon matters related to systematic or variable error that can be tolerated.

Instruments are available in the various fields of science and technology to measure factors with the most extreme precision; occasionally physical educators bemoan the fact that strength must be measured with dynamometers and tensiometers, which do not have such great precision. Yet it may be shown in the statistical analysis, for example, that little difference occurs between a manuometer that can be read to $1/10$ kg and one that can be read to $1/100$ kg, assuming that the typical range of grip-strength values in a sample of individuals is 30 kg. In other words, the addition of greater accuracy might make the investigator feel better, but the resultant gain would be trivial as related to the study's results.

The back and leg dynamometer is a cruder instrument than the manuometer, as the typical scale values are given in increments of 10 pounds. Still, this instrument is very useful in obtaining leg lift measures, where the range is likely to be 1,000 pounds and more. Much the same argument may be used when employing timers to test human performance. Reaction time and speed of movement studies have widely employed electric chronoscopes that measure to .01 sec. Actually then, times may be read to the nearest .001 sec, which obviates the necessity for more precise methods, since simple reaction time may average approximately .17 sec, with the range of values somewhere between, say, .12 and .22 sec. On the other hand, a simple stopwatch may be adequate for the timing of a short running event where the precision is to .1 sec over a range of several seconds. In longer runs, such as 300 and 400 yards, testing in full seconds may be adequate for some uses in physical education research.

1. *Systematic error.*   Error may be classified in two ways, as far as this discussion is concerned; these are systematic error and variable error. For systematic error, *true* scores may not be absolutely essential to the purposes of the investigation, so long as the error involved affects all scores in the same way. However, it is best to reduce systematic error as much as possible. Calibration of testing instruments is one way of taking care of this problem. The investigator should make such calibrations at the beginning of the experiment and as often as may be necessary during the period of data collection. Manufacturer's specifications that accompany an instrument, even dial faces, have been improperly applied or are out of alignment. Thus, all sensitive items of equipment should be compared with known standards, and a conversion chart should be prepared that can be used during testing. If this proves cumbersome, it may be permissible to use some other scheme and apply a *standard* correction later to means and standard deviations. This will not be acceptable if the error is not systematic, and it underlines the necessary for determining the instrumental precision by actual calibration. Moreover, if the instrument changes its characteristics during the course of the experiment, a corresponding lack of accuracy will result; unfortunately, such a change may go undetected.

   Other sources of systematic error may be reduced by carefully standardizing all the pertinent aspects of testing, such as subject position, placement of straps, electronics, and other devices, and keeping motivation, temperature, and fatigue constant so that the response of the subject is not influenced by tertiary factors.

2. *Variable error.*   No matter how much care is taken to ensure that the instruments are calibrated and the testing procedures standardized, a certain amount of error is inherent in the testing process. It is nearly impossible to avoid some error where human effort is involved. Yet, the investigator must do all in his or her power to reduce it to a minimum. Practice in reading instruments and interpolating between divisions will engender greater consistency and a reduction in reading error.

An important discussion of errors in measurement is presented by Henry and others, who point out that variable errors are random, varying irregularly and unsystematically, and are presumably uncorrelated.[25] Moreover, the removal of several small errors will affect the total error by only a small amount: "the elimination of any variable error no larger than a third of the total error is ordinarily a waste of time." On the other hand, large errors may disturb the data collection, so every effort must be made to reduce them through greater testing precision.

Before any investigator collects test data for a study, he or she should practice the tests under competent supervision and should demonstrate his or her testing competency. Testing competency may be demonstrated by obtaining test-retest objectivity coefficients that are equal to those reported for the test. The test should be given independently by the trainee and a competent tester to the same subjects. This process should be continued until the correlation between the two testers is satisfactory. For example, the objectivity coefficients of the various cable-tension strength tests exceed .90. Until the neophyte tester achieves this goal, he or she should not collect such strength scores for scientific studies.

Reliability

Reliability will be discussed here, as it is closely allied to instrumental procedures, although the focus of attention is on the subject rather than on the test. An additional source of error is present when the performance of human subjects is measured. Such error occurs in two forms, as trial-to-trial variability (intraindividual difference variance) and as subject-to-subject variability (interindividual difference variance), both of which are ordinarily large when compared with the error variance discussed above.

In computational terms, Henry has expressed the test-retest reliability coefficient as the "true score" variance divided by the total variance.[26] The "true" measure of individual differences is said to be the interindividual difference variance (σ_t^2), and the total variance consists of the sum of interindividual difference variance (σ_t^2), intraindividual difference variance (σ_i^2), and variable errors of measurement (σ_e^2). The calculation of the reliability coefficient will decline in proportion to the intraindividual difference and variable error variance. If the latter is small, as should be the case, it may have but slight influence on the magnitude of the correlation; thus, the reliability may well be related to the consistency from trial-to-trial of the subjects' performance. On the other hand, systematic errors, provided they

[25] Franklin M. Henry, *et al.*, "Errors in Measurement," in *Research Methods Applied to Health, Physical Education and Recreation* (Washington, D.C.: American Alliance for Health, Physical Education, Recreation, and Dance 1952), Ch. 19.

[26] Franklin M. Henry, "Reliability, Measurement Error, and Intra-Individual Difference," *Research Quarterly*, 30, No. 1 (March 1959), 21.

affect all scores in the same proportion, will have no affect at all. In order to enhance test-retest reliability, one method is to increase the replications, which will increase reliability in direct proportion to the square root of the number of trials.[27]

ESTABLISHING THE RESEARCH LABORATORY

Most large universities that offer programs for advanced degrees in physical education have well-established research laboratories, some of which rival the best in the life sciences on their respective campuses. Others are less well equipped but are nevertheless quite serviceable. These institutions are committed to the establishment of a research laboratory as a vital and essential part of faculty research and graduate study. However, not all students studying research methods will be destined for employment in such institutions, nor will they be advising graduate student research right away; yet, they may feel the need for establishing programs of their own and eventually inaugurating graduate study. For these reasons, the ensuing discussion is directed to the establishment of a research laboratory.

A persistent lament from individuals teaching in small colleges, community colleges, public schools, and in some universities is that they do not have a research laboratory and therefore—it follows—they cannot do research. Nothing is farther from the truth, for in fact, a formal and well-equipped laboratory is not of itself the most important factor in the pursuit of scholarly problems. Obviously, there will be some things that will be extremely difficult, if not impossible, to accomplish without an appropriate facility, but this is more a problem of selection and feasibility of investigations to be made. Problems can be selected for which little special equipment is needed. In such a situation, it will be necessary to start slowly and gradually increase in complexity as more money and facilities become available. The emphasis is correctly placed on getting started.

It is deplorable how few graduate students think of themselves as researchers and how many lack confidence that they can make a contribution to the field as scientists. Somehow, many feel that research is up to someone else with more qualified experience. It is understandable how master's degree candidates who are experiencing graduate study for the first time might not be imbued with the desire to do research, but it is inconceivable that this would happen with doctoral candidates. Perhaps the difficulty is in the mistaken impres-

[27]See Chapter 8 for a discussion of reliability and the determination of the standard error of the mean.

sion that teaching and research are separate entities and that when a person desires a teaching career it is at the exclusion of a research career. Obviously, such is not the case; for example, in physical education, almost every member of the Research Consortium of AAHPERD is also a teacher or professor. As outlined in earlier chapters, it is the strong belief of the authors that the most effective teacher—even of activities—is one who continually engages in some research and is conversant with the research conducted in his or her area of endeavor.

Inaugurating the Laboratory

A research laboratory is any room that is available to conduct experiments; the basic prerequisite is that it permit one to obtain valid data. Thus, a gymnasium, pool, track, or supply room might be acceptable, depending on the problem to be investigated. Equipment may be locked up with other supply items and equipment of the physical education programs. The room may be used for other classes when not used as a laboratory; or vice versa, a room may be used for a laboratory during periods of the day when it is not in use for classes, intramurals, or varsity athletics. Researchers have been known to collect data in their offices or in the shower room (where an ample supply of water is available) and even to transport equipment from school to school to test boys and girls in corners of gymnasiums, on auditorium stages, and elsewhere. The major consideration is that the data be obtained accurately. Frequently, this may be done without the use of a formal suite of rooms labeled "laboratory."

The experience of many in research when no laboratory as such was available has been to utilize whatever facilities were at hand, to be satisfied with any progress that can be made, and to maintain steady productivity. When the individual can demonstrate a sustained desire and ability to develop a problem and carry it through to completion, this demonstration constitutes a powerful argument when requesting equipment or facilities.

One of the prime times for inaugurating the research laboratory is at the time of new construction, when a new physical education facility is being planned. The inclusion of space for a research laboratory is a wise investment in the future, because at this time the room can be adequately fitted with proper electrical outlets and hot water, shielded for electrical interference, equipped with gas and vacuum lines, and so forth. Provisions may also be made for building in equipment, such as treadmills, environmental chambers, and observation rooms. Such items would be much more difficult to obtain at a later time. Frequently, approval for construction of a new building carries with it the purchase of needed equipment. Thus, this is an ideal time to obtain the essential equipment for research, as a new and functional research laboratory is instantly available.

If new facilities are contemplated, it should be made clear to the building coordinator that the laboratories represent specialized facilities that need careful planning. It is desirable that a faculty member knowledgeable in laboratory procedures be part of the building committee and participate in all related deliberations.

Finances

The manner of financing a research laboratory in physical education should be essentially the same as in other departments of the university, that is, through the departmental budget. The basic facility and primary operating equipment should be planned over a period of time and supported in a manner similar to other departmental items. Included as the laboratory staff are research laboratory assistants, technicians, and custodians.

The tendency in the past has been to obtain funds from extramural sources in the form of research grants, which, of course, is an excellent way of supporting specific research projects that sometimes last for several years. The investigator should bear in mind that grants such as these must be actively sought, correctly proposed, accurately written up, and submitted to the appropriate agency. Upon approval and funding, it is incumbent for the researcher to carry the project through to completion, including the submission of whatever written reports are required.

The appropriation of outside funds for research is very intriguing, although there is less opportunity today to obtain major items of equipment than in the past. However, the researcher may also find that intramural grants are available from his or her own institution. Although these may not be as large financially, at least they may provide basic equipment for modest projects. Known sometimes as "starter grants," their purpose for faculty members is to provide a stimulus for inaugurating a research program. The intent is to let other sources take over once the investigator has made an initial thrust. In a similar manner, such grants are often available to graduate students, particularly doctoral candidates, to assist in the completion of the thesis requirement as well as for other aspects of the research program. The student should investigate these sources on campus.

The inauguration of a research laboratory in most places will be supported by individual departments and will more than likely begin inauspiciously with a modest budget. The ultimate quality of the research is not dependent as much upon great financial support as it is on the ability of the personnel. Given properly prepared investigators, important contributions to science may be made on a low budget and modest facilities.

Suggestions for a
Comprehensive Laboratory

Standard plans for a research laboratory in physical education are not available, just as there is no standard research program. Similarities from one institution to another will be noted because there are some functions that seem to be universally accepted; even though the physical proportions of rooms differ, the utilitarian aspects are quite similar. In fact, there are some aspects of laboratory work in physical education that would resemble functions in other fields of study. For example, biochemical analysis must hold to the same rigorous standards wherever carried out. Thus the growth of laboratories proceeds first of all from the needs of the investigators who will be using them. Except in the instance where a new facility is being planned, it is essential that the laboratory be sufficiently functional to handle the collection and analysis of data for those problems most likely to be pursued. Second, expansion should accommodate those future needs—both real and proposed—that will arise as a result of faculty growth and graduate student expansion. Little is gained in spending funds that are needed for other things on a fully equipped biochemical laboratory if the technical personnel are not available. It should also be mentioned that some equipment, particularly if seldom required, may be available in other departmental laboratories on campus.

The main ingredients required in a comprehensive research laboratory parallel the subject matter in physical education as set forth in succeeding chapters and as dictated by types of problems anticipated. It would be inappropriate to predict specific needs at the start, so the facility requirements may be stated rather generally, with brief notes concerning broad categories of use. One room, of course, may be available for multiple uses. The sizes will vary, and the general architectural layout must be determined according to criteria associated with local requirements. The following facilities should receive consideration in developing a research laboratory:

1. *Biochemical laboratory.* The inclusion of such a facility as a laboratory for chemical analysis of blood, gas, tissues, and so forth, will depend upon the personnel available to support such an enterprise. An affirmative answer will mean that considerable planning is necessary for its construction. Consideration must be given to sinks and counter tops that are resistant to corrosion, gas lines, vacuum lines, hooded ovens, cabinets, and a refrigerator. Centrifuges, autoclaves, and other items of equipment, plus an array of chemicals, glassware, and other items are needed to support biochemical analyses. This facility adds considerable sophistication to research, and it provides for an ideal teaching

station for advanced experimental research. But sophisticated personnel are also needed to operate it.

2. *Cardiovascular laboratory.* The collection of data on problems in exercise physiology must take place away from the biochemical laboratory, although in planning the two may be adjacent. Depending upon whether or not chemical work is to be done, the collection of gas for analysis will require certain techniques and analyses, so the cardiovascular laboratory should require such things as environmental chambers, treadmills, recorders, and sufficient electrical outlets.

3. *Hydrostatic weighing room.* Most human performance laboratories today need to be equipped to provide measurement of body fat and lean body mass. This is sometimes performed by use of skinfold measures or other anthropometric procedures, but it is becoming increasingly necessary in research that it be done by weighing the subject under water. This requires a separate facility that should be part of the initial planning for a research laboratory if at all possible. The underwater weighing tank itself can be fashioned relatively inexpensively, if need be, but it is not always easy to provide for regulation of water temperature, filtration, and ease of managing a subject when the facility is added later. Considerations beyond those mentioned include a facility for showering and changing clothes, ready access to the tank, and ability to keep the water still and give instructions to the subject. The ceiling should be equipped with a hanging assembly for the measuring scale and the subject over the center of the tank. Provision must also be made to obtain residual lung volume at the time of hydrostatic weighing.

4. *Animal laboratory.* A trend noted today in exercise physiology is the development of research with small animals, usually laboratory rats. A room set aside for such purposes should be planned in terms of the intended use, especially with regard to the number of animals to be housed at any one time and the type of device for exercising them. In construction, consideration should be given to temperature control, automatic light control to rotate periods of light and darkness, and deodorization. This laboratory will require a supply of water and will need sinks and counter space as well as a dissection table and other accessories. At the same time, thought should be given to adequate disposal of wastes and to sterilizing cages and water bottles.

5. *Biomechanics laboratory.* The study of problems requiring motion analysis may require a slightly higher ceiling than rooms

for other research, so this should be investigated and weighed against the probable extra cost involved in construction. If at all possible, thought should be given to the question of cinematography, the placement of overhead cameras, and the lights for indoor filming. In addition, it may be necessary to screen the room or part of the room for use with electromyographic equipment.

6. ***Photography laboratory.*** More than just a darkroom, the modern photography laboratory offers facilities for developing film; enlarging prints, both in black and white and in color; analyzing motion analysis film; and meeting the general requirements necessary for high speed photography. This laboratory should be located adjacent to the kinesiology laboratory.

7. ***Motor learning or motor control laboratory.*** The basic requirement for the majority of motor learning studies is to provide an area that is quiet and relatively free of traffic—where subjects can concentrate on tasks and not be disturbed. The amount of room needed will depend upon the nature of the experimentation to be undertaken.

8. ***General testing room.*** A number of research projects of a general nature will simply require a room where testing may be done; in some instances, the gymnasium, the playing field, or the pool may be utilized. Such facilities would be needed for tests of motor fitness, motor performance, strength, anthropometry, ergometry, and circulatory-respiratory functions.

9. ***Faculty research facilities.*** Thought should be given to providing space for faculty members to do their research, either in terms of a separate laboratory or a space within the main laboratory. Perhaps a small cubicle could house specific equipment, including a desk or work table, in which the faculty member could establish a working area outside his or her main office. Such resources may be important in encouraging faculty participation in research problems.

10. ***Shop.*** One of the most important adjuncts to any experimental laboratory is a shop where repairs of equipment may be made or new equipment may be fashioned. Much of the apparatus used in research cannot be purchased commercially, so the necessity for including a shop, equipped with the necessary power tools and all the supportive paraphernalia, should not be underestimated. Sending items away for repair or contracting for each new apparatus needed is not only time-consuming but also quite expensive. Even better is the provision of a trained mechanical or electrical engineer who will maintain the shop and help plan and solve the problems of equipment raised by the investigator.

11. ***Offices.*** The well-equipped modern research laboratory should be planned with adjoining office space so that proper supervision is provided. Enough space should be included for both faculty and graduate research assistants.

12. ***Computer laboratory.*** No research facility is complete without a computer laboratory with a sufficient number of terminals to handle peak traffic in data analysis and to support courses in statistics. The area selected for this purpose may be a rather small room, in comparison with some of the others in the laboratory, but thought should be given to adequate lighting and seclusion.

SUMMARY

The largest proportion of research in physical education involves the experimental method, which uses a laboratory environment. Knowledge of the various forms of methodology is important because it assists the investigator in organizing and carrying out research. One of the most important aspects of this problem concerns an understanding of the use of adequate experimental controls; it is essential to know when to use a control group so that the magnitude of the main effects can be known.

Among the simple experimental designs, the following have been emphasized: the single-group design, the repeated-measures design, the random-groups design, and the related-groups design. The majority of experiments in the past have employed some form of these methods, although more complex designs, such as the factorial designs, have become necessary with advanced students.

The researcher must be acquainted with various means of controlling experimental factors, in addition to selection of the proper design. Subjects themselves constitute an essential part of research; matters pertaining to their randomization and selection according to age, sex, and physical ability are crucial to success in the experiment as well as to the maintaining of their motivation and interest. Beyond these factors are considerations of rotation of treatments and various means of exerting statistical control.

A major concern of the investigator is the selection of proper instruments, whether or not the testing takes place in the formal confines of a research laboratory. Questions of validity help decide the precision that is required for the measurement of selected variables; it is possible to be overly precise in some cases and yet not sufficiently exact in others. Each problem must be decided on its own merits, and each will involve considerations of systematic and variable errors. The question of error may also involve a subject's repeated response to a test as well as the variance between subjects, all of which concern reliability.

Establishing a research laboratory is a growing function of higher education, although it usually remains for the larger universities to develop the comprehensive facility. The size does not necessarily reflect negatively on the quality of the research, for very important work has grown from rather meager beginnings. When developing a laboratory, a number of considerations must be made relative to the needs and the projected type of research to be undertaken.

SELECTED REFERENCES

BEST, JOHN W., *Research in Education* (4th ed.). Englewood Cliffs, N.J.: Prentice-Hall, Inc., 1981, Ch. 4.

CAMPBELL, DONALD T., and JULIAN C. STANLEY, *Experimental and Quasi-Experimental Designs for Research*. Chicago: Rand McNally & Company, 1966.

DONNELLY, RICHARD J., "Laboratory Research in Physical Education," *Research Quarterly*, 31, No. 2 (May 1960), 232.

FISHER, R., and F. YATES, *Statistical Tables for Biological, Agricultural, and Medical Research* (5th ed.). New York: Hafner Publishing Co., 1957.

GOOD, CARTER V., *Essentials of Educational Research*. East Norwalk, Conn.: Appleton-Century-Crofts, 1966, Ch. 8.

HENRY, FRANKLIN M., "Reliability, Measurement Error, and Intra-Individual Difference," *Research Quarterly*, 30, No. 1 (March 1959), 21.

HENRY, FRANKLIN M., *et al.*, "Errors in Measurement," in *Research Methods Applied to Health, Physical Education and Recreation*. Washington, D.C.: American Alliance for Health, Physical Education, Recreation, and Dance, 1952.

MOREHOUSE, LAURENCE E., and EUGENE R. O'CONNELL, "A Plan for Gradually Equipping a Physical Education Research Laboratory," *Journal of Health, Physical Education and Recreation*, 29, No. 9 (December 1958), 28.

MORRIS, HAROLD H., "Analysis of Repeated Measures," in *Symposium Papers*, eds. Richard H. Cox and Robert C. Serfass. Reston, Va.: American Alliance for Health, Physical Education, Recreation, and Dance, 1981, pp. 5-60.

WINER, B. J., *Statistical Principles in Experimental Design*. New York: McGraw-Hill, Inc., *Book Company*, 1962.

11
Physiology of Exercise

The study of exercise and its physiology forms a sizable portion of the research activity in physical education. The methods employed are experimental, and the techniques are scientific. A wide variety of procedures is available for the solution of problems; others are being refined and continually developed to fit the multitude of special requirements dictated by current needs. This is one of the areas of research in physical education where there is a pronounced reliance upon automatic and electronic devices, and the sophistication in modern laboratories reflects the emerging depth of the discipline. The development in exercise physiology is gradually achieving the level found in physiology and biology, and, in fact, scientists in physiology and exercise physiology are sometimes indistinguishable, moving in the same circles and publishing in the same journals.

As outlined briefly in Chapter 1, the physiological factors that relate to movement, including immediate (exercise) and long-term (training) aspects typify the field of physiology of exercise. Although the bulk of past research has emphasized human performance, increasingly greater attention has been given to animal studies, notably those employing rats. At any rate, the methods and techniques needed require the same degree of care and precision for physiologist or physical educator, and certain variables appear common to both. In presenting material for this chapter some of the most common techniques are given. No single volume could contain a complete documentation of all tests considered as physiology of exercise, nor could each be completely documented. A compromise is in order for both considerations. Thus, the techniques that have been selected offer some solution to recurring problems; the references given are selective and, in many cases, offer further sources of pertinent material or equipment.

MUSCULAR STRENGTH

One of the oldest and most basic techniques to be used for research in physical education is the assessment of muscular strength. Various devices have been used, including spring scales, dynamometers, strain gauges, myometers, and tensiometers. Many combinations exist, but all serve a primary purpose: to obtain a measure of maximum strength. Perhaps the simplest and most widely used is the cable tensiometer. This instrument is small and compact and has the advantage of being extremely versatile. Adequate documentation and description of 38 strength tests are described by Clarke and Clarke.[1]

The current concern has been less with developing new devices than with understandng the characteristics of muscular contraction and relating strength to other variables. Actually, strength is becoming thought of as less an entity unto itself as the end result of the excitation-contraction coupling sequence that requires the activation of motor units. Although under conscious control of the will, volitional contraction involves coordination by higher nervous centers; thus, strength can be seen as an expression of neuromotor coordination as related to the specific task being performed.

Although the inherent properties and characteristics of the contractile elements of muscle are the primary responsibility of the biochemist and physiologist, the *in vivo* investigation of the contraction characteristics, while the muscle-tendon-joint complex remains intact, is the responsibility of the physical educator. Attempts at the quantitative assessment of the uptake and release of muscular tension have revealed the mathematical parameters to be quite distinctive and reproducible from one sample to another; these attempts have been helpful in comparing the effects of fatigue[2] and temperature[3] on the contraction.

[1] H. Harrison Clarke and David H. Clarke, *Developmental and Adapted Physical Education*, 2nd ed. (Englewood Cliffs, N.J.: Prentice-Hall, Inc., 1978), pp. 100-125.

[2] Joseph Royce, "Force-Time Characteristics of the Exertion and Release of Hand Grip Strength Under Normal and Fatigued Conditions," *Research Quarterly*, 33, No. 3 (October 1962), 444.

[3] David H. Clarke and Joseph Royce, "Rate of Muscle Tension Development and Release under Extreme Temperatures," *Int. Z. angew. Physiol. einschl. Arbeitsphysiol.*, 19 (1962), 330.

Essentially, one needs to have available a device for exerting force and at the same time recording the tension on fast moving paper. Many ways of doing so are available, which will be discussed subsequently, but the recorder must have a minimum paper speed of 150 mm per sec in order to spread out the contraction that has a half-time of approximately .08 sec. The half-time of release is faster (.04 sec), and analysis at this paper speed becomes very difficult. Once the record has been obtained, serial measures are made at intervals of convenience for adequate analysis and interpretation. These must be rather frequent, as the literature indicates the curve form to be fast-changing and to contain multiple components. The details of curve fitting will be discussed subsequently.

A search of the literature very quickly reveals the extensive manner in which strength measurements have been used in research studies. In its usual sense, this has meant maximal strength, and measures have ordinarily been isometric in nature. The trend seems further established that to assess the quantity of muscular strength of an individual, multiple tests must be given. This has been true for the construction of tests and for their application. For a presentation of the results of a large number of such efforts, the reader is directed to a monograph on the subject.[4]

MUSCULAR FATIGUE/ENDURANCE

Instrumentation

The systematic repetitive contraction of muscles is known to produce fatigue, and since the early work of Mosso,[5] it has been a prime target for research. Whether or not concern is with the reduction in strength, called fatigue, or its reciprocal, endurance, a desire to understand muscular behavior under a variety of experimental conditions has been evident. The most obvious muscle groups studied have been those of the arm and shoulder because of the ease of management and the amount of flexibility. However, the differences in muscle position about the joints make direct comparisons of performance difficult; this situation has resulted in the usual practice of employing a single muscle group for all comparisons. Apparently, rather pronounced differences in work production exist in various sites about the body so that eventually all should be studied.

[4]H. Harrison Clarke, *Muscular Strength and Endurance in Man* (Englewood Cliffs, N.J.: Prentice-Hall, Inc., 1966), Ch. 6.

[5]Angelo Mosso, *Fatigue*, trans. M. and W. B. Drummond (New York: G. P. Putnam's Sons, 1906).

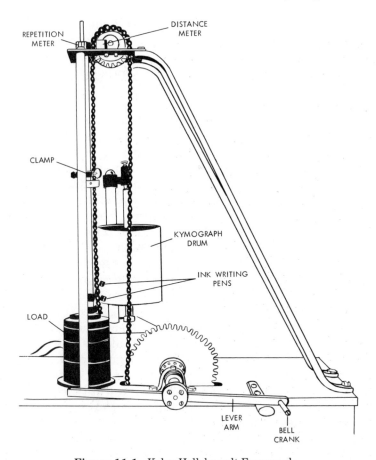

Figure 11.1. Kelso-Hellebrandt Ergograph

The basic requirement for investigating muscular fatigue is to possess an instrument that will permit the detailed quantification of repetitive effort. In the past, three types of devices have been prominent in the literature. First are the weight-loaded ergographs, such as the Kelso-Hellebrandt devices, designed for finger and wrist, radioulnar, elbow and shoulder, thumb, and grip. These ergographs are weight loaded, since weights must be placed on a carriage for the subject to raise and lower, usually according to a fixed rhythm and often at a percentage of the subject's maximal strength. The details concerning load and cadence were established by carefully controlled experimentation over a number of years, as were the conditions associated with optimum work output.[6] An illustration of the Kelso-Hellebrandt elbow-shoulder ergograph appears in Figure 11.1.

[6] Clarke, Muscular Strength and Endurance, Chaps. 3 and 4.

The second type of device is the force transducer based on strain gauges and consisting of a load cell and recorder. The load cell[7] translates changes in force into changes in voltage, the sensitive element of which is bound by special strain gauges. These form a balanced Wheatstone bridge so that changes in force on the cell will change the resistance of the gauges and thus produce a change in the output voltage, which is subsequently amplified and monitored by a recorder.[8] The advantage gained by this system is its versatility; the assembly can be adapted to nearly any muscle group desired, whether strong or weak. A special hand-grip device permits measurement of the hand and forearm flexors; standard straps, similar to those used in cable-tension strength tests, may be employed for other limb attachments. The load cell is not rigidly anchored, because tortional movements will cause spurious recordings; rather, it must be held at right angles to the limb and in direct series with any attachments. The position on the extremity of the strap or the angle of pull of the joint are matters of choice, although the optimum angles for strength application are known.[9]

The two basic exercise patterns employing force transducers have been rhythmic and static contractions. The recording of all repetitions from initial maximum to final strength allows the sampling of strength at appropriate intervals on the fatigue record. This arrangement permits a detailed mathematical analysis of fatigue and recovery.[10] They are usually found to progress toward their asymptote in an exponential manner under control of a rate constant. In other words, the progress of fatigue and its recovery are nonlinear. Knowledge of the various components that describe these curves has permitted a greater understanding of the underlying physiology that is taking place. For example, the time characteristics of blood flow in isometric contraction appear far different from those in isotonic activity. The extent of these differences can be seen more clearly by appropriate mathematical analysis.

Another form of muscular activity is the isokinetic contraction. It is similar to the isotonic contraction in that it takes the joint through its range of motion, but in this case the speed of movement is held constant. Any effort is countered by an equal opposing force, so that an increase in the contraction is simply met by increased resistance rather than increased acceleration. Thus, in this type of exercise, a high force is applied throughout the movement. Isotonic exercise, on the other

[7] Suggested source: BLH Electronics, Waltham, Mass.

[8] Suggested source: Beckman Instruments, Inc., Schiller Park, Ill.

[9] Clarke, Muscular Strength and Endurance, Ch. 2.

[10] David H. Clarke, "Strength Recovery from Static and Dynamic Muscular Fatigue," *Research Quarterly*, 33, No. 3 (October 1962), 349.

hand, usually has a peak angle where the resistance is greatest, whereas the tension may be less at other points in the range of motion. Special equipment is required to undertake research employing iso-kinetic contractions,[11] but newer problems can be investigated, such as the effects of this type of training on muscular hypertrophy and strength development, both at fast and slow movements, and the relationship between the fast contracting muscle and the percentage of its fast-twitch fibers. Relevance will also be established to various athletic groups, undoubtedly.

The following section is thus presented to acquaint the reader with the technical aspects of curve analysis as applied to the single component equation found in dynamic exercise. More complicated curve forms require additional steps. Consultation with a reference such as Riggs[12] will help by adding necessary background information and providing models for further use.

Exponential Curve Analysis

The exponential theory, as applied to dynamic muscular fatigue, operates under the assumption that a certain fraction of the available energy stores are used up by each contraction, considering only the work of the muscle over and above that of the steady state. Thus, a decrease in work output in any given contraction will always be a constant proportion of the contraction that was immediately preceding rather than a constant value. For example, if the first contraction involved 50 kg of force and there were a 10% reduction of each contraction, the second would be 45 kg, the third 40.5 kg, the fourth 36.45 kg, and so forth. In terms of units of time, the mathematical expression describing the force y at any time t would be

$$y_t = a_0 e^{-kt} + c$$

where a_0 is the amount of the first contraction above the asymptote c, e is the Naperian log base, and k is the rate constant. The numerical value of k is computed from the relationship $k = 0.693/t_{1/2}$ where $t_{1/2}$ represents the amount of time required for fatigue to progress from the initial force to one-half the amount of that force, considering only the amount of work above the asymptote. The value 0.693 derives from the fact that $e^{-0.693} = 1/2$. It should be noted that $t_{1/10}$ is frequently utilized; in this case $e^{-2.303} = 1/10$ and $k = 2.303/t_{1/10}$.

The following sequence may be employed to obtain the mathe-

---

[11]Suggested Source: Cybex, Ronkonkoma, New York.

[12]Douglas S. Riggs, *The Mathematical Approach to Physiological Problems* (Baltimore: The Williams & Wilkins Company, 1963), Ch. 6.

matical values for a single component exponential curve, with the specific aim of determining the rate constant k:

1. Plot the measured strength means for each of the experimental points on regular coordinate graph paper with force on the ordinate and time on the abscissa.

2. Estimate the asymptote (c) by visual inspection. This is not necessarily final strength or the fatigue level as an asymptote is a line that approaches a steady state but never reaches it even though extended to infinity.

3. Subtract the value of the asymptote from each of the experimental points.

4. Plot these residual values on semilogarithmic paper (two-cycle paper will probably suffice).

5. Fit a straight line by eye to the points thus plotted. An exponential curve, when plotted on a semilogarithmic graph, yields a straight line; when this line accounts for all the points, it is a single component curve. When it fits only the latter points, and the early ones depart either positively or negatively, it suggests additional components and further analysis, which is described below.

6. When the points in the latter portion of the curve fail to conform to a straight line, it may be necessary to revise the estimate of the asymptote and repeat steps 3 and 4. For example, if the points tend to fall away, lowering the asymptote will tend to bring them up; conversely, if the values rise above the line, raising the estimate of the asymptote will lower them. Because of the nature of semilogarithmic graphs, the early values are influenced by this technique less than the latter ones. It is an excellent practice to try several asymptotes to make certain that the best one is finally selected.

7. The intercept with the force at time zero is read as a_0, and represents the amount of fatigable strength at the outset of the experiment.

8. The amount of time required to drop from a_0 to one-half its value—$t_{1/2}$—is read from the graph.

9. The constant k is then computed by the half-time procedure as $0.693/t_{1/2}$.

10. In order to construct the smooth curve, the data obtained from the semilogarithmic analysis is calculated by reading the straight line intercept at each measurement point and by adding the constant value of c.

11. Each of these calculated values is plotted on coordinate graph paper as a smooth curve. The experimental points are then

superimposed on the mathematical curve. When a proper analysis has been performed, and the curve follows the exponential law, the experimental values should fall closely on or near the mathematical curve.

When the data cannot be adequately fitted to a simple component curve, the early values will depart from the trend line established on the semilogarithmic graph. When enough such points are available, this early component, if truly exponential, will appear to be curvilinear. The following steps should be followed to determine the first-component rate constant (k_1), which will then make the main rate constant determined above k_2:

1. Subtract the straight line intercept at each measurement point from the plotted experimental values. It will be clear that soon the fitted straight line will coincide with the plotted values as described above for the single-component curve. Further, there may be some circumstances in which the early values, instead of departing above the straight line, depart systematically below the line, which simply means that, rather than being a positive exponential component, it is a negative one. In this situation, simply reverse the mathematical process and subtract the experimental points from the values for the straight line intercept.

2. Plot the resultant residual values on the same semilogarithmic graph.

3. Fit a straight line through the points thus plotted. Originally this will be a shorter component, but will be significantly faster than the other component. For clarity, the intercept at time zero for this early component may be designated a_1, to differentiate it from a_2 of the original component above.

4. The amount of time required to drop from a_1 to one-half its value is read from the graph, and the constant k_1 is calculated as in step 9 of the previous process.

5. The smooth curve that is to be constructed must now take into consideration the new analysis. When this early component is positive, simply add the two straight line intercepts to the asymptote c until the first component has been completed, and proceed for the remainder as in step 11 earlier above.[13] The resultant curve can now be described by the equation

$$y_t = a_1 e^{-k_1 t} + a_2 e^{-k_2 t} + c.$$

[13]One way to determine whether the first component is positive is to calculate initial strength as follows: $a_1 + a_2 + c =$ initial strength. If negative, $(a_2 - a_1) + c =$ initial strength, the equation becomes $y_t = a_2 e^{-k_2 t} - a_1 e^{-k_1 t} + c.$

PERIPHERAL BLOOD FLOW

Instrumentation

The variation in volume of muscle resulting from exercise has been of interest since the seventeenth century. It was not until later that experiments indicated that the postexercise volume change was not due to enlargement of the muscle tissue per se but resulted from other factors. Supposedly, the hyperemia that follows exercise reflects increased blood flow, although the contraction of muscles results in temporary circulatory embarrassment. Thus, interest has been focused on the postexercise circulation changes. These changes can be assessed in two ways: by measuring volume and by measuring flow.

The instrument utilized for this purpose is the plethysmograph. A large proportion of the literature reflects its use in conjunction with the arm and hand, although it has been used successfully with the leg. Changes in volume can be measured with a volume plethysmograph and changes in blood flow with a venous occlusion plethysmograph. Of the two procedures, the volume measure is less complicated. The essence of this technique is to place the limb in a water-filled or air-filled cylinder and monitor the volume change by the amount of displacement. The measurement may be made rather accurately if an outlet is provided at the base of the cylinder at an angle along the side of the water jacket. The scores obtained can be made in convenient units (usually millimeters) if a scale is placed behind the pipette. When necessary, this can be calibrated in terms of actual volume, although for statistical purposes little advantage is gained by this procedure. If a base line is established under control or resting conditions, the amount of volume change resulting from exercise, for example, is the difference between the initial and final levels. To ensure sufficient accuracy, especially if reimmersions are to be made, marks with flesh pencil or tape are essential as an aid to standardizing the procedure.

When an air plethysmograph is employed, every care must be taken to ensure a complete air seal at the points of insertion of the extremity. Once again a connection is made with the plethysmograph and the recording device, usually through a connecting tube, which is attached to a tambour and writing unit. The expansion of the limb is transmitted via air column to the recording apparatus.

The measurement of blood flow employs the venous occlusion plethysmograph, which contains the essential ingredients of the air volume plethysmograph. In order to measure the quantity of flow, a blood pressure cuff is placed about the extremity proximal to the plethysmograph and inflated to a pressure sufficient to occlude the venous flow but not the arterial flow (40 mm Hg is sufficient). In this manner, the blood continues to enter the extremity from the systemic circulation, but it cannot leave. Thus, the volume change can be monitored as the limb swells. Calibration can be made by introducing known air samples and measuring the displacement.

Various other methods are available for recording the volume changes besides the mechanical method utilizing tambour and pen. The increased use of biomedical instrumentation permits the coupling of this phenomenon with other measures on the same recording. This may be accomplished with the use of a strain gauge pressure transducer where the change in pressure is detected and converted to an electrical signal and then magnified and reproduced on recording paper.[14]

WORK

The heart of exercise physiology is the production of work; for research purposes, the work must be measurable, or at least the task must be standardized in some way. Many activities involve work, but such things as cadence and distance traveled render most exercises useless for controlled experimental study. Thus the selection of an exercise modality must be carefully considered in light of the objectives of the study. It is likely that selection of exercise modalities will be made among several standardized procedures. The decision to employ the treadmill, bicycle ergometer, or step-bench will depend upon a number of factors, cost and availability being among them. Other matters also weigh heavily, as will be discussed.

Treadmill

One of the most widely used techniques for exercise physiology research is the treadmill. Treadmills come in all sizes and shapes, some portable and others installed permanently in the laboratory floor. The specifications may vary, but, in general, two variables should be provided—speed and inclination. The treadmill should have the capability of varying speed between 0-16 mph and inclination between 0-20%, thus providing a range of work loads that should meet the needs of most research designs. The grade is based on the incline that would result from the elevation of 100 horizontal feet; therefore, 1% grade would be the rise of the belt equivalent to a 1 foot vertical elevation taken at a distance of 100 horizontal feet.

[14]Carole A. Williams and Alexander R. Lind, "Measurement of Forearm Blood Flow by Venous Occlusion Plethsymography: Influence of Hand Blood Flow during Sustained and Intermittent Isometric Exercise," *European Journal of Applied Physiology*, 42 (1979), 141.

The treadmill has the advantages of ease of running or walking and of positioning so as to obtain various cardiopulmonary measures, although running does impart some disturbing bodily motion. Variations in belt speed and grade can be standardized for the necessary application. One difficulty is in standardizing the work done, as this amount varies directly with body weight. Maintaining constant belt speed and grade does not hold constant the work accomplished; equating body weight and treadmill speed are difficult and not at all practical. However, it is possible to calculate the work done (W) in treadmill running by application of the following formula:

$$W \text{ (kgm)} = [\text{Body Wt (kg)}] \, [\text{Total Belt Revolutions}$$

$$\times \text{ Belt Length (M)} \times \text{ Grade (\%)}].$$

For example, for a subject weighing 92.6 kg., if the total number of belt revolutions was 252, the belt length was 5.55 meters, and the grade was 6%, the total work done for 8 minutes of exercise would be

$$W = [92.6] \, [252 \times 5.55 \times .06] = 7861 \text{ kgm} = 982.6 \text{ kgm/min.}$$

Bicycle Ergometer

Another widely used device for work studies is the bicycle ergometer. In its simplest form, this ergometer is a stationary bicycle with one wheel adapted so that a belt can be passed around and attached to a spring balance. The work load can be changed while in motion simply by increasing the tension on the belt, which in turn is monitored on the scale. The addition of lead strips to the wheel gives the proper inertia for smooth operation. The ergometer can be calibrated for work load by determining the distance the rim of the wheel is moved by one pedal revolution; this amount times the product of resistance and cadence (per min) gives the total work accomplished in foot-pounds or kilogram-meters per min. The usual procedure is to employ a constant pedal rate (50-60 revolutions per min); only the resistance is varied. For the Monark ergometer,[15] for example, the wheel travels a distance of 6 m per pedal revolution; thus, if, kg resistance is applied at 50 revolutions, the resultant work would be

$$W = 50 \text{ rev} \times 6M \times 1 \text{ kg.} = 300 \text{ kgm/min.}$$

When 2kg resistance is employed, the work becomes 600 kgm/min.

A more sophisticated design is the electric-brake bicycle ergometer, although the results of testing are not necessarily better with the more elaborate instrument. The resistance is provided by increasing

[15] Suggested Source: Quinton Intruments, Inc., Seattle, Wash.

the field current through an electromagnetic brake, which is monitored by a power output meter. This meter is calibrated to determine friction losses and power output over the usable speeds and loads to be employed by comparing the results with the known power input of an electric motor.

The bicycle ergometer has certain advantages as a tool for research. First, it is rather small and compact, and most of the friction belt types are portable, although the electric-brake bicycle ergometer tends to be larger, heavier, and thus less mobile. Because it is stationary and because the subject remains seated, electrodes and gas collection equipment can be attached conveniently, with less danger of bodily movements interfering with data collection and of leaks occurring around respiratory apparatus. The most important advantage, however, is the ability to set and maintain a constant work load for all subjects. Body weight does not become a variable in work load determinations, so the investigator can study the individual differences in performance of a standard task. The load or cadence may be reduced, although here there are certain questions related to efficiency that should be studied.[16] However, with a mechanical revolution counter, the actual number of revolutions can be recorded, so that slight deviations in rhythm can be accounted for. It has been claimed that difficulty is experienced in learning to ride the bicycle and that practice sessions are needed, but the same can be said for other exercise tasks. However, once the subject has adjusted to the proper pedal rate, little difficulty is ordinarily found.

Step-Bench

The most inexpensive and simple device for work is the step-bench. The reader is undoubtedly aware of physical fitness tests utilizing this technique, so that further description is unnecessary. The height of the bench and cadence may vary, depending upon the objectives of the study and perhaps the age and sex of the subjects. The work load varies once again with body weight, and the movement of the subject makes instrumentation very difficult, although many of the problems may be overcome successfully with care. At any rate it can be used for a number of tasks requiring sustained effort or involvement of large muscles. Work load per minute is calculated by multiplying the weight of the subject (kg) by the height of the bench (m) by the number of steps per minute. Ordinarily the negative work of going down encountered in bench stepping is ignored in these calculations.

[16]Sylvia Dickinson, "The Efficiency of Bicycle-Pedalling, as Affected by Speed and Load," *Journal of Physiology*, 67, No. 3 (June 1929), 242.

ENERGY METABOLISM

Probably one of the most important laboratory skills for research in physical education is the measurement of energy expenditure. This process permeates much of the literature of exercise physiology. Modern laboratories today usually have available one or more of the instruments necessary to perform gas analysis; thus, the student who is interested in exercise physiology should learn to use these instruments. This is also true of the doctoral student who plans to teach in this area and who anticipates thesis advisement of graduate students.

The basic concepts concerning energy expenditure should already be known from undergraduate courses in exercise physiology. The student should understand the difference between direct and indirect calorimetry in measuring the amount of heat produced by the body as a result of muscular work. The direct measurement of heat requires rather expensive equipment and rigorous laboratory protocol, including the body calorimeter, which is a chamber especially equipped for measuring the heat given off by the body. The high cost and limited application to experiments involving exercise means that direct calorimetry is seldom used.

On the other hand, indirect calorimetry is the common method employed in energy cost studies. Calculation of aerobic capacity is made on the basis of oxygen consumed and carbon dioxide produced, which in turn may be converted to calories (kilocalories) if desired. More often, one is interested in oxygen uptake in liters per minute or in ml per kg of body weight per minute, rather than in calories, because the design of the experiment so often involves comparisons of one level of exercise to another or the influence of mitigating environmental or other factors. Assuming that comparable conditions are to be imposed on the subjects in the experiment, this process has been found acceptable. The open-circuit method of indirect calorimetry is described.

Open-Circuit Method

The preferred manner of obtaining data on aerobic capacity is by means of the open-circuit method. The procedure is to breathe in atmospheric air—which has known percentages of oxygen, carbon dioxide, nitrogen, and so forth—and exhale into a collection receptacle, such as a Douglas bag. The mouthpiece utilized is a three-way, high-velocity valve, permitting unobstructed inhalation of room air and exhalation into the collection assembly. Usually, several Douglas bags or meteorological balloons are used, as several samples may be collected separately. For this, a four-way or five-way valve must be used so that the exhaled air can be directed to the appropriate bag without loss of time or inappropriate mixing of the various gases.

The total volume of expired air is determined by passing the quantity of gas from each bag through a dry gas meter. Thus, if the total volume of expired gas is known, and also the percentage composition of the inspired air, the oxygen requirement will be calculated as the difference between percentage inspired and percentage expired air. Corrections must be made for standard conditions of gas temperature and barometric pressure.

The manner of analyzing the expired air in the open-circuit method provides some choice, but two methods are most frequently employed in research laboratories; both of these methods extract small gas samples from each of the collection bags and subject them to standardized analysis. The two procedures employ the Haldane[17] and the Scholander[18] apparatus; both require very careful techniques under exacting laboratory specifications. The experimenter who wishes to employ these methods must plan to spend sufficient time in the laboratory to perfect the procedures needed to obtain valid data; slight errors in these micromethods can result in large discrepancies. In addition to the basic references cited, the reader is directed to Consolazio, Johnson, and Pecora for additional specific information on equipment and procedures to be employed.[19]

Presently, a growing reliance is evident on still another procedure for obtaining O_2 and CO_2 from expired air, one which bypasses the traditional and laborious devices just described. This procedure is the continuous recording method whereby the expired air is drawn through paramagnetic oxygen[20] and infrared carbon dioxide[21] analyzers by a vacuum pump. The method has the advantages of simplicity of use and provides a continual monitoring of the changes in expired air, with apparently no serious loss of accuracy (and which may be coupled to a recorder for direct write-out). Calibration with known gases and comparisons with the Haldane or Scholander analyzers are routine matters to ascertain the acceptability of the analysis. If additional sophistication is desired, the two analyses, plus the instrumentation

[17]J. S. Haldane and J. G. Priestley, *Respiration* (New York: Oxford University Press, Inc., 1935).

[18]P. F. Scholander, "Analyzer for Accurate Estimation of Respiratory Gases in One-Half Cubic Centimeter Samples," *Journal of Biological Chemistry*, 167, No. 1 (January 1947), 235.

[19]C. Frank Consolazio, Robert E. Johnson, and Louis J. Pecora, *Physiological Measurements of Metabolic Functions in Man* (New York: McGraw-Hill Inc., 1963), Ch. 2.

[20]Suggested source: Model C-2 or E-2 Oxygen Analyzers, Beckman Instruments, Inc., Schiller Park, Ill.

[21]Suggested source: Model LB-1 Carbon Dioxide Analyzer, Beckman Instruments, Inc., Schiller Park, Ill.

for measuring expired air volume temperature and pressure can be assembled in one unit that possesses the added capability of timing the sequence of measurements and completely analyzing the results, which in turn are printed out by a programmable computer as often as every 15 seconds.[22]

The calculations required to complete the analysis of oxygen uptake (Vo_2), carbon dioxide production (Vco_2), and the respiratory exchange ration (R) are based upon obtaining the percentage of gas in the sample introduced to the Haldane or Scholander analyzers. This percentage applies to all volumes, but they in turn must be corrected for temperature and pressure. It is possible to apply a computer program to the data,[23] but the reader should be aware of the mathematics involved,[24] as follows:

1. Volume of ventilation per minute, ambient temperature and pressure, saturated ($\dot{V}E$ ATPS).

$$\dot{V}E \text{ ATPS} = \dot{V}E \times \frac{60}{ct}$$

where $\dot{V}E$ = volume of expired gas as measured.
   ct = collection time in seconds.
   60 = conversion of volume from seconds to minutes.

2. The $\dot{V}E$ ATPS is converted to volume of ventilation per minute, body temperature and pressure, saturated ($\dot{V}E$ BTPS), as follows:

$$\dot{V}E \text{ BTPS} = \dot{V}E \text{ ATPS} \times \frac{310}{273 + T} \times \frac{P_B - P_{H_2O} \text{ at } T}{P_B - 47}$$

where T = temperature in degrees centigrade,
   P_B = barometric pressure in mm Hg,
   P_{H_2O} = water-vapor tension.

The value 47 is the alveolar P_{H_2O} in mm Hg; 310 is the average respiratory tract temperature in deg K; 273 is the temperature at absolute zero in deg K.

3. The oxygen consumption per minute (BTPS) can be calculated from knowledge of the proportion (fraction, F) of the oxygen and carbon dioxide expired, along with the known values of both gases in the inspired air, as follows:

[22]Suggested source: Metabolic Measurement Cart, Beckman Instruments, Inc., Schiller Park, Ill.

[23]Jay T. Kearney and G. Alan Stull, "A Fortran Program for the Reduction of Open-Circuit Data," *Research Quarterly*, 42, No. 2 (May 1971), 223.

[24]David H. Clarke, *Exercise Physiology* (Englewood Cliffs, N.J.: Prentice-Hall, Inc., 1975), pp. 265-66.

$$\dot{V}_{O_2} \text{ BTPS} = \dot{V}_E \text{ BTPS} \times \frac{T_{IO_2} (1 - F_{ECO_2}) - F_{EO_2} (1 - F_{ECO_2})}{(1 - F_{IO_2} - F_{ICO_2})}$$

where F_{IO_2} = proportion of oxygen inspired (.2093).
         F_{EO_2} = proportion of oxygen expired.
         F_{ICO_2} = proportion of carbon dioxide inspired (.0003).
         F_{ECO_2} = proportion of carbon dioxide expired.

4. The $\dot{V}_{O_2}$ BTPS is converted to STPD, according to the following:

$$\dot{V}_{O_2} \text{ STPD} = \dot{V}_{O_2} \text{ BTPS} \times \frac{273.0}{310.0} \times \frac{P_B - 47}{760}$$

5. The $\dot{V}_{CO_2}$ BTPS may be calculated by using the following formula:

$$\dot{V}_{CO_2} \text{ BTPS} = \dot{V}_E \text{ BTPS} \times \frac{F_{ECO_2} (1 - F_{IO_2}) - F_{ICO_2} (1 - F_{EO_2})}{(1 - F_{IO_2} - F_{ICO_2})}$$

6. $\dot{V}_{CO_2}$ STPD is calculated as follows:

$$\dot{V}_{CO_2} \text{ STPD} = \dot{V}_{CO_2} \text{ BTPS} \times \frac{273.0}{310.0} \times \frac{P_B - 47}{760}$$

7. The Respiratory Exchange Ratio (R) is calculated as:

$$R = \frac{\dot{V}_{CO_2} \text{ STPD}}{\dot{V}_{O_2} \text{ STPD}}$$

CARDIOPULMONARY MEASURES

Several other cardiovascular variables are commonly studied by exercise physiologists as part of their research design, some of which are rather advanced techniques whereas others are rather pedestrian. The more technical procedures require additional laboratory training or perhaps the use of clinical technicians so that no errors are made and sterile conditions are maintained when blood is taken. A growing tendency is found today in the larger laboratories to employ personnel whose function is to assist in the collection of such data. They are also responsible for the chemical assays, as they can be trained in various biochemical techniques required for such studies.

There was a time when the researcher was expected to possess the expertise necessary to gather and treat all this experimental data. But, more and more, the tendency is to employ others for many of the more tedious and complicated laboratory processes, thus freeing the investigator of considerable time that can be spent in enlarging the project; frequently, too, the research problem can be more comprehensive. The same can be said for the use of computers in the reduction and statistical analysis of the resultant data from such multivariate studies; the repetitious and detailed treatment of the data may be accomplished in a fraction of the time and, one hopes, more accurately. Thus, the team approach used today has permitted far more sophisticated research designs than ever before.

Heart Rate

Nothing new or startling is involved in the simple determination of heart rate, as this is a time-honored and long-standing physiological parameter, among the most early of measured variables. The reason, of course, is the absolute simplicity involved in monitoring the pulse: No equipment is needed and very little training is required. In early physical fitness tests,[25] the emphasis was placed on the recovery of the heart following a given exercise task, based on the assumption that the individual with the best physical fitness was the one whose pulse would recover most rapidly. It is known now that the heart rate during exercise should be studied—that this phenomenon more adequately reflects the circulatory system in its response to the stress of exercise.

The technique today is to monitor heart rate by the use of electrodes and recorder rather than to depend upon a manual method, because of the greater chance for error when counting in the latter instance. This is particularly true during exercise, when subject movement and muscular contraction may interfere with detection of the pulse beat. An error introduced as a consequence will probably go undetected; if 10-, 15-, or 20-sec counts are taken, with conversion to minute rate, an error of 1 beat per measured interval will cause the heart rate to be off from 3 to 6 beats per min. This amount of error is intolerable in research applications, so the more sophisticated techniques are preferable.

Any number of electrocardiographic systems that give very acceptable recordings are available to the research worker. Further, telemetry may be employed in gathering data so that the subject is freed of electrode-recorder leads and can be at some distance from the receiver and still monitor his or her heart rate. Telemetry is becoming popular, as field use is possible where large-scale physical activity is involved in the exercise regimen. Care must be taken, however, that unwanted muscle action potentials do not interfere with the recording during exercise. In preparing the subject for heart rate measurement with a three electrode configuration, the skin should first be cleaned and abraded with gauze soaked in alcohol, and a small amount of

[25]Lucien Brouha, "The Step Test: A Simple Method of Measuring Physical Fitness for Muscular Work in Young Men," *Research Quarterly*, 14, No. 1 (March 1943), 31.

electrolyte jelly should be rubbed into each site. The dish of each electrode should be filled with jelly and the electrode applied to the skin. A modified V_5 arrangement would have the ground lead placed one inch below the left clavicle, another lead one inch below the right clavicle, and the third lead on the left side of the chest in the fifth intercostal space or V_5 location.

Blood Pressure

Reliable blood pressure determinations must still be obtained in humans by the usual procedure involving the sphygmomanometer and stethoscope for studies in exercise physiology. The manual method is often difficult to do successfully for the novice, so he or she should plan on sufficient practice to ensure adequate results. Even so, the dangers of variations exist in auditory acuity and in interpretation of the sound levels, as well as in the occurrence of other variables related to individual differences, strength of the heart beat, and factors related to equipment. Resting blood pressure may be given on various read-out devices, but movement artifacts are pronounced during exercise. Therefore, great care and sufficient amplification are needed for successful recording. Use of a large-face dial for the sphygmomanometer assists greatly in promoting measurement accuracy.

Cardiac Output

Considerable interest has been evident in the assessment of cardiac output, going back to the early work in 1870 by Fick, who employed a direct cardiac puncture. Although one infers blood flow from the heart rate, the amount of blood volume cannot be known from this measure alone, so it has been important to devise a technique whereby the cardiac output could be determined. Such a technique was provided by Cournand[26] by which a catheter is threaded through the basilic vein into the right side of the heart to the pulmonary artery; mixed venous blood samples are taken. Arterial puncture provides arterial blood samples; the oxygen utilization can be obtained by the Douglas bag technique. Cardiac output in ml/min is then calculated by the following formula:

$$\text{Cardiac output} = \frac{O_2 \text{ (ml/min)}}{\text{arterio-venous } O_2 \text{ difference (ml/min)}}$$

The difficulty inherent in this procedure is apparent: The heart catheterization is not routinely possible, except under the most rigidly controlled situations; therefore, its use in exercise physiology is

[26]Andre Cournand, "Measurement of the Cardiac Output in Man Using the Right Heart Catheterization," *Federation Proceedings*, 4, No. 2 (June 1945), 207.

questionable. However, these problems have been surmounted in subsequent research,[27] where an indwelling catheter proceeding from the femoral vein into the right side of the heart was utilized during a bicycle ergometer experiment.

Most feasible are the indirect measures whereby a foreign gas, notably acetylene, is used to obtain the A-V O_2 difference or some of the more popular dye dilution techniques.[28] Recently, radioisotopes have been substituted for dyes, and the cardiac output has been measured by use of external detectors.[29] Perhaps more practical for studies in physical education is a photoelectric device called an oximeter, which can continuously measure the O_2 saturation of arterial blood and can be used for obtaining mixed venous blood determinations.[30] This method has the obvious advantage of avoiding the necessity for puncturing blood vessels.

The most promising of the techniques currently in use involves the carbon dioxide rebreathing method, whereby V_{CO_2} and the arteriovenous CO_2 difference are substituted in the Fick equation.[31] Instrumentation for this procedure is not simple, and considerable preparation on the part of the researcher is required. However, its use is gaining wide acceptance as a noninvasive procedure for determination of cardiac output and, by inference, stroke volume.

Blood Gas Determinations

When blood gas measures must be obtained, the typical researcher in physical education may need to obtain assistance in securing the blood samples and in using the measurement apparatus. These procedures cannot be considered routine for exercise physiology laboratories. However, as the research becomes more sophisticated and as more research funds become available, they will undoubtedly come into greater use. When such equipment can be obtained and used, the

[27]J. Stenberg, P. O. Astrand, B. Ekblom, J. Royce, and B. Saltin, "Hemodynamic Response to Work with Different Muscle Groups, Sitting and Supine," *Journal of Applied Physiology*, 22, No. 1 (January 1967), 61.

[28]Erling Asmussen and Marius Nielsen, "The Cardiac Output in Rest and Work Determined Simultaneously by the Acetylene and the Dye Injection Methods," *Acta Physiologica Scandinavica*, 27, No. 2-3 (1952), 217.

[29]Hideo Ueda, Iwao Ito, and Masahiro Iio, "External Measurement of Cardiac Output Using Radioisotopes by Means of a Digital Data Readout Device," *American Journal of Medical Electronics*, 2, No. 3 (July-September 1963), 229.

[30]Nils J. Nilsson, "Oximetry" *Physiological Reviews*, 40, No. 1 (January 1960), 1. See also W. Sleator, J. O. Elam, W. N. Elam, and H. L. White, "Oximetric Determinations of Cardiac Output Responses to Light Exercise," *Journal of Applied Physiology*, 3, No. 11 (May 1951), 649.

[31]N. L. Jones and A. J. Rebuck, "Rebreathing Equilibration of CO_2 during Exercise," *Journal of Applied Physiology*, 35 (1973), 538.

research design may be considerably enhanced or, at least, permit the delineation of a far greater number of studies than otherwise would be possible.

The basic instrument utilized for blood gas measures is the Van Slyke-Neill manometric apparatus,[32] or, more recently, the Roughton-Scholander syringe pipette.[33] Other devices are currently available. For additional information, the reader is directed to descriptions provided by Consolazio, Johnson, and Pecora.[34]

Blood Biochemistry

Because of the importance of studying mechanisms in controlling exercise metabolism, the examination of various other constituents of the blood has become necessary. These may include such assays as blood glucose, triglycerides, cholesterol, and lactic acid. Clearly, special training is required before such biochemical methods can be employed. For details of these and other procedures, Costill and others[35] is a helpful reference.

Muscle Histochemistry and Biochemistry

There has been a great increase in research employing muscle histochemistry and biochemistry, both with human and animal tissue. In particular, the biopsy procedure has made muscle fiber typing a reality for many laboratories, even though it is primarily a medical procedure. The histochemical methods employed require extensive preparation, as do those for such assessments as glycogen, lactate and the whole array of muscle enzymes.[36]

BODY COMPOSITION

The study of the physical and chemical aspects of the body has led to a variety of techniques designed to estimate its physical composition. The concept that a body displaces an amount of water equal to its own

[32]Donald D. Van Slyke and James M. Neill, "The Determination of Gases in Blood and Other Solutions by Vacuum Extraction and Manometric Measurement," *Journal of Biological Chemistry*, 61, No. 2 (September 1924), 523.

[33]F. J. W. Roughton and P. F. Scholander, "Micro Gasometric Estimation of the Blood Gases: I. Oxygen," *Journal of Biological Chemistry*, 148, No. 3 (June 1943), 541. See also P. F. Scholander and F. J. W. Roughton, "Micro Gasometric Estimation of the Blood Gases: IV. Carbon Dioxide," *Journal of Biological Chemistry*, 148, No. 3 (June 1943), 573.

[34]Consolazio, Johnson, and Pecora, *Physiological Measurements*, Ch. 4.

[35]D. L. Costill and others, *Analytical Methods for the Measurement of Human Performance*, 2nd ed. (Muncie, Ind.: D. L. Costill, 1979), pp. 16-58.

[36]Ibid., pp. 62-128.

volume was passed down by Archimedes as long ago as the third century B.C. Even though the possibilities for estimating body composition were suggested earlier, it was not until Behnke[37] perfected a technique for ascertaining the body composition of adult males that the procedure began to gain wide acceptance. Early work by Rathbun and Pace[38] and a later review by Keys and Brozek[39] centered attention on the possibilities of the estimation of various components of the body, most notably the lean and fat contents. Inasmuch as the technique for measuring body density by immersing the body in water is a very simple one, it has become a rather important procedure to be used in research laboratories. The initial materials include a tank for water, a harness for suspension, and a scale for obtaining submerged weights. In addition, apparatus for measuring residual lung volume is needed.

As described by Siri,[40] the weight of the body in air is compared to its weight in water when totally submerged. Thus, a means must be found whereby the body can be fully immersed in water and weighted in this position. A tank of some sort will suffice; successful attempts have been made in measuring subjects suspended both vertically and horizontally. The vertical position is easier because it is a more natural one, and subject movement can be controlled more effectively. A harness is employed to lower the subject underwater directly beneath the scale. The horizontal position is probably more difficult to control, but experience has shown it to be entirely satisfactory when certain controls are incorporated. One control technique is to use a rectangular frame with nylon webbing as a stretcher on which the subject reclines. The size depends upon the dimensions of the water tank; in any event, oscillating movements can be reduced by applying bumper guards to the sides of the frame. The entire assembly can then be attached to the scale which in turn can be damped to avoid excessive indicator movement.

The prime requisite is to obtain the underwater weight of the subject when completely submerged in water. In order to do so, the subject must exhale completely before the weight is read on the scale. Extra lead weight may be necessary to hold the subject down; this weight, plus the weight of any harness, must later be subtracted.

[37]A. R. Behnke, B. G. Feen, and W. C. Welham, "The Specific Gravity of Healthy Men: Body Weight ÷ Volume as an Index of Obesity," *Journal of the American Medical Association*, 118, No. 7 (February 14, 1942), 495.

[38]Edith N. Rathbun and Nello Pace, "Studies on Body Composition: I. The Determination of Total Body Fat by Means of the Body Specific Gravity," *Journal of Biological Chemistry*, 158, No. 3 (May 1945), 667.

[39]Ancel Keys and Josef Brozek, "Body Fat in Adult Man," *Physiological Reviews* 33, No. 3 (July 1953), 245.

[40]William E. Siri, "The Gross Composition of the Body," *Advances in Biological and Medical Physics*, 4 (1956), 239.

However, this process does not account for the buoyant effect of gas in the gastrointestinal tract or for residual lung volume, both of which may affect the estimate of specific gravity. The former condition may be reduced by being weighed in the morning in the postabsorptive state, and the latter may be measured directly.[41]

The following computational procedures may be employed in determining body density. As indicated, residual air in the lungs is calculated, and corrections are made for the harness weight and for water density.

1. Weight in air (lbs)
2. Weight immersed in water, full exhalation
3. Weight of the harness in water
4. Underwater weight (item 2 − item 3)
5. Estimated volume of residual air in lungs (cc)
6. Weight of water displaced by residual lung volume (item 5 ÷ 454, the weight equivalent of this volume in lbs)
7. Water density at temperature of the water used
8. Correction for residual air and density (item 6 × item 7)
9. Net weight in water (item 4 + item 8)

$$\text{Body weight} = \frac{\text{body weight in air}}{\text{body weight in air} - \text{net weight in water}}$$

When related to the reference body which has 14% fat, the following formula may be used:[42]

$$\text{Per cent body fat} = 100 \, (4.201/\text{density} - 3.813).$$

Based upon the above determinations, other constituents of body composition can be calculated. The weight of the fat component can be assessed from knowledge of the percentage of fat. In a similar manner, the lean body weight is the residual, that is, nonessential fat, or the body weight less the body fat weight. Other combinations are possible, and further readings will elicit additional parameters of interest on this topic.[43]

Other techniques for assessing body composition have proven

[41]Behnke, "Gravity of Healthy Men."

[42]Keys and Brozek (July 1953), "Body Fat in Adult Man."

[43]Josef Brozek and Austin Henschel, *Techniques for Measuring Body Composition.* Washington, D.C.: National Academy of Sciences, National Research Council, 1961; Josef Brozek, ed., "Body Composition, Part I," *Annals of the New York Academy of Sciences,* 110 (September 1963), 1; and Josef Brozek, ed., "Body Composition, Part II," *Annals of the New York Academy of Sciences,* 110 (September 1963), 425.

successful to researchers. The estimation of nutritional status by means of skinfold measures has been done repeatedly and can be considered very useful in certain kinds of studies. However, the reader should be aware of the increasing reluctance to accept the estimation of percentage of fat from anthropometric measurements, that there is sufficient error to render these techniques less than desirable for research purposes. The technique is to sample the thickness of the skinfold at various sites on the body and then to predict the body density, or specific gravity. From this, percentage of fat and lean body mass can be obtained. Although more advanced and rather sophisticated techniques are available in the literature and have been employed by physiologists and others interested in these problems, it is doubtful that they will be available routinely to physical education research laboratories. At any rate, the more important question may be to discover if function relates to structure. Stated in another way, to what extent does knowledge of the constituents of the body enable one to predict performance ability? For further discussion of body composition as related to anthropometry, refer to Chapter 15.

ANIMAL RESEARCH

Research in exercise physiology with the use of small animals is becoming more and more popular. The obvious advantage lies in the fact that the lives of the subjects can be rigidly controlled in such important aspects as diet and exercise, which is more difficult or even impossible with humans. The analysis of far more variables is also possible where dissection and examination of a wide variety of tissues and organs may be accomplished at the end of the experiment. Thus, the use of animals extends the research possibilities into areas that would be impossible otherwise. The obvious drawback concerns the direct applicability that such studies would have on human performance; there is no guarantee that what happens with animals would occur in the same way in human studies. As the life cycle of most laboratory animals is considerably shorter than humans, the design may be telescoped in such a way as to follow changes from birth to maturity.

The usual laboratory animal in physical education has been the male albino rat, to which the following discussion will be limited. They may be purchased commercially of the same age and strain, thus assuring control of these two variables. These animals are typically assigned randomly to the experimental or control groups at the outset of the experiment. A color coding system may be established, and the tails of the animals marked appropriately so that they can be instantly identified to avoid any error of repeated treatment at a later time. A matching mark should appear on the cage to facilitate this process.

Two types of cages for rats are in general use today: those that are sedentary and those that permit spontaneous exercise. The sedentary cage is small and rectangular, permitting movement but no exercise; the activity cage is accompanied by an exercise wheel, to which the animal has access. A mechanical revolution counter attached to the cage can be set to record the number of wheel revolutions in either direction, and it may be read at intervals throughout the experiment. A method for studying the intensity of exercise per bout or the total per hour is also possible.[44]

Laboratory Care

Undertaking an animal study means accepting responsibility for their care and feeding throughout the experiment. This must be done carefully and conscientiously on a regular basis, for neglect here can result in the loss of subjects. The diet may be one of the variables to be studied, and if so, it must be rigidly followed, with caloric accounting taken of new food added plus any leftover food meausred. Otherwise, it is expected that the rats will be fed *ad libitum* from a stock diet. Specific information about the diet may be obtained from a local distributor. Water bottles should also be provided and kept full. These bottles should always be sterilized.

The animal laboratory should be isolated from the rest of the laboratory in order to assure that the animals will not be disturbed or contaminated. Thus, normal spontaneous activity will be permitted. A control over light in the laboratory is necessary so that alternating periods of light and darkness are maintained; rats are known to be more active during dark hours and to sleep during light. Normal care also requires disposal of excrement on a regular basis. Other routine problems involve proper temperature, air circulation, deodorizing, and general laboratory cleanliness. As a general rule, as few people as possible should have contact with the animals; and if the investigator has a cold or other infection, he or she should wear a hospital face mask to avoid possible contamination.

Exercise

The manner of exercise becomes very important in animal studies, as the primary reason for using animals is usually to study the effects of activity on certain parameters. Whereas humans can be

[44]Dale Hanson, Wayne Van Huss, and Gundars Strautneik, "Effects of Forced Exercise upon the Amount and Intensity of the Spontaneous Activity of Young Rats," *Research Quarterly*, 37, No. 2 (May 1966), 221.

given explicit instructions and encouraged to follow a set routine, rats are not always cooperative when it comes to an exercise routine. In fact, experienced researchers spend hours devising appropriate means to control this variable, and even then can seldom state the extent of the physical or metabolic work accomplished.

The two procedures most often employed are running and swimming. Running on a treadmill can be accomplished very readily with certain rats. Others, however, either cannot or will not run; they are even willing to undergo rather painful stimuli rather than adapt to the exercise routine. Various forms of inducement may be offered to the animal to force him to run, including electric shock, but the results have not always been favorable. In fact, the stress that is involved in forced exercise may confound the true results that are investigated.[45] Success has been obtained with a short strong blast of compressed air that is not physically traumatic but that serves to keep the rat forward in his running compartments.[46] Other variables, such as running in light or dark areas, the use of such rewards as stroking, or even housing in spontaneous activity cages, have, at best, produced only a modest improvement.[47]

Swimming has gained wide acceptance as an exercise medium, as it provides the built-in incentive that the rat will swim out of sheer self-preservation. The typical procedure is to fill a container to such a depth that the animals can neither touch the bottom with their feet nor prop themselves on their tails. Then they will perform a vertical treading motion until exhausted. Great care must be exercised, of course, that they do not drown; the briefest inattention may result in just such an accident. In order to maintain negative buoyancy, a weight may be attached to the tail, amounting from 2% to 6% of body weight. The animals may be placed in individual compartments or swim together. The water should be kept at body temperature and the animals dried before returning them to their cages.

SUGGESTED PROBLEMS

The area of exercise physiology is so broad that the identification of appropriate topics is bound only by the limits of the imagination. Upon a thorough review of the literature, the student will discover a number

[45]Henry J. Montoye, Richard Nelson, Perry Johnson, and Ross Macnab, "Effects of Exercise on Swimming Endurance and Organ Weight in Mature Rats," *Research Quarterly*, 31, No. 3 (October 1960), 474.

[46]David L. Kelley, University of Maryland, personal communication.

[47]Dale Hanson, David Clarke, and David Kelley, "Effect of Selected Treatments upon the Treadmill Running Success of Male Rats," *Research Quarterly*, 40, No. 1 (March 1969).

of worthy topics. Additional answers may well come to such questions
as the following:

1. Although training studies have been undertaken in the past, they have
   frequently involved subjects already in a state of moderate conditioning.
   What is the training pattern among physiological variables for the sedentary? How long do the effects of training persist?
2. What is the extent of physiological sex differences at various ages?
3. What are the environmental effects upon various performance criteria,
   including the effects of temperature, altitude, deep diving, and others?
4. What is the relationship between physiological variables and performance
   such as learning?
5. What is the extent of individual differences among various physiological
   parameters?
6. What is the physiological cost of varied physical activities? Can comparative values be established based on intensity of play?
7. In the area of adapted physical education, what is the energy cost of
   performance for those with handicapping conditions?

SUMMARY

The study of the underlying mechanisms that permit physical performance is known as exercise physiology and includes factors that relate
to the immediate and long-term aspects of activity. While primarily
concerned with human performance, increasing effort is being placed
on animal studies, especially when it is essential to control such
variables as diet and activity or when certain types of blood and tissue
analyses are employed.

The range of research possibilities is wide; with the advent of more
sophisticated instrumentation, the field is growing considerably.
Where formerly a single dynamometer was employed to measure
strength, a host of techniques are presently available, some electronically coupled to standard laboratory recorders that permit the investigation of muscular strength, endurance relationships, and other
characteristics of muscular contraction.

A number of devices for measurement of work are widely employed in research laboratories, but the bicycle ergometer and treadmill
are most popular. Both permit certain types of standardization, and
both may be used to study the energy cost of activity. The usual
procedure in this design is to collect expired air and submit small
samples to some gas analysis apparatus where the percentages of the
gases may be precisely determined. Increasing attention is being given
to methods of recording continuously expired air, thus providing

additional information concerning the time factor associated with oxygen uptake.

Other cardiovascular variables, such as heart rate, blood pressure, cardiac output, and various blood gas determinations, are receiving wide attention in exercise physiology laboratories as indicators of physical fitness and as a means for aiding in the assessment of performance. Heart rate in particular has been employed for years for this purpose. Recently, laboratory procedures have been employed by exercise physiologists for the analysis of tissue histochemistry and biochemistry which have greatly aided in the investigation of factors responsible for energy metabolism.

Assessing the various components of the body has involved a knowledge of body composition. The methods used for the process are rapidly becoming more accessible to researchers in physical education who are raising questions related to structure and function. The technique of densitometry can be applied to these problems, as well as other procedures designed to study relative portions of body fat and lean tissue.

SELECTED REFERENCES

ASTRAND, P.-O., "Human Physical Fitness with Special Reference to Sex and Age," *Physiological Reviews*, 36, No. 3 (July 1956), 325.

BROZEK, JOSEF, ed., "Body Composition, Part I," *Annals of the New York Academy of Sciences*, 110 (September 1963), 1.

———, "Body Composition, Part II," *Annals of the New York Academy of Sciences*, 110 (September 1963), 425.

BROZEK, JOSEF, and AUSTIN HENSCHEL, *Techniques for Measuring Body Composition*. Washington, D.C.: National Academy of Sciences, National Research Council, 1961.

CARTER, J. E. L., *The Heath-Carter Somatotype Method*. San Diego: San Diego State University, 1975.

CLARKE, DAVID H., *Exercise Physiology*. Englewood Cliffs, N.J.: Prentice-Hall, Inc., 1975.

CLARKE, H. HARRISON, *Muscular Strength and Endurance in Man*. Englewood Cliffs, N.J.: Prentice-Hall, Inc., 1966.

CLARKE, H. HARRISON, and DAVID H. CLARKE, *Developmental and Adapted Physical Education* (2nd ed.). Englewood Cliffs, N.J.: Prentice-Hall, Inc., 1978.

CONSOLAZIO, C. FRANK, ROBERT E. JOHNSON, and LOUIS J. PECORA, *Physiological Measurements of Metabolic Functions in Man*. New York: McGraw-Hill, Inc., 1963.

COSTILL, D. L., and others, *Analytical Methods for the Measurement of Human Performance* (2nd ed.). Muncie, Ind.: D. L. Costill, 1979.

KEYS, ANCEL, and JOSEF BROZEK, "Body Fat in Adult Man," *Physiological Reviews*, 33, No. 3 (July 1953), 245.

PETERS, JOHN P., and DONALD D. VAN SLYKE, *Quantitative Clinical Chemistry, Vol. II, Methods*, Baltimore: The Williams & Wilkins Company, 1932.

RIGGS, DOUGLAS S., *The Mathematical Approach to Physiological Problems*. Baltimore: The Williams & Wilkins Company, 1963.

SCHOLANDER, P. F., "Analyzer for Accurate Estimation of Respiratory Gases in One-Half Cubic Centimeter Samples," *Journal of Biological Chemistry*, 167, No. 1 (January 1947), 235.

VAN SLYKE, DONALD D., and JAMES M. NEILL, "The Determination of Gases in Blood and Other Solutions by Vacuum Extraction and Manometric Measurement," *Journal of Biological Chemistry*, 61, No. 2 (September 1924), 523.

12
Motor Learning /
Motor Control

The area of psychology of sport that deals with learning and its related topics is usually termed motor learning. It is apparent from a perusal of the psychological literature that the primary interest of psychologists is in learning per se and only incidentally in the motor aspects of performance. Thus, there has developed a growing and maturing concern for an understanding of the motor performance capabilities of individuals involved in large-scale muscular and coordinative acts. Although the line is not clearly drawn between what would be considered psychology and what would be physical education, there seems a greater concern in physical education for what may be termed gross motor activity than for fine motor ability. Motor control deals with those factors that are responsible for the learning of skilled acts. In fact, there is evidence that the research emphasis is even moving to the neurophysiological components of motor behavior, which means that advanced study in that field may be required for the student to be able to work at the frontiers of this discipline.

In contrast to the field of exercise physiology, where instrumentation is far more standardized, the motor learning specialist quite often must rely upon his or her own ingenuity for the development of suitable instruments or tests. Basic devices, such as timers and counters, and rather widely used tests of learning, such as pursuit rotors, star tracing, or mirror tracing devices, can be purchased commercially, along with other types of equipment used in psychology. However, the tasks involving learning that are used so widely in physical education seem to be of two types—those that are self-testing and require very little or no accessory equipment and those for which the device has been fashioned by the investigator for a particular task. These devices, nevertheless, are showing an increasing sophistication of design and electronic circuitry, reflecting a growing precision of measurement. Moreover, they are becoming increasingly available for sale by enterprising manufacturing concerns.

When it comes to studying motor learning, the usual sports and games so commonly taught in activity classes are notoriously poor as learning modalities in research. Aside from the obvious difficulty of obtaining adequate measures from trial to trial is the more serious concern that the individual is so practiced in the event as to in fact have learned it. It is well known that the greatest learning takes place in the early phases, and later in practice the gains are small; thus, common skills almost invariably find the individual with enough sophistication that relatively little learning occurs. What is needed then is a novel skill, one in which the subject is naive and which can be expected not to have been practiced before. Sometimes old skills may be so modified as to meet this criterion, but more often some new task must be found. Even then, there is no guarantee that it will be suitable for learning, because its level of difficulty may be such that the subject grasps it right away or it may be so difficult that extremely high trial-to-trial variability makes it unstable. The proper combination of factors seems to be a blending of the degree of difficulty and the ability of the subject to master the skill so that the trial-by-trial performances reflect a refinement of the task in a measurable manner. Some of these tasks will be discussed in this chapter, the aim being to study their applicability and their use in various other matters connected with performance psychology.

LEARNING TASKS

The decision to present selected motor learning tasks at the outset is prompted by the utilitarian purpose that once described their function can be used in later discussion. No attempt will be made to be exhaustive; rather, the tests which seem to be most commonly used in physical education will be presented. The specialist in the field of motor learning will be aware of others, and the reader may acquire sufficient insight to develop other tests that can be used to study learning. As pointed out above, the modification of known skills has proven useful and quite often permits the use of available equipment and space. Indeed, one of the most intriguing aspects of this type of study is the simplicity with which it can be accomplished and, in most cases, at a fraction of the cost of equipment generally employed, as contrasted, for example, with physiology of exercise and other experimental research. This may or may not be an important consideration, but it has given solace to those researchers operating on a limited budget.

Stabilometer

The stabilometer has been used in studies of motor learning and motor performance, sometimes as a measure of balance. The instrument is actually a horizontally pivoted board upon which the subject stands, the center of rotation being above the level of the feet so that the task is to try to maintain balance. This is done through the use of a selected number of trials. The technique is to measure the number of deviations, which may be called errors, so that in successive trials the subject reduces the error of movement. A stabilometer currently in use is shown in Figure 12.1 and has been described by Bachman as follows:

> Motion of the board was measured by a work adder. Any movement was transmitted by a 1.5 in. lever arm which was mounted on the axle. A waxed string which was fastened to the lever arm passed over the groove of a pulley 3.63 in. in net diameter that was independently pivoted, the spring being held taut by a coil spring exerting 150 gr tension. The pulley carried a flat disc 6 inch in diameter and ⅛ inch thick, with a milled or knurled edge. A pawl rested against this edge, permitting easy rotation in one direction, but preventing any movement in the opposite direction. (In the latter case, the string slipped in the pulley groove.) The disc carried a calibrated dial which was scaled in 100 arbitrary units. Each scale unit represented 12 degrees of back and forth platform tilting. Microswitches were fastened under each end of the tilting board and wired in series with an electric clock so that no time was registered during such periods as the subject had the board completely out of balance and against the baseboard and could thereby rest without movement. This provision insured that each 30-sec trial represented that much net time of actual balancing effort.[1]

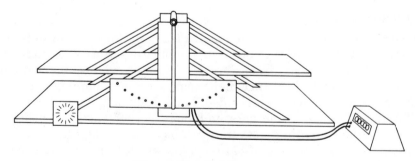

Figure 12.1 Stabilometer

[1] John C. Bachman, "Specificity vs. Generality in Learning and Performing Two Large Muscle Motor Tasks," *Research Quarterly*, 32, No. 1 (March 1961), 5. Used by permission of the author and AAHPERD.

Another way to handle the measurement of work done is to attach to the platform an electrical counting device, which is activated by the movement of an arm that mirrors the tilting of the platform. Copper electrical contacts can be so arranged as to activate a counting device at selected intervals or to time the amount of unbalances.[2]

Each trial is usually 30 sec in duration, followed by 30 sec of rest, with 10 trials being used for the learning period. When this procedure is followed, the resultant learning curve obeys mathematical laws of the exponential form.[3]

Ladder Climb

Bachman has also provided another task, original with him, consisting of a free-standing ladder upon which the subject climbs. The apparatus, described as two parallel ladders connected by a common side, is 14 inches wide, with the following specifications as given by Bachman:

> The rungs (made of 1 in. dowling, 5 in. apart) were staggered in the two sections so that the distance from the bottom of the ladder to rung number 16 (the top) was 40 inches. A vertical extension was adjusted for each subject in such a manner that its top rung could just be grasped by his upward extended hand. Climbing was done near the middle of a 5 feet by 10 feet mat to lessen fear of injury in case of a fall. Tennis shoes were worn . . . to prevent, as much as possible, slipping off the ladder rungs. In the starting position, the ladder was held by the subject directly in front of him with the toes of both feet placed on the bottom crosspiece. It was required that climbing be done one step at a time.[4]

In a manner similar to the stabilometer, the ladder climb is administered in 30 sec periods interspersed by 30 sec of rest. The task is to climb as high as possible before losing balance and then to reclimb once again, repeating as often as is necessary during each trial. The total accumulation of steps taken is utilized as the score for each testing period, and 10 trials constitute the performance. Examination of the learning curve reflects a similar mathematical model as the stabilometer performance, that is, it follows the exponential law.[5] However, as the ladder climb involves a progressive accumulation of scores, whereas the stabilometer results in a reduction, the learning curve goes

[2]Suggested Source: Lafayette Instrument Company, Lafayette, Ind.

[3]For a description of exponential curve analysis, see Chapter 11.

[4]Bachman, "Two Large Muscle Motor Tasks."

[5]John C. Bachman, "Motor Learning and Performance as Related to Age and Sex in Two Measures of Balance Coordination," *Research Quarterly*, 32, No. 2 (May 1961), 123.

upward rather than downward. There is also the addition of an extra component to the ladder climb early in performance that has been attributed to familiarity with the equipment.

Pursuit Rotor

Another technique for studying motor learning is provided by use of a pursuit rotor. Originally designed by Koerth,[6] the currently available instruments would seem to vary only in minor detail. The description given by Alderman is representative of the pursuit rotors commonly in use.

> The subject grasped a stylus handle equipped with a rigid extension attached to his forearm by means of a strap. This served to eliminate finger and wrist action. The stylus proper (a metal rod 5-inches long, with the usual ½-in. vertical bend at the ⅛-in. diameter tip) was hinged horizontally to the handle. In response to an oral command and the initiation of turntable rotation (78 rpm), the subject pursued the target with the tip of the stylus. The target was a silver disc, 1-in. in diameter, the center of which was 4 inches from the center of the turntable and flush with the surface of the turntable. The subject's task was to maintain stylus-tip contact with the target disc as much as possible during each 15-sec trial. The amount of stylus-tip contact time per trial was recorded by a ¹⁄₁₀₀-sec electric chronoscope. Each subject received a 10-sec rest between trials and each test day consisted of 60 trials.[7]

A rather large number of trials is needed to secure the best estimate of performance and to allow the appropriate learning to occur. The amount of learning is substantial when the test is administered as described; in fact, Alderman found a 440% gain in performance. It should be noted that the pursuit rotor may be obtained commercially.[8] It is also possible to enlarge the pursuit rotor so that whole body movements are involved in tracking.[9] When this is done, substantial amounts of learning take place, as is true with the conventional apparatus.

Juggling

The task of juggling is quite different from the ones mentioned so far, primarily in the method of scoring and thus in assessing per-

---

[6] Willhelmine Koerth, "Pursuit Apparatus: Eye-Hand Coordination," *Psychological Monographs*, 31, No. 1 (1922), 288.

[7] Richard B. Alderman, "Influence of Local Fatigue on Speed and Accuracy in Motor Learning," *Research Quarterly*, 36, No. 2 (May 1965), 133. Used by permission of the author and AAHPERD.

[8] Suggested source: Lafayette Instrument Company, Lafayette, Ind.

[9] L. R. T. Williams and I. R. Grbin, "The Large Pursuit Rotor: A New Gross Motor Tracking Task," *Journal of Motor Behavior*, 8, No. 3 (1976), 245.

formance. Obviously, the scoring of trials would not be the same, and thus no learning curves, as such, are available. However, it can be considered a motor task, and it is likely that few individuals have had prior experience or practice that would invalidate their inclusion as subjects.

As suggested by Knapp and Dixon,[10] the task consists of juggling 3 balls to the extent that 1 ball must be in the air at all times; if 2 balls touch a hand simultaneously, the count must be discontinued. The criterion for learning is to make 100 consecutive catches; scoring is based upon the cumulative number of minutes of practice until the criterion is met. Learning thus becomes a matter of reaching a fixed goal, with considerable variability among individual capabilities. In fact, it has been necessary to eliminate subjects simply because they failed to learn the task, even after extended practice.[11]

Ball Toss

A number of skills involving throwing are available in a variety of physical activities, some of which involve speed whereas others require accuracy. When throwing at a wall target, there may be elements of both. Whether or not these can be successful learning media is questionable, since throwing per se is a skill that most subjects have practiced. Thus, better performers exhibit higher scores and perhaps less variability, but they may not exhibit real learning. The use of an accuracy throw, as given by a ball toss, seems to offer better possibilities, particularly if the task is a novel one. Attempts have been made to modify a known task,[12] and still others have taken a standard ball and modified the skill. For instance, Egstrom, Logan, and Wallis tossed a ball over a crossbar and onto a target consisting of three concentric circles ranging from 7 inches in diameter to 35 inches.[13] Scoring was accomplished by assigning values of 5, 3, and 1 to the target areas.

More recently, Ambo modified the ball toss task so that a

[10]Clyde G. Knapp and W. Robert Dixon, "Learning to Juggle: I. A Study to Determine the Effect of Two Different Distributions of Practice on Learning Efficiency," *Research Quarterly*, 21, No. 3 (October 1950), 331.

[11]Clyde G. Knapp, W. Robert Dixon, and Murney Lazier, "Learning to Juggle: III. A Study of Performance by Two Different Age Groups, *Research Quarterly*, 29, No. 1 (March 1958), 32.

[12]Robert N. Singer, "Massed and Distributed Practice Effects on the Acquisition and Retention of a Novel Basketball Skill," *Research Quarterly*, 36, No. 1 (March 1965), 68.

[13]Glen H. Egstrom, Gene A. Logan, and Earl L. Wallis, "Acquisition of Throwing Skill Involving Projectiles of Varying Weights," *Research Quarterly*, 31, No. 3 (October 1960), 420.

continuous scoring method could be employed.[14] In order to do this, a circular board 4 feet in diameter was placed on the floor at an angle of 34°. In the center, a steel metric tape was secured so that it could rotate 360°, thus permitting a rapid measure of each trial. In order to facilitate the scoring, the target face was chalked, and the ball was dampened with water so that a clear impression was made on the board. The distance from the target center to the center of the mark was used as the measure of accuracy. To control the trajectory, a bar—placed 3 feet 11 inches from the subject and 8 feet from the target—was adjusted to 6 inches above each subject's standing height. In this particular investigation, it was deemed advisable to standardize the throwing motion so that only the movement of elbow extension and wrist flexion was possible. To do this, an adjustable platform was employed upon which the subject rested his upper arm at shoulder height; a strap helped to stabilize this position. A soccer ball was used, and each subject was given 50 trials.

A rather sizable learning occurred from this task. For 70 subjects, the improvement in accuracy amounted to approximately 50% over the first 7 trials; a steady state occurred after trial 35. The progress of learning was curvilinear, occurring rapidly at first and slower during later stages.

Mirror Tracing

As developed by Snoddy, this task consists of tracing the path of a 6-sided star while looking in a mirror (see Figure 12.2).[15] Essentially, the device is a sheet of brass, from which a star-shaped path ¼-inch wide has been cut. This is then mounted upon a heavy glass plate. Rather than a smooth-sided figure, the star is cut in an indented manner, as illustrated, to facilitate the learning, presumably by supplying feedback of information concerning errors. At any rate, it tends to force the subject out into the path. A soft copper stylus is used; an electrical connection is made between the brass plate, the stylus, and a counter so that each contact with the edge of the star is counted mechanically. The usual procedure is to obscure the hand and star from direct vision but to observe it by means of a mirror image. The subject begins at S and proceeds in the direction indicated, each trial separated by 10 sec. The usual learning curves result from 20 circuits.

[14]Dennis M. Ambo, "Individual Differences in Various Structural and Strength Measures of the Hand and Forearm and Their Relation to Accuracy of Performance," (Master's Thesis, University of Maryland, 1966).

[15]George S. Snoddy, "Learning and Stability: A Psychological Analysis of a Case of Motor Learning with Clinical Applications," *Journal of Applied Psychology*, 10, No. 1 (1926), 1.

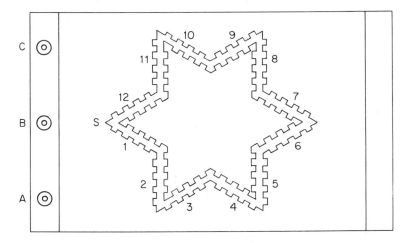

Figure 12.2. Mirror-Tracing Star Test (Reproduced by permission of the American Psychological Association. Originally published by the *Journal of Applied Psychology*.)

Ring-Peg Test

Lambert devised a ring-peg test to study motor learning. The test apparatus consists of a pegboard on which are placed 2 identical patterns of pegs situated in opposition to each other.[16] The subject can view directly the near pattern. The far pattern is obscured by a plywood panel but can be seen through a mirror that is attached to the end of the pegboard, as shown in Figure 12.3. Thus, the subject moves washers from the near, visual side, to corresponding pegs on the far, mirrored side. This is done in the sequence as given until 2 washers from each peg are distributed to the opposite side. In order to control the alternating hand sequence, the subject begins by depressing with both index fingers a key that turns off a light. The investigator then starts a stopwatch that serves as the signal to begin, and the subject proceeds with the left hand to peg 1. He or she completes the task, returns the hand to the key, goes to peg 2 with the right hand, and thus alternates throughout the board until a total of 20 washers has been placed on the far side. The watch is stopped with the positioning of the 20th washer, thus ending the first trial.

The decision to use 1 hand or 2 depends upon the experimental circumstances, as does the total number of trials. Examination of the performance curves reveals considerable learning, even beyond 40 trials.

[16] Philip Lambert, "Practice Effect of Non-Dominant vs. Dominant Musculature in Acquiring Two-Handed Skill, *Research Quarterly*, 22, No. 1 (March 1951), 50.

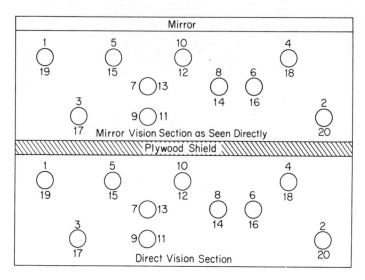

Figure 12.3. Ring-Peg Test (Reproduced by permission of Professor Philip Lambert, Director, Instructional Research Laboratory, University of Wisconsin, and AAHPERD).

Maze

A maze can be developed for use by humans as well as by animals for the purpose of studying learning. Two such attempts were made by Cratty.[17] One maze was a small stylus pattern adapted from Cook;[18] the other was a large maze, identical in pattern to the small one (see Figure 12.4) but through which the subjects could walk. Cratty gave the following description of the small maze:

> The pathway of the small maze was drilled, routed, and smoothed until it became ½ in. wide. The masonite containing the pattern was then mounted on a second piece of plywood so that a clearance between the two surfaces resulted, which allowed the lip of the stylus to pass freely. The stylus was lathe-turned with a handle 6 in. long and 1 in. in diameter; a tip was turned to ⅛ in. diameter and made ¾ in. long. The tip of the stylus was threaded and a washer 1 in. in diameter was attached so that the stylus would fit into the maze pathway and slide through without binding. The small maze was then attached to a table for stability and placed in a quiet room. The maze was covered until the subject's stylus was placed in the pathway's starting point.

[17]Bryant J. Cratty, "Comparison of Learning a Fine Motor Task with Learning a Similar Gross Motor Task, Using Kinesthetic Cues," *Research Quarterly*, 33, No. 2 (May 1962), 212. Used by permission of the author and AAHPERD.

[18]T. W. Cook, "Studies in Cross-Education: III. Kinesthetic Learning of an Irregular Pattern," *Journal of Experimental Psychology*, 17, No. 5 (October 1934), 749.

Figure 12.4. Cratty's Maze Pathway (Bryant J. Cratty, "Recency Versus Primacy in a Complex Motor Task," *Research Quarterly*, 34, March, 1963. Reproduced by permission of Dr. Bryant Cratty and AAHPERD.)

The large maze was increased 30 times in length and 96 times in width, but the original pattern was retained. The subject made contact with the pathway through the volar surface of his hand against ⅜-inch plastic tubing that was glued to wooden supports at a height of 30 inches from the ground and placed 2 feet apart. Neither maze contained blind alleys. The task was to traverse each maze as quickly as possible while blindfolded. Times were recorded with a stopwatch to the nearest ⅒ sec, with 12 trials constituting the learning period. Both tasks yielded large amounts of learning.

Coincidence-Anticipation Timer

The Basic Anticipation Timer[19] was devised to provide a means for studying such phenomena as motion prediction, velocity estimation, and motion perception. The apparatus consists of a control unit and a start- and finish-lighted runway, along with a response button. The runway consists of a series of lights that can be activated at various speeds (1-500 mph), giving a visual stimulus of apparent motion over a distance that can be varied in length. The control unit has the capability of controlling the velocity of light travel and presenting a variable foreperiod. It comes equipped with a stimulus initiate button and directional (early/late) user error clock. The runway has a subject response button.

The task requires the subject to time a response to coincide with the arrival of the signal at the target light at the end of the runway by depressing the response button. The amount of any error, positive or negative, is displayed on the clock. Suggestions for modification have been made to provide for an external stimulus initiator, to modify the warning light, to expand the number of runways, and to change the

---

[19]Suggested Source: Lafayette Instrument Company, Lafayette, Ind.

selectable velocities from 1-500 mph in 1 mph increments to 1-50 mph in 0.1 mph increments.[20]

Summary

In summary, tasks that have been developed for the study of motor learning have been presented. Before serious study may be undertaken in this field, an acquaintance with the tests that have been devised to produce measurable learning is necessary. It should be pointed out that other tasks are needed, so thought should be given to this in the future.

The remaining portion of the chapter will be devoted to a discussion of some of the more current research concepts that have been the concern of investigators in physical education. Specific references will be selected to illustrate the methodological approach undertaken, with a brief note of the findings. The selections are made not with the intention of reviewing the literature nor of emphasizing only a limited point of view but of offering examples that may serve to underscore the research technique.

DOCTRINE OF SPECIFICITY

One of the more mature developments in the field of motor performance has been the identification of the extreme specificity among tasks of motor ability. In spite of early evidence to the contrary, physical education has typically thought of coordination as being a general trait; one was either coordinated or uncoordinated. If one could be considered an athlete, for instance, this would be seen to carry over automatically from one motor task to another. Reference to the development of general motor abilities tests was supposed to measure the degree of generality in the performance of physical tasks. The difficulty was, however, that few persons evaluated the extent of the relationship of individual differences among large neuromotor coordination abilities. The establishment of the doctrine of specificity can be attributed to Henry,[21] who largely conceived the theoretical framework and then stimulated the experimental testing of hypotheses. The considerable advancement of the theory has provided insight into motor performance and human capabilities.

[20]Charles H. Shea and Alan A. Ashby, "Modifications to the Basic Anticipation Timer," *Research Quarterly for Exercise and Sport*, 52, No. 2 (May 1981), 278.

[21]Franklin M. Henry, "Specificity vs. Generality in Learning Motor Skills," *Proceedings of the College Physical Education Association*, 61 (1958), 126.

Much of the early work in theory development emanated from the study of reaction time and movement time. Typically, low (usually insignificant) correlations have been found between them. This has resulted from tests of both arm and leg tasks.[22] Apparently, individual differences in reaction time are not related to individual differences in movement time—ability to move fast is in no way dependent upon ability to react fast. These are separate coordinations involving excitation on the one hand and contraction of muscles on the other.

Strength and Speed

Perhaps the larger question concerns the contraction of muscle per se and those factors governing the physical limits of action. In an important paper on this subject, Henry and Whitley theorized that since the force (F) that would move a limb mass (m) a distance (d) in a time (t) could be given by the equation $F = 2md/t^2$, the result would be a measure of strength in action.[23] Thus, the correlation of interest would be between measured muscular strength and force estimated from the formula. When a horizontal adductive arm movement was used, it was found that the correlation was nonsignificant. Apparently, individual differences in isometric strength do not predict strength in action as given by maximal speed of movement. In other words, there is a maximum amount of specificity in such tasks, both being controlled by separate neuromotor coordination pathways of the central nervous system. Far from being an isolated finding, such results persist from sample to sample and from one study to another. In fact, when subjects are trained with weights to effect a change in strength, the correlation between changes in strength and changes in speed is still low.[24]

Memory Drum Theory

As a consequence of the experimental observations and with respect to the neuroanatomy involved, Henry proposed a memory drum (open loop) theory to explain the occurrence of planned and purposeful movement.[25] Learned acts of skill, developed as a result of practice over

[22]Leon E. Smith "Reaction Time and Movement Time in Four Large Muscle Movements," *Research Quarterly*, 32, No. 1 (March 1961), 88.

[23]F. M. Henry and J. D. Whitley, "Relationships between Individual Differences in Strength, Speed, and Mass in an Arm Movement," *Research Quarterly*, 31, No. 1 (March 1960), 24.

[24]David H. Clarke and Franklin M. Henry, "Neuromotor Specificity and Increased Speed from Strength Development," *Research Quarterly*, 32, No. 3 (October 1961), 315.

[25]Franklin M. Henry and Donald E. Rogers, "Increased Response Latency for Complicated Movements and a 'Memory Drum' Theory of Neuromotor Reactions," *Research Quarterly*, 31, No. 3 (October 1960), 448.

varying periods of time, are stored in the unconscious motor memory so that at a later time they may be tapped and brought forth in response to some stimulus. Analogous to a computer program concept, the appropriate act is programmed in some form of motor "memory drum" that will call into play appropriate coordinations when given the proper cues. Thus, an experiment was designed to test the hypothesis that the reaction time would be longer when the response movement was more complex than would be the case when the response was simple. This, indeed, was the case; undoubtedly, the more choices that are to be made in movement the more time is required to program properly the events to follow.

Specificity vs. Generality

It is essential to the interpretation of the literature in this area that the reader be acquainted with the mathematical and statistical use of the terms specificity and generality. As commonly employed, the relationship of individual differences in one task to those in another task is given by the correlation coefficient (r), provided that the influence of error variance (unreliability) is removed by the correction for attenuation. In order to assess the obtained correlation, two avenues are available: One is the test of significance, and the other is the test for specificity and generality. In the former instance, one may simply refer to a table of correlations at the appropriate degrees of freedom ($N - 2$) and either accept or reject the hypothesis that the two variables are related (or not related). In other words, this permits the investigator to determine if the correlation is essentially zero or not. It should be pointed out that since a correlation does not have to be particularly large to be significant, it does not help very much in deciding the larger issue.

The other procedure—that of determining the specificity or generality—is dependent upon the assessment of individual difference variance that is common between 2 tasks. This is done by calculating r^2; when multiplied by 100 it gives the percentage of generality. On the other hand, the amount of individual difference variance not common between 2 tasks is given by the squared coefficient of alienation k^2. Thus, $k^2 \times 100$ is the percentage of specificity. The interpretive decision that may be made will depend upon the relative balance of the 2 factors; as related to the question of motor ability, it could be argued that greater specificity than generality exists if k^2 is greater than r^2. It should be clear, therefore, that a correlation of $r - .71$ would be a rough dividing line between these 2 concepts. (See Chapter 9 for a further development of these statistical concepts.)

MOTOR CONTROL

Scholars involved in concerns over motor control have studied reaction time (RT) and movement time (MT), refining the experimentation considerably. Reaction time is defined as the time required for an individual to respond to a stimulus by making some overt movement, and MT is the time between onset of movement to completion of any motion. A stimulus (visual or auditory) starts a timer, and any limb movement stops it; if some further motion is required, an additional timer is needed, to be started at the end of RT and stopped at the end of the movement.

The quality of the neuromuscular response has been facilitated by partitioning the total RT into central and peripheral components.[26] The central component has been termed premotor time, and it is the interval between onset of stimulus and occurrence of the first action potential in the muscle group. The peripheral component, called motor time, is the remaining interval between the action potential and the initiation of movement. As was the case with RT and MT, the correlation between premotor reaction time and motor time is low, indicating a high degree of specificity between these two processes.[27]

Additional instrumentation is required to obtain these fractionated RT components.[28] It is necessary to employ surface electrodes in conjunction with an electromyograph and appropriate timers, arranged in such a way that the arrival of the first action potential can be timed.[29] The elapsed time is premotor reaction time, and when subtracted from total RT, it yields motor time. The technique requires that electrodes be placed over the motor point of the muscle in order to be in the best position to pick up the different nerve impulses.

DISTRIBUTION OF PRACTICE

The manner in which learning takes place relates to the length of time between bouts of practice and the distributions of practice schedules required to learn some act, either mental or physical. Aside from the

[26]Gary Kamen, Walter Kroll, Priscilla M. Clarkson, and Sheryl T. Zigon, "Fractionated Reaction Time in Power-Trained and Endurance-Trained Athletes under Conditions of Fatiguing Isometric Exercise," *Journal of Motor Behavior*, 13, No. 2 (1981), 117.

[27]G. Alan Stull and Jay T. Kearney, "Effects of Variable Fatigue Levels on Reaction-Time Components," *Journal of Motor Behavior*, 10, No. 3 (1978), 223.

[28]Walter Kroll, "Effects of Local Muscular Fatigue Due to Isotonic and Isometric Exercise upon Fractionated Reaction Time Components," *Journal of Motor Behavior*, 5, No. 2 (1973), 81.

[29]See Chapter 14.

practical value that it will yield information as to the most effective approach to the teaching of physical activities, it also may give basic information on the way people learn motor acts. Actually, the data available seem to divide themselves into the dichotomous functions of massed vs. distributed practice. Although these are relative terms and must be described for each experimental situation, the main question is whether or not individuals learn more effectively when trials are given with only brief intertrial rest intervals or when they are spaced by varying periods of time.

Before such a study may be undertaken, however, the investigator must have a task that provides learning, as indicated earlier in this chapter. In fact, the typical learning curves seem to be based upon massed practice, that is, the rest interval between each trial is of very short duration, usually long enough for the investigator to record the data from the previous trial and to reset timers, counters, and the like for the next trial. Whether or not the same amount of learning could be achieved with fewer practice sessions set at differing intervals is an intriguing question in the study of motor learning.

It is felt that spaced practice periods are more effective than massed periods of practice for both verbal and motor learning,[30] although Stelmach examined the efficiency of motor learning under conditions of massed and distributed practice, both with the ladder and the stabilometer.[31] Each group received the same amount of practice, but the massed groups practiced continuously for 8 minutes each session, while the distributed groups practiced under a 30-sec work/30-sec rest schedule. Following 4 minutes of rest, each group followed the distributed work schedule for 6 additional 30-sec trials. Performance was significantly improved during the initial phase of practice under the distributed practice schedules, but after the 4 minutes of rest, performance was almost identical among groups. This would suggest that the amount learned is determined more by the number of practice trials than the conditions of practice. Whitley even raised the question as to whether it was learning or just performance that was affected by the type of practice condition.[32] He employed a fine-motor task involving foot tracking. The massed practice schedule was 25 sec work and 5 sec rest, while the distributed practice schedule was 25 sec work with 35 sec rest. Both groups learned the task to a significant degree, but no significant differences existed between the 2 groups in the

[30]Joseph B. Oxendine, "Effect of Progressively Changing Practice Schedules on the Learning of a Motor Skill," *Research Quarterly*, 36, No. 3 (October 1965), 307.

[31]George E. Stelmach, "Efficiency of Motor Learning as a Function of Intertrial Rest," *Research Quarterly*, 40, No. 1 (March 1969), 198.

[32]Jim D. Whitley, "Effects of Practice Distribution on Learning a Time Motor Task," *Research Quarterly*, 41, No. 4 (December 1970), 576.

amount learned. It would seem that performance rather than learning was affected by the practice condition.

RETENTION

The retention of motor performance has been of interest to investigators who have asked the question of how long skills can be retained once they have been learned. It has been a commonplace observation that certain skills are retained for rather extended periods of time, sometimes even years. Skills learned in childhood, such as swimming, skiing, skating, and bicycling, are apparently learned so well that in later adult life they can be brought forth with reasonably good accuracy. Obviously, the amount of excellence will be impaired, but apparently the skill can be relearned rather quickly to the previous level. The characteristics of this learning are matters of prime concern to investigators in the field of motor performance, just as psychologists have studied the retention of verbal skills.

It would be naive to suggest that the problem should be studied longitudinally for years, as suggested in the previous example, since the time element would render the topic useless to most investigators. Thus, the concern has been to employ a motor learning task, apply a series of trials, and then permit rest periods to ensue, followed by more trials on the criterion task. The extent of retention, or its reciprocal, forgetting, may be dependent on the type of skill learned. For example, in a study employing a random group design, Ryan found the retention, when given 3, 5, 7, and 21 days after the original learning trials, to be greater for the pursuit rotor than for the stabilometer skills in the early retention trials, but subjects actually appeared to gain in ability (called reminiscence) for the pursuit rotor.[33] When 21-23 days elapsed in an experiment involving hitting a small rubber ball at a target with a paddle held in the nonpreferred hand, no evidence of forgetting was found, which is evidence that the retention rate for newly acquired skills is high.[34]

Apparently, the loss in ability was not related to the length of rest, a finding that prompted additional work with the stabilometer.[35] The subjects in this random group experiment were retested at intervals of 3 months, 6 months, and 12 months in order to study not only the amount

---

[33]E. Dean Ryan, "Retention of Stabilometer and Pursuit Rotor Skills," *Research Quarterly*, 33, No. 4 (December 1962), 593.

[34]Richard S. Rivenes and Martha M. Mawhinney, "Retention of Perceptual Motor Skill: An Analysis of New Methods," *Research Quarterly*, 39, No. 3 (October 1968), 684.

[35]E. Dean Ryan, "Retention of Stabilometer Performance over Extended Periods of Time," *Research Quarterly*, 36, No. 1 (March 1965), 46.

of retention but also the pattern of relearning. All 3 groups lost considerable proficiency, ranging from 50% to 81%; the subjects with the longest interval retained the least ability. In fact, the 12-month rest period apparently impaired the relearning phase, as this group failed to recover their performance to the extent of the other groups. Purdy and Lockhart found that college women retained gross-motor skills even after a time lapse of 1 year, and they also discovered that relearning to previously attained levels of skill took place very rapidly.[36]

REMINISCENCE

Very closely allied to problems of practice distribution and retention is the question of reminiscence. Reminiscence may be described as the increase in performance or an increase in learning that may occur following the cessation of practice. As pointed out above in the study by Ryan, such reminiscence occurred in the condition of retention for the pursuit motor skill; however, it is not always present, as attested to by studies employing the stabilometer and the ladder.[37] When performance is adversely affected, it is called warm-up decrement.[38]

A number of attempts have been made to explain the occurrence of reminiscence. The reader will find the review by Fox and Young[39] helpful in dealing with this phenomenon. A single theory that would broadly apply to studies in the motor learning field does not seem feasible at this time, inasmuch as so little is known of the neurology involved in learning. However, several variables are generally regarded as important. These include the degree of massing of prerest practice, the amount of prerest practice given, and the length of the rest period itself.

Perhaps it is the potentiality for change that is vital, and the interpolation of rest must come before all of the learning has taken place. Inasmuch as learning curves tend to be exponential, the closer one gets to the asymptote, the less change in performance can be expected. Thus, a period of rest given late in learning will result more in

[36]Bonnie J. Purdy and Aileene Lockhart, "Retention and Relearning of Gross Motor Skills after Long Periods of No Practice," *Research Quarterly*, 33, No. 2 (May 1962), 265.

[37]Judith L. Meyers, "Retention of Balance Coordination Learning as Influenced by Extended Lay-Offs," *Research Quarterly*, 38, No. 1 (March 1967), 72.

[38]John F. Catalano, "The Effect of Rest Following Massed Practice of Continuous and Discrete Motor Tasks," *Journal of Motor Behavior*, 10, No. 1 (1978), 63.

[39]Margaret G. Fox and Vera P. Young, "Effect of Reminiscence on Learning Selected Badminton Skills," *Research Quarterly*, 33, No. 3 (October 1962), 386.

forgetting, whereas that given earlier would be more apt to exhibit reminiscence. Whether or not this will occur is a matter for experimentation.

For tasks such as the Bachman ladder and the stabilometer, it seems that reminiscence is greatest during rest pauses following massed rather than distributed practice schedules.[40] In fact, it has been reported that a rest period following massed practice of a continuous task such as tracking with a stylus increased performance, demonstrating reminiscence.[41] When rest followed massed practice of a discrete task such as one involving positioning, the performance was lowered, exhibiting warm-up decrement.

TRANSFER

One of the most prevalent constructs in education today is the anticipation that things learned will carry over to practical endeavors—that the underlying elements present in one situation will be available for application in another. In other words, there are basic elements that can be expected to exhibit transfer. It should be pointed out that much of this is undocumented and speculative, and the precise terms of its acceptance must remain somewhat tentative until more evidence becomes available.

Similar strong feelings exist in physical education that elements in motor skills may be transferred. This is implied by the emphasis upon the so-called elements in general motor fitness that has persisted for so long. If one is able to accept the doctrine of specificity, however, it is difficult to imagine that a high degree of transfer occurs in the area of neuromotor coordinations, except where there are like elements. Even then, there is controversy as to whether or not teaching progression should always be from simple to complex or whether mastery of the more complex is equally justified, thus obviating the necessity for presenting the simple skills. This is especially intriguing if the complex activity includes the simple skills.

By way of illustration, in 1962 Cratty employed the practice of learning of a small maze to determine if this facilitated learning of a large maze.[42] One group of subjects was given practice on a stylus maze that was identical to the large maze, while another group practiced on one that was a reversal of the large maze, and still another group

---

[40]George C. Stelmach, "Motor Learning as a Function of Intertrial Rest."

[41]John F. Caralano, "Effect of Rest Following Massed Practice."

[42]Bryant J. Cratty, "Transfer of Small-Pattern Practice to Large-Pattern Learning," *Research Quarterly*, 33, No. 4 (December 1962), 523.

practiced on a stylus maze completely unrelated to the large maze. A control group received no stylus maze practice, thus completing the random-group's design. Apparently, practice on the similar pattern resulted in improved large maze scores, illustrating the positive transfer effects of such practice. Negative transfer also occurs, as shown by the retarding effect on learning from practice of the reverse pattern stylus maze.

Later, Rivenes experimented with the possibility of multiple-task transfer, whereby subjects learning several skills would be examined for transfer effects.[43] He devised an apparatus resembling a modified shuffleboard. The subject stood with his back to the apparatus and received his visual cues from a mirror; the nonpreferred hand was used in performing the skill. Target distances were graded into degrees of difficulty; three were shorter than the transfer task, and three were longer. The practice sequence provided various multiple- and single-task conditions. Apparently, the multiple-task practice of relatively easy tasks facilitated transfer, although with the more difficult tasks, single-task practice would appear to be most effective in causing transfer.

Clearly, the amount of transfer depends upon the similarity of the two tasks; the more similar they are the greater the transfer. This was illustrated in a study using a discrete tracking task and examining differences in stimulus input and task strategy.[44] Significant transfer was found when going from large to small targets, but when there were differences in stimulus input, as given by changes in target speed, no transfer occurred. In the former instance, the change in stimulus did not cause task strategy changes, and it may be this element that is crucial in deciding on whether transfer will take place.

Transfer can also be examined between limbs. Dunham devised a coincidence-anticipation task consisting of a small visible ball that traveled down a 16-foot track past a metal target flag.[45] The subject tracked the ball and activated a control switch with his foot at the precise instant the front edge of the ball was tangent with the edge of the target flag. Subjects in the transfer group performed 5 trials with the right foot, followed by 25 trials with the left foot, and finally with 5 more trials with the right foot. The control group omitted the middle 25 trials and instead read unrelated material. The results failed to substantiate the notion that this type of performance with the right

[43]Richard S. Rivenes, "Multiple-Task Transfer Effects in Perceptual-Motor Learning," *Research Quarterly*, 38, No. 3 (October 1967), 485.

[44]Jan P. Livesey and Judith I. Lasgio, "Effect of Task Similarity on Transfer Performance," *Journal of Motor Behavior*, 11, No. 1 (1979), 11.

[45]Paul Dunham, "Effect of Bilateral Transfer on Coincidence-Anticipation Performance," *Research Quarterly*, 48, No. 1 (March 1977), 51.

foot was facilitated by practice with the left foot. The coincidence-anticipation task resulted in no bilateral transfer, but such transfer has been found for other types of learning tasks.

MENTAL PRACTICE

Motor acts, to be learned, must first be conceived, usually a visual process that involves certain cognitive processes of the higher nervous centers. Physical education teachers have long believed that this cognition is enhanced by demonstration of the skill to be learned, usually after a brief description. The more complicated the skill, the more explanation and demonstration is required; along the same lines, the more advanced the performer, the less rehearsal is needed. Novel skills, such as those usually used in the study of motor learning, probably obtain needed feedback from the performance itself, although the subject may anticipate the task to varying degrees, depending upon previous experience and ability.

Aside from these considerations is the question of the role of mental practice per se on the ability to learn motor skills. It is a rather commonplace observation among individuals that they can conjure up the mental image of a skill, and thus, in a sense, rehearse it prior to the actual performance. This type of kinesthetic organization must draw upon some sort of mental proprioception to guide later response. The question is not whether mental practice is effective but how effective it is and under what circumstances it can be expected to operate. The reader is directed to two excellent reviews on this subject by Richardson.[46]

By way of illustration, Smith and Harrison utilized the experimental approach with an eye-hand coordination task.[47] They employed a three-hole punchboard that counted the number of hits made by the subject with a metal stylus; stress was given to speed and accuracy of movement. Five groups were used with learning situations assigned as follows: first, interpolated motor practice; second, visual practice; third, reversed-visual practice; fourth, mental practice; and fifth, guided practice. An additional control group that received no practice was included, and only the initial and final tests given all subjects were administered to them. The results showed that mental practice and

---

[46]Alan Richardson, "Mental Practice: A Review and Discussion, Part I," *Research Quarterly*, 38, No. 1 (March 1967), 95; and Alan Richardson, "Mental Practice: A Review and Discussion, Part II," *Research Quarterly*, 38, No. 2 (May 1967), 263.

[47]Leon E. Smith and John S. Harrison, "Comparison of the Effects of Visual, Motor, Mental, and Guided Practice upon Speed and Accuracy of Performing a Simple Eye-Hand Coordination Task," *Research Quarterly*, 33, No. 2 (May 1962), 299.

visual practice improved performance significantly by achieving more correct hits and fewer errors in the criterion task.

Such studies have also been attempted using total body performance. In fact, Jones employed a gymnastic skill, the hock-swing upstart, selected because it could be scored on a pass-fail basis, thus obviating subjective estimates.[48] The mental practice was carried out in two forms, both given before the subjects were permitted to practice the skill. One group of subjects was given directed mental practice, during which the experimenter controlled most of the mental practice by reading instructions aloud; the second group received essentially undirected mental practice. After six successive sessions, the criterion task was administered for the first time. It was found that the group given undirected mental practice achieved a significantly greater skill in the performance.

TIMING

The ability to time movements is an important ingredient in the performance of physical activities. It is notably lacking in early childhood; as youngsters grow older, they make rapid improvements so that they can catch, kick, or hit a ball with some implement. Each of these skills, and a host of others, requires the individual to mentally plot the path of some moving object and then to intercept its flight at some critical point. Learning to do this successfully may indeed occupy an individual's attention and require continual practice for years, as attested to by the degree of excellence required by contemporary athletics.

The common feature of most of these tasks is to anticipate the arrival of some object and then to plan ahead so that it may be anticipated at the correct moment. This is generally referred to as coincidence-anticipation and implies that considerable attention must be given to the learning of perceptual cues that dictate the special characteristics of a motor program but some also to the temporal factors.[49]

The illustration as explained by Slater-Hammel is pertinent.

As a means of illustrating the nature of coincidence-anticipation, let it be supposed that a subject (S) is given the simple task of moving his hand off

[48]John Gerald Jones, "Motor Learning without Demonstration of Physical Practice, under Two Conditions of Mental Practice," *Research Quarterly*, 36, No. 3 (October 1965), 270.

[49]Craig A. Wrisberg and Michael R. Ragsdale, "Further Tests of Schmidt's Schema Theory: Development of a Schema Rule for a Coincident Timing Task," *Journal of Motor Behavior*, 11, No. 2 (1979), 159.

a signal key at the instant a moving marker passes across a fixed marker. In performance of this task there are two possible procedures available to S. First, S may take exact coincidence of the markers to be the stimulus for his response, and second, S may attempt to make his response simultaneous with coincidence using coincidence-anticipation; under this operating rule the inevitable delays in human sensory-response systems will enter, and S's response will always be one reaction time late. If the second procedure is followed, S may be said to be using coincidence-anticipation, and it is only by anticipating coincidence of the markers that S can possibly avoid being late.[50]

Thus a variety of experimental situations could be devised to study timing control. Grose elected to study movements of the finger, arm, and whole body in response to a moving target.[51] His target was a pointer that moved along a track at a rate of 4.15 feet per sec; the 3 tasks were to intercept the moving pointer by pressing a contact plate with the hand, by moving the arm, or by stepping forward two steps and kicking a target. The individuals in all 3 tasks tended toward early estimates of coincidence. Apparently, coincidence timing exhibits greater task specificity rather than generality. Also of interest was the finding that individual differences in reaction time were not related to coincidence-timing ability.

In order to study the problem associated with simultaneous timing of arms and legs, Norrie developed a target board that contained a series of 2-inch diameter metal discs, accompanied by appropriate microswitches that activated marking pens.[52] The tasks were a series of simultaneous movements involving various combinations of hand and foot actions to be performed as quickly as possible, each requiring contact with certain discs on the target board. For the more complicated tasks, starting time differences and contact time differences were significantly longer than for the simpler tasks. There also seemed to be rather considerable generality between the time measures.

A number of studies concerned with tracking have linked subject response with proprioceptive feedback. Additional references on these and related topics can be found in Adams and Schmidt.

A number of studies concerned with timing and the response of a subject to proprioceptive feedback have employed a linear slide

[50]A. T. Slater-Hammel, "Reliability, Accuracy, and Refractoriness of a Transit Reaction," *Research Quarterly*, 31, No. 2 (May 1960), 217. Used by permission of the author and AAHPERD.

[51]Joel E. Grose, "Timing Control and Finger, Arm, and Whole Body Movements," *Research Quarterly*, 38, No. 1 (March 1967), 10.

[52]Mary Lou Norrie, "Timing of Two Simultaneous Movements of Arms and Legs," *Research Quarterly*, 35, No. 4 (December 1964), 511.

positioning apparatus.[53] This consists generally of a metal bar up to 100-cm long mounted firmly on a frame. A metal slide is mounted on the bar with ball bearings to give it smooth action and is fitted with a handle. The subject grasps the handle and is able to slide the assembly to some predetermined point. A rather large number of research paradigms have been designed to employ this equipment, since learning occurs in estimating position or times of movement over trials. The instrumentation ordinarily can be rather complex and sophisticated, but easily accommodated in the more established motor learning laboratories.

KINESTHESIS PROPRIOCEPTION

An area of special concern to those interested in the experimental psychology of performance has been that of kinesthesis. Essentially, this involves the perception of movement, the sensation of position, or the control of motor performance. It is a developmental phenomenon that is mostly lacking or undeveloped in infancy and quite often well developed in the adult. Babies and young children are typically uncoordinated in their responses and have poor balance. As they grow during childhood, they become better at proprioceptive adjustments and develop the awareness of spatial relationships, both with their own bodies and in relation to their external environment. It is largely held that the introduction of physical skills in childhood will lead to enhanced adult ability, although the evidence for this may be fragmentary. Observation would have it, though, that youngsters in their preadolescent years achieve rather high levels of skill in certain types of athletics. Presumably, this is a result of large amounts of practice.

Whether or not there is any such single entity as "kinesthetic sense" is questionable, and just how proprioceptive feedback is utilized by the individual is not clearly understood. However, it is reasonable to believe that certain adjustments can be made, but the extent of the performer's awareness of them is not always clear. Muscular adaptation to changing external stimuli is often reflexive and many times involves just a monosynaptic relay in the central nervous system for adjustment of muscular tension. At any rate, this ability must be marked by a high degree of individual differences, judging by the range of performance capabilities exhibited by the general population.

Physiologically, the proprioceptors that are of importance to muscular function include: the muscle spindles, which monitor muscle

---

[53]Jack A. Adams, Daniel Gopher, and Gavan Lintern, "Effects of Visual and Proprioceptive Feedback on Motor Learning," *Journal of Motor Behavior*, 9, No. 1 (1977), 11.

length; the Golgi tendon organs, which monitor muscular tension; the pacinian corpuscles in joints and articular cartilages, which monitor joint and limb position in space; and a series of free nerve endings present in muscles, tendons, ligaments, and joints, whose function in kinesthesis may be a result of muscular tension. The vestibular receptors of the inner ear are also extremely important in balance control, especially in those activities involved in tumbling, diving, and the like.

Because kinesthesis is such a general term, a rather large number of tasks have been used in research to represent its function. The reasoning seems to be that if kinesthesis means muscular control, then administration of a test involving body or limb position or muscular adaptation would seem to suffice as a measure of kinesthesis. The description of a substantial number of these tasks can be found in studies by Wiebe[54] and by Scott.[55] It is interesting to note, however, that the findings in both studies reflected a lack of relationship among the various tests used. In other words, the low correlations obtained would indicate a small amount of generality and thus would support the doctrine of specificity of motor performance. It would seem, then, that there may actually be no such single entity as kinesthesis but rather that it is made up of a large number of specific items.

The relationship of kinesthesis to other performance abilities has also resulted in rather low correlation. Roloff correlated a battery of tests, including balance stick, arm raising, weight shifting, and arm circling, against the Scott motor ability test.[56] The resulting coefficient of .42 is low, although it is both significant and positive. Witte gave 7- to 9-year-old boys and girls the 4 kinesthetic tests of forward arm raising with the preferred and nonpreferred arms and sideward arm raising with the preferred and nonpreferred arms.[57] The correlation with certain ball handling measures was .28, indicating that no real relationship existed between these two functions as measured.

In order to study the effectiveness of feedback of visual information on kinesthetic learning, Morford[58] employed a modification of the

[54]Vernon R. Wiebe, "A Study of Tests of Kinesthesis," *Research Quarterly*, 25, No. 2 (May 1954), 222.

[55]M. Gladys Scott, "Measurement of Kinesthesis," *Research Quarterly*, 26, No. 3 (October 1955), 324.

[56]Louise L. Roloff, "Kinesthesis in Relation to the Learning of Selected Motor Skills," *Research Quarterly*, 24, No. 2 (May 1953), 210.

[57]Fae Witte, "Relation of Kinesthetic Perception to a Selected Motor Skill for Elementary School Children," *Research Quarterly*, 33, No. 3 (October 1962), 476.

[58]W. R. Morford, "The Value of Supplementary Visual Information during Practice on Dynamic Kinesthetic Learning," *Research Quarterly*, 37, No. 3 (October 1966), 393.

apparatus designed by Henry[59] to study the dynamic muscular response to changing external tensions. One group received practice while given kinesthetic information only, and the two other groups were given varying amounts of supplementary visual cues (random-groups design). It was found that the feedback of visual information facilitated subsequent kinesthetic performance.

The question of perceptual recall of visual tactual information has been of interest to investigators, and it seemingly represents a growing interest in such phenomena for the future. For example, Cratty and Hutton sought to determine if a configural aftereffect was produced when subjects traversed, while blindfolded, curved and straight pathways.[60] It was concluded that this was indeed possible. This concern has been extended to the field of muscular performance, where the immediate effects of various overloads on contraction have been studied. Nelson and Nofsinger gave overload trials ranging from 15% to 45% of maximal strength and then tested the speed of movement of the elbow flexor muscles.[61] Although no actual change in performance was noted, the subjects experienced a kinesthetic illusion of greater speed.

Closed-Loop Theory.   In 1971, Adams proposed a closed-loop theory of movement which held that slow, self-paced, graded movements were governed by two independent memory states.[62] One was termed the memory trace and the other the perceptual trace. The former was said to be responsible for selecting and initiating a movement, which means that it was responsible for calling forth the movement required and the direction in which it was to proceed. The perceptual trace, on the other hand, determined the extent of movement and evaluated its accuracy. Thus, it compared proprioception feedback from the ongoing movement with the memory of previous movements. These are said to be analogous to recall and recognition in the context of verbal memory. The two are thus subject to development and reinforcement. The memory trace strengthens as a result of knowledge of results and practice of movement, while development of the perceptual trace is a result of knowledge of results and movement practice, but also with various feedback stimuli from the movement itself, such as

[59]Franklin M. Henry, "Dynamic Kinesthetic Perception and Adjustment," *Research Quarterly*, 24, No. 2 (May 1953), 176.

[60]Bryant J. Cratty and Robert S. Hutton, "Figural Aftereffects Resulting from Gross Action Patterns," *Research Quarterly*, 35, No. 2 (May 1964), 116.

[61]Richard C. Nelson and Michael R. Nofsinger, "Effect of Overload on Speed of Elbow Flexion and the Associated Aftereffects," *Research Quarterly*, 36, No. 2 (May 1965), 174.

[62]Jack A. Adams, "A Closed-Loop Theory of Motor Learning," *Journal of Motor Behavior*, 3, No. 2 (1971), 111.

audition, vision, and proprioception. The theory holds that the percep- tual trace functions according to feedback stimuli, but the memory trace does not. The closed-loop theory, then, proposed theoretically that any stimulus is able to "stamp in" a perceptual trace, the strength of which is a function of knowledge of results and amount of practice. The individual performing the movement task receives a certain amount of feedback from the task and compares it to the perceptual traces of previous responses.

Schema Theory. Schmidt developed motor learning theory fur- ther by pointing out certain difficulties with the closed-loop theory, especially with respect to the problem of novelty of task.[63] In some movements, there may be no reference of correctness against which to judge future responses and thus provide for appropriate feedback. The schema theory proposes two separate states of memory, which may depend slightly on the type of task to be undertaken.[64] The recall schema involves the generation of impulses to the musculature, while the recognition schema evaluates the feedback produced from the movement to provide error information. Thus, the recall schema is the relationship between the result of a movement and the specifications for the response, so that after a number of trials there develops an association between the two variables that is updated on each trial. Eventually, one can see where this schema would become well estab- lished; when one wishes to bring forth a new movement he or she enters a schema that has the proper response specifications. The recognition schema operates with variables that are concerned with the sensory consequence and knowledge of results (KR), which are paired on each trial. During a movement, the subject may specify the desired outcome and is able to predict the sensory consequences. The actual sensory consequences are compared with the expected sensory consequences, and any discrepancy represents an error in the movement. Thus, it is possible to be provided information about the suitability of movement without actually having been given KR.

SUGGESTED PROBLEMS

In addition to the investigation of the numerous topics listed in this chapter, several questions remain that are of interest in the study of motor learning and motor performance.

[63]Richard A. Schmidt, "A Schema Theory of Discrete Motor Skill Learning," *Psychological Reviews*, 82 (1975), 225.

[64]Richard A. Schmidt, "The Schema as a Solution to Some Persistent Problems in Motor Learning Theory," in *Motor Control: Issues and Trends*, ed. G. E. Stelmach (New York: Academic Press, Inc., 1976), Ch. 2.

1. New learning tasks are needed, especially those that require large muscle involvement. What are the characteristics of those individuals who learn rapidly as compared with those who learn slowly?
2. Is there a substantial relationship between motor learning and other forms of learning, for example, verbal?
3. What degrees of consistency exist in the trial-by-trial performance of a motor learning task?
4. Does learning change with increasing age? Are the characteristics of retention dependent upon the growth processes?
5. Based upon electromyographic data, can the pattern of skilled behavior be described?
6. What environmental or other mitigating influences alter the rate of learning? Can learning be facilitated?

SUMMARY

Motor learning involves the repeated practice of some act that leads to improved performance. The dividing line between what may be called motor learning and what is learning per se, such as verbal or other cognitive processes, is not always clear, nor is it fully understood just what factors operate to bring about learning in the first place. What is known is that learning of motor acts will occur with practice only if the task itself is novel to the performer; the usual skills taught in physical education are inappropriate for studies in motor learning because of subject familiarity.

The tests of motor learning apparently are few in number, if one differentiates between learning on the one hand and performance on the other. Many performance tests exist, but whether or not they result in learning depends upon what happens when a series of trials is given. The typical learning curve reflects rapid gains at first, gradually tapering off as a steady state is approached. The number of trials required will be determined by the type of task and the subjects employed, data that are available for several learning tests.

Psychomotor performance is seen to involve several rather clearly defined areas for which research opportunities exist. For example, the distribution of practice relates to the length and concentration of practice schedules, ordinarily with the intention of seeking the arrangement that gives optimum learning. Ultimately, this involves the additional question of retention of performance, which examines the degree of impairment resulting from various periods of rest. This may even involve measurement of relearning following retraining.

Important corollary concepts of interest to the researcher include reminiscence and mental practice. Reminiscence is the increased performance that occurs in some tasks following the cessation of practice, whereas mental practice is the nonperformance rehearsal of a skill that leads to enhanced ability. The conditions under which these operate is vital to a full understanding of this field. This is also true of the transfer of one task to another. How much of what is learned in one task is transferred to another may very well depend upon how similar are the elements in both.

The study of timing control, tracking, and anticipation of movement are receiving attention in current research, and motor control specialists have put forth various theories to assist in explaining learning phenomena. So many activities performed by individuals require fine adjustments to coordinate motion successfully; in some, the subject may be approaching a stationary object, and in others an object may be moving while the subject remains stationary. At any rate, the ability to understand one's position in space, to control muscle function, may be described as kinesthesis, and a rather substantial number of tests have been employed at one time or another to assess its function. How these matters relate to balance, motor skills, and proprioception has been the subject of some investigation.

SELECTED REFERENCES

ADAMS, JACK A., "A Closed-Loop Theory of Motor Learning," *Journal of Motor Behavior*, 3, No. 2 (1971), 111.

———, "Human Tracking Behavior," *Psychological Bulletin*, 48, No. 1 (January 1961), 55.

BILODEAU, EDWARD A., ed., *Acquisition of Skill*. New York: Academic Press, Inc., 1966.

CATALANO, JOHN F., "The Effect of Rest Following Massed Practice of Continuous and Discrete Motor Tasks," *Journal of Motor Behavior*, 10, No. 1 (1978), 63.

FLEICHMAN, EDWIN A. and JAMES F. PARKER, "Factors in the Retention and Relearning of Perceptual-Motor Skill," *Journal of Experimental Psychology*, 64, No. 3 (September 1962), 215.

HENRY, FRANKLIN M., and DONALD E. ROGERS, "Increased Response Latency for Complicated Movements and a 'Memory Drum' Theory of Neuromuscular Reactions," *Research Quarterly*, 31, No. 3 (October 1960), 448.

KROLL, WALTER, "Effects of Local Muscular Fatigue Due to Isotonic and Isometric Exercise upon Fractionated Reaction Time Components," *Journal of Motor Behavior*, 5, No. 2 (1973), 81.

SCHMIDT, RICHARD A., "Anticipation and Timing in Motor Performance," *Psychological Bulletin*, 70, No. 6 (1968), 631.

———, "A Schema Theory of Discrete Motor Skill Learning," *Psychological Reviews*, 82, (1975), 225.

———, *Motor Skills*. New York: Harper & Row, Publishers, 1975.

SHEA, CHARLES A., and ALAN A. ASHBY, "Modifications to the Basic Anticipation Timer," *Research Quarterly for Exercise and Sport*, 52, No. 2 (May 1981), 278.

STELMACH, GEORGE C., "Efficiency of Motor Learning as a Function of Intertrial Rest," *Research Quarterly*, 40, No. 1 (March 1969), 198.

———, ed. *Motor Control: Issues and Trends*. New York: Academic Press, Inc., 1976.

13
Psychological Studies

The research problem undertaken in psychological studies is not apt to be designed in quite the straightforward manner as those found in motor learning or in motor control, because the instruments generally employed are not as precise. For example, where learning may be judged almost exactly by improvement in performance as measured to a fraction of a second, personality traits must be estimated somewhat less objectively. Moreover, some psychological tests require special training that puts their use beyond the reach of individuals who are not adequately prepared in the subject matter.

The fact that there are certain difficulties and limitations in some types of psychological research should serve to stimulate a greater desire for excellence. A constant search for new techniques and better refinements of old ones is needed; such will not occur unless interest is shown in really studying various types of psychological problems. Mental and emotional characteristics are complex, human drives and motives are deep-seated, and social and psychological traits are difficult to define. Yet, human overt behavior is determined by underlying forces: the need to be accepted by one's peer group, the drive toward greater personal success, and the decisions that are made on hundreds of questions during one's lifetime. All these forces serve to indicate the need for careful examination of the many topics that are presented in this connection.

The physical educator becomes interested in psychological studies because of the belief that personality plays a role in the selection of and participation in physical activities and sports and that somehow the involvement in physical education and sports contributes to personal and social adjustment. At any rate, the development of personality and the achievement of desirable social values have been objectives of physical education since early leaders led the profession away from the formalized type of program that emphasized gymnastics, calisthenics, and marching.

The psychological tools available frequently provide only an indirect method of bringing data to bear on this subject, and so the analysis that is made is often tentative. In fact, the finding that athletes are different from nonathletes may not mean that athletics *causes* enhanced personality characteristics. It may be just as tenable to conclude that athletics attracts the more well-adjusted individuals in society (or perhaps rejects maladjusted persons). As is true with other forms of research, causation is often difficult to determine.

In some instances, rather direct methods of dealing with psychological problems are available. For example, use of sociometric questionnaires, teachers' ratings, differential motive-incentive conditions, and others provide useful technical tools for the researcher. Many of these techniques are discussed in this chapter, together with selected research studies that are intended to serve as a stimulus for more careful examination of current topics.

GENERAL PERSONALITY TECHNIQUES

Projective Techniques

The individual's overt response to a situation is made up of a number of factors, some of which he or she is undoubtedly aware and some that are deep-seated and perhaps hidden in the depths of unconscious memory. Drives and motives are complex, and the single response to a single stimulus may be conditioned to a considerable extent by tertiary considerations. At any rate, the assessment of the basic elements of personality may be approached in a number of ways, the most difficult of which is through use of projective techniques.

Projective techniques were developed originally to help assess psychological disorders, and they have since gained increasing acceptance as tools for the estimation of various degrees of normal personality. The tendency in research is to create as objective a situation as possible (questions are answered that can be scored numerically, etc.), but projective devices are relatively unstructured, so the response of the subject must be interpreted very carefully. The individual's perception of things or events will be conditioned by basic drives and then projected to the external test situation, whether it be an interpretation of ink blots or a description of events portrayed in a picture. Regardless of the method employed, the investigator should be prepared to study these matters very carefully under proper guidance of trained evaluators. A number of hours of advanced work in psychology will be necessary before adequate data interpretation can be made. The following tests are currently in use and are suggested, along with an original reference source:

1. Rorschach (Ink Blot) Test[1]
2. Thematic Apperception Test[2]
3. Sentence Completion Test[3]
4. House-Tree-Person Test[4]
5. Rosenzweig Picture-Frustration (P-F) Study[5]

Inventory Techniques

The most widely used method of obtaining data on a variety of psychological characteristics is by means of inventory or questionnaire. In this manner, subjects answer a host of questions designed to bring out the basic elements of personality, mental health, and the like. The advantages gained over the projective techniques are the simplicity of testing and ease of scoring. Thus, several subjects may be tested simultaneously, as long as the proper testing decorum is maintained, the environment is quiet and conducive to proper introspection, and some confidence is imparted by the test administrator. The subject must be assured that results will be kept in the strictest confidence, that the best answer in any situation must be given honestly, and that there are no right or wrong answers (unless otherwise specified by the test). The data are certain to be invalidated by improper testing conditions that permit talking or moving about or encourage frivolous responses.

[1] Samuel J. Beck, Anne G. Beck, Eugene E. Levitt, and Herman B. Molish, *Rorschach's Test: I. Basic Processes* (New York: Grune & Stratton, Inc., 1961).

[2] Leopold Bellak and Eileen Ort, "Thematic Apperception Test and Other Perceptive Methods," in *Progress in Clinical Psychology*, Vol. 1, ed. Daniel Brower and Lawrence E. Abt (New York: Grune & Stratton, Inc., 1952), Ch. 9.

[3] James Quinter Holsopple and Florence R. Miale, *Sentence Completion: A Projective Method for the Study of Personality* (Springfield, Ill.: Charles C. Thomas, Publisher, 1954).

[4] John N. Buck, "The H-T-P Test," *Journal of Clinical Psychology*, 4, No. 2 (April 1948), 151: "The H-T-P Technique: A Qualitative and Quantitative Scoring Manual," *Journal of Clinical Psychology*, 4, No. 4 (October 1948), 317.

[5] Saul Rosenzweig, "The Picture-Association Method and Its Application in a Study of Reactions to Frustration," *Journal of Personality*, 14, No. 1 (September 1945), 3.

Similarly, if the proper instructions are not given, or if the respondents are not assured that the data will be used statistically rather than personally, the subjects may choose to mask their true feelings, giving what they think is wanted rather than what actually may be their true choices.

The indiscriminant use of inventory techniques is one of the principal criticisms in psychological research. If a test fails to measure the traits it purports to measure, or if improper application is made in research, no amount of care in testing can save the data. For example, a test designed solely for use with psychiatric patients or for individual counseling purposes may not be appropriate for examining large groups where statistical procedures are employed and where the population may contain no subjects classified as mentally ill. The essential consideration here should be to evaluate every test carefully to assure its applicability to the problem selected and then to employ the most favorable testing protocol. It is growing increasingly evident that the study of personality in groups such as athletes should involve evaluative tools that are task specific, in this case those designed for the athletic environment. The broad use of personality tests should be employed only after careful consideration.

Some of the more important tests are briefly reviewed below. The specific needs of the research problem will dictate which ones are most applicable. The usual procedure is for the subject to respond to a number of questions on a yes-no or true-false basis. The responses are scored with a key provided with the test manual. The answer sheet may be submitted to automatic scoring, so this process should be investigated and the appropriate procedures applied. The various Mental Measurements Yearbooks will prove helpful in securing additional material appropriate to such research, as well as critical reviews concerning test acceptability.[6]

California Psychological Inventory. The California Psychological Inventory is a 480-item true-false questionnaire designed to test nonpathological subjects 13 years of age and above.[7] The 18 scales of the inventory were identified as the following: dominance (Do), capacity for status (Cs), sociability (Sy), social presence (Sp), self-acceptance (Sa), sense of well-being (Wb), responsibility (Re), socialization (So), self-control (Sc), tolerance (To), good impression (Gi), communality (Cm), achievement via conformance (Ac), achievement via

---

[6]Oscar Krisen Buros, ed., *The Sixth Mental Measurements Yearbook* (Highland Park, N.J.: The Gryphon Press, 1965). Other Yearbooks were published in 1938, 1940, 1948, 1953, and 1959.

[7]Harrison G. Grough, *California Psychological Inventory* (Palo Alto, Calif.: Consulting Psychologists Press, Inc., 1956).

independence (Ai), intellectual efficiency (Ie), psychological-mindedness (Py), flexibility (Fx), and femininity (Fe). These scales have been cross-validated and are based on the test responses of individuals considered to exhibit various kinds of effective behavior. Norms have been constructed from data gathered on over 13,000 cases spread geographically over 30 states.

Cattell's Sixteen Personality Factor Questionnaire. One of the most widely used tests in the assessment of personality is Cattell's Sixteen Personality Factor Questionnaire (16 P-F).[8] The factors for college students are as follows:

A Reserved vs. outgoing
B Less intelligent vs. more intelligent
C Affected by feelings vs. emotionally stable
E Humble vs. assertive
F Sober vs. happy-go-lucky
G Expedient vs. conscientious
H Shy vs. venturesome
I Tough-minded vs. tender-minded
L Trusting vs. suspicious
M Practical vs. imaginative
N Forthright vs. shrewd
O Self-assured vs. apprehensive
Q_1 Conservative vs. experimenting
Q_2 Group-dependent vs. self-sufficient
Q_3 Undisciplined self-conflict vs. controlled
Q_4 Relaxed vs. tense.

Bernreuter Personality Inventory. The Bernreuter Personality Inventory contains 125 questions designed for high school and college students and adults, adapted largely from Laird's C_2 Test of Introversion-Extroversion, Allport's A-S Reaction Study, Thurstone's Neurotic Inventory, and Bernreuter's Self-Sufficiency Test.[9] The 6 traits are as follows: neurotic tendency, self-sufficiency, introversion-extroversion, dominance-submission, sociability, and confidence.

Bell Adjustment Inventory. The revised student form of the Bell Adjustment Inventory measures personal and social adjustment in the

[8]Raymond B. Cattell, H. W. Eber, and M. M. Tatsuoka, *Handbook for the Sixteen Personality Factor Questionnaire*, in *Clinical Educational, Industrial and Research Psychology* (Champaign, Ill.: Institute for Personality and Ability Testing, 1970).

[9]Palo Alto, Calif.: Consulting Psychologists Press, Inc.

following 6 categories: home adjustment, health adjustment, submissiveness, emotionality, hostility, and masculinity-femininity. High scores indicate an unsatisfactory adjustment, whereas low scores denote a satisfactory adjustment.[10] The reliability of the 200 statement inventory is reported to be satisfactory (.80 or above). An adult form is also available that includes an additional scale for occupational adjustment but does not contain the hostility and masculinity-femininity scales.

Eysenck Personality Inventory. The Eysenck Personality Inventory was developed to describe 2 major patterns of psychological behavior, grades 9-16.[11] These 2 dimensions are extraversion-introversion (E scale) and neuroticism-stability (N scale). The Inventory consists of 57 yes-no responses, with a lie scale. Test-retest reliabilities range from .80 to .97, with split-half reliabilities between forms A and B ranging between .75 and .91. The test has been extended to grades 7-15 with the *Junior Eysenck Personality Inventory.*

Personality Studies

The literature relative to personal and social adjustment and various physical factors seems characterized by diversity. A wide variety of social and psychological instruments has been employed, many of the inventory type and some using projective techniques. In addition, the physical and motor variables have varied, depending in part upon the intention of the study in question, which makes generalization difficult. A few of these studies will be given in this section with the hope that it will stimulate further research.

In an investigation of the psychological characteristics of athletes and nonparticipants at three educational levels, Schendel administered the California Psychological Inventory to 334 subjects in junior high school, senior high school, and college.[12] Significant differences were found between the means of 8 of the scales for the athletes and nonparticipants in the ninth grade, on 4 scales of twelfth graders, and on 9 scales of the subjects in college. Nearly all significant differences were in favor of the athletes; on the other hand, few differences in psychological characteristics were found between athletes rated as substitutes, regular players, or outstanding performers.

[10] Hugh M. Bell, *Bell Adjustment Inventory*, Revised 1962 Student Form (Palo Alto, Calif.: Consulting Psychologists Press, Inc., 1962).

[11] H. J. Eysenck and Sybil B. G. Eysenck, *The Eysenck Personality Inventory* (San Diego: Educational and Industrial Testing Service, 1963).

[12] Jack Schendel, "Psychological Differences between Athletes and Nonparticipants in Athletics at Three Educational Levels," *Research Quarterly*, 36, No. 1 (March 1965), 52.

The personality traits of female and male college athletes were investigated by O'Connor and Webb.[13] Of the 55 subjects, 41 were intercollegiate athletic team members selected from such sports as basketball, gymnastics, swimming, and tennis. The Cattell 16 P-F test was administered to the athletes and a group of nonathletes serving as a control group. Results revealed that the subjects differed in 4 of the personality factors. The athletes were found to be more intelligent (Factor B), more inclined to experiment (Factor Q_1), more self-sufficient (Factor Q_2) and more disciplined (Factor Q_3) than their nonathlete counterparts.

Young and Ismail examined male adults who exercised regularly over a four year period.[14] They assessed their physiological status and administered Cattell's P-F test to the subjects, including two groups who were less active. The two groups who were regularly active increased their physical fitness significantly, and the most active subjects were significantly more self-assertive (Factor O) than the less active group. In a similar program of shorter duration (14 weeks), Buccola and Stone administered an exercise program of jogging and cycling to two groups of men aged 60-79 years.[15] They were given a battery of physiological tests and the Cattell 16 P-F questionnaire. Results indicated that both groups significantly increased their aerobic capacity and decreased their systolic and diastolic blood pressure. While a significant decrease in percentage of fat occurred only in the cycling group, an increase in flexibility was found only for joggers. In personality, the cyclers showed no changes; the joggers became significantly less surgent (Factor F) and more self-sufficient (Factor Q_2) as a result of the exercise program.

In a specific experiment involving pain tolerance, arousal, and personality between college age athletes and nonathletes, Ellison and Freischlag administered the Bernreuter Personality Inventory along with the galvanic skin response.[16] The subjects performed a task involving protracted muscular contractions to determine pain tolerance. Data analysis revealed no differences in pain tolerance between

[13]Kathleen A. O'Connor and James L. Webb, "Investigation of Personality Traits of College Female Athletes and Nonathletes," *Research Quarterly*, 47, No. 2 (May 1976), 203.

[14]John Young and A. H. Ismail, "Comparison of Selected Physiological and Personality Variables in Regular and Nonregular Adult Male Exercisers," *Research Quarterly*, 48, No. 3 (October 1977), 617.

[15]Victor A. Buccola and William J. Stone, "Effects of Jogging and Cycling Programs on Physiological and Personality Variables in Aged Men," *Research Quarterly*, 46, No. 2 (May 1975), 134.

[16]Kerry Ellison and Jerry Freischlag, "Pain Tolerance, Arousal, and Personality Relationships of Athletes and Nonathletes, *Research Quarterly*, 46, No. 2 (May 1975), 250.

groups, and when these values were constant no differences were found in arousal or in personality traits. These factors are thus essentially similar between athletes and nonathletes.

Husman administered several projective techniques, including the Rosenzweig Picture Frustration Study, a portion of the Thematic Apperception Test, and a sentence completion test, to study aggression of boxers, wrestlers, and cross-country runners.[17] These tests were given before the season, before and after an athletic contest, and at the end of the season. The data indicated that boxers were significantly less aggressive and less extrapunitive, and they tended to be more intrapunitive than other subjects tested. Husman concluded that boxing and wrestling did not attract aggressive personalities.

By use of the House-Tree-Person Test of personality, Johnson and Hutton studied the personalities of eight college wrestlers before a wrestling season, four to five hours before the first intercollegiate match of the season, and the morning after the first match.[18] A decrease in functioning intelligence and an increase in aggressive feelings and neurotic symptoms were evident in the before-match situation. A general return to the preseason personality level occurred by the following morning.

ANXIETY

Concern for the role that emotions play on the individual has prompted a number of theories and a rather extensive number of research studies, as well as fairly wide interest among sport psychologists. They have argued that athletic competition itself produces an anxious state, following the description of Selye.[19] His general adaptation syndrome (G.A.S.) stated that stress causes changes to occur in the organism, some of which are manifestations of the body's adaptive reactions. He specifically postulated three stages of the G.A.S.: alarm reaction, stage of resistance, and stage of exhaustion. It is felt that anxiety is one form of stress and is a psychological variable that can be studied.

State-Trait Anxiety

Spielberger has defined anxiety as 2 distinctly different forms. *State anxiety* is a transitory state that fluctuates over time, and it is characterized by an emotional response to a situation viewed by an

[17]Burris F. Husman, "Aggression in Boxers and Wrestlers as Measured by Projective Techniques," *Research Quarterly*, 26, No. 4 (December 1955), 421.

[18]Warren R. Johnson and Daniel C. Hutton, "Effects of a Combative Sport upon Personality Dynamics as Measured by a Projective Test," *Research Quarterly*, 26, No. 1 (March 1955), 49.

[19]Hans Selye, *The Stress of Life*, rev. ed., (New York: McGraw-Hill, Inc., 1976).

individual as personally dangerous or frightening.[20] This is known as A-State and will elicit feelings of tension, including elevations in heart rate, blood pressure, and galvanic skin response. The other, *trait anxiety*, known as A-Trait, is a personality factor that is more stable, representing a latent disposition toward anxiety when situations are seen as threatening.[21] The State-Trait Anxiety Inventory (STAI) evaluates feelings of tension, nervousness, worry, and apprehension (A-State scale) and consists of 20 items to which the subject indicates on a 4-point scale how he or she feels at a particular moment in time. The A-Trait scale consists of 20 statements that ask the subject to indicate how he or she feels in general. Thus, the A-State scale can be adapted to a given experimental situation by asking the subject to report feelings experienced as a result of a stressful condition.

Anxiety Studies

The relationship between trait and state anxiety, movement satisfactory, and participation in physical activities was investigated by Burton.[22] Male and female college students in selected activity classes were given the State-Trait Anxiety Inventory (STAI) and the Movement Satisfaction Scale before and after a 15-week activity course. The high A-Trait subjects had higher A-State scores along with lower movement satisfaction scores than did the low A-Trait subjects on both pretests and posttests. No change was found in the A-State level of the low A-Trait group, but the A-State level of the high A-Trait group decreased significantly over the treatment period. The correlations between STAI and Movement Satisfaction at both pretest and posttest ranged from $r = .25$ to $-.44$.

Gruber and Beauchamp administered a 10-item short form of the State Anxiety Inventory, called the Competitive State Anxiety Inventory (CSAI) to 12 members of a university women's varsity basketball team on 16 different occasions: before and after 2 practice sessions (base-line data), and before and after 3 easy and 3 crucial games.[23] It was found that state anxiety was significantly reduced after the 3 easy games the players won, but remained high after the 3 crucial games

[20]Charles D. Spielberger, "Trait-State Anxiety and Motor Behavior," *Journal of Motor Behavior*, 3, No. 3 (September 1971), 265.

[21]C. D. Spielberger, R. L. Gorsuch, and R. E. Lushens, *The State-Trait Anxiety Inventory (Test Manual)* (Palo Alto, Calif.: Consulting Psychologists Press, Inc., 1970).

[22]Elsie Carter Burton, "Relationship between Trait and State Anxiety, Movement Satisfaction, and Participation in Physical Education Activities," *Research Quarterly*, 47, No. 3 (October 1976), 326.

[23]Joseph J. Gruber and Diane Beauchamp, "Relevancy of the Competitive State Anxiety Inventory in a Sport Environment," *Research Quarterly*, 50, No. 2 (May 1979), 207.

they lost. The subjects exhibited significantly more anxiety before the crucial games than before the easy games.

Wankel employed a pursuit rotor tracking task to study the way in which trait anxiety and number of observers affected state anxiety and motor performance.[24] Subjects were placed in a high-anxious group and a low-anxious group, based on the trait anxiety scale of the STAI. They were placed in one of 3 treatment conditions: tested alone, tested in front of two observers, or tested before 5 or 6 observers. They were given 30 massed 10-sec trials on the pursuit rotor under the appropriate condition and then completed the STAI state anxiety scale. A 2×3 analysis of variance (A-trait $\times$ audience reaction) revealed that trait anxiety significantly affected both A-state and pursuit rotor performances; no significant audience effects or interaction effects were found. Hall used a simple motor tapping task involving speed and accuracy of a forearm movement to compare postperformance A-state of internals and externals.[25] Subjects were initially classified as internals and externals by use of the Locus of Control Scale and randomly assigned to success-failure situations. A-trait and preperformance A-state were assessed by the STAI prior to and following the experimental treatment. It was found that externals scored significantly higher on A-trait than internals; and significant relationships were found for A-trait and pre- and postperformance A-state.

PEER STATUS

Support is mounting for the concept that peer evaluation of an individual may be a better indicator of his or her group behavior and may reveal more about inner drives than the inventory technique. The rating given by one's peers concerning social acceptance may well provide greater insight into a subject's effective relationships with people than can be ascertained by more devious means. Perhaps the compromise is between types of data obtained; peer status and mental health, for example, certainly are two separate entities. The choice of instruments must match the problem, but the selection of a research study itself must also be approached realistically. Little is gained by using invalid tools no matter how urgent the research.

Sociometric Questionnaire. The use of the sociometric technique has not been employed extensively as a measure of social adjustment

[24]Leonard M. Wankel, "Audience Size and Trait Anxiety Effects upon State Anxiety and Motor Performance," *Research Quarterly*, 48, No. 1 (March 1977), 181.

[25]Evelyn Gay Hall, "Comparison of Postperformance State Anxiety of Internals and Externals Following Failure or Success on a Simple Motor Task," *Research Quarterly for Exercise and Sport*, 51, No. 2 (May 1980), 306.

in physical education. The systematic investigation of group structure and the position of the individual had its chief origin in the work of Moreno,[26] first published in 1934. He defined sociometry as "the mathematical study of psychological properties of populations."

The sociometric test consists of asking an individual to choose associates for any group of which he or she is, or might become, a member. For example, the individuals within a group might be asked to choose from the group those members whom they wish to have with them in the formation of some new group, whether it be one of recreation, work, or study. When Moreno first introduced this technique, it was no more than a tentative, qualitative, and rough outline. The results were diagrammed with individuals represented as triangles or circles with respect to sex, and the lines drawn from one to another representing choices. As the number of persons thereon increased, these sociograms became extremely complex and resistent to analysis. Furthermore, at the time of the original study, no specific rules for the construction of the sociogram were available, so they could be composed in many diverse ways.

Soon after the appearance of Moreno's basic work, attention was given to methodology in sociometric research. Moreno and Jennings were responsible for early work in this area, studying deviations from chance expectancy; their paper was notable for the stimulus it provided.[27] Lemann and Solomon investigated certain group characteristics by means of data obtained from sociometric tests and rating scales, using as subjects the members of three small dormitories at a woman's college.[28] Emphasis was placed on methodology and the improvement of sociometric techniques; a method of determining status groups was developed which took into account both choices and rejections and which yielded meaningful and workable divisions into high, middle, and low status groups. Those subjects who were "highly noticed" by others were more likely to be noticed unfavorably than favorably—that is, they were more likely to have low status than high status. Those who were "very unnoticed" by the group were more likely to be liked than disliked.

A sociometric questionnaire was developed and utilized in the Medford Boys' Growth Study[29] in which each boy was asked to list as

[26]J. L. Moreno, *Who Shall Survive?* (New York: Beacon Press, 1934).

[27]J. L. Moreno and H. H. Jennings, "Statistics on Social Configurations," *Sociometry*, 1, No. 3-4 (January-April 1938), 342.

[28]Thomas B. Lemann and Richard L. Solomon, "Group Characteristics as Revealed in Sociometric Patterns and Personality Ratings," *Sociometry*, 15, No. 1-2 (February-May 1952), 7.

[29]See Chapter 15.

many other boys in his homeroom as he wanted in each of the following five categories.

Friends: List your good boy friends and boys you would like for friends.
Movies: List the boys you would like to go to the movies with.
Sports: List the boys you would like to play sports with.
Homework: List the boys you would like to study homework with.
Party: List the boys you would like to invite to a birthday party.[30]

The manner of scoring the questionnaire is relatively simple. For example, if unlimited choices are given, as noted above, two possibilities may be employed: (1) itemizing the number of times each subject is chosen by other boys, and (2) itemizing the number of different boys each subject has chosen from those in his group. In this manner, two different numerical values are available for each subject; in the event different numbers of subjects are involved, the percentage of choices can be utilized. It may also be permissible to restrict to three the number of choices that may be made and to include a negative question such as to list those individuals with whom they do not wish to associate. Breck found two methods of scoring sociometric questionnaires to be particularly valuable: (1) tabulating only expressions of choice, assigning one point to each expression; and (2) tabulating expressions of choice and deducting expressions of rejection, assigning one point for each acceptance and subtracting one point for each rejection.[31]

Peretti administered a sociometric questionnaire to 15 boys and girls in a sixth grade classroom. They were asked to choose 3 students they would like to sit near and 3 they would not like to sit near. They were also asked to select words or terms most frequently associated with personality impressions of one student to another.[32] The data revealed that the girls were more frequently chosen as accepted members of the class, while boys were more frequently rejected. It was found that choices of acceptance and rejection were based on perceived personality impressions. The personality characteristics of the classmates who were accepted tended to center on pleasantness, sharing, and concerned behaviors, while those of the classmates who were

[30]H. Harrison Clarke and David H. Clarke, "Social Status and Mental Health of Boys as Related to Their Maturity, Structural, and Strength Characteristics," *Research Quarterly*, 32, No. 3 (October 1961), 326.

[31]Sabina J. Breck, "A Sociometric Measurement of Status in Physical Education Classes," *Research Quarterly*, 21, No. 2 (May 1950), 75.

[32]Peter O. Peretti, "Perceived Personality Impressions in Student Acceptance and Rejection Interaction Patterns in the Classroom," *Research Quarterly*, 46, No. 4 (December 1975), 457.

rejected tended to center on self-destruction and ego-centered behaviors.

BEHAVIOR RATING

Another approach to social and psychological evaluation may be made through various types of behavior ratings. This would imply knowledge of the subject by the evaluator, so its use by teachers has proven successful in assessing pupil behavior. If the instrument is carefully prepared and if the method of rating is clear, it should prove useful as an adjunct in understanding the status of the subject in a social environment. The main limitation that should be kept in mind is that the adult tends to assign rather different values to certain behavior than might the peer group or the individual. For example, a student who is in conflict with the adult value system may receive wide acceptance within the peer group, a fact that might lead to reinforcement of his or her own behavior. The fact that this may occur at different ages and for different reasons makes the study of social and psychological problems all the more intriguing; it might well serve to stimulate research concerning the role that sports and games play in this process.

The usual precautions must be taken in the use of behavior rating scales as in other subjective measures where an individual must make decisions that are not always clear and obvious and where precision may be lacking. If the investigator is not performing the rating but must rely upon others who are acquainted with the subjects, he or she must carefully instruct them on the meaning of questions and the applicability of the rating categories. Inasmuch as the data may be pooled from several raters, the need for standardization of use is acute. This is eased somewhat if several persons can judge the same subject, providing each rater has an adequate opportunity for observation.

A precaution that should be mentioned concerns the "halo effect," which occurs when the rater tends to give high ratings in every category to pupils he or she likes and, conversely, tends to rate all traits very low for those individuals whom he or she does not like. One must strive to be as objective as possible in this regard and not permit deficiencies of a subject in one category to influence decisions in all categories. That such a condition may exist is shown by Grant, who found high positive intercorrelations between items in a rating scale.[33] On the other hand, if the items themselves do not discriminate among

[33]Donald L. Grant, "An Exploratory Study of the Halo Effect in Rating" (Ph.D. diss., Ohio State University, 1952).

traits of behavior, such a finding might be expected. Langlie found that sex differences in ratings exist, as both men and women teachers tend to rate girls as superior to boys, even though test records do not verify this trend.[34]

Blanchard scale. Blanchard employed 85 trait actions, had them evaluated by 16 physical education teachers, and selected the 45 that received the highest ratings.[35] From this group, 24 were finally selected for the behavior frequency rating scale shown in Figure 13.1. The reliability of this battery is .71, and the intercorrelation of 1-trait action with the rest of the items in its category is .93.

Cowell Social Behavior Trend Index. Cowell developed 12 pairs of behavior "trends" representing good and poor adjustments, after studying factors that differentiate junior high school boys who tend to participate wholeheartedly in physical education from those who tend to participate reluctantly.[36] From a factor analysis, 10 of the pairs of positive and negative behavior trends were retained as common factors underlying good and poor adjustment. Forms A and B, representing positive and negative scales, appear in Figure 13.2. Cowell recommended that 3 teachers rate each pupil on both forms at different times; a pupil's social adjustment score is the combined total of the ratings of the 3 teachers. Thus, a socially well adjusted pupil would get a high positive score, a socially maladjusted pupil would receive a high negative score. These raw scores can be transposed to percentile values from scales presented by Cowell and Schwehn.[37]

SELF-IMAGE

A growing interest has developed in recent years in the concept of self-image. The concern is that an individual's impression of himself or herself may reflect various personality factors or be related to his or her performance capabilities. There have been a few such studies in physical education, some of which have used inventory techniques and

[34]T. A. Langlie, "Personality Ratings: I. Reliability of Teachers' Ratings," *Journal of Genetic Psychology*, 50 (1937), 339.

[35]B. E. Blanchard, "A Behavior Frequency Rating Scale for the Measurement of Character and Personality in Physical Education Classroom Situations," *Research Quarterly*, 7, No. 2 (May 1936), 56.

[36]Charles C. Cowell, "Validating an Index of Social Adjustment for High School Use," *Research Quarterly*, 29, No. 1 (March 1958), 7.

[37]Charles C. Cowell and Hilda M. Schwehn, *Modern Principles and Methods in High School Physical Education* (Boston: Allyn & Bacon, Inc., 1958), pp. 305-8.

Name:...Grade:...................Age:................Date:............
School:...Name of Rater:.......................................

Behavior Rating Scale

Personal Information	No Opportunity to Observe	Never	Seldom	Fairly Often	Frequently	Extremely Often	Score
Leadership							
1. Popular with classmates		1	2	3	4	5	
2. Seeks responsibility in the classroom		1	2	3	4	5	
3. Shows intellectual leadership in the classroom		1	2	3	4	5	
Positive Active Qualities							
4. Quits on tasks requiring perseverance		5	4	3	2	1	
5. Exhibits aggressiveness in his relationship with others.................................		1	2	3	4	5	
6 Shows initiative in assuming responsibility in unfamiliar situations		1	2	3	4	5	
7. Is alert to new opportunities		1	2	3	4	5	
Positive Mental Qualities							
8. Shows keenness of mind....................		1	2	3	4	5	
9. Volunteers ideas...........................		1	2	3	4	5	
Self-Control							
10. Grumbles over decisions of classmates.........		5	4	3	2	1	
11. Takes a justified criticism by teacher or classmate without showing anger or pouting		1	2	3	4	5	
Co-operation							
12. Is loyal to his group		1	2	3	4	5	
13. Discharges his group responsibilities well		1	2	3	4	5	
14. Is co-operative in his attitude toward his teacher		1	2	3	4	5	
Social Action Standards							
15. Makes loud-mouthed criticism and comments		5	4	3	2	1	
16. Respects the rights of others		1	2	3	4	5	
Ethical Social Qualities							
17. Cheats		5	4	3	2	1	
18. Is truthful		1	2	3	4	5	
Qualities of Efficiency							
19. Seems satisfied to "get by" with tasks assigned...		5	4	3	2	1	
20. Is dependable and trustworthy.................		1	2	3	4	5	
21. Has good study habits.......................		1	2	3	4	5	
Sociability							
22. Is liked by others..........................		1	2	3	4	5	
23. Makes a friendly approach to others in the group		1	2	3	4	5	
24. Is friendly		1	2	3	4	5	

Figure 13.1. Blanchard's Behavior Rating Scale.

Cowell Social Behavior Trend Index (Form A)

Date:_____Grade:_____
School: _____Age: _____
Describer:_____

Last Name   First Name

INSTRUCTIONS:—Think carefully of the student's behavior in group situations and check *each behavior trend* according to its degree of descriptiveness.

	Descriptive of the Student			
Behavior Trends	Markedly (+3)	Somewhat (+2)	Only Slightly (+1)	Not at All (0)
1. Enters heartily and with enjoyment into the spirit of social intercourse___				
2. Frank; talkative and sociable, does not stand on ceremony___				
3. Self-confident and self-reliant, tends to take success for granted, strong initiative, prefers to lead___				
4. Quick and decisive in movement, pronounced or excessive energy output ___				
5. Prefers group activities, work or play; not satisfied with individual projects ___				
6. Adaptable to new situations, makes adjustment readily, welcomes change___				
7. Is self-composed, seldom shows signs of embarrassment ___				
8. Tends to elation of spirits, seldom gloomy or moody___				
9. Seeks a broad range of friendships, not selective or exclusive in games and the like ___				
10. Hearty and cordial, even to strangers, forms acquaintanceships very easily				

Cowell Social Behavior Trend Index (Form B)

Date:_____Grade:_____
School: _____Age:_____
Last Name   First Name   Describer: _____

INSTRUCTIONS:—Think carefully of the student's behavior in group situations and check *each behavior trend* according to its degree of descriptiveness.

	Descriptive of the Student			
Behavior Trends	Markedly (−3)	Somewhat (−2)	Only Slightly (−1)	Not at All (−0)
1. Somewhat prudish, awkward, easily embarrassed in his social contacts___				
2. Secretive, seclusive, not inclined to talk unless spoken to ___				
3. Lacking in self-confidence and initiative, a follower___				
4. Slow in movement, deliberative or perhaps indecisive. Energy output moderate or deficient ___				
5. Prefers to work and play alone, tends to avoid group activities ___				
6. Shrinks from making new adjustments, prefers the habitual to the stress of reorganization required by the new___				
7. Is self-conscious, easily embarrassed, timid or "bashfull"___				
8. Tends to depression, frequently gloomy or moody ___				
9. Shows preference for a narrow range of intimate friends and tends to exclude others from his association___				
10. Reserved and distant except to intimate friends, does not form acquaintanceships readily ___				

Figure 13.2. Cowell Social Behavior Trend Index.

some of which have used a more direct approach. For a discussion of body image and the self-concept, the reader is directed to Fisher and Cleveland.[38]

Instruments

Body Cathexis Test. One technique for assessing an individual's attitude toward his or her body is through use of a Body Cathexis Test. As developed by Secord and Jourard,[39] a 46-word questionnaire was employed consisting of a wide variety of terms describing the various parts of the body and their functions. The subject was instructed to indicate on a 5-point scale whether or not he had strong positive feelings (1), strong negative feelings (5), or was more moderately disposed (2, 3, 4). A quantitative score could be obtained by summing the values for each item. Thus, a subject with a high score was not as satisfied with his body as one with a low score.

Body Rating Scale. The Body Rating Scale was developed originally as a Semantic Differential Test by Osgood and others, who provided the subject with a word stem (my body is) and then gave a series of bipolar adjectives that could be rates on a 7-point scale (e.g., masculine 1—2—3—4—5—6—7 nonmasculine).[40] The sum of the values for each response constituted a score for this test; a low score indicated that the subject favorably perceived his body.

Martinek-Zaichkowski Self-Concept Scale. The Martinek-Zaichkowski Self-Concept Scale is nonverbal and designed primarily to measure various social, psychological, intellectual, and physical components of a child's self-concept.[41] It consists of 25 items that are appropriate for elementary and middle school children. The overall internal consistency, as determined by the Hoyt estimate of reliability, is .88.[42]

Adjective Check List. The Adjective Check List for college students consists of 300 adjectives commonly used to describe attri-

[38]Seymour Fisher and Sidney E. Cleveland, *Body Image and Personality* (Princeton, N.J.: D. Van Nostrand Company, Inc., 1958).

[39]Paul F. Secord and Sidney M. Jourard, "The Appraisal of Body-Cathexis: Body-Cathexis and the Self," *Journal of Consulting Psychology*, 17, No. 5 (October 1953), 343.

[40]Charles E. Osgood *et al.*, *The Measurement of Meaning* (Urbana: University of Illinois Press, 1957).

[41]T. Martinek and L. D. Zaichkowski, *Manual for the Martinek-Zaichkowski Self-Concept Scale for Children* (Jacksonville, Ill.: Psychologists and Educators, Inc., 1977).

[42]T. Martinek and S. B. Johnson, "Teacher Expectations: Effects on Dyadic Interactions and Self-Concept in Elementary Age Children," *Research Quarterly*, 50, No. 1 (March 1979), 60.

Name: _____   Date: _____

School: _____   Grade: _____

Directions: These are words that are often used to describe children. Please check the ones that apply to you.

_____Afraid	_____A Good Pupil	_____Polite
_____Bad	_____A Good Sport	_____Quiet
_____Bossy	_____A Hard Worker	_____Selfish
_____A Brat	_____Helpful	_____Silly
_____A Bully	_____Honest	_____A Show Off
_____Careless	_____Kind	_____A Sissy
_____Cheerful	_____Lazy	_____A Sloppy Worker
_____Clean	_____A Leader	_____A Smart Aleck
_____Clever	_____Not Eager To Learn	_____A Sore Loser
_____Clumsy	_____Loving	_____Smart
_____A Copy Cat	_____Mean	_____Stupid
_____A Crybaby	_____Neat	_____A Time Waster
_____Dependable	_____Nervous	_____A Trouble Maker
_____Fair	_____Noisy	_____Unhappy
_____Forgetful	_____Not Alert	_____Not Eager To Study
_____Friendly	_____Outstanding	_____Willing
_____Generous	_____A Pest	

Figure 13.3. Davidson Adjective Check List

butes of a person and it may be employed by an individual to rate himself or herself or to be rated by others.[43] Twenty-four scales and indices are available for use with this instrument.

In 1960 an adjective checklist was developed by Davidson and Long to determine a child's self-perception.[44] Fifty different adjectives were selected for this checklist on the basis that they were often used as traits to describe children, such as afraid, noisy, forgetful, and friendly. An early form of the Davidson-Long Adjective Check List has been employed in the Medford Boys' Growth Study and is illustrated in Figure 13.3.

Self-Image and Physical Ability

Tests of self-image are beginning to be employed in physical education to study the relationship between what an individual thinks of himself or herself and his or her ability in physical tasks. For example, Sloan gave the Body Cathexis Test and the Body Rating Scale to a group of college men and selected two groups, one scoring low

[43]Harrison G. Gough and Alfred B. Heilbrun, *The Adjective Check List Manual* (Palo Alto, Calif.: Consulting Psychologists Press, Inc., 1965).

[44]Helen H. Davidson and Gerhard Long, "Children's Perceptions of Their Teachers' Feelings toward Them Related to Self-Perception, School Achievement and Behavior," *Journal of Experimental Education*, 29, No. 2 (December 1960), 107.

(the desired direction) and one scoring high.[45] These groups were given the following physical performance tests: medicine ball put, wall pass, zig-zag run, standing broad jump, and 60-yard dash. Based upon an analysis of the difference between the means of these two groups in physical ability, he concluded that an individual possessing a positive body-image would be more likely to have a higher level of motor ability than his counterpart who had a negative attitude toward his body.

Women athletes and nonathletes were measured for psychological well-being and body image (modification of the Body Cathexis Test) by Snyder and Kivlin.[46] A separate analysis was performed on women gymnasts and basketball players. It was found that the women athletes scored significantly higher than the nonathletes on both psychological well-being and body image. However, no significant differences existed between gymnasts and basketball players in psychological well-being; the results of the body-image test failed to reveal any differences.

Reynolds formed groups of 13-year-old boys who checked and who did not check each of the 50 adjectives on the Davidson-Long Adjective Check List; the differences between the means on 16 physical and motor tests for the groups thus formed were tested for significance.[47] The adjectives showing greatest differentiation in descending order were: crybaby, stupid, bossy, leader, mean, nervous, and sissy. For example, those boys who marked the word crybaby were significantly weaker in arm strength and cable-tension strength and scored significantly lower in pullups, Physical Fitness Index, and the standing broad jump than did those who did not check this adjective.

An interesting technique was devised by Broekhoff to assess the body image of boys.[48] At 16 years of age, the subjects were asked to identify their own physique from a series of somatotype photographs (faces obscured) in the following sequence: (1) Each selected a "look alike" physique from pictures of 16-year-old boys, ranging from the extreme endomorphic physique through mesomorphic somatotypes and midtypes to the extreme ectomorphic physique. (2) Each did the

[45]William W. Sloan, "A Study of the Relationship between Certain Objective Measures of Body-Image and Performance on a Selected Test of Motor Abilities" (Master's thesis, University of Maryland, 1963).

[46]Eldon E. Synder and Joseph E. Kivlin, "Women Athletes and Aspects of Psychological Well-Being and Body Image," *Research Quarterly*, 46, No. 2 (May 1975), 191.

[47]Robert M. Reynolds, "Responses on the Davidson Adjective Check List as Related to Maturity, Physical, and Mental Characteristics of Thirteen-Year-Old Boys" (Ph.D. diss., University of Oregon, 1965).

[48]Jan Broekhoff, "Relationships between Physical, Socio-psychological, and Mental Characteristics of Thirteen-Year-Old Boys" (Ph.D. diss., University of Oregon, 1965).

same for a similar series of photographs of 13-year-old boys. (3) From both series, they selected their "ideal" body type. (4) From a third series of photographs, each tried to identify his own picture at 13 years of age. Even though they failed to recognize their own somatotype pictures, they nevertheless selected body builds closely resembling their actual body type. Moreover, these boys appeared to have a definite image of an ideal physique; the great majority selected a well-balanced meso-morphic physique as the ideal body type.

The study of the effects of 2 teaching models on the development of specific motor skills and self-concept was conducted by Martinek and others,[49] who drew a sample from a pool of 600 children in grades 1-5 who were given instruction over a 10-week period. One group received a vertical model of instruction, and the other received a horizontal model; a control group received no treatment. A body-coordination test was employed to measure development of motor skills; the Martinek-Zaichkowski Self-Concept Scale was used to measure self-concept. Results indicated that a teacher-directed approach (vertical model) was best for the development of skills, while a student-sharing approach (horizontal model) had a beneficial effect on the development of self-concept.

LOCUS OF CONTROL

The term *locus of control* refers to the manner in which individuals perceive control over their lives, in a sense control over what happens to them. Locus of control is viewed as a continuum from internal control on the one hand, in which the person has control over his or her complete destiny, to external control, whereby an individual has no control over his or her life. Thus, externally controlled persons perceive successes and failures to be determined by chance, fate, or some other powerful force. Internally controlled persons, on the other hand, view themselves as the primary agents of their own self-control, able to regulate and feel responsible for most events in their lives. Rotter developed an internal-external locus of control scale which consisted of 23 forced-choice items plus 6 filler items.[50] High scores indicate externality and low scores indicate internality. A locus of control scale for children was later developed by Nawicki and Strickland.[51]

[49]Thomas J. Martinek, Leonard D. Zaichkowski, and John T. F. Cheffers, "Decision-Making in Elementary Age Children: Effects on Motor Skills and Self-Concept," *Research Quarterly*, 48, No. 2 (May 1977), 349.

[50]Julian B. Rotter, "Generalized Expectancies for Internal Versus External Control of Reinforcement," *Psychological Monographs*, 80, No. 1 (1966), 1.

[51]Stephen Nawicki and Bonnie R. Strickland, "A Locus of Control Scale for Children," *Journal of Consulting and Clinical Psychology*, 40, No. 1 (1973), 148.

Finn and Straub compared the locus of control of highly skilled Dutch and American female softball players, and administered the Rotter internal-external locus of control scale.[52] The Dutch players were significantly more external than the American athletes. When analyzed for positions played (infield, outfield, or battery), it was found that the American battery subjects were significantly more internal than each group of Dutch players. Employing the Nawicki-Strickland locus of control scale on fifth and eighth grade children, Aushel designed a study to determine the effects of positive and negative feedback on six weeks of pursuit rotor practice.[53] Subjects were classified and placed into high-internal and high-external groups, irrespective of gender. It was found that subjects across all age groups who received positive feedback performed better than those who were given negative feedback. The significant locus of control by feedback interaction indicated that high-internal subjects were superior to high-externals under positive feedback conditions, but that negative feedback produced inferior performance by internals and improved performance by externals. It was further noted that neither age group shifted its locus of control response to the positive and negative feedback.

LEVEL OF ASPIRATION

A technique of personality evaluation that has proven fairly successful involves an assessment of level of aspiration. Essentially this is a technique whereby the subject performs some task—either mental or physical—and then reveals the score he or she would attain if there could be a second trial. It represents to some extent an objective judgment of probable future performance, the individual differences in aspiration level in an experimental situation being readily measured and sufficiently generalized to appear in dissimilar tasks. Thus, the possibility is presented for enhancing the understanding of human drives and motivation.

People evaluate themselves for future performance in one of three possible ways: They feel that they can perform better than previously; they feel they can do as well; or they feel they will not do as well. Asking such a question following tests of speed printing, spatial relations, and accuracy of quoit throwing, Frank obtained aspiration scores by subtracting from the average of individual levels of aspiration the

[52]Joan A. Finn and William F. Straub, "Locus of Control among Dutch and American Women Softball Players," *Research Quarterly*, 48, No. 1 (March 1977), 56.

[53]Mark H. Aushel, "Effect of Age, Sex, and Type of Feedback on Motor Performance and Locus of Control," *Research Quarterly*, 50, No. 3 (October 1979), 305.

median of the performance that preceded each of them.[54] The ratio between the level of aspiration and the level of performance remained constant, irrespective of the test being employed, and thereby represented a stable element of the personality.

In 1938 Gardner measured the level of aspiration of 32 college men following the administration of 4 tasks: card sorting, digit-symbol substitution, a multiple-choice test of opposites, and a complicated activity consisting of cancellation performed while counting backward by 3s.[55] After each trial, a score was reported to the subject; he was then asked to set his aspiration level for the next trial. Reliabilities of the measures ranged from .76 to .98, most of them being above .90. Intercorrelations between tasks for these measures ranged from .42 to .69 when corrected for attenuation. However, in studying individual differences in aspiration level and ratings on 8 personality variables of high school boys, Gardner obtained low and, for the most part, insignificant correlations, which would indicate that the level of aspiration represents a specific trait of personality.[56]

In general, experiments involving level of aspiration have used mental rather than physical tasks, since the technique originated in psychology. An early study in physical education was conducted by Smith, who studied the influence of athletic success and failure on the level of aspiration of the participants.[57] Members of a freshman football team were interviewed prior to each game and were asked to indicate quantitatively their immediate aspiration level—the number of minutes they thought they would play in that game—and their ultimate aspiration—the number of minutes they thought they would play in some game before the season ended. Among the findings were the following: a tendency for successful players to raise their levels of aspiration and for failing players to lower their levels; a trend for players to escape from failing-producing situations after having experienced failures; a tendency for players with somewhat higher levels of aspiration to maintain some hopes of success; and a trend for players with highest aspiration levels to experience success repeatedly even though they raised their goals.

A level-of-aspiration test based upon maximum grip strength was

[54]Jerome D. Frank, "Individual Differences in Certain Aspects of the Level of Aspiration," *American Journal of Psychology*, 47, No. 1 (January 1935), 119.

[55]John W. Gardner, "Individual Differences in Aspiration Level in a Standard Sequence of Objective Success and Failure Situations," *Psychological Bulletin*, 35, No. 8 (October 1938), 521.

[56]John W. Gardner, "The Relation of Certain Personality Variables to Level of Aspiration," *Psychological Bulletin*, 36, No. 6 (June 1939), 540.

[57]Carnie H. Smith, "Influence of Athletic Success and Failure on the Level of Aspiration," *Research Quarterly*, 20, No. 2 (May 1949), 196.

utilized in the Medford Boys' Growth Study. The following protocol was followed:

1. After instruction in grip testing technique, the subjects grip strength is taken (P–1). He is then informed of his score.
2. The subject is asked to estimate what score he believes he can attain on a second grip strength effort. This score is recorded as his first aspiration score (A–1).
3. A second grip strength test is administered and recorded (P–2), and the subject is informed of this score.
4. Steps 2 and 3 are repeated to obtain a second aspiration score (A–2) and a third grip strength measure (P–3).

Two useful level-of-aspiration scores available are

1. *First aspiration discrepancy* (AD–1). The difference between P–1 and A–1.
2. *Second aspiration discrepancy* (AD–2). The difference between P–2 and A–2.

Clarke and Clarke administered such a test to 98 9-year-old boys and formed 3 groups comprised of those with the highest positive scores on AD–1 and AD–2, those with zero discrepancies (P–1 and A–1 being the same), and those with the greatest negative scores.[58] It was found that the boys in a high AD—1 group had a significantly greater Physical Fitness Index mean than did boys in zero and low AD–1 groups. Where high and zero groups were compared, the high group was significantly superior in the following five additional tests: standing height, body weight, McCloy's Classification Index, McCloy's arm strength score, and Strength Index. Apparently, the 9-year-old boy who strives to attain higher goals is physically superior in size and strength to others his own age who are not willing to risk the chance of failure and who thereby choose the aspiration level that seems to ensure at least some measure of continued success.

On the other hand, Clarke and Stratton found the second aspiration discrepancy (AD–2) to be the most representative of the various performances, aspirations, and discrepancies studied.[59] It correlated

[58]H. Harrison Clarke and David H. Clarke, "Relationship between Level of Aspiration and Selected Physical Factors of Boys Aged Nine Years," *Research Quarterly*, 32, No. 1 (March 1961), 12.

[59]H. Harrison Clarke and Stephen T. Stratton, "A Level of Aspiration Test Based on the Grip Strength Efforts of Nine-Year-Old Boys," *Child Development*, 33, No. 4 (December 1962), 897.

relatively well with performance discrepancy, aspiration discrepancy, and grip strength performance scores. This discrepancy measure differentiated best between the three basic groups—high-positive, low-positive to low-negative, and high-negative—formed on the basis of magnitude and direction of aspirations to achieve grip strength scores.

Schiltz and Levitt employed a simple motor task on fifth and sixth grade boys that involved moving small blocks from one board to another to determine if the level of aspiration of high-skilled and low-skilled groups differed under prearranged conditions of failure.[60] Preceding each of the trials, the subject indicated how many blocks he thought he could move in the next trial. Failure was induced by systematically stopping the subject before he attained his stated goal. It was found that the level of aspiration of the high- and low-skilled groups differed significantly only on the last of the three trials, that failure had a significant negative effect on both groups. The high-skilled subjects expressed higher levels of aspiration than did the low-skilled subjects, although this difference was not significant.

MOTIVATION

The student of psychology will be aware of the numerous theories that explain personality and will identify many of the causative factors that underlie behavior. The study of these basic drives and interrelated aspects of psychology is best left to the psychologist, although it does form the substructure for the discipline in physical education that seeks to answer questions presented by physical performance. At this point, it is the physical educator's responsibility to develop and expand the literature in the psychology of sport so as to gain a greater understanding of the factors associated with movement and physical capabilities.

One such major aspect may be called motivation, although human drives and motives are so pervasive that great injustice may be done by separating them from other topics mentioned previously. The motivation theories of Freud, Hull, Hebb, Maslow, and others may be regarded as essential sources in the study of personality; the presentation by Johnson and Cofer will prove helpful in understanding the theoretical aspects of personality dynamics.[61]

[60]Jack H. Schiltz and Stuart Levitt, "Level of Aspiration of High- and Low-Skilled Boys," *Research Quarterly*, 39, No. 3 (October 1968), 696.

[61]Warren R. Johnson and Charles N. Cofer, "Personality Dynamics: Psychological Implications," in *Science and Medicine of Exercise and Sport*, 2nd ed., eds. Warren R. Johnson and E. R. Buskirk (New York: Harper & Row, Publishers, 1974), Ch. 28.

Action Motivation

The discussion of motivation here will be restricted to those studies, usually experimental in design, that seek to alter performance by manipulating certain psychological factors. In other words, circumstances exist that may enhance or perhaps interfere with overt action; and, although the usual emphasis is to seek ways of causing improvement, examination of those factors that inhibit behavior may be just as valid. At any rate, anyone who has tested subjects on physical tasks is aware of the problem posed by motivation; the instructions usually adopted suggest that all subjects be given the same degree of motivation, so this factor is at least held constant. This practice does not guarantee that all subjects will be motivated equally, however, because there may well be wide individual differences in such a trait: some subjects are normally aggressive when it comes to performance of physical tasks and others seem more reticent. The conditions that pertain in such situations should prove provocative to the investigator.

The results of this study are in contrast to those of Nelson, whose subjects were subjected to exhaustion exercise on an elbow-flexion ergograph.[62] Ten motivational situations arranged in a random-groups design were applied as follows:

1. *Normal Instructions.*   The subjects were instructed to exercise as long as possible.

2. *Verbal Encouragement.*   The investigator gave continual verbal encouragement during the exercise bout.

3. *Individual Competition.*   Two subjects were asked to compete against each other to attain the highest endurance score.

4. *Group Competition.*   The subjects were encouraged to determine their fitness by being shown a scale that purported to show ergographic performances of college men.

5. *Obtainable Goal.*   Each subject was directed to exercise for a total of 40 repetitions, a goal that was obtainable.

6. *Observer's Presence.*   After the exercise began, an official-looking observer walked in and observed the exercise with apparent interest.

7. *Instructor Interest.*   The subject's class instructor urged him to do as well as possible and to report his score after testing.

[62]Jack K. Nelson, "An Analysis of the Effects of Applying Various Motivational Situations to College Men Subjected to a Stressful Physical Performance" (Ph.D. diss., University of Oregon, 1962); in H. Harrison Clarke, *Muscular Strength and Endurance in Man* (Englewood Cliffs, N.J.: Prentice-Hall, Inc., 1966), pp. 101-9.

8. ***Ego Involvement.*** In a casual manner, before exercise was started, each subject was told that junior high school pupils had averaged 62 repetitions and that senior high school students had averaged more than 70 repetitions. The investigator made it clear that the subject was expected to do better, even though these norms were fictitious and extremely high.

9. ***Air Force Space Program.*** The subjects were told that they were part of the Air Force space program that was determining standards for future astronauts.

10. ***Competition with Russian Students.*** The subjects were told that they were participating in a nationwide program to compare performances of American and Russian students.

The analysis, based on the total work accomplished, resulted in the identification of three motivational groups. The low group consisted of those subjects given normal instructions, verbal encouragement, and instructor interest; the moderate group was composed of those given an obtainable goal, observer's presence, group competition, and competition with the Russians; and the high group consisted of ego involvement, Air Force space program, and individual competition. Thus it was demonstrated that applying different motivations did affect the performances of college men in stressful physical performance involving exercise to the point of volitional exhaustion.

Weinberg and Jackson randomly assigned male and female subjects to a reward or no-reward condition, where they either received success or failure feedback during competition.[63] The task was to perform trials on a stabilometer, and the subjects were told prior to performance that this type of activity was an excellent predictor of success in sports. Money was promised as a reward for achieving a given level. After completing the 10 stabilometer trial , the subjects received either success or failure feedback and were given 3 questions which were rated on a 7-point scale designed to assess their intrinsic motivations during the task. The questions asked the subjects to rate the task on interest, excitement, and enjoyment. Also, they were asked to respond to attribution questions dealing with ability, effort, luck, and task difficulty. Results revealed a significant overall effect for feedback, with subjects exhibiting more intrinsic motivation after success than after failure. In terms of intrinsic motivation, the subjects found the task more interesting, more exciting, and more enjoyable after success than after failure. For the attributional data, it was found

---

[63]Robert S. Weinberg and Allen Jackson, "Competition and Extrinsic Rewards: Effect on Intrinsic Motivation and Attribution," *Research Quarterly*, 50, No. 3 (October 1979), 494.

that the subjects rated themselves as having higher ability, trying harder, and having more luck after success than after failure.

In a companion study, Weinberg and Ragan randomly assigned male and female subjects to either a face-to-face competition or competition against a standard of excellence, where they received either success or failure feedback during competition.[64] The task was performance on the pursuit rotor, and the subjects were told that it measured hand-eye coordination, perceptual motor ability, and predicted success in sports. Subjects competing against a standard of excellence were told that norms had been developed and that they would be informed on how well they had performed. Two subjects in a condition of face-to-face competition were brought together and were told after each trial who had won and who had lost. A noncompetitive condition served as control. Subjects in each of the two experimental conditions were randomly assigned to either success or failure feedback conditions. They were also asked to rate their motivation in terms of enjoyment, whether it was more like work or leisure; they were also asked to rate their degree of intrinsic interest in the task. Results indicated a significant overall feedback effect. Subjects viewed the task as more like leisure time after success than after failure; they also saw the task as more intrinsically motivating after success than after failure. Subjects also displayed more intrinsic motivation during competition than when not in competition. Males were more intrinsically motivated when not competing, but no differences were found for females.

Hypnosis

Special mention should be made of the technique of hypnosis. Although hypnosis is not a research procedure available to everyone, some pertinent studies have been made utilizing hypnosis and posthypnotic suggestion in connection with certain physical performance variables. By the very nature of the method, it should be clear that rather extensive training should be undertaken prior to experimentation. Used indiscriminately, rather severe repercussions and possible mental health hazards may result, so employment by novices should be discouraged. A student desiring to use hypnosis should obtain assistance from competent professional sources. The reader will find a discussion of this process by Morgan to be helpful.[65]

The discussion of hypnosis in connection with motivational

[64]Robert S. Weinberg and John Ragan, "Effects of Competition, Success/Failure, and Sex on Intrinsic Motivation, *Research Quarterly*, 50, No. 3 (October 1979), 503.

[65]W. P. Morgan, "Hypnosis and Muscular Performance," in *Ergogenic Aids and Muscular Performance* ed. W. P. Morgan (New York: Academic Press, Inc., 1972), Ch. 7.

studies is not intended to imply that this is the only use to which it may be put. There have been a number of studies designed merely to investigate the effects of hypnosis on a variety of bodily functions and other factors, including exercise.[66] However, several reports in physical education are notable for the emphasis placed on large-muscle performance. In one of these, Johnson, Massey, and Kramer investigated the effect of posthypnotic suggestion on all-out rides for 100 revolutions on a loaded bicycle ergometer.[67] Ten subjects were selected on the basis of their ability to learn to enter a trance quickly and to carry out posthypnotic suggestions. They were placed under a trance before each of 2 rides, but before 1 of these they were given the suggestion that they would be unusually strong and resistent to fatigue. The difference between the means of the 2 criterion exercises was not significant. Later, Massey, Johnson, and Kramer employed hypnosis to control the psychological variable so often present in warm-up studies.[68] Utilizing the ergometer task described above, they gave 15 subjects warm-up exercises involving generalized activity and no warm-up for the task. However, prior to both conditions the subjects were placed in a deep hypnotic state so that there was no conscious awareness of this period of time. Upon arousal they were tested on the all-out ergometer ride. Once again, no statistically significant differences were found.

Rating of Perceived Exertion

The literature in psychology of sport contains a number of references to attempts to quantify the sensation of effort. This has culminated in a simple rating scale known as the *rating of perceived exertion* (RPE), which consists of a 15-point graded category scale[69] as follows:

6

7 very, very light

8

---

[66]Johnson and Cofer, "Personality Dynamics," pp. 552-54.

[67]Warren R. Johnson, Benjamin H. Massey, and George F. Kramer, "Effect of Posthypnotic Suggestions on All-Out Effort of Short Duration," *Research Quarterly*, 31, No. 2 (May 1960), 142.

[68]Benjamin H. Massey, Warren R. Johnson, and George F. Kramer, "Effect of Warm-up Exercise upon Muscular Performance Using Hypnosis to Control the Psychological Variable," *Research Quarterly*, 32, No. 1 (March 1961), 63.

[69]Gunnar A. V. Borg, "Perceived Exertion: A Note on 'History' and Methods," *Medicine and Science in Sports*, 5, No. 2 (1973), 90.

9 very light

10

11 fairly light

12

13 somewhat hard (heavy)

14

15 hard (heavy)

16

17 very hard (heavy)

18

19 very, very hard (heavy)

20

The ratings correlate well with exercise heart rate; when a zero is added to the RPE it yields values which are nearly the same as the exercise heart rate.[70] Therefore, there is an interrelationship between the physiological response to exercise and the psychological awareness of that stress.

SUGGESTED PROBLEMS

The researcher interested in personality dynamics and psychological traits in general may wish to probe the following questions:

1. Can the tests of personality presently in use be improved or new ones constructed? Is it possible to identify personality through physical behavior?
2. In what ways can motivation be determined? Can a physiological basis be used to predict motivational change?
3. What are the individual and group patterns of changes in personality with age?
4. What factors determine academic achievement in school?
5. What are the characteristics of subjects in the extreme categories of personality? What cultural factors play a role in personality development?

---

[70]William P. Morgan, "Psychophysiology of Self-Awareness during Vigorous Physical Activity," *Research Quarterly for Exercise and Sport*, 52, No. 3 (October 1981), 385.

6. Does the pattern of social acceptance change with age and physical ability? Is there a change in individual social acceptance as boys and girls change physically or develop athletic skills?

SUMMARY

A variety of research procedures involving psychological problems is available. The main purpose of this chapter was to stimulate study of that aspect of psychology concerned with personality as related to physical performance, as well as to encourage the development of related topics.

The measurement of psychological characteristics ordinarily is not accomplished in the objective manner that marks the majority of research procedures in physical education, because psychological variables are more elusive and sometimes difficult to define clearly. Internal drives and motives are often unclear to the individual, so the methods of obtaining adequate data are complex and perhaps indirect. The use of projective techniques provides an example of the difficulty experienced by the novice; they should not be attempted without sufficient training and experience in this type of evaluation.

Inventory techniques are characterized in general by their ease of application and scoring but are marked in many cases by questionable validity. Ample precedence is evident for their use in psychological studies, and their relevance to physical performance seems logical. The proper selection of tests, along with extreme care in their administration, is essential for success in this type of research.

Anxiety is a well-known psychological state that has relevance to a variety of life situations including sports and athletics. State anxiety is viewed as a transitory state that fluctuates over time, while trait anxiety is a more stable personality factor, representing an inherent disposition toward anxiety.

The evaluation of peer status appears to be fairly direct, especially when ratings are made by acquaintances. The sociometric questionnaire has been employed as a measure of social adjustment with apparent success for a number of years, and in one form or another it asks subjects to list individuals with whom they would like to be associated. Thus, social acceptance and rejection can be evaluated. Closely related to this technique are the various behavior rating scales used by trained observers.

The area of self-image, self-concept, and locus of control is receiving some attention due to the feeling that an individual's body concept may reflect his or her physical ability. This is reinforced by the various studies involving level of aspiration and other attempts at the measurement of motivation including ratings of personal exertion.

SELECTED REFERENCES

ALLEN, ROBERT M., *Personality Assessment Procedures: Psychometric, Projective, and Other Approaches.* New York: Harper & Row, Publishers, 1958.

BUROS, OSCAR KRISEN, ed., *The Eighth Mental Measurements Yearbook,* Highland Park N.J.: The Gryphon Press, 1978.

CLARKE, H. HARRISON, *Application of Measurement to Health and Physical Education* (5th ed.). Englewood Cliffs, N.J.: Prentice-Hall, Inc., 1976.

CRONBACH, LEE J., *Essentials of Psychological Testing* (3rd ed.). New York: Harper & Row, Publishers, 1970.

FERGUSON, LEONARD W., *Personality Measurement.* New York: McGraw-Hill, Inc., 1952.

FISHER, SEYMOUR, and SIDNEY E. CLEVELAND, *Body Image and Personality* (2nd ed.). New York: Dover Publications, Inc., 1968.

JOHNSON, WARREN R., and E. R., BUSKIRK, eds., *Science and Medicine of Exercise and Sport* (2nd ed.). New York: Harper & Row, Publishers, 1974, Chaps. 28 and 29.

MORGAN, WILLIAM P., "Psychophysiology of Self-Awareness during Vigorous Physical Activity," *Research Quarterly for Exercise and Sport,* 52, No. 3 (October 1981), 385.

MORGAN, WILLIAM P., "The Trait Psychology Controversy," *Research Quarterly for Exercise and Sport,* 51, No. 1 (March 1980), 50.

14
Biomechanical Research

An area of research in physical education that has been developed largely as a direct result of the efforts of scholars within the field is that of biomechanics. The term has been coined to represent the study of human movement, which would seem to describe much of the research in physical education; however, biomechanics as the subject field can be more rigorously defined.

As constituted here, biomechanical research deals largely with the anatomical, mechanical, and electrophysiological analysis of performance, both in terms of local muscular action and gross body movement. No attempt is made to resolve all the questions raised by such a designation, for the analysis of performance might take directions other than purely biomechanical. For example, take the choreographer's terminology in describing movements in the dance or the historical researcher's description of ancient rites. Certain arbitrary decisions must be made, and the types of research considered to be biomechanical here may be something quite different in other frames of reference. It should also be pointed out that much of the earlier literature employs the term *kinesiology*. No distinction between kinesiological and biomechanical research is implied, but since *biomechanics* is a term receiving international recognition today, it is used here.

Two points of view seem evident from the current instructional efforts in the teaching of biomechanics. One can be described as anatomical, in which movement is depicted in terms of muscle action with strong emphasis on the description of actions through muscle origin and insertion. The second approach, often superimposed upon the first, is the description of action in terms of known physical laws. Thus, the appropriate laws of motion, mechanical principles, and the like are brought to bear to give the fullest possible understanding of human movement. It is pointless to argue the merits of either approach, but one can indicate that the tendency today is to utilize the most appropriate means to gain the fullest possible analysis of performance.

The modern biomechanist employs the camera, the electromyograph, the timer, the goniometer, and any other device that will yield information on the way people move. Considerable overlapping will be inevitable among disciplines particularly between biomechanics and physiology of exercise. The electromyograph is widely used to study the functional state of muscles and yields information of muscle excitation, a matter of concern in physiology. It also tells the biomechanics specialist about the patterning of muscle action and helps him or her to decide about questions related to movement sequence. As will be described later, such overlapping serves to underlie the difficulty in designating specific areas of research in physical education.

Although the trends in biomechanics reflect greater concentration on mechanical and cinematographical analysis, this does not mean that developments no longer take place in the field of anatomy. Perhaps the research is less voluminous, but nonetheless there is a concern that differences among individuals may exist in so-called muscle origin and insertion, which in turn may account for differences in performance. Thus, anatomical structure may bear upon mechanical analysis, a fact well known to the comparative anatomist,[1] although not so well documented for various human males and females. This situation, coupled with increasing attention to the relative contributions made by separate muscles within a well-defined group, offers an intriguing area for study in physical education.

ELECTROMYOGRAPHY
EQUIPMENT AND USE

A motor unit is composed of the nerve cell, its motor nerve, and the muscle fibers that it innervates. When an impulse from the spinal cord travels down the nerve fiber and is propagated beyond the myoneural junction, all the muscle fibers of the motor unit contract simultaneously, which action is accompanied by an electrical potential that

---

[1] Milton Hildebrand, "Motions of the Running Cheetah and Horse," *Journal of Mammalogy*, 40, No. 4 (November 1959), 481.

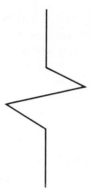

Figure 14.1.   Diphasic Spike

can be detected, amplified, and recorded. The number of motor units in a muscle may run into the thousands, and the number of muscle fibers per motor unit will vary, probably from a very few to several hundred, depending upon the muscle selected. It has been difficult to assess adequately the number of fibers in a unit because of the overlapping of motor units (one motor neuron may innervate fibers belonging to several motor units), as well as the presence of intrafusal fibers.

The elements associated with the propagation of the nerve impulse result in a change in electrical potential of the muscle membrane. This is known as the action potential, and the record obtained of this activity is known as the electromyogram. A wave of negative electricity accompanies the contraction of a single muscle fiber; two electrodes placed in close proximity to each other along the fiber will monitor this wave in quick succession. The well-known diphasic spike (Figure 14-1) results, in which the initial peak signals the passage of the wave under the first electrode and the opposite peak marks the passage of the wave under the second electrode. In order to understand the use of electromyography in biomechanics research, acquaintance with some of the problems associated with obtaining an acceptable recording is first necessary.

Electrodes

Electrodes may be of two general types: needle electrodes or skin electrodes. The criteria for selecting one or the other depend upon the function that is to be assessed. The value of the former is that it provides a means of recording the action potential produced by a single motor unit or by even a single muscle fiber.[2] It consists of an ordinary stainless steel hypodermic needle with an insulated wire inserted into

[2] Gerald G. Hirschberg and Arthur S. Abramson, "Clinical Electromyography," *Archives of Physical Medicine*, 31, No. 9 (September 1950), 576.

the lumen so that it is flush with its bevel. Thus, the needle becomes one electrode and the wire the other; because they are so close to each other, they may reach the same motor unit. This is known as a coaxial needle electrode, and it will produce a diphasic spike. The advantage gained by using this type of electrode stems from the fact that more specific motor unit activity may be assessed, a function of vital importance in medicine, where information on lower motor neuron lesions, muscular atrophies, and so on can be a diagnostic and prognostic value. Among the disadvantages of such a study in physical education is the problem associated with needle insertion, involving important considerations of subject acceptance and asepsis.

Employment of surface electrodes is probably much more feasible and, in the long run, may prove more desirable from the standpoint of the information needed. Where large muscles are to be investigated, the additive recording of a large number of motor units may be desirable, especially when they are to be monitored over a period of, say, a few seconds of contraction time. Skin electrodes consist of small, metal (e.g., silver) discs that are placed over the belly of the muscle to be monitored, usually separated by a distance of 1 mm to 1 inch or more, depending upon the size of the muscle to be monitored; the smaller the muscle, the smaller and more closely spaced will be the electrodes.[3] The site selected may straddle the motor point, although it is not essential to do this in all cases, since muscle excursion is certain to alter this relationship during contraction. Nevertheless, the location of various motor points may be accomplished by electrical stimulation or by reference to standard positions, such as those designated by Walthard and Tchicaloff.[4] Although the precise anatomical site of each motor point varies slightly among subjects, the relative position follows a fairly fixed pattern.

The electrodes are secured in place by some sort of adhesive so that they do not shift in position or disturb the conductance from the skin. Electrolyte gel is ordinarily used to promote the contact between electrodes and skin. The biopotential skin electrodes and adhesive collars designed by Beckman Instruments, Inc., have proven satisfactory for use in *EMG* research. These contain an electrolyte reservoir space between the electrode space and a silver/silver chloride pellet inside the electrode. Thus, when electrolyte gel is squeezed into the reservoir holes, a closed connection is formed between skin and pellet. Disposable adhesive collars form a hermetic seal to hold the entire

[3] A. L. O'Connell and E. B. Gardner, "The Use of Electromyography in Kinesiological Research," *Research Quarterly*, 34, No. 2 (May 1963), 166.

[4] Karl M. Walthard and Michel Tchicaloff, "Motor Points," in *Electrodiagnosis and Electromyography*, 2nd ed., ed. Sidney Licht (New Haven, Conn.: Elizabeth Licht, Publisher, 1961), Ch. 6.

assembly in position on the subject so that it will be impervious to movement and perspiration and consequently insure a stable baseline on the recording throughout the testing sequence. The plan for a simple surface electrode designed especially for vigorous movements may prove to be helpful, especially if cost is a factor, and if the electrodes currently in use tend to come loose or be dislodged.[5]

Once again, the question of number of electrodes arises. For each muscle group investigated, it would be possible to use a single electrode, but the monopolar recording is more likely to pick up unwanted current from other muscles than the bipolar electrodes. The choice may then be to use two surface electrodes placed across the belly of the muscle. This will ensure a restricted field of sensitivity, a condition highly desirable in this type of research. In addition, a third (indifferent) electrode will be required to be placed at some remote site on the body, which will serve to reduce interference (such as the cardiac potential).

A source of additional resistance to current flow is found in the skin itself, where layers of metabolizing and nonmetabolizing cells offer obstacles to the conduction of electricity, so there must be some attention given to the skin preparation prior to electrode placement. In general, it has been found satisfactory to shave off all hair, sand the skin lightly with fine sandpaper to remove the layer of horny and dead cells, clean with alcohol, and apply electrode paste. To test the skin resistance, an ohmmeter can be employed after the electrodes have been secured in place. Although the amount of impedance that can be tolerated varies with the equipment used, it is generally advisable to reduce it to 10,000 ohms or even 5,000 ohms if possible. If intolerable resistance is noted, reapplication of electrodes will help reduce it to acceptable limits. A discussion of these and other problems associated with electromyographic research will be found in a report by Davis.[6]

One of the problems in electromyographic testing has been the difficulty in repeating conditions of electrode placement in studies that require a retest. Since all necessary conditions cannot be achieved, such repeated measures designs should be used only with the most extreme caution. In short, it is necessary to rule out any discrepancy associated with the mechanics of recording the electromyogram. This may be possible, however, under certain conditions. Deutsch and coworkers reapplied electrodes and compared the resultant *EMG* of the biceps brachii muscle during submaximal (50%) static contractions

[5] Tom Corser, "A Simple Surface Electrode Specially Suited for Electromyographic Studies of Vigorous Movements," *Research Quarterly*, 46, No. 2 (May 1975), 140.

[6] John F. Davis, "Manual of Surface Electromyography," *WADC Technical Report, 59-184* (Wright-Patterson Air Force Base, Ohio: Wright Air Development Center, December 1959).

taken twice a week for two weeks.[7] No significant differences were found for trials, days, or interactions when the amount of tension did not vary, so under certain circumstances consistent reapplication of electrodes is possible.

Recording

A variety of devices is available for detecting and reproducing the electromyogram for research and other applications, ranging from single-channel to multiple-channel recorders. The number of channels required will depend upon the number of muscle groups tested—hence, the number of electrode sets. Some of the 8-channel recorders, for example, offer tremendous versatility for most needs of the investigator in a wide variety of applications. Perhaps in the future one could envision a greater requirement than this, but it is difficult to see how more than 8 sets of muscles would be tested simultaneously.

At any rate, the investment in multiple-channel recording equipment for a laboratory can reap important dividends in the versatility that it provides, because, for a fraction of the initial cost, other physiological parameters may be included by purchasing additional coupling devices. These needs will be dictated by the experimental design. Actually, only one channel may be required and be entirely adequate for a host of research investigations. This illustrates the thin dividing line between studies of a biomechanical nature and those oriented more physiologically or medically. Whereas the biomechanist may need to know the relative interaction between muscle groups during a movement, the physiologist may be more interested in the quality of the electromyographic response. This will be illustrated subsequently.

Among the devices useful to demonstrate the action current that accompanies the contraction are the loud speaker and the oscilloscope. The simplest is the loud speaker, which has its greatest value as a diagnostic medical adjunct. A physician trained in its use can interpret the character of the sound and relate it to the appropriate abnormality. This sound may even be put on magnetic tape for subsequent evaluation. Its use for physical education research cannot be encouraged, however, for obvious reasons. On the other hand, the cathode ray oscilloscope offers the possibility for the most accurate method of obtaining the necessary record. Its advantages over the direct-writing method are that it does not have to overcome the inertia of a pen, and it

---

[7] Helga Deutsch, G. Wayne Marino, and Terrence Andres, "Consistency of Submaximal Integrated Electromyographic Tracings," *Research Quarterly*, 46, No. 4 (December 1975), 410.

will provide much greater fidelity of response. A camera may be employed to photograph the tracing on the screen.

Beyond this, however, there is ordinarily an operational requirement that some sort of write-out device be available in more convenient form so that the investigator can obtain immediately a record of the electrical activity. Several such systems can be incorporated to meet this demand, depending once again upon the experimental requirements. One of these has been described by de Vries, who sought a device that would have extremely high sensitivity and would thus detect the low-level motor unit activity in resting muscle with the use of surface electrodes.[8] As a result, an *EMG* monitor was designed that possessed a precision of ± 0.01 μv at the 10-μv level and ± 0.05 μv at the 1.0-μv level. A voltage gain amplifier feeds a voltage controlled oscillator, the frequency output of which is related linearly to the integral of the muscle action potential and is counted as pulses by an electronic counter. The count registered per unit time is related to the mean *EMG* voltage according to the equation

$$\mu v \text{ root mean square } (RMS) = \frac{\text{counter reading (total pulses)}}{\text{integration period (sec)}}.$$

Thus, a testing sequence may be followed during active contraction so that during one interval (e.g., 1 sec) the muscle action potentials are counted, and during a second interval they are read. This can be alternated for the period of time selected.

Monitoring the integrator with an oscilloscope for artifacts due to 60 cps interference, the electrocardiogram, or other factors, is also appropriate; it is often necessary to enclose the subject in a room shielded by copper or bronze screening. However, de Vries feels bipolar electrodes do not discriminate changes in *EMG* activity for his research as well as unipolar leads and therefore uses a single vacuum cup electrode and ground. For a further description of these and other factors, an additional reference will prove helpful.[9]

Another method to be mentioned here is the usual pen-writing system that results in a permanent, written record of the *EMG*. This is quite satisfactory when surface electrodes are employed, and the record obtained may be analyzed later according to the procedures established by the investigator. Equipment available for such purposes should be selected with care, and the manufacturer's specifications should be followed very closely. As indicated earlier, the problem that

[8]Herbert A. de Vries, "Quantitative Electromyographic Investigation of the Spasm Theory of Muscle Pain," *American Journal of Physical Medicine*, 45, No. 3 (June 1966), 119.

[9]Herbert A. de Vries, "Muscle Tonus in Postural Muscles," *American Journal of Physical Medicine*, 44, No. 6 (December 1965), 275.

arises is to amplify a small signal from the muscle to such an extent that there is an appropriate pen deflection. This requires precision, fidelity, and compatibility of the various components if the resultant record is to be meaningful. Fortunately, the further possibility remains that the action potentials may be integrated electronically so that the tremendous difficulty in measuring manually the individual amplitudes of a large number of muscle action potential spikes can be alleviated. Although the task of measuring records will not be eliminated, the investigator should carefully explore the question of providing an automatic means of measuring the so-called "area under the curve" by instrumental integration; this method averages such factors as number, amplitude, and duration of the action potentials. The reader will find Basmajian helpful in dealing with various types of recorders.[10]

Measurement

After the problems associated with instrumentation, electrode placement, and testing procedure have been solved, the last question has to do with measurement of the record. It cannot be emphasized too strongly that this is meaningless if the greatest care has not been taken in obtaining the data in the first place. Nothing can be done with the record if there have been errors introduced at some earlier point, so the researcher should plan the design to control all essential factors and then provide time to practice with the equipment. If multiple-channel operation is anticipated, this will compound the difficulties and probably require greater care and longer practice. Experience suggests that the investigator will need assistance in using the equipment and helping the subject; hopefully, a laboratory technician who understands the electronic and practical aspects of electromyography will be available.

Thus, with careful planning, the kind of record to be obtained will be known. In fact, a clear decision should be made in advance on the manner of measuring the records in order to coordinate it with the testing procedure. Literally yards and yards of *EMG* tracings may be obtained in the course of an experiment, but probably only certain portions are crucial. Again, this will depend upon the experimental design, but testing should not begin until these problems have been solved.

In general, some sort of sampling procedure is used to obtain the estimate of *EMG* activity, and this may well be obtained by proper timing. For example, it may be sufficient to measure the middle 3 sec of

[10]J. V. Basmajian, *Muscles Alive* (Baltimore: The Williams & Wilkins Co., 1962), Ch. 1.

a 5-sec contraction, or to sample at intervals during a sustained contraction, or even to monitor the activity through a range of isotonic movement. It should be clear that the basic element is time, and there must be a way of coordinating the subject and record. If these are not standardized, confusion and error may result, especially later when the investigator is working on the data and finds there is no point of reference. Two devices on the electromyograph may be helpful in this task: a time marker and an event marker. The time marker, given in standard intervals (e.g., sec), gives a visual indication of testing duration; and the event marker, operated by the tester, can be used to indicate special matters of interest (e.g., subject activity). If greater synchronization is required, procedures have been described that will accomplish the task by coupling camera to pen recorder.[11]

The method of measuring the record itself will require some thought. For the nonintegrated *EMG*, it may be possible to overlay an appropriate scale, calibrated according to the settings on the gain control, and to read the amplitude of the pen deflections, converting them into microvolts if necessary. However, when an integrated electromyogram (*IEMG*) is to be obtained, several investigators have employed a planimeter. Essentially, this process involves running the planimeter from point to point along the wave form created by the pen deflections and returning to the starting point. The resultant "area under the curve" may be converted to some appropriate unit or may remain in arbitrary values. No further accuracy is obtained by converting to some standard value, so investigators commonly express their result as an *EMG* unit.[12] Moreover, it may be useful to normalize the *IEMG* for each subject, using maximum as 100%. This sometimes makes intersubject comparisons more explicit.

ELECTROMYOGRAPHICAL STUDIES

Once the practical matters have been settled successfully, the investigator is ready to begin the experimental work. The type of problem selected may take a number of directions, the review of literature in electromyography being quite voluminous. It should be stressed that the *EMG* technique itself is important only to the extent that it

[11]Randall J. Bevan, "A Simple Camera Synchronizer for Combined Cinephotography and Electromyographic Kinesiology for Use with a Pen Recorder," *Research Quarterly*, 43, No. 1 (March 1972), 105.

[12]H. J. Ralston. "Uses and Limitations of Electromyography in the Quantitative Study of Skeletal Muscle Function," *American Journal of Orthodontics*, 47, No. 7 (July 1961), 521.

contributes to solution of a problem, that it exists as a means to achieve some goal—in this case, the fullest possible understanding of some aspect of human movement. In order to assist in appreciating this concept, a sampling of research will be presented to illustrate the range of subject matter that exists in this field.

Muscle Function

Familiarity with the many studies performed by physiologists who have attempted to understand the action of the motor unit as well as factors associated with the so-called small motor nerve system gives an indication of the extent that electromyographic research may be carried. For example, Buchthal, Guld, and Rosenfalck employed 2 multielectrodes to chart the territory of a motor unit in human biceps muscles.[13] These electrodes were inserted at right angles to each other; 12 leads, each 1.5 mm long, were placed at distances of .5 mm along their length. The first multielectrode was so inserted that the maximum action potential magnitude was recorded on leads 5 to 7; the second was inserted as close as possible to the first and turned so as to obtain maximum amplitude of the potentials. The action potentials were found to belong to the same motor unit if their time relationships were identical, irrespective of the frequency of discharge. Thus it was determined that the action potentials of a motor unit spread over an area approximately circular in shape, the average territory determined to be 4 to 6 mm. Of interest, also, was the finding that as many as 6 different motor units intermingled, and 3 motor units overlapped completely.

Stubbs and others studied the action of the sartorius and tensor fascia latae muscles in male and female subjects in a variety of movements, both unweighted and against resistance.[14] Fine-wire electrodes were inserted with standard 27-gauge hypodermic needles into the muscles at specific locations. Integrated recordings were made with an electromyograph, all testing being carried out in a copper-lined room. Results revealed that the sartorius functioned in flexion and abduction at the hip joint, in flexion of the knee joint from 90° to pull flexion, and as a trunk flexor. The tensor fascia latae also functioned in flexion and abduction at the hip joint, during flexion of the trunk, and only slightly during medial rotation of the femur.

In a companion study fine-wire electrodes were placed in the

[13]Fritz Buchthal, Christian Guld, and Poul Rosenfalck, "Multielectrode Study of the Territory of a Motor Unit," *Acta Physiologica Scandinavica*, 39, No. 1 (1957), 83.

[14]Nancy B. Stubbs, Edward K. Capen, and Gary L. Wilson, "An Electromyographic Investigation of the Sartorius and Feusor Fascia Latae Muscles," *Research Quarterly*, 46, No. 3 (October 1975), 358.

gluteus minimus and gluteus medius muscles and the *EMG* recorded during a variety of movements.[15] It was found that the gluteus minimus was active during abduction and medial rotation of the thigh, that it served as an extensor of the thigh in some subjects, a flexor of the thigh in others, and in still others was active during both flexion and extension. The gluteus medius functioned most effectively in abduction and extension of the hip joint, but served in medial rotation in only about half of the subjects tested.

Relation of EMG to Tension

One of the most pressing issues has been the relationship between the electrical activity created during contraction and the tension produced. At first glance, one might assume that the two would be equivalent, but it must be remembered that the events associated with excitation on the one hand and contraction on the other are sequential, actually representing two distinct phenomena. There is no question that they are closely tied together, but the question remains as to whether or not they are actually equivalent.

In 1952, Inman and others investigated the *IEMG* during an isometric contraction of the biceps of a cineplastic amputee whose muscle had bee: freed from its insertion and connected directly to a dynamometer.[16] It was noted that the two factors, *EMG* and tension, paralleled each other. The same results were obtained in normal subjects in isometric contractions of the elbow flexors and ankle dorsi flexors, irrespective of the type of electrodes (skin, wire, or needle) employed, so long as care was taken that the muscle length did not change during contraction. However, this relationship failed to exist when the muscle was allowed to vary in length.

During the same year, Lippold studied the integrated activity of the gastrocnemius-soleus muscles in 30 human subjects during a series of isometric contractions.[17] When the data from 10 experiments were plotted according to a line of best fit, a linear relationship was found. Moreover, when the experimental values were correlated with the expected value obtained by fitting, the relationship was quite high ($r = .93$ to $.99$). The author noted considerable variation among the

---

[15]Gary L. Wilson, Edward K. Capen, and Nancy B. Stubbs, "A Fine-Wire Electromyographic Investigation of the Gluteus Minimus and Gluteus Medius Muscles," *Research Quarterly*, 47, No. 4 (December 1976), 824.

[16]Verne T. Inman and others, "Relation of Human Electromyogram to Muscular Tension," *Electroencephalography and Clinical Neurophysiology*, 4, No. 2 (May 1952), 187.

[17]O. C. J. Lippold, "The Relation between Integrated Action Potentials in a Human Muscle and Its Isometric Tension," *Journal of Physiology*, 117, No. 4 (August 1952), 492.

regression lines, however, which would indicate that some caution should be exhibited in interpretation of the correlations.

Extending the concept to the relation between the action potential of a muscle and its tension under conditions of constant velocity and constant tension, Bigland and Lippold tested 5 young adult males and females. A special dynamometer was constructed to permit isotonic contractions of the calf muscles in plantar flexion so that the subject could control the velocity of contraction.[18] Integrated action potentials were recorded by using surface suction electrodes. It was found that at constant velocity of either shortening or lengthening, the electrical activity was directly propotional to the tension, although the amount of electrical activity was less during lengthening. At constant tension, the electrical activity increased in a linear manner with velocity of shortening but seemed almost independent of speed during lengthening. The correlation of the observed points to the straight line during the condition of constant velocity of shortening was .93. It was of interest to note, also, that Bigland and Lippold compared the results of surface electrodes and needle electrodes and obtained essentially the same results. Later, de Jong and Freund studied the amplitude of the action potential and isometric twitch tension of the adductor pollicis brevis muscle when given graded electrical stimulation.[19] When the data were plotted for 15 subjects, a linear relationship between *EMG* and tension occurred; the correlation was .693.

In an effort to determine if differences in electromyographic activity occur during isometric, isotonic, or isokinetic contractions, Hinson and Rosentswieg applied bipolar surface electrodes to the biceps brachii and rectus femoris muscles.[20] Skin preparation reduced impedance levels below 5,000 ohms; *EMG* data were displayed both on an ink recorder and in digital form on an electronic counter (u volt/sec). Each isometric contraction was held for 5 sec, and the isotonic and isokinetic contractions were taken through the full range of motion for elbow flexion and for 90° for knee extension. Maximum efforts were required for each method. It was found that none of the contraction types produced the greatest muscle action potential for every subject, that a great deal of specificity was revealed. The authors concluded

[18]Brenda Bigland and O. C. J. Lippold, "The Relation between Force, Velocity and Integrated Electrical Activity in Human Muscles," *Journal of Physiology*, 123, No. 1 (January 1954), 214.

[19]Rudolph H. de Jong and Felix G. Freund, "Relation between Electromyogram and Isometric Twitch Tension in Human Muscle," *Archives of Physical Medicine and Rehabilitation*, 48, No. 10 (October 1967), 539.

[20]Marilyn Hinson and Joel Rosentswieg, "Comparative Electromyographic Values of Isometric, Isotonic, and Isokinetic Contraction," *Research Quarterly*, 44, No. 1 (March 1973), 71.

that since it requires a full range of motion and on the average produces greater action potentials, the isokinetic method should be favored over the isotonic method of muscular contraction.

The electromyograph has also been used to study the changes within muscle that occur with fatigue. As indicated in Chapter 11, the operational definition of fatigue is the observable impairment in performance. What happens is subject to conjecture unless some way is found to monitor motor unit activity. Thus, Edwards and Lippold studied the action potentials in human calf muscles that held a continuous isometric contraction at 25% of maximum for a period of 4 min.[21] Electromyographic recordings were made for 5 sec every 10 sec of contractions. When compared with the slope of the line for normal tension versus *EMG*, a linear relationship was found, but the slope of the regression line was different. In fact, more electrical activity was required to maintain a given tension in the fatigued state. This was related to the recruitment of motor units required to compensate for the decrease in force of contraction in the fatigued muscle fibers.

The efficiency of a muscular contraction may be increased during a sustained isometric contraction when auditory *EMG* feedback is provided. Lloyd applied bipolar silver/silver chloride surface electrodes over the long head of the biceps muscle on 30 male subjects.[22] Resistance across the electrodes was 5,000 ohms or less on all trials. The data were recorded on an ink recorder as well as on an FM analog tape, and further fed into an audio amplifier for feedback to the subject. Maximum isometric elbow flexion strength was determined; the subjects subsequently were asked to sustain a contraction force of 50% for as long as possible. The experimental group received auditory *EMG* feedback, and the control group was given no feedback. During the fatigue bout subjects were asked to indicate on a 5-point subjective scale the amount of pain they experienced. It was found that auditory *EMG* feedback did not significantly increase endurance time, but it did significantly reduce the amount of muscle activity required to sustain the contraction. No differences among groups occurred in the stated estimates of pain. Thus the auditory EMG enhanced the muscular efficiency of this endurance task.

Pattern of Movement

Beyond the functional details of the neuromuscular apparatus lies another important use of electromyography—that of motion analysis. Various ways of studying this problem are available; others will be

[21] R. G. Edwards and O. C. J. Lippold, "The Relation between Force and Integrated Electrical Activity in Fatigued Muscle," *Journal of Physiology*, 132, No. 3 (June 1956), 677.

[22] Andree J. Lloyd, "Auditory EMG Feedback during a Sustained Submaximum Isometric Contraction," *Research Quarterly*, 43, No. 1 (March 1972), 39.

discussed later in this chapter. However, the *EMG* possesses an important advantage in ability to reflect rather precisely in time the interplay of the musculature participating in a movement. Although the physical educator seems more prone to examine the so-called large-motor sports skills, it should be pointed out that some of the more basic actions remain to be thoroughly researched. This is not to decry the interest in movement analysis but to indicate that a host of varied research topics is available.

Inman, Saunders, and Abbott provided some of the first electro-myographic results of movement analysis.[23] They studied muscles of the shoulder joint, depicting the pattern of individual response throughout a range of motion and revealing the angle at which the action potentials was greatest. Emphasis was placed on interrelated patterns of behavior; the statement that there is no such thing as a prime mover, at least as ordinarily understood, will prove thought provoking to the reader of this study.

Although the muscular action of the elbow joint tends to be taken for granted, since the joint is ginglymus and permits only flexion and extension, the action of the various muscles has received limited study. In 1957 Basmajian and Latif evaluated the role of both heads of the biceps, the brachialis, and the brachioradialis in flexion, extension, pronation, and supination at the elbow joint.[24] Bipolar concentric needle electrodes were employed in a wide variety of movements and positions, both freely moving and with a 2-pound load. Aside from the detail of muscle function provided, a lack of unanimity of action was noted. This finding should prove of interest to investigators in physical education who have found a great deal of specificity in a range of physical activities of the body as a whole. Such findings as the fact that the biceps does not act as a chief flexor of the elbow when the forearm is pronated, even with a 2-pound load, and does not supinate the forearm when the elbow is extended unless strongly resisted also provide very basic biomechanics data.

A number of studies have been undertaken to examine normal and pathological walking, both by physicians and others who have been concerned with basic gait patterns. For instance, in physical medicine, the proper development of prosthetic devices had to wait for research to be completed on the normal walking process. Then it became possible to make comparisons with ambulatory patterns while wearing the prosthesis. One such study by Sheffield, Gersten, and

[23] Verne T. Inman, J. B. de C. M. Saunders, and Leroy C. Abbott, "Observations on the Function of the Shoulder Joint," *Journal of Bone and Joint Surgery*, 26, No. 1 (January 1944), 1.

[24] J. V. Basmajian and A. Latif, "Integrated Actions and Functions of the Chief Flexors of the Elbow," *Journal of Bone and Joint Surgery*, 39-A, No. 5 (October 1957), 1106.

Mastellone examined 12 muscles of the foot in 10 adult male subjects during walking.[25] They employed both surface and needle *EMG* electrodes and placed 3 small microswitches in a specially adapted shoe. This latter procedure permitted the investigators to know precisely the time sequence of foot movement; such information as heel strike, metatarsal strike, and toe strike was transmitted to the recorder, and the *EMG* evaluation of gait pattern was then synchronized with the foot movements. The details of muscle function from such an analysis revealed the precise interplay of action of agonist and antagonist in human walking.

Various exercises can be examined electromyographically, as shown by Rosentswieg, Hinson, and Ridgway for an isokinetic bench press.[26] Since speed is controlled in the isokinetic contraction, there is an interest in learning just how the muscles accommodate to the movement. Bipolar surface electrodes were placed on the anterior deltoid, pectoralis major, biceps brachii, and triceps muscles after the skin was prepared by rubbing with alcohol and lightly sanding. Impedance levels were less than 5,000 ohms. Integrated *EMG* data were obtained through use of a bioelectric monitor and electronic digital counter (u volts/sec). The bench press employed an isokinetic apparatus, and the subjects pressed from a starting point of 30° elbow flexion to full extension at 180°. Three speeds were selected, so that the complete 3-foot excursion of the movement would occur in 1.5 sec, 2.0 sec, and 3.5 sec. Results indicated that muscle action potentials increased significantly with the slower speeds, thus verifying the concept of muscle accommodation.

The manner in which *EMG* can help in the understanding of skilled movement is illustrated in a study by Anderson, who compared the overarm throw and the tennis serve.[27] Subjects were skilled in throwing, in serving, or in both, as evidenced by throwing and serving speed. Bipolar surface electrodes were placed on 10 muscles: 2 on the trunk, 4 on the shoulder girdle, and 4 on shoulder joint. Three 16 mm cameras operating at 100, 67, and 64 frames/sec simultaneously recorded the two actions from the side, rear, and overhead. A timer was seen in the field of vision of all 3 cameras, and a corresponding time mark at .2-sec intervals was electronically transmitted to the *EMG* record.

[25]Fred J. Sheffield, Jerome W. Gersten, and Aniello F. Mastellone, "Electromyographic Study of the Muscles of the Foot in Normal Walking," *American Journal of Physical Medicine*, 35, No. 4 (August 1956), 223.

[26]Joel Rosentswieg, Marilyn Hinson, and Mary Ridgway, "An Electromyographic Comparison of an Isokinetic Bench Press Performed at Three Speeds," *Research Quarterly*, 46, No. 4 (December 1975), 471.

[27]Margaret B. Anderson, "Comparison of Muscle Patterning in the Overarm Throw and Tennis Serve," *Research Quarterly*, 50, No. 4 (December 1979), 541.

Results indicated that similar joint actions were employed, and during the later stages of the preparatory phase and force production phase subjects activated the same number of muscles. However, the range of movement, time, and sequence for each segment varied considerably. Regardless of skill level, subjects initiated the segments earlier in the tennis serve, which emphasized the conclusion that the two activities placed different demands on the neuromotor system, and suggested that it may not be acceptable to practice the overarm throw to improve the tennis serve.

In summary, although the concept of electromyography is not new, the availability of more versatile and flexible equipment has placed this type of research within the investigatory capabilities of more laboratories than ever before. No longer is it necessary to build homemade equipment or fashion electronic devices to cope with these problems, nor is it essential that one know all the circuitry that enters into their construction. In the same manner that one carefully chooses a high fidelity audio system, the investigator must know enough to make the proper choices and then study the literature to thoroughly understand the specifications and capabilities called for by his or her research design. Consultation with manufacturers representatives and electronic engineers and examination of basic references will also assist in successfully conducting electromyographic research.[28]

CINEMATOGRAPHIC EQUIPMENT AND USE

The art of photographing human movement known as cinematography is widely employed in biomechanics as a means of recording the events associated with muscular action. In the larger context, it provides a pictorial record of events that occur so rapidly that careful analysis is impossible by observation alone. The human eye is a notoriously poor recorder; accounts of the same action by several observers frequently result in discrepancies. However, with the use of special photographic equipment, a record can be obtained of the movement that can be used later for detailed analysis. Properly done, motion pictures provide data that will yield to lengthy analysis; in fact, they may be so extensive that a major difficulty is to delimit the problem to manageable proportions. The filming of the action is probably the least time consuming part of cinematography; more time is required to handle the host of details surrounding such things as selection of equipment, calibration of camera, setting up of proper experimental protocol, and analysis of data.

---

[28]E. E. Suckling, *Bioelectricity* (New York: McGraw-Hill, Inc., 1961).

Equipment Requirements

The actual selection of a problem usually rests with the interests of the experimenter. Judging by past research, one would strongly suspect that the analysis of sports skills has depended upon the type of sport engaged in by the researcher, which would seem logical considering his or her insight into the activity; in addition to greater motivation, there is the added knowledge gained by participation. This is certainly no prerequisite, and the study of sports skills is by no means the only use of cinematography, although it does form the bulk of published research in physical education. In reality, almost anything that needs to be timed may be a subject for these techniques if the proper type of camera is used and especially if it is not feasible to employ other timing devices. For example, the timing of running events, arm or leg movements, and such things as reaction time will be more successfully determined by the use of standard timers plus appropriate microswitches that can be operated mechanically. These devices have the added features of simplicity of testing, ease of recording, and reduced cost.

A difficulty of cinematographic research is the expense of providing the equipment, including the purchase and development of film; if the camera is operating at high speed, film will be moved at a rather rapid rate. Consider the footage required in a simple speed of movement task if a rather large number of subjects are to be given several trials. Then calculate the amount of time that will be required to determine the factor of speed once the film has been developed. It will be found that both time and cost mount quickly. As problems become more complex, more sophisticated equipment must be employed.

Aside from the factor of timing is the matter of providing information about other parameters of interest to the researcher. Obviously, photography itself is just a means to an end; the resultant film is meaningless until the appropriate analysis has been completed. Inasmuch as the basic element in any sequence is time (i.e., the number of elapsed frames at known speed of film), other factors may be calculated, such as velocity, acceleration, force, distance, power, and so on, according to known mechanical principles. In the case of body or implement motion, knowledge of mass may also be essential, but ordinarily this information can be made quickly available and usually remains constant throughout any single sequence. These principles were employed in an early study to determine mechanical expenditure of energy during running.[29]

Forming the central core of investigations in this field is the descriptive analysis of skilled movements. It is considered essential by

[29] W. O. Fenn, "Mechanical Energy Expenditure in Sprint Running as Measured by Moving Pictures," *American Journal of Physiology*, 90, No 2 (October 1929), 343.

many kinesiologists that a rather complete "library" of documented research studies describing in detail the pattern of sports skills be developed. Inasmuch as physical education deals with movement, the argument is brought forth that fully effective teaching is hampered until as much is known about as wide a variety of skills as possible. Many of the textbooks in biomechanics are incomplete because of a lack of technical data, and so often descriptions of movements are empirical, fragmentary, and devoid of theoretical insight. Moreover, comparative data are lacking on the differences between skilled and unskilled performers, and the decision on what is proper "form" is often made on inconclusive evidence.

These and other matters fall within the purview of the cinematographer and make continued emphasis on such research techniques essential. In carrying out the basic responsibilities, several types of problems will be encountered and must be solved before a study may be undertaken. Some of these will be discussed.

Selection of Equipment

Ample consideration should be given to the purchase of proper cinematographic equipment, including cameras and accessories, stroboscopic equipment, floodlights, and various tripods. The expenditure of money for high quality material will pay important dividends in the quality of the research produced and will also tend to serve for a long time without difficulty or loss of precision. Also, inferior quality may cause a premature lack of accuracy and render the equipment useless for research at an early date.

At the same time, thought should be given to the manner in which film is to be processed with consideration of the possibility of providing a darkroom and equipment for developing film. Such facilities give greater flexibility to the investigator, who may wish to experiment with different procedures for developing film as well as to work out problems associated with various camera settings and lighting techniques. Nothing is more exasperating than waiting several days for commercial processing to be completed, only to find that the film is either too light or too dark for use.

The usual requirements for cinematographic research in the past have been to employ two cameras, one placed in front of the subject and one facing his or her side. Thus a two-dimensional view is obtained, and analysis of movement in two planes can be accomplished. Although this will be discussed more fully subsequently, a growing need is evident to consider three-dimensional photography,[30] which

[30] James [sic Jerome] Noss, "Control of Photographic Perspective in Motion Analysis," *Journal of Health, Physical Education and Recreation*, 38, No. 7 (September 1967), 81.

will require three cameras, the third to be placed directly overhead. In so doing, the three cardinal planes can be viewed simultaneously and all portions of the movement accounted for.

Two considerations for human movement studies through cinematography involve film size and shutter speed; to satisfy these needs, the choice may be 16 mm film with the camera capable of operating at 64 to 128 frames per sec. Once again, this will be dictated by the design of the experiment, but a deviation from this standard should be though out carefully. For example, film readers are designed primarily for this film size, and if the camera is actually operating at, say, 64 frames per sec, the time per frame is of the order of .0156 sec, usually sufficient to detect the significant aspects of movement. Although, these cameras are generally spring driven, it is possible to expand operations to electronically driven cameras capable of moving film at a rate of thousands of frames per sec.[31] Consideration may also be given to the use of stroboscopic photography.[32]

The additional equipment needed includes tripods and floodlights, especially if filming indoors, and other accessories dictated by the requirements of the research. These items, as well as the type and quantity of film, can be obtained at the usual photographic stores or perhaps through an outlet on campus, such as the audiovisual department. Perhaps even more important to the novice is the possibility that technical help may be obtained from these sources in the form of advice on a host of operational problems that can arise during the study. Arrangements can also be made to rent or borrow cameras if they are not already available.

Calibration of Cameras

Aside from the problems associated with obtaining the proper equipment are those involved with understanding and standardizing their operation. Most notably, the cameras must be calibrated so that their speed is known precisely; even though they may be advertized at 64 frames per sec, this does not guarantee that they are actually going at exactly that rate. The investigator is solely responsible for checking camera speed at the time of filming in order to be able to make the correct conversions of his data. This does not become much of a problem when an electrically driven camera is employed with a built-in timing device. In such an instance, time may be automatically recorded

[31] Red Lake Laboratories, Santa Clara, California 95051.

[32] Janice S. Merriman, "Stroboscopic Photography as a Research Instrument," *Research Quarterly*, 46, No. 2 (May 1975), 256. See also Richard C. Nelson, K. L. Petak, and Gary S. Pechar, "Use of Stroboscopic-Photographic Techniques in Biomechanics Research," *Research Quarterly*, 40, No. 2 (May 1969), 424.

on each frame of film. However, timing in cinematography may require less expensive methods.[33]

The usual spring-driven camera may be calibrated in one of two ways. The first is least expensive and consists of photographing an object (usually a ball) falling from a known height. Thus, the time t may be calculated according to the formula

$$s = \tfrac{1}{2}gt^2$$

where s is the distance, and g is the constant acceleration of gravity (32.2 feet/sec^2). The amount of film elapsing during the time of fall can be converted to frames per sec. One of the difficulties of this technique is in making the correct decision as to ball contact, which can occur between frames; therefore, it may be necessary to repeat the procedure several times and take an average value.

The second method consists of photographing the sweep hand of a clock (e.g., a hundredth second timer) and then counting the number of frames elapsing between seconds. This can be repeated for several seconds merely by permitting the camera to run, and it is much more accurate than the ball-drop technique. It also permits the calculation of lag at the beginning of the film as the camera begins its operation and may help decide upon differences in film movement at varying spring tensions. Interesting methods of synchronizing various film views in triaxial cinematography by using timing devices are available.[34]

Experimental Protocol

The experimental methodology is dependent upon the nature of the research design, but certain problems should be anticipated. Decisions to film outdoors may depend upon the indoor space available. say, for a large-scale activity common to certain sports skills, and thus the environmental conditions of lightness-darkness are subject to wide variation. Placement of cameras must be made carefully so as to obtain optimum light. Indoors, the use of floodlights or a "sun gun" must be studied with the ultimate aim of reducing shadows to a minimum. It is sometimes difficult to differentiate the precise outline of a subject if he or she seems to blend into the background, which becomes even more

---

[33] John Newton, John Provancher, and Sue Lewis, "Inexpensive Timing Method for Cinematography," *Research Quarterly*, 48, No. 2 (May 1977), 484. See also Les Saunders, Stan Johnson, and Linus J. Dowell, "Construction of an Inexpensive Internal Timing Device for Film Speed Determination," *Research Quarterly for Exercise and Sport*, 51, No. 3 (October 1980), 576.

[34] David L. Blievernicht, "A Multidimensional Timing Device for Cinematography," *Research Quarterly*, 38, No. 1 (March 1967), 146. See also James S. Walton, "A High Speed Timing Unit for Cinematography," *Research Quarterly*, 41, No. 2 (May 1970), 231.

difficult when the subject is moving. Once again, these problems can be alleviated by careful study and practice before the actual filming begins and by seeking professional advice if difficulty persists.

The background of the subject is quite important, as may be surmised, since much of the evaluation depends upon a clearly defined image. When photographing outdoors, there is less opportunity to choose the background than indoors; but, even so, good and poor outdoor backgrounds may be found. Essentially, one is desirous of obtaining a proper contrast so that the subject stands out well. If the subject blends into trees, buildings, or the like it may make analysis very difficult. This may even be a problem of proper camera setting—permitting too much light in the picture—or it may be the type of overcast day that gives poor contrast. These situations can be standardized indoors much more effectively, but the difficulty then comes in some restrictions of the activities to be filmed, as space is much more restrictive indoors in ordinary research laboratories.

One of the most important considerations for later analysis is to place some sort of grid at the average subject position from the cameras to serve as a frame of reference for measurement of distance. A common standard for the grid is 1 foot—that is, a marker sectioned in 1-foot segments (along with various subdivisions as needed) is placed in the photographic field so that the investigator can calculate a distance multiplier by dividing the projected distance by the known distance. It should be pointed out that if the subject is moving away from this standard, it will not be accurate; this is especially true when several cameras are employed.

The ultimate decision to use more than one camera in cinematographic research is the result of a desire to secure a more complete analysis of the activity in question if possible. Therefore, if the motion takes place in planes other than perpendicular to one camera, then another camera will be required. In this manner, the simultaneous recording of movement in two planes can be obtained, each of the two cameras situated perpendicularly to a different plane of the body. In actual practice, these two cameras are usually placed so that one photographs the side view and the other the front view. The decision as to whether or not this is sufficient will depend upon whether or not the action actually takes place in just two planes; if the answer is negative, then it may be essential to employ a third camera (placed overhead in this instance). This will permit the description of rotary movements that are so prevalent in human mechanics.

Inasmuch as the analysis of the data will involve the measurement of body angles, Noss makes a special plea for triaxial photography to correct the distortion that is produced in any angle when the angle of incidence is varied.[35] In fact, any angle may be seen to vary in a photograph from 0° to 180°, depending upon the angle of incidence. For this reason, triaxial analysis is especially valuable where the mean angle obtained from the 3 cameras will equal the true value of the subject angle. By way of illustration, suppose in Figure 14.2 that the subject angle is actually 45° but is so arranged in the photographic field that the cameras record angles of 27°, 36°, and 72°, none of which is correct. The average of the 3 (45°), however, is the true angle, and is obtained only by triaxial perspective. Other procedures should also be investigated, since it may be theoretically better to adopt alternative strategies for such calculations from the axial cinematographical data.[36] A technique in which the coordinates of a point can be determined from any 2 of 3 cameras was presented by Miller and Petak.[37] A linear transformation method originally designed for still cameras to obtain spatial coordinates of points during human movement has been developed for high-speed cinematography.[38]

The difficulty with the three-camera system is the necessity for precise camera location. Not all filming opportunities will permit such a laboratory procedure to be carried out. In fact, there has been substantial interest in filming the expert performances of superior athletes in competition, such as would be found in the Olympic Games or other championships. Bergemann developed and validated a three-dimensional technique employing two or more cameras placed in any position.[39] The only requirement was that a common point of origin be visible to all cameras, and that the optical axes intersect. The reader will find a description of the procedures instructive.

An additional problem created by subject movement in the photographic field is parallax (see Figure 14.3). With the camera placed at F, camera-to-subject is a distance b; if the subject moves to X or Z, the distance becomes a or c, respectively. Because of the greater distance, the calibration of the subject in position Y is no longer applicable at the other positions x and z. This situation may be relieved in part by

[35] James Noss, "Control of Photographic Perspective in Motion Analysis," *Journal of Health, Physical Education, Recreation*, 38, No. 7 (September 1967), 81.

[36] C. A. Putnam, "The Tri-axial Cinematographical Method of Angular Movement," *Research Quarterly*, 50, No. 1 (March 1979), 140.

[37] Doris I. Miller and Kenneth L. Petak, "Three-Dimensional Cinematography," in *Kinesiology III*. (Reston, Va: American Alliance for Health Physical Education, Recreation, and Dance, 1973), pp. 14-19.

[38] Robert Shapiro, "Direct Linear Transformation Method for Three-Dimensional Cinematography," *Research Quarterly*, 49, No. 2 (May 1978), 197.

[39] Brian W. Bergemann, "Three-Dimensional Cinematography: A Flexible Approach." *Research Quarterly*, 45, No. 3 (October 1974), 302.

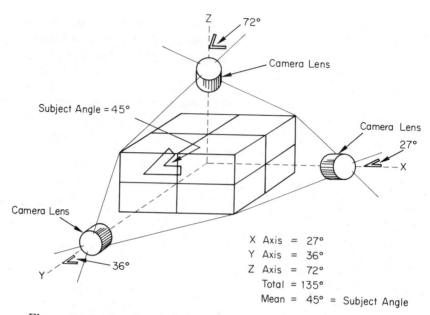

X Axis = 27°
Y Axis = 36°
Z Axis = 72°
Total = 135°
Mean = 45° = Subject Angle

Figure 14.2 Tri-Axial Analysis (Reprinted from James [*sic* Jerome] Noss, "Control of Photographic Perspective in Motion Analysis," *Journal of Health, Physical Education and Recreation*, 38, No. 7 (September, 1967, 81). Used by permission of the author and AAHPERD.

lengthening the subject-to-camera distance, but the danger of this practice may be sacrifice of detail. A method of evaluating errors resulting from voluntary or involuntary camera misalignments is available.[40] The practice of "panning," employed in the usual motion pictures, would alter the photographic field entirely.

In order to synchronize the action, it is necessary to do something that will be observed simultaneously by all cameras. A usual practice has been to fire a flashbulb at the beginning of each sequence so that later analysis can be coordinated properly.

[40]Bart Van Ghelowe, "Errors Caused by Misalignment of the Cameras in Cinematographical Analyses," *Research Quarterly*, 46, No. 2 (May 1975), 153.

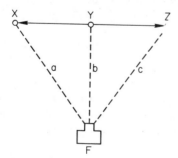

Figure 14.3. Parallax.

Preparation of the subject should also receive careful attention. If the analysis is to include changes of limb position, changes of body angles, and so on, a clear differentiation of specific body parts in the film must be made. One way of doing so is to place contrasting markings (perhaps in the form of black tape) on selected bony prominences. In order to be effective, clothing should not obscure the limbs; placing marks over loosely fitting clothing is certain to result in errors of measurement.

The question of sample size in cinematographic research is pertinent, as it is with other types of studies. Ordinarily, the decision will be based upon feasibility, since the investigator must balance such factors as time and cost with sampling reliability. Inasmuch as the analysis of data may be quite time consuming and the production costs of filming rather high, the tendency is to employ very few subjects. In fact, many investigators have used expert performers of the skill, electing to film several sequences of the same act rather than photograph several different subjects whose ability may not be reflective of "optimum" performance. The highly skilled athlete is characterized by low intertrial variability, so the chances are enhanced that the actions will be more representative, at least for that one subject. The question of studying individual differences through cinematography has not been resolved adequately, but it has permitted the basic analysis of skills with some comparisons between the highly skilled and poorly skilled performers.

Analysis of Data

Once the photographing has been done and the film developed, the analysis of data may proceed according to the investigator's plan. There may be two important contributions to be made in the analysis: the overall description of the skill and the detailed presentation of the technical patterns of motion. In either event, a decision must be made as to which frames of film are to be selected for measurement. To make this determination, the investigator will view the film through a projector in order to get an impression of the usable sequences and to make a choice for additional analysis.

Analysis of the film must be precise for research purposes. As much care must be taken in this process as was put into filming in the first place. One of these procedures involves the use of a film reader (e.g., Recordak Model 310A)[41] and plotting, frame by frame, the change in the selected body parts. The decision as to exactly which frames need be examined will depend upon how rapidly movement is occurring. Obviously, human motion tends to flow from one body part to another,

---

[41]Eastman Kodak Company, Rochester, N.Y.

so sequential analysis is very important; in fact, such may be an extremely vital part of the description. Further questions of velocities, accelerations, angular changes, and so forth will be answered for each body part selected, provided that the factors of time and distance are known. As indicated earlier, these problems should be anticipated and solved in the preparatory experimental phases. It also serves to emphasize the need for a fixed standard of measurement in the photographic field, for this permits the accurate alignment of the film in the film reader from one frame to the next.

Motion analysis utilizing these methods is laborious and time consuming and has been supplanted in many laboratories by use of a digitizer. Thus, the film is projected on a digitizing tablet and the investigator uses a pen or other device to mark the position of a joint or body segment. The digitizer automatically displays the x-y coordinates.[42] Such a system can have a number of sophisticated electronic and computerized adjuncts, such as the use of an analog/digital converter and storage or magnetic tape. These may be relatively expensive alternatives, although the requirements for accuracy and ease of cinematographic analysis can actually be met with a relatively modest cost.[43]

CINEMATOGRAPHIC STUDIES

A number of cinematographic studies are available in the related literature. Unfortunately, not enough of them have been published in the research journals, so that, if a review of literature is undertaken, the reader should exhaust sources of unpublished studies. For example, microform publications and the various volumes of *Completed Research in Health, Physical Education and Recreation*[44] contain references to a number of theses and dissertations that will prove of interest. The ones selected here for inclusion are readily available and can be considered somewhat representative of research in this area; rather than an exhaustive list of the literature, these references serve to illustrate the range of investigations undertaken and in turn may serve as guides for the future.

Walking. Some of the early work in cinematography was directed to the detailed study of walking in an attempt to understand the

---

[42]John M. Cooper, Marlene Adrian, and Ruth B. Glassow, *Kinesiology*, 5th ed. (St. Louis: The C.V. Mosby Company, 1982), p. 174.

[43]A. Dainis, "Construction of a Film Analyzer and Digitizer," *Research Quarterly*, 49, No. 4 (December 1978), 542.

[44]See Chapter 3.

mechanical principles and to assess the muscular pattern involved in human locomotion. In 1939 Elftman utilized an apparatus that measured the point of application of foot pressure but also assessed the magnitude of force in several components.[45] In addition, the subject was photographed at the rate of 92 exposures per sec as he walked behind a rectangular grid. The positions of the hip, knee, and ankle were plotted from successive frames, and values were calculated at intervals of 0.02 sec. In this manner, it was possible to determine such things as reversed effective force (defined as ma, where m = mass and a = acceleration), torque, and the rate at which energy is transferred in the various components of the system. Apparently, the transfer of energy in the leg occurs when it is in the middle of its swing and again while the foot is on the ground.

More recent impetus for the study of walking resulted from the treatment of orthopedic disabilities. For example, the rehabilitation of lower extremity amputees was speeded by the care, precision, and construction of prosthetic devices, but, in order to evaluate gait patterns, normal ambulation had to be defined. Such studies as that of Eberhart and Inman reflect the sophistication in design of such experiments.[46] Of interest here was obtaining triaxial views while employing only 2 cameras. This feat was accomplished by having the subject move across a glass walkway, beneath which, and inclined at an angle of 45°, was a mirror. Thus, 1 camera photographing the side view would also obtain the bottom view, while a second camera was placed at the end of the walkway to obtain the front view. In this case, the cameras were operated, synchronously, using 35 mm film exposed at a rate of 48 frames per sec.

Another technique employed by the same investigators was called "interrupted lights," in which small ophthalmic electric bulbs (illuminated by a 3-volt battery carried by the subject) were attached at certain joint centers, and the subject walked in a darkened room in front of the open lens of a camera. This in turn was synchronously interrupted 30 times per sec. Thus, a sequence of selected points was traced on the same negative, and accurate determinations of velocity and acceleration were obtained. The reader will find descriptions of pin attachment to bone, high-speed cinematography (400-700 frames per sec), X-ray moving pictures, electromyographic, and force plate studies helpful in designing biomechanics research.

[45]Herbert Elftman, "Forces and Energy Changes in the Leg during Walking," *American Journal of Physiology*, 125, No. 2 (February 1939), 339.

[46]Howard D. Eberhart and Verne T. Inman, "An Evaluation of Experimental Procedures Used in a Fundamental Study of Human Locomotion," *Annals of the New York Academy of Sciences*, 51, Art. 7 (January 1951), 1123.

Running. Although humanity's interest in running may be traced to earliest times, the traditional concern seems to have been with techniques to produce greater speed rather than with understanding propulsion per se. With the latter aim in mind, Deshon and Nelson studied the relationships between running velocity and factors associated with leg positions and stride length.[47] With a 16 mm Bolex camera operating at 64 frames per sec (with 35 mm lens setting between f—4.0 and f—5.6 using Kodachrome Type II film), 19 subjects were filmed for precisely 100 frames (approximately 15 yards) after accelerating to maximum speed. Intercorrelations were computed for velocity, the length of one full running cycle, the angle of leg at the touchdown, and the height of the leg lift. The correlations ranged from .31 to .71. In general, reliabilities were high, showing that runners maintained rather consistent styles from one cycle to the next.

Analysis of the role played by the ground leg during sprinting was presented by Mann and Sprague by employing 15 highly skilled sprinters who were filmed at least 3 times while running at maximum velocity.[48] A 40-meter running start was given before entering the filming field. A 16 mm camera operating at 100 frames per sec was used, positioned at a distance of 11.9 m from the subject. Film speed was corroborated by utilizing a 100-cycle/sec pulse generator built into the camera. A 1-meter marker was filmed in the movement plane as a scale for later film analysis. The subjects were marked at wrist, elbow, shoulder, hip, knee and ankle joints, iliac crest, and foot center of gravity. Film analysis was accomplished with the use of a digitizer and computer. The authors summarized their results by noting that during ground contact in sprinting the muscular dominance of the hip, knee, and ankle appears to be integrated in a manner that permits efficient use of force during the critical moment of foot strike and take off. When this does not occur, sprinting speed is lessened.

Nelson and Gregor sought to determine biomechanical changes in running technique in a longitudinal study of collegiate distance runners over a 5-year period.[49] They were filmed running at various speeds on an outdoor synthetic track with a 16 mm camera, positioned at a distance of 65 feet and operating at 160 frames per second. The precise camera speed was determined from marks made along the film edge by internal timing lights operated by a pulse generator at a frequency of 100 Hg. Appropriate markings were placed on the subjects

[47]Deane E. Deshon and Richard C. Nelson, "A Cinematographical Analysis of Sprint Running," *Research Quarterly*, 35, No. 4 (December 1964), 451.

[48]Ralph Mann and Paul Sprague, "A Kinetic Analysis of the Ground Leg during Sprint Running," *Research Quarterly for Exercise and Sport*, 51, No. 2 (May 1980), 334.

[49]Richard C. Nelson and Robert J. Gregor, "Biomechanics of Distance Running: A Longitudinal Study," *Research Quarterly*, 47, No. 3 (October 1976), 417.

so that the investigators could determine changes in stride rate, stride length, time of support, time of nonsupport, and total stride time. All trials were digitized by a motion analyzer, punched on paper tape, and analyzed by a special computer program. Significant differences occurred in all variables over the duration of the study, leading to the conclusion that training for distance running does result in changes in the running mechanics of experienced distance runners.

The effects of fatigue on components of the running cycle were investigated by Elliot and Ackland.[50] Runners were 8 highly skilled performers in a championship 10,000 meter run. Two complete running cycles were filmed with a high-speed 16 mm camera at laps 2, 10, 17, and 24. A large sweep hand clock was included in the photographic plane to permit calculation of film speed; a reference marker to convert film measurements to standard values was filmed before the race. The film was digitized and computerized, and the data were subjected to analysis of variance to test for significant differences among the 4 stages of the run. Among the results it was found that besides a linear decrease in running speed from the second to fourth leg, there was a significant reduction in stride length, while stride rate changed very little. It was concluded that fatigue caused an alteration in running technique, although this was not considered excessive.

Jumping. The triple jump was analyzed by Fukashiro and associates in an effort to follow the changes in velocity of the center of gravity and mechanical energy.[51] Fifteen outstanding triple-jumpers were filmed by 8 high-speed cameras set to operate at 100 frames/sec and calibrated from a 100 Hg timing signal. They were positioned 2.5 meters apart along the run-up path and 17 meters from the subject, thus covering the whole action from the end of run-up to the landing. The film was run through a film analyzer, which plotted the flight of the center of gravity. Mechanical energy was calculated from the sum of kinetic energy and potential energy. The maximum height of the center of gravity was about 10% lower in the step than in the hop and jump. The horizontal velocity decreased during the first half of each take-off and increased during the second half, but gradually decreased during the overall event. On the other hand, the vertical velocity increased at about the same rate during each take-off, reaching its greatest value at the end of the take-off in the jump. Mechanical energy decreased progressively during flight after each phase of the triple jump.

[50]Bruce Elliot and Tim Ackland, "Biomechanical Effects of Fatigue on 10,000 Meter Running Technique," *Research Quarterly for Exercise and Sport*, 52, No. 2 (May 1981), 160.

[51]Senshi Fukashiro and associates, "A Biomechanical Study of the Triple Jump," *Medicine and Science in Sports and Exercise*, 13, No. 4 (1981), 233.

Vaulting. Some interest has been shown in studying pole vault-ing from a cinematographical point of view. Fletcher, Lewis, and Wilkie obtained records on 5 skilled pole vaulters by photographing with a camera operating at 64 frames per sec at a distance of 100 feet.[52] Calibration was established by placing bright metal stakes at 2-foot intervals from the uprights—the uprights themselves were marked off in feet. In order to establish trajectory, the center of gravity was estimated with the use of a manikin placed in the various body positions encountered. When plotted, the trajectory formed a smooth line, suggesting that the procedure employed was acceptable. The subjects approached the vault at velocities of 21-31 feet/sec, and were moving at a rate of 5-10 feet/sec at the top of their flight. The authors indicated that the vaulter stores kinetic energy during the approach and uses the pole to alter direction and convert kinetic energy into potential energy. Apparently, a high initial speed is associated with a net loss of energy during the vault so that the better performers actually take off at moderate speed and perform more work while riding the pole.

Prompted by the advent of the more flexible Fiberglas pole, Hay studied various factors related to the magnitude and direction of force at take-off with particular emphasis on the bend of the pole.[53] The subject was photographed from the side at 128 frames per sec and from the front at 24 frames per sec. The usual timer and distance markers were placed in the field of vision for calibration purposes; the subject performed 6 trials at each of 5 heights. Such variables as horizontal and vertical velocity, angle of take-off, hand spread, distance from top hand to take-off foot at the instant of leaving the ground, and pole-bend were intercorrelated and found to vary between .03 and .68. It was felt that horizontal velocity was principally responsible for pole-bend.

Commenting on the paucity of biomechanical research available in gymnastics, Dainis studied female gymnasts in the handspring vault.[54] The horse was set at regulation height (1.2 meters) and the filming was accomplished using a camera operating at 64 frames per sec and including in the field of view the take-off board, the horse, and the landing area. The film was digitized and the coordinates trans-mitted directly to computer for analysis. The subjects were marked so as to permit configuration of the big toe, hip joint, shoulder joint, and wrist, and they were analyzed from the time of take-off until the feet

[52]J. G. Fletcher, H. E. Lewis, and D. R. Wilkie, "Human Power Output: The Mechanics of Pole Vaulting," *Ergonomics*, 3, No. 1 (January 1960), 30.

[53]James G. Hay, "Pole Vaulting: A Mechanical Analysis of Factors Influencing Pole-Bend," *Research Quarterly*, 38, No. 1 (March 1967), 34.

[54]G. Dainis, "Cinematographic Analysis of the Handspring Vault," *Research Quarterly*, 50, No. 3 (October 1979), 341.

made contact with the landing mat. Results revealed that vertical velocities at initial horse contact varied considerably, even though the variables assessed at the moment of take-off were very similar. During the contact base, all gymnasts lost horizontal speed, angular momentum, and mechanical energy.

Swimming. Illustrative of the cinematographical studies in swimming is the investigation of the dolphin stroke by deVries, who photographed two subjects through an observation window with a camera operating at 128 frames per sec.[55] Comparisons between subjects were made for various distance, time, and velocity components of the stroke cycle.

MECHANICAL ANALYSIS OF MOVEMENT

As indicated, an important aim in biomechanical research is to obtain as full an understanding of movement capabilities as possible, and much of this information is gained through analysis by cinematography and by electromyography. Both techniques yield insight into the mechanical aspects of movement in such a manner that motion may be analyzed by known physical laws. However, such techniques, useful as they may be, are required only if certain special circumstances prevail. A considerable number of studies are available in the literature that required neither method but employed other means to study the mechanical principles of muscular action. For example, the provocative work of A. V. Hill, performed largely on frog muscle, gave a very important impetus to physiologists and others interested in the dynamics of muscle contraction.[56] His finding that the shape of the force-velocity curve was governed by the manner of energy release during shortening was verified by thermal measurements. In order to explain the slow rise in tension of muscle, he postulated a two-component system, one consisting of active contractile structures and the other of series elastic elements. Although a number of studies have been conducted in this area, they have quite largely employed excised animal muscle; however, they are in general agreement that the relation between force and velocity is curvilinear.

Extending the research to human intact performance is the logical next step, one of the first investigations to do so being that of

[55] Herbert A. de Vries, "A Cinematographical Analysis of the Dolphin Swimming Stroke," *Research Quarterly*, 30, No. 4 (December 1959), 413.

[56] A. V. Hill, "The Heat of Shortening and the Dynamic Constants of Muscle," *Proceedings of the Royal Society of London*, Series B, 126, No. B 843 (October 1938), 136.

Dern, Levene, and Blair, who examined the relationship of force and velocity of elbow flexion.[57] They developed an apparatus called an isotonic lever, which was designed to give constant force or torque to oppose the arm movement. In such a manner, a variety of tensions could be produced and voluntary maximal contraction could be studied. The curves contained three phases: an increasing initial segment, a period of constant torque, and a final period of decreasing tension. Apparently, the results were independent of sex, muscular strength, and training of the subject.

In a comprehensive study of the force and velocity of human elbow flexor muscles, Wilkie[58] found that the curve could be represented by Hill's equation,

$$(P + a)(v + b) = (P_0 + a)b$$

where P represents force of contraction, v the velocity of shortening, P_0 the isometric tension, with a and b constants. Subsequently, Hubbard studied the difference in control of slow (complex) and fast (ballistic) movements to determine if there were a critical velocity separating them or if overlapping occurred.[59] Acceleration and velocity of finger, wrist, and forearm were imparted to a kymograph, and action potentials were recorded electromyographically. In describing reciprocal ballistic motion, it was of interest to note the differentiation into phases of acceleration, momentum, and deceleration, as well as the discussion of the activity of agonists and antagonists.

Among the investigations of various sports skills, several have provided theoretical insight into the mechanical aspects of the activity. In 1951, Henry and Trafton[60] studied the exponential nature of the time-velocity curve of sprint running, as well as individual differences in the curve constants, according to the integral form of the equation of motion:

$$y = v\left(t + \frac{1}{k}e^{-kt} - \frac{1}{k}\right).$$

This says that the distance (y) obtained by the runner at any time (t) upon approaching a maximum velocity (v) is controlled by the velocity

[57]R. J. Dern, Jack M. Levene, and H. A. Blair, "Forces Exerted at Different Velocities in Human Arm Movements," *American Journal of Physiology*, 151, No. 2 (December 1947), 415.

[58]D. R. Wilkie, "The Relation between Force and Velocity in Human Muscle," *Journal of Physiology*, 110, No. 3-4 (December 1949), 249.

[59]A. W. Hubbard, "The Upper Limits of Slow Movements and the Lower Limits of Ballistic Movements" (Ph.D. diss., University of Illinois, 1950).

[60]Franklin M. Henry and Irving R. Trafton, "The Velocity Curve of Sprint Running," *Research Quarterly*, 22, No. 4 (December 1951), 409.

constant (k) according to the exponential law (e is the Naperian log base). The runner ($N = 25$) broke an electric circuit by contacting a series of 10 light bamboo sticks spaced throughout a 50-yard course, set up in such a manner that they all recorded sequentially on the single pen of a chronograph. Confirmation of the distance covered by the average runner was obtained by means of the formula. Further, reliable individual differences were found in the individual curve constants for velocity (v) and for the rate constant (k), although these 2 factors were found to be independent of each other. The reader will find an analysis of the force-time factors involved in the sprint start to be of concern to this discussion as well.[61]

In order to study water resistance and propulsion in crawl-stroke swimming, Alley constructed an apparatus that controlled velocity and permitted the measurement of drag, towing force, and the force required over and above the water resistance at a given velocity (called surplus-propulsive force), as well as the calculation of other variables.[62] Essentially, this consisted of a motorized system that was connected to the swimmer and that at the same time kymographically recorded the forces exerted during a variety of kicking and stroking experiments. Among the findings was the note that the bow wave was important in limiting speed of swimming; also, when the swimmer was resisted by the apparatus (causing zero velocity), the effective-propulsive force of the whole stroke was approximately the same as for the arm stroke alone.

The mechanical principles were brought to bear by Heusner in a study of the racing dive to determine optimum angles of take-off.[63] He developed a mathematical equation to express such factors as the diving time, the glide, and the time taken to swim one length (25 yards); validation was by photographically recording the start and the one-length swim of 17 trained swimmers. The correlation between computed time and measured time was .975; the optimum angle of take-off was 13°. Estimates were also made of the ability to swim if certain physical characteristics of body size were altered and changes in some of the experimental variables were made. The reader will find the derivation of the formula helpful in understanding the mathematical concept as applied to this problem.

The study of human movement, then, can be seen to take on several important characteristics with a variety of procedures avail-

[61] Franklin M. Henry, "Force-Time Characteristics of the Sprint Start," *Research Quarterly*, 23, No. 3 (October 1952), 301.

[62] Louis E. Alley, "An Analysis of Water Resistance and Propulsion in Swimming the Crawl Stroke," *Research Quarterly*, 23, No. 3 (October 1952), 253

[63] William W. Heusner, "Theoretical Specifications for the Racing Dive: Optimum Angle of Take-Off," *Research Quarterly*, 30, No. 1 (March 1959), 25.

able to obtain reliable data so that they may be reduced to meaningful terms that can be expressed quantitatively. In the present instance, the range of studies that has been discussed illustrates some of the ways in which a mechanical analysis may be pursued. Whether the intent is to examine rather discrete limb movements or whole body activities is irrelevant, provided that the problem is adequately designed and the proper procedures are followed. The logical result, eventually, will be to amass sufficient information to complete descriptions of muscular activity; as seen from the biomechanical point of view, this is still a long way from fruition.

CENTER OF GRAVITY

One of the techniques frequently of concern to the researcher in biomechanics is the determination of center of gravity. As applied to problems of motion, plotting the flight of the center of gravity through space is often helpful in order that the proper arrangement of body parts can be made. Although the center of gravity will follow a predetermined path—depending upon such factors as velocity and angle of take-off—the body may be performing certain coordinative movements. Since this is likely to be the central focus of the investigation, a complete analysis may require serial determinations of the path of the center of gravity.[64]

Such matters as these would logically be dealt with in undergraduate courses in biomechanics, so discussion here is limited. The treatment provided in Cooper, Adrian, and Glassow will prove helpful to the investigator in this respect.[65] One of the primary considerations to keep in mind is the transient nature of the center of gravity in other than stationary objects; since it is defined as the center of a mass, its position relative to body segments will vary as an individual moves. However, in a fixed part, the center of gravity will remain quite stationary, and in fact it may be located separately in various portions of the limbs and trunk.[66] One might even be quite successful in determining the exact center of the mass of the body in the standing position in the sagittal and frontal planes, but unless the experimental

[64]Robert E. Johnson, "A Technique for Determining the Path of the Whole Body Center of Gravity," *Research Quarterly*, 48, No. 1 (March 1977), 222.

[65]John M. Cooper, Marlene Adrian, and Ruth B. Glassow, *Kinesiology*, 5th ed. (St. Louis: The C. V. Mosby Company, 1982), Ch. 12.

[66]Wilfred Taylor Dempster, "Space Requirements of the Seated Operator," *WADC Technical Report*, 55-159 (Wright-Patterson Air Force Base, Ohio: Wright Air Development Center, July 1955). See also Micheline Gagnon and Diane Rodriguez, "Determination of Physical Properties of the Forearm by Anthropometry, Immersion, and Photography Methods," *Research Quarterly*, 50, No. 2 (May 1979), 188.

subject remains in this position, it will be of little value. Therefore, marking the subject with a piece of tape on some anatomical site and then plotting the path of this mark during the movement would not yield data of the true path of the center of gravity. It can readily be shown that the center of gravity of flexed segments of the body (e.g., knee flexion or trunk flexion) will even fall outside the body, making it necessary to calculate this point in each new position.[67] In practice, this may require that the investigator select certain frames of a cinematographical film and duplicate the positions in the laboratory. A template may be employed for such determinations.[68] For a detailed center-of-gravity determination, attention is directed to a discussion by Hay.[69]

FLEXIBILITY AND JOINT MOTION

Flexibility has long been of concern to biomechanists and anatomists in the study of joint and muscle capabilities, as well as to the teacher and coach who could envision advantages of increased flexibility to the performance of certain sports skills. Hurdlers and gymnasts, for example, require more joint range of motion in their activities than might be needed in other kinds of skills. The importance of flexibility as a factor in general performance is not clearly understood, although its inclusion in certain fitness test batteries is well known. A practical flexometer has been provided by Leighton for measuring the range of motion of most joints of the body.[70]

With the advent of the electrogoniometer, as developed by Karpovich,[71] the position of joints can be monitored continuously during activity, and the patterns of motion can be studied in considerable detail. It may be especially valuable in reducing errors sometimes found in cinematographical techniques.[72] As described, the electro-

---

[67] Marian Williams and Herbert R. Lissner, *Biomechanics of Human Motion* (Philadelphia: W. B. Saunders Company, 1962), pp. 46-56.

[68] James S. Walton, "A Template for Locating Segmental Centers of Gravity," *Research Quarterly*, 41, No. 4 (December 1970), 615.

[69] James G. Hay, "The Center of Gravity of the Human Body," in *Kinesiology III* (Reston, Va.: American Alliance for Health, Physical Education, Recreation, and Dance, 1973), pp. 20-44.

[70] Jack R. Leighton, "Flexibility Characteristics of Four Specialized Skill Groups of College Athletes," *Archives of Physical Medicine and Rehabilitation*, 38, No. 1 (January 1957), 24.

[71] Peter V. Karpovich, Everett L. Herden, and Maxim M. Asa, "Electrogoniometric Study of Joints," *United States Armed Forces Medical Journal*, 11, No. 4 (April 1960), 424.

[72] Marjorie G. Owen and Gerald E. Tripard, "Electronic Differentiation of Electrogoniometer Output," *Research Quarterly*, 47, No. 3 (October 1976), 557.

goniometer consists of a small potentiometer of 0-10,000 ohms resistance placed directly over the center of rotation of the joint; the 2 arms of the potentiometer are positioned along the shafts of the articulating bones. Descriptions of the methods of calibration and techniques of testing when connected electronically to a recorder are helpful in gaining insight into this type of research. A simple electrogoniometer has been described by Korb.[73] With the invention of the flexometer, too, Leighton has provided a device for measuring the range of motion of most joints of the body.

SUGGESTED PROBLEMS

The approach to problems of a biomechanical nature reflects a need for understanding equipment and procedures for obtaining meaningful data. Among the questions asked are the following:

1. What are the basic patterns for skilled movement in the currently employed physical activities, including, but not limited to, sports skills?
2. What is the difference between the highly skilled and the moderately skilled or the poorly skilled performer?
3. Are there anatomical differences between individuals that suggest functional advantages? Can high speed of limb movement, for example, reflect more favorable muscle-tendon-joint arrangements than those exhibiting slow speed?
4. What is the relationship between energy expended as calculated mechanically and that actually obtained by direct measurement?
5. Can the problems be solved for the ready use of cinematographical techniques so that adequate sampling procedures can be employed?
6. What are the individual differences among various performers in the manner of execution of sports skills?

SUMMARY

Research in biomechanics is essentially designed to study the characteristics of human movement, by means of both a functional and a mechanical analysis of behavior patterns. Although a clear line of differentiation cannot be drawn between what may be technically physiology of exercise and what is considered biomechanics, the aim of the latter is seen to rely more on the appropriate physical laws of motion than on the underlying physiology to describe activity. There-

---

[73]Robert J. Korb, "A Simple Electrogoniometer: A Technical Note," *Research Quarterly*, 41, No. 2 (May 1970), 203.

fore, before research can be undertaken in this field, the individual must acquire the appropriate theoretical undergraduate preparation upon which will be superimposed graduate work in this area.

Electromyography is a major technical advancement that has permitted the detailed evaluation of the electrical activity associated with muscular contraction, thus providing information concerning the precise interplay of various skeletal muscles involved in specific movements. Electromyographic methods must be understood before application can be made to research. Associated problems seem to be centered around the choice and application of electrodes and the recording and measurement of signals detected during testing. Knowledge of the literature would involve not necessarily that of electromyography per se, but of specific research topics; the decision to solve them by *EMG* would be made only if this provided an adequate means to such an end. In the past, typical research has involved studies of muscle function, the relation of *EMG* to tension, and the examination of specific patterns of movement.

Cinematography is another major tool of the biomechanics, as it provides a means of detecting movement that is not possible under ordinary visual circumstances. An activity filmed by high-speed camera can be analyzed frame by frame if necessary; the data can be employed to describe such factors of motion as velocity, acceleration, force, distance, and power. Analysis may be done for limbs and trunk separately or may be used to describe whole body activity; the result would be a complete analysis of movement. The investigator must deal with such problems as selection and calibration of equipment and the proper design and preparation of the experimental environment, all with the objective in mind of providing data that can be analyzed with the use of a film reader. Previous studies have dealt with topics ranging from walking and running to a host of activity skills.

The techniques of biomechanics research may take other forms than these, for the mechanical analysis of movement may be made simply by employing timers or other devices that serve to record muscle action or body activity. The decision will always be based upon the exigencies of experimental design rather than upon instrumentation. In other words, the researcher must use the most appropriate tools to solve the problem selected.

SELECTED REFERENCES

BASMAJIAN, J. V., *Muscles Alive*. Baltimore: The Williams & Wilkins Co., 1962.
COOPER, JOHN M., MARLENE ADRIAN, and RUTH B. GLASSOW, *Kinesiology* (5th ed.). St. Louis: The C. V. Mosby Company, 1982.

DAINIS, A., "Construction of a Film Analyzer and Digitizer," *Research Quarterly*, 49, No. 4 (December 1978), 542.

DAVIS, JOHN E., "Manual of Surface Electromyography," *WADA Technical Report*, 59-184 (Wright-Patterson Air Force Base, Ohio: Wright Air Development Center (December 1959).

DEWHURST, D. J., *Physical Instrumentation in Medicine and Biology*. New York: Pergamon Press, Inc., 1966.

HAY, JAMES G., "The Center of Gravity of the Human Body," in *Kinesiology III*. Reston, Va.: American Alliance for Health, Physical Education, Recreation, and Dance, 1973, pp. 20-44.

MILLER, DORIS I. and KENNETH L. PETAK, "Three-Dimensional Cinematography," in *Kinesiology III*. Reston, Va.: American Alliance for Health, Physical Education, Recreation, and Dance, 1973, pp. 14-19.

O'CONNELL, A. L., and E. B. GARDNER, "The Use of Electromyography in Kinesiological Research," *Research Quarterly*, 34, No. 2 (May 1963), 166.

SUCKLING, E. E., *Bioelectricity*. New York: McGraw-Hill, Inc., 1961.

WILLIAMS, MARIAN, and HERBERT R. LISSNER, *Biomechanics of Human Motion*. Philadelphia: W. B. Saunders Company, 1962.

15
Growth and Development

HISTORICAL PERSPECTIVE

Man's interest in body structure and growth has a long history among scientific endeavors. Long before the establishment of formal research, ancient artisans demonstrated that matters of body size were important in a very practical way. Egyptian and Greek sculptors showed concern for the manner in which they emphasized relative proportions of limb and trunk, and for the way they highlighted and molded the musculature. Scholars of history have noted that athletic prowess was depicted in ancient artifacts and relics. They not only have archaeological value but serve as reminders of the interest in human physique as well.

Much later, the study of man through the anthropological observations of early naturalists and comparative anatomists fostered development of fields of study where body size was of vital concern. Knowledge of man and animal species depended in large part upon relative bone sizes and configurations. Although more advanced techniques helped decide evolutionary dates, the transition from archaeological remains to descriptions of function was made partly on the basis of relative sizes.

From a practical standpoint, one may also look to those artisans who became concerned with the sizing of clothes and who, as a consequence, became vitally interested in human dimensions. It has always been necessary to account for relative body proportions in the clothing industry; such concerns as the ratio of trunk length to arm length, trunk length to leg length, and so on, have had to be understood.

The period 1650-1750 marks the time that anthropometry began to be employed intermittently as an investigative tool in the emerging science of human biology. Defined narrowly as the systematized measurement of the human body, anthropometry became a matter for serious study, resulting in substantial number of investigations. At the same time, a concern for the developmental aspects of human growth emerged to the extent of expanding upon the structural changes with age to include aspects of maturity. Thus, the examination of pubescence and interrelated topics has blended the structural and functional aspects of growth and development.

Primary emphasis in the past has been placed upon those physiological changes that have accompanied the onset of puberty and, of course, on the accompanying practical concern relative to the chronological age at which these occur for boys and girls. Thus, a social factor was introduced that has educational implications for curriculum development. This is notably true in physical education, where separation of the sexes occurs at early ages and where decisions relative to type of activity are made for boys and girls.

What makes a knowledge of growth and development important is the necessity to make intelligent decisions about human characteristics as one grows older. Education is still plagued with "chronological confusion"; many really important decisions are made on the basis of a child's chronological age without respect to his or her maturity. The age of entering school is usually set by birth date, the curriculum presented by grade, and so forth. Only recently have educational dicta permitted classroom teachers the flexibility of dealing with students on the basis of their abilities. Such innovations as team teaching and flexible scheduling are helping to solve the problem raised by rigidity of the graded system.

Physical education is recognizing these difficulties and attempting to deal with them, although the support for inventive scheduling and classification is far less widespread. The irony is that actual physical danger may exist when students varying widely in size (regardless of their chronological age) compete against one another in games or athletics. The wise teacher discerns the potential danger and takes steps to equalize the abilities of individuals for participation and competition. The necessity for some equalization has been recognized in interscholastic athletics, where sports such as boxing and wrestling utilize weight limitations and where schools compete in leagues based upon school population.

Physical and motor traits are now held to be significant in the growth and development of children and youth. Still, until fairly recently, it has not been given adequate attention in volumes on growth and development. However, the data available have prompted the publication of two books written by physical educators. In 1967 Espenschade and Eckert wrote on motor performances from prenatal development through infancy, childhood, and adolescence to adulthood and old age.[1] In 1973 Rarick edited a volume on physical activity as related to growth, development, and health of children and youth.[2] Also, Rarick recently reported on the growing knowledge base in motor development.[3] These publications may be considered milestones for physical education in the expanding field of growth and development.

GROWTH STUDIES

Issues of the *Review of Educational Research* have contained innumerable references devoted to growth and development. Much of this research was sponsored in child-study divisions of universities and with helpful grants from government agencies and foundations. Several extensive growth centers have been established to study the long-term aspects of growth and development. Although the early studies concentrated on physical growth patterns, other information pertaining to social, psychological, and mental parameters was frequently included. Certain of the early growth centers did include variables of significance for physical education; recently, longitudinal growth studies have been conducted by physical educators. Only growth investigations with special relevancy for physical education will be mentioned here.

Iowa Child Welfare
Research Station

The Iowa Child Welfare Research Station was established in 1917 under the direction of Bird T. Baldwin for the purpose of studying the physical growth of children from birth to maturity.[4] Employing large numbers of subjects, the investigators collected data on a variety of

[1] Anna S. Espenschade and Helen M. Eckert, *Motor Development* (Columbus, Ohio: Charles E. Merrill Publishing Co., 1967).

[2] G. Lawrence Rarick, ed., *Physical Activity: Human Growth and Development* (New York: Academic Press, Inc., 1973).

[3] G. Lawrence Rarick, "Motor Development: Its Growing Knowledge Base," *Journal of Physical Education and Recreation*, 51, No. 7 (September 1980), 26.

[4] Bird T. Baldwin, "The Physical Growth of Children from Birth to Maturity," *University of Iowa Studies in Child Welfare*, 1, No. 1 (June 1921), 1.

anthropometric variables, breathing capacity, and strengths of the muscles involving the grip, wrist, and elbow. Use was made of roentgenograms as criteria of anatomical age. Baldwin reported correlation coefficients between measures of strength, weight, height, and lung capacity, finding them to be highest during early adolescence and lowest at 17 years of age. Two physical educators produced monographs developed at the Iowa Station: Charles H. McCloy, *Appraising Physical Status: The Selection of Measurements*, 1936, and *Appraising Physical Status: Methods and Norms*, 1938; and Eleanor Metheny, *Breathing Capacity and Grip Strength of Pre-School Children*, 1940. Howard V. Meredith and Virginia B. Knott prepared age-height-weight charts which were published by the American Medical Association.

Fels Research Institute

The Fels Research Institute was established in 1929 at Antioch College, Ohio, by Samuel S. Fels and directed by Lester W. Sontag[5] to study factors of structure, function, and behavior of children as related to their environment and heredity. Approximately 300 children and their families were studied longitudinally, with data collected on body structure, growth, and health, utilizing the interdisciplinary approach through medicine, anthropology, psychology, genetics, biochemistry, biology, and psychophysiology. This project permitted description of average growth curves, including familial patterns, by comparing similarities between triplets, identical twins, siblings, and unrelated children. The determination of such physiological-biochemical measures as the excretion of sex hormones and other ketosteroids, blood enzyme levels, and other variables have helped in the understanding of the mechanics and significance of differences in the growth process.

Institute of Child Welfare, University of California

The Institute of Child Welfare, founded in 1927, conducted 3 separate long-term developmental investigations at the University of California at Berkeley under the direction of Harold E. Jones.[6] These investigations included the Berkeley Growth Study, the Child Guidance Study, and the Adolescent Growth Study. The Berkeley Growth Study initially enrolled some 30 boys and 30 girls at their birth and successfully followed about 20 of each sex to their maturity. Twenty-

[5] Lester W. Sontag, "Biological and Medical Studies at the Samuel S. Fels Research Institute," *Child Development*, 17, No. 1-2 (March-June 1946), 81.

[6] Harold E. Jones and Nancy Bayley, "The Berkeley Growth Study," *Child Development*, 12, No. 2 (June 1941), 167.

two physical measurements, photographs, hand-wrist X rays, and various psychometric data were obtained. The Child Guidance Study was essentially a psychological and sociological study. However, 4 physical strength measures were given: right and left grip strengths, push strength, and pull strength. In the Adolescent Growth Study, longitudinal data from extensive anthropometry, photographs, physiological measures, and dynamometric strength tests were collected from 70 boys and 75 girls annually from 9 to 17 years. In association with this institute, Espenschade presented a monograph on motor development in adolescence, published in 1940 by the Society for Research in Child Development.

Of special import for physical education, Jones reported from the Berkeley Growth Studies that boys high in physical strength were prone to have good physiques, to be physically fit, and to enjoy favored social status in adolescence.[7] Boys who were low in strength showed a tendency toward asthetic physiques, poor health, social difficulties, lack of status, feelings of inferiority, and personal maladjustment in other areas. Thus, boys at the strength extremes were superior or deficient not in one but in several aspects of size, build, health, and fitness; and, respectively, these advantages or disadvantages were reflected not only in physical activity but also in social participation and in the individual's own attitudes and self-appraisal. Similar results were found for girls but with diminished relationships.

Medford, Oregon, Boys' Growth Study

The Medford Boys' Growth Study was conducted from 1956 to 1968 by the Physical Education Research Laboratory, University of Oregon, in cooperation with the Medford, Oregon, public schools.[8] The purposes of this study follow:

1. To construct physical and motor mean growth and growth acceleration curves for boys 7 through 18 years of age and to study the nature, scope, and significance of individual differences of tests representing body structure, muscular strength, muscular endurance, muscular power, speed and agility, and reaction time.
2. To relate these physical and motor growth factors to physiological maturity, physique type, nutritional status, sociopersonal adjustment, interests, and scholastic aptitude and achievement.

[7]Harold E. Jones, "Physical Activity as a Factor in Social Adjustment in Adolescence," *Journal of Educational Research*, 40 (December 1946), 287.

[8]H. Harrison Clarke, *Physical and Motor Tests in the Medford Boys' Growth Study* (Englewood Cliffs, N.J.: Prentice-Hall, Inc., 1971).

3. To identify those physical and motor factors that are the most significant growth indicators, particularly as related to adolescence.
4. To contrast all traits in the study for boys who make and who do not make athletic teams competing in interschool competition; to make the same contrast for boys who score high and low on strength tests and batteries, agility and speed, muscular power, and reaction time.
5. To revise and construct strength and other tests for boys of all ages; and to determine the interrelationships of the factors included in the study at various ages.

During the first year of the Medford study, approximately 100 boys were tested at ages 7, 9, 12, and 15 years, and 40 boys at ages 10, 11, 13, and 14 years. In each subsequent year, the 100-subject groups were retested until graduating from high school. Four types of analyses were made, as follows: (1) cross-sectional, with 40 boys at each age from 9 to 15 years inclusive; (2) longitudinal, with boys followed until high school graduation; (3) convergence, as proposed by Bell,[9] at the end of 4 years, in which the boys in the longitudinal phases were joined at the overlapping years of 9, 12, and 15 years; (4) single year, in order to hold constant the effect of chronological age on those variables that change with age. (The accumulation of subjects at the older ages as the longitudinal phases progressed resulted in numbers at individual ages ranging from 223 to 340.) For all tests, except of scholastic aptitude and achievement, the subjects were tested within 2 months of their birthdays, in order to assure reasonable homogeneity as related to chronological age. The test items included in the study were as follows:

1. *Maturity factors.* Chronological age, skeletal age, pubescent development.
2. *Physique type.* Sheldon's somatotype components.
3. *Body size measures.* Body weight, standing and sitting heights, leg length, hip width, girths of upper arm, chest, abdomen, buttocks, thigh, and calf, lung capacity, Wetzel Grid, and skinfold measures over triceps, apex of scapula, lateral abdomen. Combinations of these measures were also used as indices.
4. *Strength elements and batteries.* Grip strength, back lift, leg lift, pull-ups, bar push-ups, Rogers' Strength and Physical Fitness Indices, 11 cable-tension strength tests of muscle groups throughout the body.

[9] Richard Q. Bell, "An Accelerated Longitudinal Approach," *Child Development,* 24, No. 2 (June 1953), 144.

5. *Motor tests.* 60-yard shuttle run, standing broad jump, and total-body reaction and movement times.

6. *Scholastic aptitude and achievement.* Grade point average and the following tests depending on age: California Mental Maturity (Forms S and Secondary), Otis Quick-Scoring Gamma, Stanford Achievement (Elementary, Intermediate, and Advanced), Gates Reading (Primary and Advanced), Iowa Test of Educational Development.

7. *Psycho-personal adjustment.* The following tests depending on age: Sociometric Questionnaire, Cowell Personal Distance Scale, Cowell Social Behavior Trend, Adjective Check List, California Psychological Inventory, Mental Health Analysis, Level of Aspiration.

8. *Interest.* The following depending on age: Children's Interest Blank, Adjective Check List, Dreese and Mooney Interest Inventory, What I Like To Do, Kudor Preference Record (Forms D and Vocational), Garretson and Symonds Interest Form, Strong Vocational Interest Blank.

Wisconsin Growth Study

The Wisconsin Growth Study was conducted by Rarick over a period of 6 years, ages 7 through 12 and again at age 17.[10] The following measurements were taken annually on 25 boys and 24 girls:

1. *Anthropometric.* Weight, standing and sitting heights, total and lower leg lengths, total and upper arm lengths, biachromial and bi-iliac diameters, and girths of chest, upper arm, and calf.

2. *Strength.* Eight cable-tension strength tests of the upper and lower extremeties.

3. *Motor.* 30-yard dash, velocity overarm baseball throw, and standing broad jump.

4. *Radiographs (first three years).* Hand-wrist and soft tissue on leg.

In the report by Rarick and Smoll, height, weight, and physique showed relatively stable growth trends from 7 to 12 years of age and from childhood years to age 17 years. Growth in dynamometric strength of muscles of the upper extremeties was variable, that of the lower extremeties less so. Standing broad jump performance showed relatively stable growth trends, but velocity throwing performance was highly variable.

[10]G. Lawrence Rarick and Frank L. Smoll, "Stability of Growth in Strength and Motor Performance from Childhood to Adolescence," *Human Biology*, 39, No. 3 (September 1967), 295. Also, personal correspondence, September 14, 1981.

PROBLEMS PERTAINING
TO GROWTH AND DEVELOPMENT

The common concept characterizing growth and development studies is that they are limited to the determination of changes in boys and girls as they grow up. Of course, this determination is a major function of such studies, but it need not nor should not be so limited. The following questions indicate the scope that is possible in this area of research as applied to physical education:

1. What are the shapes of mean growth curves and growth acceleration curves for various measures of such traits as body size and proportion, muscular strength, muscular endurance, and motor ability performances?
2. In what ways and to what extent do boys and girls differ in maturity, physique type, body size, strength, endurance, and motor ability elements? What significance have these differences for physical education?
3. What degrees of consistency exist for the various measures from age to age as children grow up?
4. What are the individual and group growth patterns of physical and motor traits for boys and girls who become athletes, honor-roll students, school dropouts, leaders, delinquents, and the like?
5. What relationships exist between physical and motor traits and physiological maturity, physique type, nutritional status, socio-personal adjustment, socioeconomic status, interests, and scholastic aptitude and achievement?
6. What are the significant age and sex differences found among the various growth and development parameters?
7. What is the extent of individual differences in maturity, physique type, body size, relative and gross strength, and motor abilities for each chronological age? What significance do these differences have for athletic success, peer status, sociopersonal adjustment, and scholastic achievement?
8. Based on maturity assessments made at an early age, what rate of growth change occurs for those boys and girls who are advanced as compared with those who are retarded?
9. What differences in growth patterns exist for children who demonstrate high strength or high motor ability at a young age as compared with those who score low on such measures?
10. What changes in growth and development occur during the life cycle from childhood and youth to maturity and through adulthood to old age? What differences in mental achievement and sociopersonal traits are associated with such changes?

11. What differences in maturity, physical, and motor parameters exist between sexes and between various cultural and racial groups?

Once oriented to growth and development research, the astute student will think of many other significant questions in need of answers. Further, all sorts of comparative and relationship studies can be conducted. Thus, growth studies can be and usually are much more than just a succession of means for various tests over a period of years which indicate the changes taking place as children grow up.

MATURITY

Performances in physical activities are influenced to a considerable extent by the degree of progress made toward full maturity by an individual. Certainly, this is a factor in athletics: The more mature individuals for their age have advantages in making varsity teams and in playing regularly. This concept may be extended to many other physical education, as well as education, endeavors.

According to Greulich, the chronological age of a child is often little more than an indication of the length of time he or she has lived; it does not necessarily bear a close relationship to the amount of progress made toward maturity.[11] Tanner has stated ". . . the bald statement that a boy is age 14 is in most contexts hopelessly vague."[12] Consequently, some means other than chronological age is needed to assess the maturation of children in growth studies.

Skeletal Age

A commonly used indicator of maturity utilized in growth studies is skeletal age, the degree of development of the skeleton as shown by X rays. Each bone begins as a primary center of ossification and passes through various stages of calcification, enlargement, and shaping. The process continues until adult status is reached. These changes can be seen in an X ray, which distinguishes ossified areas from areas of cartilage, where ossification has not yet occurred. In theory, any or all parts of the skeleton can be used to provide an assessment of maturity. In practice, however, the hand-wrist area is the most convenient and commonly utilized. This practice has been found acceptable, since

[11] W. W. Greulich, "The Relationship of Skeletal Status to the Physical Growth and Development of Children," in *Dynamics of Growth Processes*, ed. Edgar J. Boell (Princeton, N.J.: Princeton University Press, 1954), 213.

[12] J. M. Tanner, *Growth at Adolescence*, 2nd ed. (Springfield, Ill.: Charles C. Thomas, Publisher, 1962), 55.

investigators have shown that the hand-wrist ossification pattern closely approximates the degree of total skeletal ossification.

Greulich and Pyle have presented an atlas containing hand-wrist X-ray reproductions separately for boys and girls.[13] Age standards are provided for each 3 months during the first year and for each 6 months thereafter until maturity is reached (set at 19 years). In assessing skeletal age, some 30 bones and epiphyses of an obtained X ray are compared with those in the atlas. The average of all assessments is taken as the individual's skeletal age, usually given in months. Skeletal age corresponds to chronological age: If a 15-year-old boy has the typical hand-wrist X ray of boys 15 years of age, his skeletal age is also 15; if his X ray conforms to those typical of boys more or less than 15, he is respectively advanced or retarded in maturity.

Difficulties to be encountered in obtaining the hand-wrist X ray are related to equipment and safety precautions. If the investigator must rely upon commercial or medical facilities, the cost is probably prohibitive and would make field testing difficult. However, portable equipment may be obtained that can be set up quickly and used by trained operators. Darkroom facilities, if already available, would solve the problem of film development. X-ray development resources, especially if located on campus, as in the Student Health Center, might not be too great an expense if a large number of X rays could be processed at one time.

The portable X-ray machine used in the Medford study had maximum rated capacity of 80 K.V.P. and 20 milliamperes. Maximum protection from radiation was provided as follows: (1) placement of a lead unit with oblong opening in the aluminum cone of the X-ray machine, which restricted radiation to the area of the X-ray films; and (2) incorporation of lead shields into all sides and the bottom of the box into which the hand was placed through a slit. The standards followed to produce satisfactory roetgenographs are as follows:

1. *Type of film exposure holder.* no-screen cardboard holder for 8″ × 10″ X-ray film.
2. *Focal distance.* the lower edge of the aluminum cone placed a distance of 30 inches directly above the cardboard holder.
3. *Amperage.* 15 milliamperes.
4. *Voltage.* 110 kilovolts.
5. *Exposure time.* 1 sec.

---

[13]William Walter Greulich and S. Idell Pyle, *Radiographic Atlas of Skeletal Development of the Hand and Wrist*, 2nd ed. (Stanford, Calif.: Stanford University Press, 1959).

Reports from inspections made by the Occupational Health Section, Oregon State Board of Health, indicate that the amount of X-ray radiation with this equipment and under these conditions is slight and well within tolerance limits. Before using X ray in research, safety checks such as these should be made.

The process of film evaluation is quite time consuming. Reasoning that if the hand and wrist could be taken as indicative of growth of the whole skeleton, then it might be possible that fewer than approximately 30 sites (depending on age) on the X ray would give an accurate assessment of the total. Considerable advantage would result if a reduction could be achieved without losing appreciably in the validity of the ratings. In order to test this hypothesis, Clarke and Hayman tested 273 boys 9 through 15 years of age, intercorrelated the skeletal ages of the individual bones, and then correlated them with the total hand-wrist assessment.[14] A multiple correlation of .9989 was obtained between the skeletal age of all bones and the following 4 bones located longitudinally in the center of the hand, as shown in Figure 15.1: the capitate, metacarpal III, proximal phalanx III, and middle phalanx

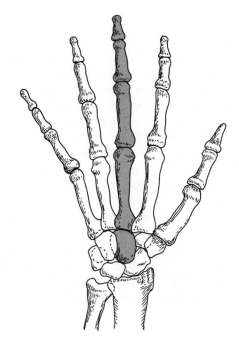

Figure 15.1 Four Bone Assessment of Skeletal Age

[14]H. Harrison Clarke and Noel R. Hayman, "Reduction of Bone Assessments Necessary for the Skeletal Age Determination of Boys," *Research Quarterly*, 33, No. 2 (May 1962), 202.

III. The difference among the skeletal age means by assessment of the four bones was .15 month (about five days); the t ratio was .03.

Great differences exist in the skeletal ages of boys and girls of the same chronological age. In the Medford study, boys were tested within 2 months of their birthdays at each age from 7 through 17 years. The standard deviations fluctuated between 11.9 and 15.1 months. The ranges varied from a low of 58 months at 17 years (where some truncation at the higher level occurred) to a high of 85 months at age 13 years; the median range was 71 months, nearly 6 years. Illustrating the magnitude of these differences at age 14 years, is the fact that approximately two-thirds of 168 boys tested had skeletal ages between 12 and 16 years; yet, these same boys did not vary more than 4 months in chronological age. The skeletal age range for these 14-year-old boys, of course, was much greater—between 10.3 and 16.9 years. From studies of the significance of individual differences in maturity in the Medford series, the following generalizations can be made: The more mature boys were taller, heavier, and stronger and had a greater potential for success in interscholastic athletics; they were prone to higher levels of aspiration and better psychological adjustment.[15]

Pubescent Assessment

Once boys and girls enter adolescence, pubic assessment may be utilized to evaluate their maturity. For boys, the transition to the pubescent state is gradual, evident by the rapid growth of fine pubic hair, which becomes pigmented; eventually pubescence ends when the pubic hair becomes coarse and kinky. Other secondary sex characteristics also occur, such as deepening of the voice and an increase in development of the genitalia, but these are not as satisfactory as pubic hair for maturity assessment. For girls, the age of menarche is usually used as the index of pubescence, although the first appearance of pubic hair precedes menarche by a year or more.

One of the earliest attempts to standardize a rating scheme of pubescent assessment was by Crampton, who divided pubescence into three stages: the growth of fine pubic hair, the pigmentation of the hair, and the appearance of the kink or twist.[16] Subsequently, a 5-point scale was devised by Greulich and others in such a manner that $1 =$ prepubescence, $2 =$ appearance of fine pubic hair, $3 =$ pigmentation,

[15]Clarke, *Medford Boys' Growth Study*, Ch. 2.

[16]C. Ward Crampton, "Physiological Age—A Fundamental Principle," *American Physical Education Review*, 13, No. 3-6 (May-June 1908), reprinted in *Child Development*, 15, No. 1 (March 1944), 1.

4 = appearance of kinky or curly hair, and 5 = postpubescence with the development of the external sexual characteristics of adults.[17]

These categories are useful in grouping the population under study but are only general approximations of physiological maturity. They do not indicate how long an individual has been in each stage, and the adolescent period, defined as the time between puberty and maturity, is short in comparison with the preadolescent and postadolescent periods. Thus, a person is classified as category 1 until he exhibits the first signs of puberty and is given 5 for any time after achieving maturity. During the interim time, however, these designations may prove useful.

Clarke and Degutis compared the skeletal ages and various physical and motor factors with the pubescent development of 10-, 13-, and 16-year-old boys.[18] Physical maturation was differentiated by pubescent assessment most effectively at 13 years of age, although it was not so sensitive to maturational changes as was skeletal age. Although the distribution by pubescent assessment of 13-year-old boys disclosed some boys at this age in each of the 5 pubescent categories, most of them were equally distributed in pubescent groups 2 and 3, according to the classification of Greulich referred to before. At 10 years of age, nearly all boys were classified in group 1; at age 16 years, they appeared mostly in group 5 but with some in group 4. Considerable overlapping occurred in the skeletal age ranges of adjacent pubescent groups at each chronological age. With few exceptions, 13- and 16-year-old boys who were advanced in pubescent development for their respective ages had higher mean scores on body size, strength, and motor tests. At 16 years of age, a significantly greater percentage of ectomorphs were found in group 4 than in group 5.

PHYSIQUE TYPE

Body build has been a matter of interest to scholars in the field of growth and development for a long time, as efforts have been made to account for human performance and behavior. A variety of descriptive terms has been employed with varying degrees of success over the

[17]W. W. Greulich, and others, "Somatic and Endocrine Studies of Puberal and Adolescent Boys," *Monographs of the Society for Research in Child Development*, 7, No. 3 (1942).

[18]H. Harrison Clarke and Ernest W. Degutis, "Comparison of Skeletal Age and Various Physical and Motor Factors with the Pubescent Development of 10-, 13-, and 16-Year-Old Boys," *Research Quarterly*, 33, No. 3 (October 1962), 356.

years; terms such as respiratory (asthmatic), cerebral (bookworm), plethoric (phlegmatic), and phthisic (energetic) illustrate attempts made along these lines. In 1925, Kretschmer suggested the terms *pyknic* to represent the fat body type, *athletic* to designate the muscular individual, and *asthenic* for the lean person.[19]

After extensive research, Sheldon, Stevens, and Tucker proposed that human beings could not be classified into just 3 physique types, but that nearly all individuals were mixtures.[20] However, they did designate 3 primary components of body build that provide first-order criteria for differentiating among individuals. These components are briefly described as: *endomorphy*, predominance of soft roundness throughout the various regions of the body; *mesomorphy*, heavy, hard, and rectangular physique with rugged, massive muscles, and large prominent bones; *ectomorphy*, frail, delicate body structure with thin segments, anteroposteriorly. Each of the components is rated on a 7-point scale to indicate its relative predominance in the total physique; half-units are used for finer differentiation. The first numeral in a series refers to endomorphy; the second, to mesomorphy; the third, to ectomorphy. Thus, a 4-4-4 describes a physique with an equal and moderate amount of all 3 components.

The entire somatotyping process is described in an atlas by Sheldon, Dupertius, and McDermott.[21] Descriptive materials have also been presented by Clarke;[22] various modifications of somatotyping are included, especially those by Carter and Health, Cureton, and Parnell. The atlas by Sheldon and others describes and illustrates 88 somatotypes (using whole numerals) as found among a large sample of 46,000 adult males. Although an altas does not exist for women, the same descriptive process employed for males is applied; the somatotype difference between men and women is in their respective distributions. Somatotyping procedures were satisfactorily applied to boys from 7 through 18 years, as demonstrated in the Medford study.[23]

Clarke, Irving, and Heath found that endomorphs and endomesomorphs exceeded the other somatotype categories in the body bulk measures of body weight, Wetzel physique channel, upper arm

[19]William H. Sheldon, S. S. Stevens, and W. B. Tucker, *The Varieties of Human Physique* (New York: Harper & Row, Publishers, Inc., 1940).

[20]Sheldon, Stevens, and Tucker, ibid.

[21]William H. Sheldon, C. W. Dupertius, and Eugene McDermott, *Atlas of Men* (New York: Harper & Row, Publishers, Inc., 1954).

[22]H. Harrison Clarke, *Application of Measurement to Health and Physical Education*, 5th ed. (Englewood Cliffs, N.J.: Prentice-Hall, Inc., 1976), 87.

[23]Clarke, *Medford Boys' Growth Study*, Ch. 3.

girth, chest girth, and hip width:[24] in general, the mesomorphs had higher means on these measures than did the ectomorphs and midtypes. Due to their excessive weight, the endomorphs were at a great disadvantage in performing pull-ups and push-ups; their means for these tests were .06 and 2.1 times, respectively. The mesomorphs showed superiority over the other categories in Strength Index and Physical Fitness Index, as well as pull-ups and push-ups. The ectomorphs and midtypes had higher Physical Fitness Index means than did the endomorphs and endo-mesomorphs.

Munroe, Clarke, and Heath[25] and Sinclair[26] found that relationships between somatotype components and measures of body structure were markedly greater than corresponding zero-order correlations where structural measures were partialed out for each age 9 through 17 years. For example, at 12 years of age the correlation between endomorphy and weight was .71; with height held constant, the partial correlation was .86. Also, the correlation between ectomorphy and height was insignificant: with weight held constant, the partial correlation rose to .93. These results demonstrated a logical deduction that physique type is independent of body size; a mesomorph can be small or large, young or old. Further, high multiple correlations between somatotype components and anthropometric variables were reported; regression equations to predict the components at the various ages appear in these studies. Of interest, zero-order correlations between .92 and .97 for these ages were obtained by Sinclair.

Sinclair studied the stability of the somatotype components of boys: 2 groups of boys served as subjects, 9 through 12 and 12 through 17 years of age. The highest interage correlations were found for adjacent ages: .75 to .85 for endomorphy, .83 to .93 for mesomorphy, and .85 to .90 for ectomorphy. The lowest correlations were for the 5-year gap, 12 to 17 years; these correlations were .50, .60, and .57 respectively for the 3 components. The differences between component means for ages 9 through 12 years were not significant; some signifi-

[24]H. Harrison Clarke, Robert N. Irving, and Barbara Honeyman Heath, "Relation of Maturity, Structural and Strength Measures to the Somatotypes of Boys 9 through 15 Years of Age," *Research Quarterly*, 32, No. 4 (December 1961), 449.

[25]Richard A. Munroe, H. Harrison Clarke, and Barbara H. Heath, "A Somatotype Method for Young Boys," *American Journal of Physical Anthropology*, n.s. 30, No. 2 (March 1969), 195.

[26]Gary D. Sinclair, "Stability of Physique Types of Boys Nine through Twelve Years of Age" (Master's thesis, University of Oregon, 1966); and Gary D. Sinclair, "Stability of Somatotype Components of Boys Twelve through Seventeen Years of Age and Their Relationships to Selected Physical and Motor Factors" (Ph.D. diss., University of Oregon, 1969).

cant differences were found for the older ages. The correlations between endomorphy and mesomorphy were not significant for ages 9 and 17 years; for the intervening ages, the correlations ranged between .21 and .37. Ectomorphy correlated negatively with both endomorphy and mesomorphy; the correlations were comparable, between −.64 and −.76.

From many analyses in the Medford study, the following generalizations may be made. Endomorphic boys are handicapped by excessive body bulk, by low strength relative to size, by inability to perform arm-shoulder muscular endurance tests, and inability to make and be successful on athletic teams. They have negative self-images, but seem psychologically well adjusted. Mesomorphic boys have advantages related to greater gross and relative muscular strength, muscular endurance, successful athletic participation, peer status, and psychological adjustment. Ectomorphic boys have disadvantages related to less body bulk and gross strength, but they have advantages related to relative strength and arm-shoulder muscular endurance. They show some lack of peer status and psychological adjustment and some favorable self-image characteristics. Skeletal age had significant but low correlations with somatotype correlations; the range of correlations for boys 9 through 12 years of age was .22 to .35 for endomorphy, .21 to .26 for mesomorphy, and −.27 to −.33 for ectomorphy.

ANTHROPOMETRY

Anthropometry, measurements of body structure, is the oldest type of body measurement known, dating back to the beginning of recorded history. It was also an early type of testing in physical education. On the theory that exercise should be prescribed to affect muscle size, emphasis was placed upon muscle symmetry and proportion. In 1861 Hitchcock, and later Sargent, produced profile charts to reveal how individuals compared with their standards. Sargent's chart contained 44 anthropometric measurements, as well as a number of strength tests. Fifty such tests were recommended by the American Association for the Advancement of Physical Education.

Numerous anthropometric measures are available and have been used in various growth studies. One use of these measures is to show a succession of annual means during the growth period. Figure 15.2 illustrates a mean anthropometric growth curve, which represents mean body weight obtained from 2 longitudinal groups of boys, one sample from 7 to 12 years and the other from 12 to 17 years. Contrasting curves may also be utilized to compare the growth patterns of boys and girls or of those from different races or cultures.

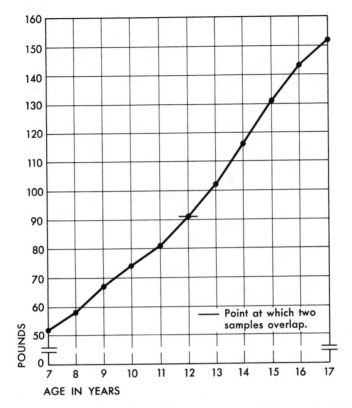

Figure 15.2 Growth Curve for Body Weight

Another use of anthropometry is to determine relationships between body structure and motor performance. Observations of such relationships are commonplace: observe the well-proportional bodies of wrestlers and gymnasts, the superstructure of great basketball competitors, the solidarity of top-flight football athletes, the wiriness of champion distance runners, and the massive builds of great shot-putters and discus throwers. On a less grand scale, relationships with flexed-tensed arm girth illustrate this use; the test is performed as shown in Figure 15.3. In the Medford study, the correlations of this test with other girth measures were mostly in the .80s for each age, 7 through 18 years. For these same ages, the correlations with gross strength batteries, the Rogers' Strength Index and the average of 11 cable-tension strength tests, varied between .35 and .65. Further, boys with the highest arm girths were 50% to 100% greater than boys with the smallest girths at the various ages.

A difficulty faced by the researcher contemplating work in the

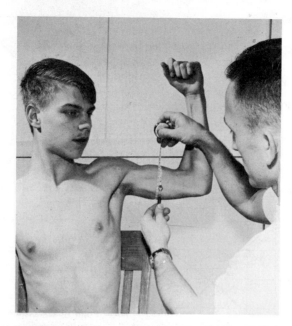

Figure 15.3 Flexed-Tensed Arm Girth Test

field of anthropometry is that of site selection. As yet, no established test routine is available in anthropometry, so the choice is dependent upon the desires of the investigator. Not only are sites not specific, but the manner of obtaining the precise measures is still largely nonstandardized. Attempts have been made from time to time to reach some agreement concerning methods in the field of anthropometry. In fact, the first proposals were made at the congress of the German anthropological societies in 1874, and later in France and Russia.[27] At the 13th International Congress of Prehistoric Anthropology and Archeology held in Monaco in 1906, serious consideration was given to this problem, resulting in the formation of an International Agreement on Anthropometry. This work was continued by the British Association for the Advancement of Science and culminated with another agreement at the 14th Congress in 1912 at Geneva. As a result, certain general principles were established, many landmarks were descriptively located, and numerous body measurements were defined.

These efforts notwithstanding, it cannot be claimed today that uniformity exists in anthropometric testing. In order to reduce misunderstanding as much as possible, measurement procedures must be

[27]T. D. Stewart, ed., *Hrdlicka's Practical Anthropometry*, 4th ed. (Philadelphia: The Wistar Institute of Anatomy and Biology, 1952), pp. 12-17.

defined precisely. For example, even though body weight seems a straightforward test, at least three important sources of error bear upon the measure for research purposes: (1) The first source concerns the amount and type of clothing worn by the subject. The use of nude weight would solve the problem. However, if this is found undesirable, a minimum of gymnasium clothing, less shoes, would be acceptable; all subjects should be dressed alike. (2) The second source concerns the accuracy required. If weight is to be recorded to the nearest half-pound, this should be made clear. (3) The third source is proper scale calibration. It might be argued that a small systematic error in scale calibration in a cross-sectional study would affect all subjects in an equal manner and thus do no serious injustice to a statistical treatment of the data. However, even if one could rationalize this point of view, the acceptance of such error in longitudinal studies would be hazardous, since all data must be directly comparable. Further, valid comparisons of results by different investigators require proper calibration of instruments.

Although the example of body weight has been used, it should be obvious that the same concepts are applicable to other anthropometric variables. Standardization of testing technique is essential in growth studies, as often different members of a testing team become involved from time to time. Assurance must be obtained that *exactly* the same procedures are employed at all times. This should require practice testing of different subjects to insure adequate repeatability of measures. In such instances the correlation coefficient between two separate tests will help decide upon testing consistency, as described in Chapter 10.

The types of instruments that are required for anthropometric research are usually few in number and ordinarily quite simple. Height—both standing and sitting—is measured by a stadiometer or other device; breadth measures are obtained by use of sliding wooden or metal calipers; circumference of limbs is taken by a cloth or steel tape; and skinfolds are determined with fat calipers.

Inasmuch as the instruments themselves may remain constant, the selection of a site must be rigidly defined and then precisely measured. Clothing must not interfere in any of the anthropometric measures for obvious reasons. When dealing with girths where the tape must be placed around soft tissue, care must be taken to exert the same tension on the ends of the tape at each administration. Tapes with a built-in calibrated spring handle (Gulick handle as shown in Figure 15.4), serve best for this testing. Variables such as chest circumference will fluctuate slightly with the breathing cycle; it is often expedient to carefully estimate the midpoint between extremes of quiet inhalation and exhalation and use this figure. Fat folds are frequently difficult measurements for the novice tester, but once again care must be taken to administer the test properly without including muscle in the skinfold or deviating from the site as defined. Since many of these items are included in tests of nutritional status or as determiners of body composition, errors of testing may be compounded when introduced into regression formulas.

SKINFOLDS

Skinfold thickness has long been a technique for estimating total body fat in humans. In addition to representing fat changes during growth, they are a useful indicator of nutritional status, especially when more sophisticated body composition procedures, such as the densiometric method described in Chapter 11, are lacking. From skinfold measures, an estimation of total body fat can be made.

Several skinfold calipers are available. The recommended amount of pressure to be applied to the skinfold is 10 grams per square mm; the size of the contact surface of the caliper may vary from 20 to 40 square mm, depending in part on the shape of the contact surface.[28] Three calipers that meet these specifications are the Vernier, the Harpenden, and the Lange. The skinfold sites generally accepted for determination of body fat are at the back of the arm and at the subscapular position on the back; a third site is suggested on the midaxillary line at the level of the umbilicus. The procedure for testing skinfolds is illustrated in Figure 15.4; the site is at the back of the arm over the triceps muscle at a point midway between the tip of the shoulder and the tip of the elbow.

A common technique for determining percentage of fat is by use of the formula developed by Keys and Brozek:[29]

Per cent fat = 100 (4.201/specific gravity − 3.813).

The specific gravity in this instance may be obtained by use of the following calculations:

Specific Gravity = $1.1017 - (0.000282)(A) - (0.000736)(B)$

$- (0.000883)(C)$

where A, B, and C are the abdominal, chest, and arm skinfolds, respectively. Instructions for obtaining these skinfolds indicate right side measures at the following sites:

[28]Josef Brozek, ed., *Body Measurements and Human Physique* (Detroit: Wayne State University Press, 1956), p. 10.

[29]Ancel Keyes and Josef Brozek, "Body Fat in Adult Man," *Physiological Reviews*, 33, No. 3 (July 1953), 245.

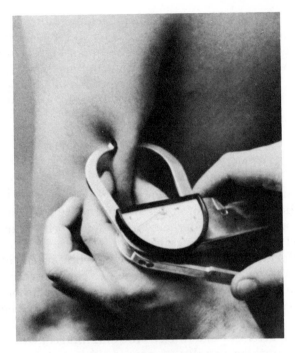

Figure 15.4 Skinfold Test over Back of Arm

1. *Abdominal skinfold.* At the midaxillary line at waist level.
2. *Chest skinfold.* At the level of the xiphoid in the midaxillary line.
3. *Arm skinfold.* At the midposterior, midpoint between the tip of the acromion and the tip of the olecranon with the elbow in 90° flexion and the arm hanging at the side.

Following the calculation of percentage of fat, the total amount of fat may be determined as the appropriate percentage of body weight. The difference between fat weight and body weight is lean body weight.

Fat tests may also be made on X-ray photographs, although it may not be required since the correlation between X-ray measures of adipose tissue and skinfolds obtained by caliper ranges from .79 to .88.[30] The relationship of skinfold measures of 12-year-old boys to

---

[30]H. Harrison Clarke, L. Richard Geser, and Stanley B. Hunsdon, "Comparison of Upper Arm Measurements by Use of Roentgenogram and Anthropometric Techniques," *Research Quarterly,* 27, No. 4 (December 1956), 379; and Stanley M. Garn and E. L. Gorman, "Comparison of Pinch-Caliper and Teleoroentgenogrammetric Measurements of Subcutaneous Fat," *Human Biology,* 28, No. 4 (December 1956), 407.

various maturity, physique, strength, muscular endurance, and motor ability characteristics was investigated by Geser.[31] When correlated with physique components, endomorphy had a high positive correlation of .824 with adipose tissue, while ectomorphy correlated negatively, −.657. The remainder of the correlations of adipose tissue with maturity, mesomorphy, strength, and motor measures were relatively low.

MUSCULAR STRENGTH

Strength tests have not been commonly employed in longitudinal growth studies. The work of Jones at the Institute of Child Welfare, University of California, Berkeley, is a noteworthy exception. His strength tests were limited to right and left grips and arm pull and push, all performed with a manuometer which had special attachments for the pull and push tests. However, Jones considered his results so significant as to warrant a monograph, in which he presented the results of his strength studies of boys and girls from 7 through 17 years of age.[32]

Muscular strength is defined as the maximal contractive power of muscles. Strength is usually measured with a dynamometer or a tensiometer. Dynamometric tests include right and left grips and back and leg lifts. These tests, along with lung capacity, pull-ups, and push-ups, comprise a gross battery, the Rogers' Strength Index; by relating the Strength Index to norms based on the individual's sex, age, and weight, a relative battery is obtained.[33] While the Strength Index increases with growth, the Physical Fitness Index does not, due to the norming process. Tensiometer tests are available for testing the strength of 38 muscle groups throughout the body.[34] It should be noted that, while strength increases with age, it is also affected by developmental activities. The separation of growth and development effects would be difficult and has not been attempted in growth studies which include strength variables. Logically, this situation may not be serious where developmental activities in the population sampled are com-

---

[31]Leo Richard Geser, "Skin Fold Measures of Twelve-Year-Old Boys as Related to Various Maturity, Physique, Strength, and Motor Measures" (Ph.D. diss., University of Oregon, 1965).

[32]Harold E. Jones, *Motor Performance and Growth* (Berkeley: University of California Press, 1949).

[33]H. Harrison Clarke, *Application of Measurement to Health and Physical Education*, 5th ed. (Englewood Cliffs, N.J.: Prentice-Hall, Inc., 1976), Ch. 7.

[34]H. Harrison Clarke and David H. Clarke, *Developmental and Adapted Physical Education*, 2nd ed. (Englewood Cliffs, N.J.: Prentice-Hall, Inc., 1978), pp. 100-27.

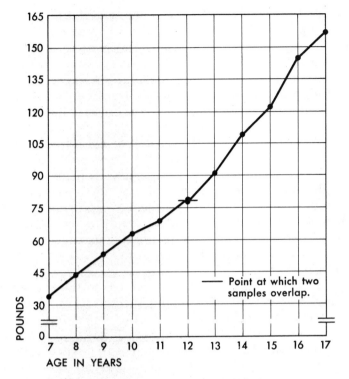

Figure 15.5 Growth Curves for 11 Cable-Tension Strength Tests

monly applied. Still, growth curves of populations with varying developmental exposures may be comparable, although the mean strength scores at the various ages would differ.

Figure 15.5 illustrates a mean strength curve, which represents the average of 11 cable-tension strength tests from the 2 overlapping longitudinal samples of boys from which the body weight curve was prepared (Figure 15.2). As can be seen, the increase in strength is reasonably linear from the youngest to the oldest age. The individual differences in strength were pronounced. At each of the 11 ages, the strongest boy was 2 to 3 times stronger than the weakest; at most ages the range of strength scores nearly reached or exceeded their respective means.

The specificity of the strength of muscle groups throughout the body, as contrasted with an interlacing strength communality, has been demonstrated.[35] Both interrelations of strength tests and their factor analyses support this observation. Seldom did such interrela-

[35]Clarke, *Medford Boys' Growth Study*, Ch. 5.

tions exceed .80; some were so low as to be insignificant. In factor analyses by principal axis solutions with varimax rotations, not one but the following factors were identified for boys 9 through 16 years of age: arm-shoulder strength, leg-back strength, lower-leg strength, and grip strength. In factor analyses of 25 cable-tension strength tests for boys and girls at various school levels from fourth grade through college, single tests were found on 74% of the rotations. Despite this specificity of the strengths of muscle groups, a small number of such tests will reflect the total musculation of the body. Multiple correlations of .95 and above were obtained between the average of 25 cable-tension tests and 3 or 4 tests for boys and girls separately in upper elementary, junior high, and senior high schools, and for men and women in college. In this context, the most frequently appearing strength tests were: shoulder extension, knee extension, and ankle-plantar flexion for boys; shoulder extension and flexion, hip extension and flexion, trunk flexion and extension, and ankle-plantar flexion, depending on school level, for girls.[36]

Muscular strength is intricately related to the entire physical-motor complex of individuals, including their maturity, physique, body size, and motor and athletic abilities. In the Medford study, gross strength (SI) was among the best differentiators of athletic ability at all school levels and in all interscholastic sports. Stronger boys also showed better psychological development, greater peer status, and enhanced self-image. Outstanding athletes in football, basketball, and track had superior relative strength scores (PFI), especially at the elementary and high school levels. The PFI showed positive relationships to motor ability tests; high PFI boys had greater peer status, positive self-image, and good psychological adjustment.

MUSCULAR ENDURANCE

Muscular endurance is defined as the ability of muscles to perform work, such as lifting a constant load as many times as possible as in weight training. Muscular endurance must assume some muscular strength: to do a pull-up test, for example, the person must have sufficient strength in the arms and shoulders to lift the body. However, muscle groups of the same strength may possess different degrees of endurance. Further, the relationships between strength and absolute and relative endurance of the muscles differ drastically. To show this differentiation: the correlation between strength and endurance is

[36]H. Harrison Clarke and Richard A. Munroe, *Test Manual: Oregon Cable-Tension Strength Test Batteries for Boys and Girls from Fourth Grade through College* (Eugene, Oregon: Microform Publications in Health, Physical Education, and Recreation, 1970).

around .90 when the load is a constant amount for all individuals (absolute); the correlation is about −.40 when the load is a proportion of the strength of each individual's muscles (relative).[37]

Although seldom utilized in growth studies, several muscular endurance tests are available for this purpose. In the Medford study, pull-ups, parallel-bar push-ups, and Rogers' arm strength scores were included as tests of the endurance of the arm and shoulder girdle muscles. Modified forms of these tests are appropriate for girls. Pull-ups and push-ups may be considered as measures of relative muscular endurance since only the number of repetitions is counted; the weight of the subject and the distance the body is lifted are not considered in the score. The Rogers' arm strength score is a gross muscular endurance measure, since these factors are credited in the performance; the formula for this score is as follows:

$$[.1 \ (Weight) + (Height - 60)] \ [Pull\text{-}ups + Push\text{-}ups]$$

The growth curve for bar push-ups for boys 8 through 17 years of age is shown in Figure 15.6; as for body weight, two overlapping longitudinal samples of boys were tested (Figure 15.2). This curve shows a slow rise from ages 8 to 12 years; starting at age 12, a sharp rise occurred with sizable increases each year. The ranges were erratic due to the presence of extremely high scores at some ages. Truncation was found at all but 3 ages, as indicated by zero scores. Skewness of distribution may be inferred from the fact that the highest scores at the various ages were 3 to 5 times their respective means. A similar pattern was evident for the pull-up test; however, the age means were lower and the truncation at the various ages was greater. These factors should be understood in selecting tests for growth studies, as they point to some weaknesses for this purpose. Also, as for muscular strength, muscular endurance can be improved through use and conditioning of the muscles, so the separation of growth and development effects during the growing years is difficult, if not impossible.

MOTOR PERFORMANCE

Motor performance is a broad term that includes a wide variety of physical tasks, such as running, jumping, throwing, and the like, and it extends to a number of athletic events, such as track and field and swimming. The development of such abilities through childhood to maturity should be of interest to those in physical education, as they have been to those studying other developmental traits.

[37]H. Harrison Clarke, "Muscular Strength-Endurance Relationships," *Archives of Physical Medicine and Rehabilitation*, 38, No. 9 (September 1957), 584.

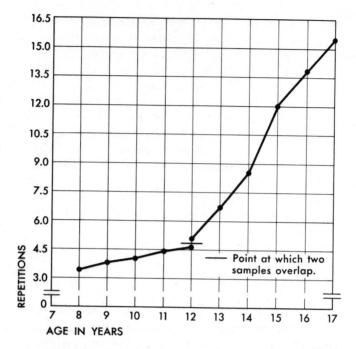

Figure 15.6   Growth Curve for Boys' Bar Push-ups

Several growth studies have utilized various motor performance tests. To indicate the nature of such tests, those in a 1940 study by Espenschade[38] and in the Wisconsin and Medford studies are listed. All 3 investigations included the standing broad jump. Espenschade and Wisconsin used a 50-yard and a 30-yard sprint, respectively; a 60-yard shuttle run was administered in the Medford series, a test which involves agility as well as speed. Other motor tests were: Espenschade, vertical jump, target throw, softball distance throw, and Brace's Test of Motor Ability (a stunt-type test, identified by McCloy as a test of motor educability); Wisconsin, velocity overhand baseball throw; Medford, total-body and arm-hand reaction and movement times. Two of these tests, standing broad jump and 60-yard shuttle run, are considered here.

Standing Broad Jump

In all 3 growth studies mentioned, standing broad jump performance was scored as the distance the body is projected horizontally from a standing position. This is the method customarily employed in administering the test in physical education. The test is generally

[38]Anna Espenschade, *Motor Performance in Adolescence* (Washington: Monograph of the Society for Research in Child-Development, 1940).

accepted as an indication of the explosive power of the leg muscles. When scored as distance jumped, relative rather than gross power is involved, as the amount of the weight projected is not incorporated into the score. The standing broad jump curve for the overlapping samples in the Medford study rose linearly from ages 7 through 17 years; the age means increased from 46 inches at 7 years to 88 inches at 17 years. This linearity provides justification for using standing broad jump as a growth measure, as muscle power compensated positively with age increases in body weight.

By correlational analysis, Clarke and Degutis studied the relationship between standing broad jump distance and various maturity, structural, and strength measures of 12-year-old boys.[39] The multiple correlations obtained were: (a) anthropometry: .41 with body weight, leg length, and lung capacity; (b) cable-tension strength: .52 with elbow flexion and hip extension; (c) combined variables: .69 with elbow flexion strength, body weight, hip extension strength, ankle plantar flexion strength, and leg length.

For adolescent boys and girls in Espenschade's study, correlations in the .60s were obtained between this jump and the 50-yard dash and the Brace test. In the Medford series, distance jumped was a consistent differentiator of the athletic abilities of upper elementary, junior high, and senior high school boys in the interscholastic sports of football, basketball, track and field, and baseball.

Flynn studied various methods of scoring the standing broad jump performances of 12-year-old boys and obtained the following correlations (in parentheses) and multiple correlations (R) with physical and motor traits:[40]

R	SBJ Scoring	Physical and motor tests
.917	Distance × weight	Weight (.84), Strength Index (.64), skinfold total (.44), abdominal girth (.63).
.908	Weight/distance	Abdominal girth (.87), Physical Fitness Index (−.44), skinfold total (.79)
.717	Leg length/distance	Physical Fitness Index (.50), leg length (.45), 10-foot run (.33), skinfold total (.44)

[39]H. Harrison Clarke and Ernest W. Degutis, "Relationships between Standing Broad Jump and Various Maturational, Anthropometric, and Strength Tests of 12-Year-Old Boys," *Research Quarterly*, 35, No. 3 (October 1964), 258.

[40]Kenneth W. Flynn, "Relationship between Various Standing Broad Jump Measures and Strength, Speed, Body Size, and Physique Measures of Twelve-Year-Old Boys," (Master's thesis equivalent, University of Oregon, 1966).

_R_	SBJ Scoring	Physical and motor tests
.690	Distance	Physical Fitness Index (.47), 10-foot run (−.42), sitting height (.22), skinfold total (−.33), cable-tension strength average (.35).

Sixty-Yard Shuttle Run

The 60-yard shuttle run was utilized in the Medford study as a measure of speed and agility in a running situation; the shuttle distance was 10 yards. The justification for choosing this agility run was based on research by Gates and Sheffield, who experimented with 18 tests, 15 of which involved change of direction while running and 3 of which were motor ability elements.[41] A criterion measure was established consisting of the sum of T scores of the subjects on all tests. The 60-yard shuttle run correlated .81 with this criterion for boys in each grade 7 through 9. Lawson obtained similar results with a 40-yard shuttle run for girls ages 7 through 12; her criterion consisted of Hull-scale totals on 12 obstacle and shuttle runs.[42]

Two problems encountered in administering shuttle runs in order to obtain consistency and comparability of results are the stabilization of the running surface and provision of a tight turn by the runner at the end of each traverse. These problems can be solved by providing a common running surface of prescribed width. To do so, 2 strips of rubberized matting, each 38' by 3', can be laid side by side on the floor; thus, the running surface is 38 feet long and 6 feet wide. The strips may be secured to the floor with tape. Four feet from each end and at the junction of the 2 mats—30 feet apart—an erect wand is located; this wand can be held upright by use of a "plumber's helper." The subjects are required to stay on the mat while performing the shuttle run; they run in their bare feet.

The 60-yard shuttle run growth curves for the 2 overlapping samples in the Medford study showed a straight line rise from ages 8 to 14; a plateau occurred from ages 14 to 15; after that the line continued to rise but at a decelerated rate. From the standpoint of individual differences, the standard deviations and ranges were reasonably consistent for the various ages.

[41] Donald D. Gates and R. P. Sheffield, "Tests of Change of Direction as Measurement of Different Kinds of Motor Ability in Boys of the Seventh, Eighth, and Ninth Grades," _Research Quarterly_, 11, No. 3 (October 1940), 136.

[42] Patricia A. Lawson, "An Analysis of a Group of Motor Fitness Tests Which Purport to Measure Agilities as They Apply to Elementary School Girls" (Master's thesis, University of Oregon, 1959).

The relationship between maturity, physique type, structural, strength, and motor ability items and the 60-yard shuttle run performance of 14-year-old boys was examined by Radcliff.[43] Seventy-eight percent of the correlations between the shuttle run and the experimental variables were significant at or beyond the .05 level. The highest correlation with the time element of the shuttle run was −.57 for standing broad jump. The highest coefficient of 5 multiple correlations computed with the 60-yard shuttle run was .65; the independent variables were standing broad jump, Physical Fitness Index, and total-body reaction time.

SUMMARY

Interest in growth and development has existed for a long time. The remains of ancient societies reveal that body size and physical dimension were understood and appreciated by sculptors and artisans. From accounts of athletic contests, it has become apparent that human physique and strength were important physical attributes. The seventeenth century saw the emergence of the field of anthropometry in the science of human biology.

A number of growth studies have been undertaken in the past to provide serial data collection over several years. The major intent of most of these studies has been to obtain measures of physical dimensions and proportions of boys and girls during childhood and adolescence. Occasionally, variables of physical strength and motor ability were included. Such factors as body structure, maturity, coordinated strength elements and batteries, agility, speed, and muscular power have been included in such studies conducted by physical educators.

Maturity measures give a different picture of the development of children than either chronological age or size factors taken separately. The skeletal age can be determined by taking the hand-wrist X ray and comparing the degree of ossification of the bones and epiphyses with known standards. Pubescent assessment, on the other hand, can be determined by evaluation of the onset of secondary sex characteristics and can be divided into various stages that categorize the population under study. Although less exact than skeletal age in differentiating maturity, the pubescent assessment does reveal important information during the adolescent period.

The most commonly used technique for determining physique

---

[43]Robert A. Radcliff, "Relationships between the Sixty-Yard Shuttle Run and Various Maturity, Physique, Structural, Strength, and Motor Characteristics of Fourteen-Year-Old Boys" (Master's thesis, University of Oregon, 1965).

type is the somatotype, in which the body is categorized into degrees of endomorphy, mesomorphy, and ectomorphy. The performance capabilities of individuals, given certain body classifications, have been the subject of investigation, thus linking the important factors of body form and function.

Anthropometry is the systematized measurement of the human body. No unanimity exists among researchers concerning the selection of sites or the method of obtaining data, but certain sources of error should be anticipated and every effort made to eliminate them. Such matters as interfering clothing, accuracy of measurement, and instrument calibration must be rigidly standardized if serial determinations are to be comparable from one examination to another. Skinfold measures by use of calipers are a means of identifying the amounts of fat deposits in the body. Total body fat is determined through calculation of specific gravity from skinfolds taken at specified sites.

Measures of muscular strength are valuable in growth studies; dynamometric and tensiometric tests are available for this purpose. Growth curves of gross strength follow the general trend of the organism as a whole. This situation does not apply to relative strength, as for Rogers' Fitness Index, since the norms utilized to derive this index are based on sex, age, and weight. The gross strength differences among individuals of the same age are pronounced. Muscular strength is interwoven within the entire physical-motor complex of individuals, including their maturity, physique, body size, and motor and athletic abilities.

Muscular endurance tests, such as pull-ups and push-ups, have appeared in a limited number of growth studies. The growth curve for the endurance of the arm and shoulder muscles shows a slight rise from 8 to 12 years, after which sizable increases occur each year to age 18. Both muscular strength and muscular endurance can be improved through use and conditioning of the muscles, so the differentiation of growth and development effects during the growing years is difficult, if not impossible.

The motor ability elements presented in this chapter are the standing broad jump and the 60-yard shuttle run. Other motor tests utilized in various growth studies are the vertical jump, the 30-yard and 50-yard sprints, the baseball target throw, the softball distance throw, the baseball velocity throw, the total-body and hand-wrist reaction and movement times, and the Brace Test of Motor Ability.

SELECTED REFERENCES

BROZEK, JOSEF, ed., *Body Measurements and Human Physique.* Detroit: Wayne State University Press, 1956.

CLARKE, H. HARRISON, *Application of Measurement to Health and Physical Education* (5th ed.). Englewood Cliffs, N.J.: Prentice-Hall, Inc., 1976.

CLARKE, H. HARRISON, *Physical and Motor Tests in the Medford Boys' Growth Study.* Englewood Cliffs, N.J.: Prentice-Hall, Inc., 1971.

ESPENSCHADE, ANNA S., and HELEN M. ECKERT, *Motor Development.* Columbus, Ohio: Charles E. Merrill Publishing Co., 1967.

RARICK, G. LAWRENCE, "Motor Development: Its Growing Knowledge Base," *Journal of Physical Education and Recreation*, 51, No. 7 (September 1980), 26.

RARICK, G. LAWRENCE, ed., *Physical Activity: Human Growth and Development.* New York: Academic Press, Inc., 1973.

part v

The Research Report

16
Preparation
of the Research Report

INTRODUCTION TO PART V

The final part of this book contains a single chapter, Preparation of the Research Report. This chapter is written primarily for the graduate student undertaking his or her first research writing. The main topics deal with the organization of the research thesis by sections and chapters, the use of written and oral sources, the construction and use of tables and graphs, forms for footnotes and bibliography, and publication based on the thesis.

The culmination of any research venture is a written report. For the graduate student, the entire degree may hinge upon successful completion of the written thesis or dissertation. Although each study is marked by individuality and usually has unique features, there are guidelines that help to expedite the writing process. Many institutions, and sometimes departments or colleges within an institution, have their own preferred form for thesis writing. In the larger universities, format guides are published and available to the student; these are helpful because they provide organizational consistency and procedures for handling numerous minor details. Obviously, the graduate student should investigate such sources and follow them appropriately.

ORGANIZATION OF THE THESIS REPORT

Quite obviously, the thesis report is organized into chapters, each of which serves a distinctive purpose. Preceding the chapters are certain "front" materials, followed by other items of essential information. Institutions vary somewhat in detail as to how the various parts of the report should be handled but agree in general practice. Some appropriate suggestions pertaining to the overall thesis organization are given in this section.

Front Materials

Several items typically appear in the front of the thesis report; some may not be required at all institutions, and others may be optional with the student.

Vita.   Some institutions require a vita as the first typed page in the thesis, inserted between a blank flyleaf and the title page. The vita includes such information about the investigator as the following, presented in outline form: (1) full name of the author and place and date of birth; (2) undergraduate and graduate schools attended and degrees awarded, with dates; (3) relevant professional experiences; (4) awards and honors received and professional offices held; (5) list of professional publications with complete bibliographical references.

Title Page.   The institution where the thesis is written dictates the form of the title page. However, it is a single page containing the title of the thesis, the author's full name, and a statement indicating the college or university, name of the degree, and date the degree was awarded. The following illustration is compressed; it should be spaced over a complete page.

TITLE OF THESIS

by

Name of Student

A THESIS

Presented to the College of Health, Physical Education,
Recreation, and Dance
and the Graduate School of the University of Oregon
in partial fulfillment
of the requirements for the degree of
Master of Science
June 1984

The title of the study should be kept as short as possible consistent with a clear indication of the subject. Some words and phrases are redundant, such as "A Study of . . ." and "An Analysis of. . . ." The use of articles, such as "A" and "The," to precede the title are unnecessary: for example: not "A Comparative Study of . . ." but "Comparison of. . . ." Illustrations of some satisfactory titles are:

Estimation of Body Fat in Middle-Aged Women Using Skinfolds and Densitometry

Cultural Significance of Sport in Colonial Chesapeake and Massachusetts

Three-dimensional Cinematographic Analysis of Selected Full Twisting Movements in Gymnastics

Longitudinal Analysis of Strength and Motor Development of Boys Seven through Twelve Years of Age

Influences of Varying Combinations of Arm and Leg Work on Maximal Oxygen Uptake

Approval Page.   Again, the institution at which the thesis is written specifies the form of the approval page. Typically, it is centered on a single sheet, immediately following the title page, and bears only the following:

$$\text{APPROVED: } \frac{\text{(Signature of thesis adviser)}}{\text{(Typed name of thesis adviser)}}$$

At some institutions, only the adviser of the thesis signs the approval sheet; at other colleges and universities, all members of the thesis (examining) committee sign.

Dedication.   Dedication of the thesis is usually optional and is entirely a personal matter. However, many graduate students find use of the dedication an opportunity to recognize someone who has been a source of help and encouragement during the arduous period of study for the graduate degree. Subjects for dedications have been parents, wife or husband, children, and others who may have given significant support to the student. The dedication should not be a eulogy but a simple designation, centered on a separate page following the approval page.

Acknowledgments.   Usually, the graduate student has had significant help from others in completing the thesis requirement. Certainly, such would be true for the thesis adviser and, possibly, members of the committee. Acknowledgments of this indebtedness on a separate page following the dedication are a thoughtful and gracious gesture on the part of the graduate student. Other sources of acknowledgments, when applicable, are: fellow graduate students who may have helped with testing or in other ways; subjects in toto if they participated repeatedly; administrators or teachers in schools where the study may have been conducted or testing accomplished; and sources of financial support if any. Acknowledgments should be simple and direct and not effusive.

Table of Contents.　The table of contents should include chapter titles with major subheads and, possibly, minor subheads. Inasmuch as the thesis does not contain an index, the table of contents should be sufficiently detailed to help the reader locate readily any section in which he or she is interested. The chapter headings are usually typed in capital letters and their subdivisions in small letters, with the first letters of principal words capitalized. The relationship between main headings and subheads is shown by proper indentions. The page numbers should be entered during the final typing.

List of Tables.　When tables appear in the thesis, a list of them should be provided next. In each instance, the exact and complete title as it appears in the text should be given. The numbering of tables is usually by Arabic numerals, although Roman numerals are used at some institutions.

List of Figures.　In the event illustrations are employed in the thesis, they should also be listed separately, with page numbers. As for tables, the titles should be given exactly as given in the body of the thesis. Usually figures are numbered with Arabic numerals.

Chapters

Although circumstances alter practice, most theses contain five chapters, as follows: Chapter I, Statement of the Problem; Chapter II, Review of Related Literature; Chapter III, Research Procedures; Chapter IV, Results of the Study; Chapter V, Summary and Conclusions. In studies that result in a short, concentrated report, certain of these chapters are combined; in others, where the results are very extensive and a logical division exists, more than one "results" chapter may be utilized. Assuming that there will be five chapters, the following contents are appropriate.

Statement of the Problem.　Although the formal statement of the problem may be delayed until later in the chapter, an indication of the nature of the problem should come early, preferably in the first paragraph. Thus, although the thesis title gives a sketchy indication, some elaboration is helpful to the reader at the outset in order to facilitate an understanding of the subsequent discussion.

As introductory to the problem statement, the investigator should orient the reader to the importance and need for the study. Some justification for undertaking the study should be provided. This statement should lead logically and smoothly into the statement itself.

The purpose of the study should be stated clearly and concisely. It must indicate exactly what the investigator intends to do, as he or she will be held rigidly to this intention after the study is completed; the entire study emanates from this assertion. A problem statement should be made and any limitations or delimitations should be clarified. Relevant hypotheses should be stated; or, if convenient and appropriate, questions to be answered by the study may be asked. Definitions of terms may be included, but only those not generally understood or those that could be misinterpreted.

The following examples are given to illustrate statements of purposes of studies:

1. To relate the personality traits of 16-year-old boys, as revealed by the individual adjectives on the Davidson Adjective Check List, to their maturity, physique type, body size, strength, and motor ability characteristics.

2. To determine the relationship between academic achievement and intelligence and the maturity, physique type, body size, muscular strength and endurance, and motor ability of the same boys 9 through 17 years of age.

3. To investigate selected aspects of the sociological backgrounds of athletes who represented the United States in the XII Winter Olympic Games, 1976.

4. To monitor the effect of supramaximal interval training on the aerobic and anaerobic fitness of women.

5. To contrast the maturational, structural, strength, and motor factors of elementary and junior high school boys with different levels of athletic ability disclosed in interscholastic competition.

6. To explore muscular strength interrelationships and to select by correlational methods the minimum number of cable-tension tests that reflect the total strength of various muscle groups of upper elementary, junior high, and senior high school girls.

Literature Review.   If only a limited literature exists relative to the problem, the review may be included in Chapter I. Otherwise, a separate chapter is indicated. A discussion of the literature search is contained in Chapter 3 of this text. The report of the literature should not be merely a chronological succession of abstracts of completed studies. Rather, it should be a synthesis of reports on a given related topic; there will usually be a succession of these syntheses.

Research Procedures. The research procedures employed in the study should be explained in sufficient detail that another investigator would be able to repeat the study precisely if desired. The nature of the study will dictate how these descriptions are made. The process varies for different kinds of studies, such as those involving the historical, philosophical, survey, or experimental method. But, in all instances, the types and sources of evidence utilized and the methods by which the evidence was evaluated must be presented.

Thus, for a historical study, the primary and secondary sources consulted and their evaluation by external and internal criticisms should be described. For a philosophical study, the hypotheses formed and the evidence employed to evaluate them should be stated. For surveys by questionnaire or interview, the construction of the inquiry forms, the selection of the individuals or institutions to be surveyed, the method of conducting the survey, and the means of analyzing the replies should be presented.

In scientific studies, testing instruments are utilized, subjects are tested, and test data are analyzed statistically. For an experimental study, a single group may be used or two or more groups may be formed; for a relationship study, a criterion of some sort is usually employed and experimental variables are related to it; for comparative studies, specific groups are identified and evaluated with appropriate tests. In all instances, these procedures must be carefully described, including the process of selecting subjects, descriptions of tests employed and their evaluation, the qualifications and training of testers, the application of the particular scientific method adopted, the experimental controls employed, and the statistics employed in analyzing the data. Common formulas need not be given; unusual ones, however, might well be listed and their use justified.

Any unique circumstances encountered in conducting the study should be described. Examples follow.

1. If the subjects are unusual in any way, additional descriptions of them may be desirable; consequently, generalizations will be limited to such samples as described. To illustrate: One of the authors, while at Springfield College, used physical education majors in studies; therefore, the samples were not only indicated as random at that institution but percentile bar graphs were presented showing their height, weight, and Physical Fitness

Index patterns, and three-dimensional shields were provided showing their somatotype distributions.

2. In longitudinal growth studies, subjects drop from the sample for various reasons, especially leaving the schools when parents move from the community. Whether or not this unavoidable attrition appreciably changes the sample is a moot question. In the Medford Boys' Growth Study, this effect was checked by comparing those who continued with and those who dropped from the original sample by comparisons with several representative tests.

3. If a pilot study was conducted, its description and results should be included.

4. Any method that was tried and abandoned and the reasons why it was inadequate or valueless should be stated.

5. If new apparatus and equipment or variations of old ones are employed, the validity and reliability of these tests should be established; detailed descriptions and drawings of them may frequently be indicated.

Research Results.   Usually, the research results are contained in a single chapter, although one or more additional chapters may be used if the situation warrants. Such additional chapters may be desirable when the results are especially extensive and fall into essentially discrete divisions. Seldom, however, is more than one chapter employed for this purpose.

Specific directions cannot be given for organizing this chapter because of the wide variety of studies and the kinds of data that exist. In an historical study, a narrative is told through a series of chronological and/or topical subjects. Philosophical reports center around hypotheses or principles, with rational support from existing evidence and its critical appraisal. Survey results usually consist of appropriate tables and charts portraying the status of the conditions investigated. Experimental and relationship studies focus upon tables and, possibly, graphs containing analyses of test data and the application of tests of significance.

The discussion in the results chapter must be presented systematically, which necessitates a logical flow of information. Generally, comparisons with other studies should not be included in this chapter but should be reserved for the final chapter; straight reporting of results should be the purpose. When test data are utilized in studies, the raw scores should not be included, although some investigators preserve them for possible future reference by placing them at the end of the thesis in an appendix. Instead, tables and graphs are employed to report the statistical analyses of the raw scores. The information in such tables and graphs is not detailed in the text. Rather, the investigator presents the salient features of the results and interprets for the reader what the facts mean. This process may be quite simple when tables contain only several entries, but it may be complex when several hundred entries are made, as in an intercorrelational matrix with a large number of variables.

Summary and Conclusions.   The final chapter should give an overview of the study. Briefly, the purpose of the study, the methods employed, and the results should be summarized, and the conclusions should be stated and supported.

If extensive statistical analyses have been employed, tables that summarize the prominent features from several related tables presented in the results chapter will prove effective for this purpose. To illustrate: In a study by Jarman,[1] a series of high and low scoring groups of 20 boys each were formed separately on the basis of 3 strength and 2 growth measures at each age, 9, 12, and 15 years; each of the 15 pairs of high and low groups was equated by use of intelligence quotients. The differences among means on standard academic achievement tests and grade point averages were tested for significance by application of the t ratio. The numerous t ratios are shown in Table 16.1 in order to summarize these results in a single table. For these comparisons, a t ratio of 2.00 is significant at the .05 level. The essential results of the entire study can be seen readily from examination of this table.

TABLE 16.1   Illustration of a Summarizing Table of t Ratios between Academic Performance Means

Experimental variables	Achievement tests			Grade point averages		
	9 yrs.	12 yrs.	15 yrs.	9 yrs.	12 yrs.	15 yrs.
Strength Index	3.00	.83	.13	5.69	1.53	1.10
Physical Fitness Index	2.31	.19	.03	.94	3.14	2.00
Rogers' Arm Strength Score	.76	.85	.33	1.94	1.21	2.19
McCloy's Classif. Index	2.06	1.17	1.86	1.84	.56	1.20
Wetzel Dev. Level	.83	1.07	2.22	1.67	1.27	.85

[1] Boyd O. Jarman, "Academic Achievement of Boys Nine, Twelve, and Fifteen Years of Age as Related to Various Strength and Growth Measures" (Master's thesis, University of Oregon, 1959).

Comparison of the results of the study should be made with those obtained by other investigators. Although a study rarely precisely duplicates another, nevertheless some bases for comparison may exist. For example, studies of the characteristics of athletes have been conducted by several investigators. Another study may use some of the same or similar variables or different ages or levels of athletic ability may be involved, and comparisons should be made. Further, the unique contribution of the investigation should be fitted into the body of knowledge in the study area.

In the conclusions, the purposes of the study as stated in Chapter I should be satisfied. What were the results in regard to the purposes to be achieved? If hypotheses had been stated, their tenability should now be indicated. If questions had been asked to define the scope of the study, they should be answered. Any shortcomings or deficiencies in the study should be noted. Any contradictions encountered should be resolved insofar as the evidence permits; speculation is permissible but only when so indicated. Frequently, suggestions for future studies may be desirable, although not mandatory.

Back Materials

Bibliography. A bibliography should be included, immediately following the last chapter of the research report. The bibliography should contain all references appearing in footnotes throughout the thesis but need not be so restricted. Any other materials particularly pertinent to the research may be included at the discretion of the investigator. However, loading a bibliography with irrelevant or insignificant references is contraindicated; it should contain only those references that the author found useful in the conduct of the study.

The bibliography should be alphabetized by authors' last names. If an author has more than one reference, they should be arranged alphabetically under his or her name by title. If an author has published with others, his or her single references should be listed first; then joint publications should appear alphabetized by associate authors. If the bibliography is especially lengthy, some classification scheme may be desirable. Such schemes could be by topic or historical period or type of publication, such as books, articles, and theses.

Appendix. An appendix is not always utilized in the thesis report. However, one or more appendices may be useful when cumbersome or voluminous material not essential to understanding of the text needs to be recorded. Examples are raw data from testing, questionnaires, test forms, descriptions of tests (especially when many are used), form letters, lists of cooperating individuals or institutions, and daily exercise regimens. The appendix should not be a depository for miscellaneous or irrelevant materials; each entry should be justified as needed for an adequate understanding of the thesis.

Chapter Organization

Time spent at the start, before actual writing begins, in organizing the research report will be valuably spent. The first thing most thesis advisers look at is the sequential and orderly presentation of the material: whether or not it flows smoothly from item to item throughout. Any time duplication occurs, the researcher should examine its necessity; usually duplication can be avoided. However, an occasional cross-reference may be desirable, either to material elsewhere in the report or as a brief summarization introducing the presentation of new but relevant material.

The broad organization of the thesis by units and chapters was discussed in the preceding section. The use of headings and subheadings within each chapter will prove most beneficial in aiding the reader to follow the thesis presentation and will make easy the location of specific materials within the chapter. Headings may be designated as orders. A four-order system meets most organizational situations. These orders are

First order: center heading
Second order: marginal heading
Third order: paragraph heading
Fourth order: numbered items under third-order headings

In this section of this chapter, the first-order heading is "Organization of the Thesis Report." The second-order headings are: "Front Materials," "Chapter," "Back Materials," and "Chapter Organization." All but the last of the second-order headings have third-order headings; under "Back Materials," they are "Bibliography" and "Appendix."

A given order should not be employed unless two or more subheads of the order are desired. As can be seen in the above, the numbers in the various orders are: first order, one (but more will follow in this chapter); second order, three; third order, eight, five, and two for the respective second-order headings; fourth order, not appearing in this chapter, but can be found elsewhere in this book.

The student inexperienced in thesis writing should examine recently completed studies at his or her institution, especially those in the field and allied to his or her problem. A completed, acceptable report will provide the novice not only with an overview of an investigation properly put together but will supply many hints on how tricky problems may be resolved. The way tables and graphs are constructed, employed, and summarized will be particularly helpful, as will be the handling of hypotheses, the formulation of generalizations, and the drawing of supportable conclusions.

WRITING SUGGESTIONS

Writing a thesis is quite different from writing a nontechnical composition. The purpose is not to entertain, amuse, or persuade the reader; nor is it concerned with merely discussing opinions related to a problem or philosophizing on its solution. Rather, thesis writing requires clear, concise, and objective statements of fact and analyses of evidence. Perhaps never before has the neophyte researcher been held so rigidly to such expression; by itself, this discipline is well worth experiencing.

Although the writing must be direct and precise, it need not be dull and pedantic. Even profound ideas can be explained in simple language. Here are some suggestions to follow in writing a thesis or other scientific paper:

1. The report should describe and explain rather than try to convince or move to action. Slang, hackneyed, or flippant phrases and folksy style should be avoided.
2. Sentences should be short and coherent, not long and involved. In draft writing, when long sentences occur, they should be broken into one or more shorter ones. Sometimes, in order to hold the thought closer, long sentences may be divided by use of the semicolon, as is frequently done in this book, even in this section.
3. The past tense should be used when referring to former work by the researcher and other investigators. The present tense is appropriate when referring to tables under discussion and when mentioning general truths and well-established principles. Style books do not always agree exactly on the same rules. However, after a style is adopted, it should be followed consistently throughout the thesis.
4. Personal pronouns should not be used (I, me, you, our, us); rather, writing should be in the third person. For example: Instead of saying, "I randomly selected a sample of 100 ninth grade girls," say "One hundred ninth grade girls were randomly selected."
5. Abbreviations are not usually employed in textual materials, but may be used in footnotes, bibliography, appendices, tables, and figures.
6. Numbers of less than 100 are spelled out (although some styles

suggest ten and below), as are ordinals, fractions, and any number that begins a sentence. Exceptions are use of numerals in a technical or statistical discussion involving frequent use of numbers or in a presentation containing numbers both under and over 100; use of a fraction as part of three or more digits; use of numerals for percentages, decimals, and dates; and use of numerals in tables and figures. If small and large numbers appear in a series, numerals are used for all of them.

7. Ordinarily, standard statistical formulas, such as for the mean, the standard deviation, and the coefficient of correlation, are not presented in the research report. If an unusual formula is used in the analysis of data, it is appropriate to include it. Computations are not included in the account.

8. Only last names of cited persons are used. Titles such as *Dr.*, *Prof.*, and *Dean* are omitted.

9. Percent is spelled out except in tables and figures.

10. Ordinary rules of correct language usage should prevail throughout the research report. References to a good dictionary and a thesaurus will be helpful.

In addition to a possible style manual by an institution's graduate school or department, manuals have been published solely for the purpose of presenting detailed form and style for writing theses, as well as reports and term papers. Four such manuals are as follows:

1. Campbell, William G., and Stephen V. Ballou, *Form and Style: Theses, Reports, and Term Papers*, 6th ed. Boston: Houghton Mifflin Company, 1982.

2. *Publication Manual of the American Psychological Association.* Washington: The Association, 1974.

3. Turabian, Kate L., *A Manual for Writers of Term Papers, Theses, and Dissertations*, 4th ed. Chicago: University of Chicago Press, 1973.

4. University of Chicago, *A Manual of Style*, 13th ed. Chicago: University of Chicago Press, 1982.

Proper and effective thesis writing is a difficult task. Good research reports require considerable time to write. Even experienced writers revise their reports several times before submitting them for publication.

USE OF SOURCES

A matter of grave concern to the writer is the proper use of sources. No research report is complete without ample evidence that the sources of pertinent information have been examined. The great bulk of such material will appear as a review of the literature, but other sections of the thesis will contain various references appropriate to the study as well. The investigator bears the responsibility for making proper selections and must see that they are cited correctly. The point cannot be stressed too strongly that each citation must be absolutely correct, both in terms of the footnote or bibliographical entry and in content.

An author will make a number of decisions in presenting material, chief among them being the selection of references. A discussion of the review of literature was presented in Chapter 3 of this text, so it will be assumed that this task has been completed. The important thing now is to put it into writing. One of the important requisites is to give proper credit to sources utilized. This extends from the abstracting of appropriate results of various investigations to the use of ideas garnered from various authorities. Failure to do this is considered plagiarism and cannot be condoned.

No clear distinction can be given to help the writer make all decisions of this sort; certainly, the flagrant use of another's words and phraseology as one's own constitutes a breach of ethics. On the other hand, certain concepts of a scientific nature may be so well-established as to be considered in the public domain. If the author is speaking from his or her general knowledge of the subject matter gained over a period of several years or is discussing theoretical matters that are not particularly controversial, no citation to a source may be required. However, in discussing new findings or rather poorly established theory, the author should give credit to the authors of such information. Little can be said for the practice of documenting facts by giving as reference undergraduate textbooks, unless it is considered essential to establish the premise that something is widely purported to be true. In such an instance, the author may be preparing the way to suggest new findings or interpretations of a contradictory nature.

Thus, it is incumbent that the author give credit where credit is due, according to the procedures established for proper citation. One major point should be mentioned, however, which seems to cause much difficulty with beginning writers: when to quote and when not to quote. Differences of opinion may occur on this point, but the basic premise here is to avoid the use of quotations as much as possible. A far better technique is to paraphrase and cite the reference. If the author's words must be preserved, if the statement is so concise and technical that paraphrasing would destroy the full impact of what is being said, then it may be desirable to quote the text exactly, once again citing the reference. Such a practice should be followed judiciously and the passages selected with great care. Excessively long quotes are usually unnecessary in research, although the examination of sources in historical research may justify their greater use. Actually, reliance upon quotations is not evidence of high scholarship, for it serves as a crutch to the writer who rationalizes that since the original author said it so well, why change it. In most cases, such passages can be paraphrased to fit the context of the writer's discussion and many times far better than by direct quotation. Further, in reporting on the literature, materials from several sources may be synthesized in a single paragraph, which is superior writing to stringing out a series of quotes.

When short quotations, say three lines or less, are used, the passage should be included in the paragraph and enclosed in double quotations marks; a quotation within the quotation is identified by single quotation marks. Periods, commas, and question marks ending quotations are within the quotation marks; colons and semicolons at ends of quotations are outside the quotation marks. Footnote reference numbers are outside the quotation marks, unless appearing with the author's name when mentioned.

Long quotations are set off from the text in a separate passage. They should be indented four typewriter spaces from the margin and single spaced. Quotation marks are omitted. The usual footnote reference is needed as for short quotations.

Quoting from oral sources, as from a speech or conversation, presents certain hazards, especially concerning the accuracy of the quotation. A good policy in such instances is to submit the quotation to the author for approval of authenticity. The usual acknowledgements are necessary.

If the writer wishes to delete certain words, phrases, or portions of the original statement, he or she may do so by inserting ellipsis dots with a typewriter space between each (. . .). Conversely, when it is considered desirable to add to the original quotation in some way, the interpolation can be made within squared brackets []; parentheses should not be used for this purpose, as they may appear in the original quote, so the differentiation between a quote and an interpolation would be obscure. When using either ellipses or interpolations, the burden of responsibility for such alterations is solely with the writer, who must not change the meaning or intent of the original statement.

Italicized words in a quotation, as elsewhere, are underlined. If the writer wishes to italicize words not italicized in the original, this may be done but must be so indicated. Such an indication may be made in a footnote or in squared brackets immediately after the italicization, such as [italics note in original].

TABLES

Tables are frequently utilized in research reporting. In some reports, a large number of tables may be used, especially in comparative, relationship, growth, and survey studies. In experimental research, the number will usually be fewer, and they may not be employed at all in historical and philosophical studies. The novice researcher, therefore, should become familiar with the use of tables and their construction.

Construction

Various points in the construction of tables are as follows:

1. Emphasize only one significant fact in each table. Each table should present results as simply and concisely as possible.
2. Avoid crowded tables. If tables become too crowded, ways should be considered to make logical divisions of them or to arrange the material into more than one table.
3. Arrange tabulations in a logical manner. Space columns of figures so they can be easily read.
4. Construct the tables so that they can be read from right to left.
5. Although other arrangements are permissible, one acceptable way of ruling the table is as follows:
   (a) Horizontal line at the top, under the table title.
   (b) Horizontal line to separate the column headings from the table data.
   (c) Vertical lines to set off the main divisions of the table, although these may be omitted in simple tables. In some complex tables, vertical lines may also be used to mark off minor subdivisions.
   (d) Omit vertical lines at both right and left margins.
   (e) Use either a horizontal line or a double space after every fifth row of figures in a long table.
   (f) Draw horizontal line at bottom of the table.
6. Align right-hand digits in columns of figures, except when decimal points are used. Decimal points must always be aligned.
7. Use superior letters ([a], [b], [c], etc.) to mark footnotes to a table, and place these notes directly beneath the table.

8. Label the table in sufficient detail that it may be read and understood without supplementary explanation. Use a single phrase and avoid use of unnecessary words.
9. Place the table number and title at the top of the table. All letters in the title should be capitalized.

In the textual discussion, the writer should refer to the table by number; the relevancy of the salient information in the table should be explained. The table itself should appear after its mention in the text at the first convenient location. Generally, it should not interrupt a paragraph but should be placed after the paragraph, on the same page if space permits; if space is not sufficient for the complete table, it should be located on the following page. If the table is wider than it is long, it may be placed broadside on the page if desired; this arrangement is preferable to using a second page.

Long tables of a page or more should occupy separate pages, starting at the top of the first one. Pages for a long table should be consecutive; the table title need not be repeated but merely indicated as *Table, continued*, giving the number. Pages of wide tables may be pasted together and folded in.

Illustrated Tables

Illustrations of actual tables utilized in research reports will be given. Many unique situations may be encountered, so the coverage by the illustrations is very limited. The student should study a number of research reports, especially in the area of his or her study, in order to gain some insight into ways by which various problems pertaining to tables have been resolved by others.

Simple Table. Brose and Hanson studied the effects of overload training on velocity and accuracy of throwing a regulation baseball for college men.[2] As one phase of the investigation, correlations were computed to determine the relationship between successive test days for velocity and accuracy scores for both pretraining and posttraining sessions. The table presented by these investigators has been adapted slightly and is shown in Table 16.2.

As can be readily seen from the table, the correlations for the velocity rates were high, between .92 and .98. The correlations for accuracy were lower but especially low at the pretraining level.

---

[2]Donald E. Brose and Dale L. Hanson, "Effects of Overload Training on Velocity and Accuracy of Throwing," *Research Quarterly*, 38, No. 4 (December 1967), 528.

TABLE 16.2   Pre-Training and Post-Training Reliability for
Velocity and Accuracy

| | Pre-Training | | Post-Training | |
Source	Velocity	Accuracy	Velocity	Accuracy
Day 1 vs 2	.98	.23	.94	.65
Day 2 vs 3	.94	.54	.93	.69
Day 3 vs 4	.92	.24	.92	.55

Complex Pattern.   The handling of tables in an analysis of variance problem and subsequent tests of significance for paired means when a significant F ratio is obtained is fairly complex. Stafford made single-age and longitudinal comparisons of the intelligence and academic achievement of elementary and junior high school athletes and nonparticipants.[3] Athletes were judged by their coaches on their performances in interscholastic athletics, as follows: 3, outstanding athlete; 2, regular player; and 1, substitute. All other boys were designated as *NP*, nonparticipant; when individual sports were considered, boys who were athletes in other sports but not in the one under scrutiny were classified *NPA*. One phrase of the study consisted of analysis of variance for Iowa Test of Educational Development means for 15-year-old track athletes in junior high school. The results of this analysis of variance not only for the composite score on the ITED but also for the means of the various parts of the test are shown in Table 16.3.

The F ratios for Reading in Social Studies, Composite Score, and Sources of Information were significant at the .05 level. Consequently, the Scheffe test to determine the significance between all pairs of means was made for each of these tests. The results of this analysis for Composite Scores on the ITED are given in Table 16.4. As can be seen, the mean of the *NP*s was significantly higher than the mean of the *NPA*s and the 2-plus-3 athletes. The means of the 1-rated athletes were significantly superior to all other groups.

The major problem in the development of these tables was to reduce the essential analysis of variance and Scheffe test information to a minimal amount. If all available information had been included, many more tables would have been necessary: one for each analysis of variance and one for each Scheffe test. Actually, Stafford's dissertation contained 92 tables; had the above method not been used, the number of tables would have been well over 500.

[3] Elba G. Stafford, "Single-Age and Longitudinal Comparisons of Intelligence and Academic Achievement of Elementary and Junior High School Athletes and Nonparticipants" (Ph.D. diss., University of Oregon, August 1968).

TABLE 16.3 Analysis of Variance for Iowa Test of Educational Development; Comparison of Fifteen-Year-Old Nonparticipants, Nonparticipating Athletes, and Track Athletes

ITED	Means				Mean Squares		F Ratio[a]
	NP	NPA	1	2,3	Within	Between	
Basic social concepts	18.21	16.38	18.00	17.25	31.179	33.546	1.08
Background natural science	16.48	15.84	18.00	14.75	30.392	30.161	.99
Corr. and approp. expression	13.93	13.41	15.71	13.56	21.060	18.969	.90
Quantitative thinking	15.35	14.92	16.21	15.00	29.573	6.284	.21
Reading in social studies	15.06	12.35	18.22	10.82	37.354	130.549	3.50[b]
Reading in natural sciences	14.94	13.05	18.22	11.36	43.844	96.754	2.21
Literary materials	13.29	14.00	14.78	12.94	32.026	14.242	.45
General vocabulary	15.69	15.22	17.36	14.94	28.220	18.678	.66
Composite scores	16.04	12.95	19.33	12.09	32.558	137.411	4.22[b]
Sources of information	15.59	13.00	18.22	10.73	36.011	133.960	3.72[b]

[a] F ratio needed for significance at .05 level between 2.65 and 2.69 depending on degrees of freedom.
[b] Significant.

TABLE 16.4   Scheffe Test for ITED Composite Score:
Comparison of Fifteen-Year-Old Nonparticipants,
Nonparticipating Athletes, and Track Athletes

Means				Diff.	Confidence limits[a]	
NP	NPA	1	2,3	means	Lower	Higher
16.04	12.95			3.09	.84	5.34[b]
16.04		19.33		−3.29	−6.55	−.03[b]
16.04			12.09	3.95	1.17	6.73[b]
	12.95	19.33		−6.38	−10.11	−2.65[b]
	12.95		12.09	.86	−2.12	3.84
		19.33	12.09	7.24	3.07	11.41[b]

[a] Confidence interval amount, 2.25 to 4.17 depending on degrees of freedom.
[b] Significant.

FIGURES

The use of illustrations in research is widely endorsed and extensively practiced. There are occasions when the serial measurements of various functions can be presented more appropriately by a well-designed figure than by verbal description. In fact, this makes the presentation in the text much easier and clearer and conveys information to the reader more quickly. The researcher should anticipate the possibility of using graphic materials in the planning stage of the study and then prepare the data for use in this way when appropriate. Illustrations are most likely to appear in two places, namely, the methodology and the results chapters. In the thesis, the former is likely to occur in Chapter III dealing with procedure, and the latter will be an integral part of Chapter IV when presenting research results.

Purposes

Apparatus and Techniques.   The use of an illustration to show the apparatus, positioning of subject, and other technical matters pertaining to the conduct of the study can frequently be accomplished with a photograph far more effectively than by reliance upon verbal description. Such illustrations should be reserved for those techniques that are essential to a full understanding of the methodology and then only if they are rather unique. The simple and well-known procedures will not require this treatment, although it cannot be considered wrong to do so.

When taking photographs, careful attention should be given to all procedures essential to obtaining clear, accurate pictures. Lighting, background, arrangement of apparatus are among the factors to be considered. When nothing of real value can actually be seen in the photograph, it may be better to abandon the effort; likewise, if poor background and unnecessary objects or equipment appear, it may obscure the desired technical details. A suggestion in such an instance is to employ a line drawing based on the photograph, in which extraneous and distracting items can be eliminated. An illustration of such a drawing is contained in Figure 16.1, which shows the technique of administering the shoulder flexion strength test by cable-tension methods.

Data presentation.   The second major purpose for using illustrations in a thesis, the portrayal of results, is far more technical and requires much greater precision. The basic consideration in making effective graphs is to present the results in the simplest and most meaningful way, in order to provide the greatest impact in the shortest space. This is accomplished by such things as utilizing a curve to represent a succession of values, by presenting several curves on one graph for comparative purposes, or by combining more than one variable on the same graph. The student may profitably examine a

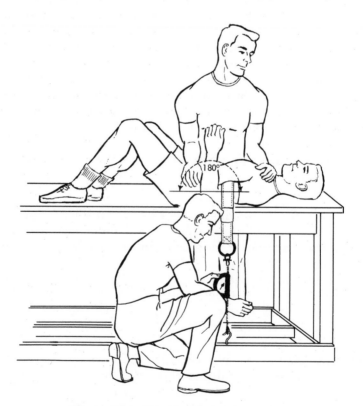

Figure 16.1. Shoulder Flexion Strength Test

number of journals in the area of his or her study to gain some familiarity with and suggestions for constructing his or her own graphs. Many other types of graphs are available to the researcher, as will be noted from the review of research literature.

Construction

Points to keep in mind in the logical construction of graphs to portray the results of research studies are as follows:

1. Select the type of graph that will best show the points to be emphasized.
2. Stress only one significant point in each graph.
3. Arrange the graph so that it can be read from left to right.
4. As a general rule, show the zero line on the graph. If the nature of the data is such that presentation of the zero line gives the graph a long-drawn-out and unbalanced appearance, show the zero line and then place just above it on the scale two short wavy lines indicating a break in it.
5. Place the scale line at the left, except in especially wide graphs, in which it may be placed on both sides.
6. Distinguish clearly the line or lines of the graph from other rulings on the graph; other rulings should be kept at a minimum and only used when necessary for clarity.
7. Construct graphs that are pleasing in appearance, well spaced and proportioned, and centered on the page.
8. Title the graph as clearly and completely as possible, using a single phrase and avoiding unnecessary words. Suggested proportion: height, approximately three-fourths of width.
9. As a rule, place the title below the body of the graph.

Illustrations

The key to successful graphic presentation is to arrange the data in the most meaningful way, consolidating the values appropriately first and then arranging the ordinate and abscissa in an attempt to utilize the space as effectively as possible. The most successful figures are those that leave a minimum of unused area and are easily read. Obviously, this arrangement will depend upon the nature of the study and the type of data obtained. The following suggestions, however, may prove helpful. As usual, the examples employed are selected simply to illustrate the principle rather than to serve as models of excellence.

1. It is incumbent that the investigator utilize the correct statistical treatment of the data, which has been mentioned repeatedly in this text. This trend is followed in graphic illustrations and is evidenced by the usual requirement of reducing plotted values to some measure of central tendency, notably the mean. When a number of subjects are employed, it is useless to consider the subject-by-subject response, since the serial mean response gives a much clearer picture. Questions of significance are answered separately as required.

2. Special mention should be made of the method of handling plotted data, especially serial determinations designed to illustrate progressive effects, such as would result from trials or successive measurements of a function over time. The tendency is to connect points on a dot-to-dot basis; this is an acceptable practice, especially when but a few points are involved. However, it may be more desirable to utilize a smooth curve in order to demonstrate linearity or curvilinearity. When each point is connected, the broken and erratic effect may confuse the analysis. A simple technique is to fit a line by visual inspection, a sort of least squares effect attempting to minimize error, and to seek an average of their positive and negative values. In the case of the exponential curve analysis discussed in Chapter 11, the smooth curve in Figure 16.2 is actually constructed mathematically, thereby taking on a specific value that is useful in making direct comparisons between conditions.

3. Frequently, more than one set of data may be incorporated in a

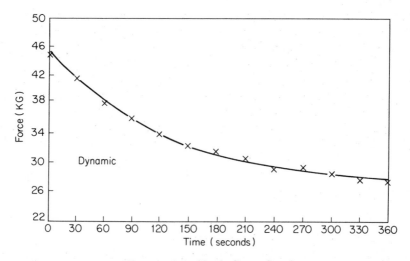

Figure 16.2. Single Curve Graph

single illustration, thus saving space and making comparisons more meaningful than if presented separately. In this situation, at least one set of values must be in common between the different measures; this is ordinarily placed on the abscissa, although the reader will find examples of all sorts of combinations in the literature. The example in Figure 16.3 illustrates this principle.

4. Occasionally, available space can be utilized to amplify some particular aspect of the figure. These amplifications are called inserts and, properly proportioned, serve to add balance to the illustration (see Figure 16.4). Sometimes, this space is useful for presenting the legend or for recording portions of the data.

5. Finally, the author must make certain that the figure is clearly labeled, including the designation of units of measurement. They must coincide with tabular material, so if the data are a function of time, the use of minutes, seconds, and so forth must correspond in the illustration.

Artwork

When the author is unable to do finished artwork, he or she must employ a professional or at least someone with skill and experience. In such a case, the work must be supervised carefully and detailed instructions must be provided concerning format, size of lines, lettering, and so on, since the artist will not understand the theoretical implications of the data. Therefore, a perfect copy must be provided. On the other hand, something can be said for the practice of the exper-

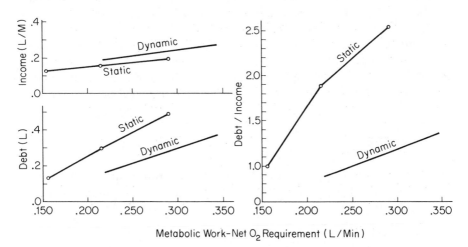

Figure 16.3. Multiple Curves Graph (David H. Clarke, "Energy Cost of Isometric Exercise," *Research Quarterly*, 31, No. 1 (March 1960), 3.)

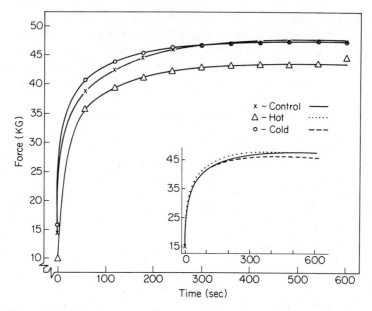

Figure 16.4. Graph with Insert (David H. Clarke and George E. Stelmach, "Muscular Fatigue and Recovery Curve Parameters at Various Temperatures," *Research Quarterly*, 37, No. 4 (December 1968), 468.)

imenter developing the ability to prepare his or her own graphs. Certainly, if the investigator anticipates a career in which research plays a part, practice in drawing, inking, lettering, and preparing final copy of his or her work will not only save time and ensure accuracy but will cost less. In this respect, the use of lettering equipment, drafting tools, and the like can be mastered with practice, and the illustrative work will take on a professional appearance.

Most journals will accept a photograph or a multilith copy of the figure for reproduction, in which case the journal itself should be consulted for further specifications. At the same time, it may be desirable to have slides made for future use in lectures or in research presentations.

FOOTNOTES

The use of footnotes is inevitable in research writing. As a consequence, the investigator must acquire considerable facility in their formulation.

Purposes

The footnote may be used in the research report for a number of purposes, especially the following:

1. *Source reference.* Acknowledgements should be made to all sources utilized throughout the study, preferably by footnote reference. As in this book, footnote references are constantly made to articles, books, theses, and the like. Acknowledgements need to be made when the materials of others or when ideas uniquely developed by others are utilized. However, such references are not necessary when made to facts of general knowledge; the same situation prevails for statistical formulas commonly used, such as the mean, standard deviation, and coefficient of correlation. This purpose of footnotes is the most prevalent by far.

2. *Amplification of the discussion.* On occasion, the writer may wish to add information relative to a point under consideration in the text but does not want to interrupt the thought under development; the footnote can be utilized for this purpose. Illustrations of this footnote use are: giving the distributor's name and address for an item of research equipment, listing the members of a committee, and adding an historical note. Footnotes of this type should be kept at a minimum, as usually things important enough to be said should be placed in the body of the report.

3. *Cross-reference.* Where the author wishes to refer to materials appearing elsewhere in the report, a good way to do this is by footnote.

Procedures

Although institutions may differ in their requirements, the footnote usually appears at the bottom of the page where the citation is made. For reader convenience, this method is best since the reference is immediately available without seeking it elsewhere, such as at the end of the chapter. The following suggestions are made for the preparation of footnotes:

1. A raised Arabic numeral is placed in the text identifying the footnote. If the author's name is mentioned, the numeral can follow the name without spacing (e.g., Cureton[1]). If the author's name is not given in the text, the numeral may appear at the end of a paraphrase or quotation. The numeral may be placed after the key noun or major statement but not after a verb or a possessive pronoun.

2. Footnotes are separated from the text by a line 1½ inches long from the left margin. This line should be one double space below the last line in the text; the footnote should start one double space below the line.

3. A footnote numeral precedes each footnote, corresponding with the one in the text. Again, it is a raised numeral (one-half typewriter space) with no spacing between it and the footnote.
4. Footnotes are single spaced in paragraph form; double spaced between footnotes.
5. Footnotes are numbered consecutively from 1 throughout each chapter.

Form

In writing a thesis, the graduate student should adopt an acceptable form for citing references as footnotes; once adopted, the form should be followed consistently throughout. In making such a selection, any regulations established by the institution's graduate school should be checked. If specific regulations do not exist, the student can adopt a plan from one of the form books mentioned above or adopt the practice given below.

Books. The order of items in a reference to a book is: author's name as it appears on the title page, with last name last; title of book and edition, if other than the first; city of publication; name of publisher; date of publication; chapter or page referred to. Illustrations of footnotes to books for various situations encountered follow:

1. One author: Brian J. Sharkey, *Physiology of Fitness* (Champaign, Ill.: Human Kinetics Publishers, 1979), 70.
2. Two or three authors: M. J. Ellis and G. J. L. Scholz, *Activity and Play of Children* (Englewood Cliffs, N.J.: Prentice-Hall, Inc., 1978), 26-31.
3. More than three authors: Ruth Evans *et al.* [or, and others], *Physical Education for Elementary Schools* (New York: McGraw-Hill Book Company, 1958), Ch. 4.
4. No author given: *Author's Guide* (Englewood Cliffs, N.J.: Prentice-Hall, Inc., 1962), p. 76.
5. Edited book: Warren R. Johnson, ed., *Science and Medicine of Exercise and Sports* (New York: Harper & Row, Publishers, 1960).
6. Book editions: John W. Best, *Research in Education* (3rd ed.) (Englewood Cliffs, N.J.: Prentice-Hall, Inc., 1977), Ch. 9.

Articles, Chapter, Monograph Series. The order of items in reference to an article in a journal is: author's name; title of article, title of journal; volume number; number of issue; date of publication; page number. Below are illustrations of footnotes not only to articles but to chapters in a book and to monographs in a series.

1. Article: G. Lawrence Rarick, "Motor Development: Its Growing Knowledge Base," *Journal of Physical Education and Recreation*, 51, No. 7 (September 1980), 26.
2. Chapter in book: Henry J. Montoye, "Health and Longevity of Athletes," in *Science and Medicine of Exercise and Sport* (2nd ed.), Warren R. Johnson and E. R. Buskirk, eds. (New York: Harper & Row, Publishers, 1974), Ch. 27.
3. Monograph Series: Charles H. McCloy, *Appraising Physical Status: The Selection of Measurements*, University of Iowa Studies in Child Welfare, Vol. 12 (Iowa City: University of Iowa Press, 1936).

Unpublished materials. Footnotes for various kinds of unpublished materials follow.

1. Thesis or dissertation: Jan Broekhoff, "Relationships between Physical, Socio-Psychological, and Mental Characteristics of Thirteen Year Old Boys," Doctoral Dissertation, University of Oregon, 1966.
2. Mimeographed material: H. Harrison Clarke, "Contributions and Implications of the Medford, Oregon, Boys' Growth Study" (4th ed.), School of Health, Physical Education, and Recreation, University of Oregon, April 20, 1968. (Mimeographed)

Abbreviations in Footnotes

A number of abbreviations are used in footnotes to reduce or eliminate the necessity for repeating the same reference when cited more than once. The full biographical reference should appear in the footnote when it is used for the first time in a chapter. Thereafter, one of the following may be substituted.

Ibid. is an abbreviation of *ibidem*, which means "in the same place." This abbreviation is used when succeeding consecutive citations are made to the same reference; no intervening references should occur. It may be used by itself if the reference is to the same page; if the reference is to a different page, the proper page must be added.

Op. cit. is an abbreviation of *opere citato*, which means, "in the work cited." This abbreviation preceded by the author's last name, is used when other references intervene between different citations of the same reference. The citation should be to a different page, so the page number should be given.

Loc. cit. is an abbreviation for *loco citato*, which means "in the place cited." This abbreviation is used when citation is made to exact nonconsecutive references.

In the following, the footnote abbreviations are illustrated in a variety of situations:

[1]C. H. McCloy and Norma D. Young, *Tests and Measurements in Physical Education* (3rd ed.) (New York: Appleton-Century-Crofts, 1954), p. 319.

[2]*Ibid.*

[3]*Ibid.*, pp. 218-25.

[4]Marie R. Liba, "Factor Analysis of Strength Variables," *Research Quarterly*, 38, No. 4 (December 1967), 649.

[5]McCloy and Young, *op cit.*, p. 183.

[6]*Loc. cit.*

BIBLIOGRAPHY

As for footnotes, no universally accepted style for bibliographical entries exists. The style books mentioned above provide forms for this purpose. Minor differences exist between the forms for footnotes and bibliographical references. One such difference is that the first surname is listed first in a bibliography. The entries are single spaced with double space between them. Each reference starts flush with the left-hand margin; subsequent lines are indented four spaces. If an author's name is repeated, an unbroken line seven spaces in length is substituted. Other differences can be seen in the following examples taken from those given earlier as footnotes.

Author's Guide. Englewood Cliffs, N.J.: Prentice-Hall, Inc., 1962.

Broekhoff, Jan, "Relationships between Physical, Socio-Psychological, and Mental Characteristics of Thirteen Year Old Boys," Doctoral Dissertation, University of Oregon, 1966.

Clarke, H. Harrison, "Contributions and Implications of the Medford, Oregon, Boys' Growth Study" (4th ed.), School of Health, Physical Education, and Recreation, University of Oregon, April 20, 1968. (Mimeographed)

Ellis, M. J., and G. J. L. Scholz, *Activity and Play of Children.* Englewood Cliffs, N.J.: Prentice-Hall, Inc., 1978.

McCloy, Charles H., "Appraising Physical Status: The Selection of Measurements," *University of Iowa Studies in Child Welfare*, Vol. 12. Iowa Press, 1936.

Montoye, Henry J., "Health and Longevity of Athletes" in *Science and Medicine of Exercise and Sport* (2nd ed.), Warren R. Johnson and E. R. Buskirk, eds. New York: Harper & Row, Publishers, 1974, Ch. 27.

Rarick, G. Lawrence, "Motor Development: Its Growing Knowledge Base," *Journal of Physical Education and Recreation*, 51, No. 7 (September 1980), 26.

THESIS REPRODUCTION

A number of choices are available to the student for duplicating a thesis. No longer is the time-honored practice of utilizing carbon copies the only acceptable procedure for supplying the number of copies required by the graduate schools. In fact, the least desirable form is the carbon copy, since some carbons are indistinct, the paper is usually of poorer and more fragile grade, and they are susceptible to smudging. The requirements established locally should be consulted to determine the number of copies needed as well as the acceptable methods of reproduction.

The most widely used alternate means of obtaining additional copies of the thesis are the multilith and Xerox processes. For these processes, the original copy of the manuscript is the only one that must be typed, as the remaining copies are made from it. Excellent reproductions on high quality paper will result, making all copies essentially originals. Usually, a number of extra copies can be obtained at a fraction of the original cost, which in turn may serve as working copies for future reference.

FOLLOW-UP PUBLICATION

No discussion of research writing would be complete without suggesting that the investigator follow up his or her thesis or dissertation with a condensed paper submitted to a journal for publication. If the research is sound in the first place, then it is incumbent that the author make it more widely available so that others may have the benefit of the results. Such is the case whether or not it is a master's or a doctoral study; the decision must be made on scientific worth more than anything else. If the reader shares the belief that the primary means of supporting the body of knowledge of his or her discipline is through published research, then he or she must realize that the effort required to take this additional step is a vital one. Assuredly, the results of the thesis in his or her institutional library may be microfiched or microfilmed and may be abstracted, but these are not considered the same as a publication. The impact of the research is much greater when the study has met the editorial standards of a scholarly journal.

The writer should keep in mind that research journals do not publish theses, only articles; therefore, the thesis must be rewritten in article form. Ordinarily, this means extensive condensation, and in many cases, whole portions of the original thesis are omitted. The decision depends upon the nature of the study itself and the data that have been obtained.

The choice of the journal for submitting the manuscript depends on the type of study conducted. In physical education the *Research Quarterly for Exercise, and Sports* of the American Alliance for Health, Physical Education, Recreation and Dance is the most available one for most researchers, although a number of other journals might be equally acceptable. Perhaps it is a question of which audience would profit most from the data collected. A glance at the list of periodicals in Chapter 3 will disclose the many sources for publication that exist in physical education, health, recreation, and related disciplines.

Format. The format to be employed for publication will depend upon the particular journal selected, as mentioned earlier. Some journals do not publish their "Guide to Contributors" in every issue but do so once in each volume (thus, once each year). The author should consult the latest statement as a format guide in order to avoid the possibility of rewriting to conform to a new format if one should have been adopted. In all instances, the directions should be followed precisely in order to facilitate reviewing and processing the manuscript.

In addition to the question of publication is the possibility of presenting the study at some scholarly meeting, perhaps at a state, district, or national convention of the American Alliance for Health, Physical Education, Recreation, and Dance. The experience gained from such a presentation is quite valuable and provides further opportunity to condense a study. Ten to 15 minutes is typically allotted for each paper, so the author is forced to make some rather critical decisions as to the content to be included.

Authorship. A sensitive question in publishing research articles may be authorship. In the traditional situation, an individual publishes the results of his or her investigation alone; today, however, this practice has changed considerably. The tendency today is for multiple authorships to occur more frequently than before, largely due to the natural result of group research activity. Therefore, group projects have sprung into existence, fostered by relatively easy access to funds. In such cases, it is highly legitimate for colleagues to work together on large problems of common interest.

The question may be raised concerning what the graduate student should do with the article that he or she wishes to publish resulting from his or her thesis or dissertation. The student will note that the practice varies from one situation to another. The advice received on the thesis, sometimes amounting to considerable help from the stage of problem formulation to final writing, may result in a desire to coauthor the article with an advisor. This is perfectly legitimate, as is the fact that the student may be the sole author; in this latter instance, the student should acknowledge both the institution and the advisor by means of a footnote reference.

An exception to the above rule is related to the problem created by funded research projects. In this situation, the professor inaugurates and actively directs a large research endeavor supported from a substantial grant received over a period of several years. The plan calls for a number of technicians to implement the gathering of data; typically, graduate students are involved and develop their graduate studies from the project. Such a situation is prevalent in many departments on campus and is a modern day departure from the typical procedure whereby each student on his or her own initiative goes through the formal steps of problem formulation, seeking a topic in a new area, constructing equipment, testing subjects, and so forth. The research experience gained from association with a large under-taking is sufficiently valid to receive widespread support. In such a situation, the project director must fulfill his or her contract and protect the grant. Since the project plan and overall procedures were developed by the director and the financing was from project funds, he or she will quite likely retain partial publication rights. Thus, research papers emanating from such a project will in all likelihood be coauthored, with the faculty member serving as principal investigator.

SUMMARY

This chapter presented in some detail procedures for writing the research report, with primary emphasis on the graduate thesis. Attention was given to the organization of the report, centered around five chapters: Chapter I, Statement of the Problem; Chapter II, Review of Related Literature; Chapter III, Research Procedures; Chapter IV, Results of the Study; Chapter V, Summary and Conclusions. Front and back sections of the thesis were also considered. Chapter organization was presented, as was the formation of the bibliography. Instructions on the uses and construction of tables and figures were illustrated.

SELECTED REFERENCES

BEST, JOHN W., *Research in Education* (4th ed). Englewood Cliffs, N.J.: Prentice-Hall Inc., 1981.

BOOKWALTER, CAROLYN, KARL W. BOOKWALTER, and MARJORIE PHILLIPS, "Writing the Research Report," in *Research Methods in Health, Physical Education, and Recreation* (2nd ed.), ed. M. Gladys Scott. Washington: American Alliance for Health, Physical Education, Recreation, and Dance, 1959, Ch. 16.

CAMPBELL, WILLIAM G., and STEPHEN V. BALLOU, *Form and Style: Thesis, Reports, and Term Papers*. Boston: Houghton Mifflin Company, 1974.

Publication Manual of the American Psychological Association, 2nd ed. Washington: The Association, 1974.

TURABIAN, KATE L., *A Manual for Writers of Term Papers, Theses, and Dissertations*. Chicago: University of Chicago Press, 1973.

UNIVERSITY OF CHICAGO, *A Manual of Style* (13th ed.). Chicago: University of Chicago Press, 1982.

Index